Metropolitan Governance and Spatial Planning

Metropolitan Governance and Spatial Planning explores the relationship between metropolitan decision-making and strategies to coordinate spatial policy. This relationship is examined across 19 city-regions of Europe and the similarities and differences are analysed.

Cities are having to formulate their urban policies in a very complex and turbulent environment. They are faced with numerous new pressures and problems and these often create contradictory conditions. This book provides a theoretical framework for exploring these issues and links this to a detailed investigation of each city-region. In the context of globalisation, cities in the last twenty years have experienced new patterns of activity and these usually transcend political boundaries. The management of these changes therefore requires an effort of coordination and different cities have used different approaches.

The nation states in Europe have handed over many responsibilities to the European Union while also increasing devolution to regions and cities. Government has therefore become a more complex multi-level activity.

There has also been a move from government to governance. Many different public, quasi-public and private bodies are now involved in making decisions that affect urban development. The exploration of the 19 city-regions shows that many face similar difficulties while some also provide interesting examples of innovative practice. This book concludes that the way forward is to find strategies to link the different spheres of metropolitan action through 'organising connectivity'.

City-regions covered: London, Birmingham, Cardiff, Stockholm, Berlin, Frankfurt, Hanover, Stuttgart, Amsterdam, Rotterdam, Prague, Vienna, Venice, Milan, Paris, Brussels, Marseilles-Aix, Barcelona, Madrid.

Willem Salet is Scientific Director of Amsterdam Studycentre for the Metropolitan Environment (AME). **Andy Thornley** is Director of Planning Studies at the London School of Economics and Political Science. **Anton Kreukels** is Professor of Urban and Regional Planning at the University of Utrecht.

Metropolitan Governance and Spatial Planning

Comparative Case Studies of European City-Regions

Edited by Willem Salet,
Andy Thornley and
Anton Kreukels

Spon Press
Taylor & Francis Group

LONDON AND NEW YORK

First published 2003
by Spon Press
11 New Fetter Lane, London EC4P 4EE

Simultaneously published in the USA and Canada
by Spon Press
29 West 35th Street, New York, NY 10001

Spon Press is an imprint of the Taylor & Francis Group

Typeset in Times and Frutiger by
HWA Text and Data Management, Tunbridge Wells
Printed and bound in Great Britain by
TJ International Ltd, Padstow, Cornwall

British Library Cataloguing in Publication Data
A catalogue record for this book is available from the British
Library

Library of Congress Cataloging in Publication Data
Metropolitan governance and spatial planning : comparative
case studies of European city-regions / edited by Anton
Kreukels, Willem Salet and Andy Thornley.
    p. cm.
Includes bibliographical references and index.
  1. Metropolitan government–Europe–Case studies.
  2. Regional planning–Europe–Case studies. I. Kreukels,
Anton. II. Salet, W. G. M. III. Thornley, Andy.

JS3000 .M46 2002
320.8´5´094–dc21   2002026841

ISBN 0–415–27448–6 (hbk)
ISBN 0–415–27449–4 (pbk)

Contents

Contents

Contributors

Jeremy Alden Professor of International Planning Studies and Pro-Vice Chancellor at Cardiff University in the UK.

Mike Beazley Lecturer at the Centre for Urban and Regional Studies, University of Birmingham. Chair of West Midlands Branch of the Royal Town Planning Institute (RTPI). Published on planning and urban regeneration, community involvement and the impacts of urban development on communities.

Dave Carter Mr Carter joined Birmingham City Council in 1986. Head of the Strategic Planning Group in the Development Planning Division of the Planning Department, responsible for City-wide planning and liaison with local authorities in the West Midlands.

Bodo Freund Professor of Human Geography, Humboldt Universität zu Berlin. Prior to 1993 he was professor in Frankfurt and Lisbon. Published on economic and social geography, highly skilled migrants, offices and urbanism, locational dynamics in metropolises.

Dietrich Fürst Professor of spatial planning and regional research at the University of Hanover (Germany), trained in Economics and Public Administration.

Marisol García Urban sociologist at the University of Barcelona. Member of the Editorial Board of the International Journal of Urban and Regional Research. Publications on Cities and Citizenship.

Enrico Gualini PhD grade in urban and regional planning at Politecnico di Milano. Currently senior researcher at Amsterdam study centre for the Metropolitan Environment (AME), Universiteit van Amsterdam. Published on multi-level governance, regional cooperation, European integration and planning theory.

Alan Harding Professor of Urban and Regional Governance and co-director of the Centre for Sustainable Urban and Regional Futures, University of Salford.

Björn Hårsman Managing Director of Inregia AB and Professor of Regional Economic Planning at the Royal Institute of Technology, Stockholm. He is the author of several books and articles on regional economics and governance issues.

Contributors

Hartmut Häussermann Sociologist, Professor for Urban and Regional Research at Humboldt Universität zu Berlin. Published on post-communist transformation of cities, changes in Berlin, spatial development and social exclusion, urban politics.

Susanne Heeg Assistant Professor, Institute of Geography, University of Hamburg, Germany. Main research interests economic geography, in particular urban economy and town planning.

Anton Kreukels Professor of Urban and Regional Planning and Head of the Department of Urban and Regional Planning, Utrecht University. From 1986 through 1992 Member of the Netherlands Scientific Council for Government Policy, The Hague, The Netherlands.

Evert Lagrou 1963–80 planner in a private consultancy with official planning tasks in Belgium, Africa and Asia. Since 1980 professor at the Department Architectuur Sint-Lucas, Hogeschool Wetenschap en Kunst, Brussels. Involved in official local planning committees.

Jesús Leal Maldonado Professor of Urban Sociology, Universidad Complutense de Madrid. Author of the 1985 Urban Plan of Madrid and the 1997 Housing Plan of the Strategic Plan of Madrid Community. Published 'La Dimensión de la Ciudad' (1995), Madrid.

Christian Lefèvre Professor of Urban Studies at the French Institute of Urban Affairs, University of Paris 8 and Research Fellow at the LATTS. Published on metropolitan governance focusing on the political and economic dynamics of territorial reforms in European Cities.

Karel Maier Professor of Urban Planning and Vice-Dean Czech Technical University, Faculty of Architecture, Department of Urban Design and Planning. Member of the Czech Chamber of Architects. Experience: urban and regional planning, local strategic planning, urban economy.

Alain Motte Professeur des Universités en Aménagement de l'espace, urbanisme. Directeur Institut d'Aménagement Régional (Université Aix-Marseille III, France).

Alan Murie Professor of Urban and Regional Studies at the Centre for Urban and Regional Studies at the University of Birmingham. Published on issues related to the development of housing provision and housing policy and did major research in the West Midlands region and Birmingham.

Amy Rader Olsson Doctoral candidate in regional planning at the Royal Institute of Technology, Stockholm and is a consultant with Inregia AB. Her research interests include fiscal federalism and effective institutions for regional governance.

Michaela Paal Worked as lecturer at the Department of Geography, University of Innsbruck and as a scientist at the Austrian Academy of Sciences. Since 2001 she is full professor for Urban Geography and Regional Planning at the Philipps-University of Marburg.

Beth Perry Peel Fellow, Centre for Sustainable Urban and Regional Futures, University of Salford.

Turiddo Pugliese Graduated in Town Planning in 1977. Presently responsible for the Strategic Plan of the City of Venice, after working for 15 years with a local research agency.

Ansgar Rudolph University degree in Landscape and Environmental Planning at Hanover University, 1994. Assistant Researcher for the universities of Oldenburg and Hanover. Currently Regional Manager for the Goslar District, Lower Saxony, Germany, since 2002.

Willem Salet Professor of urban and regional planning and Director of Amsterdam Studycentre for the Metropolitan Environment (AME), Universiteit van Amsterdam.

Andy Thornley Director of Planning Studies, London School of Economics and Political Science. He worked as a professional planner for many years before moving to academia. His main interest is in the interaction between politics and urban planning and he has written numerous books and articles on different dimensions of this subject.

Mariolina Toniolo Town planner with the City of Venice Planning Department since 1994. Her previous experiences concerned research on regional and metropolitan development.

Stuart Wilks-Heeg Lecturer in Social Policy at the University of Liverpool.

Preface

This book explores the relationship between the arrangements for metropolitan decision-making and the coordination of spatial policy, through an examination of 19 major city-regions of Europe. The main objective is to explore the inter-relationship between the formulation of strategic spatial perspectives for the whole metropolitan area and the arrangements of governance that enable decisions to be made. In order to achieve a comprehensive strategic policy, a considerable amount of coordination is required. This coordination has three dimensions:

a) Spatial – to ensure that the different levels of policy, from national through regional and metropolitan to local, are consistent with each other. The policies of the local areas within the metropolitan region also need to be integrated.
b) Functional – the different land uses and activities that combine and interact in a strategy have to be linked, e.g. housing, transport, economic development and environmental sustainability.
c) Sectoral – the intentions and resources of the public, private and voluntary sectors need to be brought together to maximise the coherence of the strategic policy and ease its implementation.

This coordination task requires special institutional structures if it is to be fulfilled. There have been considerable changes in these structures in European metropolitan regions in recent years. The key issue for this research is the extent to which these governmental changes aid or hinder the process of coordination in the production of metropolitan spatial policy.

Therefore the principal questions for the research on each city are: is there a mismatch between the coordination of strategic policy and the structures of governance? How did arrangements of governance evolve and how did they influence the process of coordination? Drawing together the results for each city, it is then asked: what are the similarities and differences in the policy/governance relationship between cities? How far are these effectuated by national differences? Are some changes in governance better able to contribute to strategic coordination than others?

In order to explore these relationships, experts from the 19 regions analyse the spatial development patterns of their region by determining the emerging spatial

Preface

metropolitan configurations as a result of socio-economic changes. They then focus on strategic spatial policy by investigating what policies have been formulated and what has been the relative involvement of national, regional, metropolitan and local governments, and what other interests have influenced these policies. Finally, the authors focus on strategies of metropolitan governance. They investigate what changes have taken place, who initiated these changes and what were the stated reasons for them. The analyses take into account national and European conditions to public and private action.

Concepts of the chapters were intensely debated in Amsterdam in February 2001, at a seminar organised by the Amsterdam study centre for the Metropolitan Environment (AME). We express our thanks to the many people who helped us to produce this book, and in particular to Joost Molenaar for the coordination of the project and the editing of the contributions. The graphics were prepared by I/O-Graph, Utrecht.

The Editors

PART I

General introduction

1 Institutional and spatial coordination in European metropolitan regions

Willem Salet, Andy Thornley and
Anton Kreukels

Introduction

In this book a comparative analysis is made of spatial planning strategies and metropolitan coordination of public and private action in 19 major city-regions of Europe. The crucial challenge of metropolitan policy coordination is the spatial complexity of social and economic activities in the context of institutional fragmentation and the resultant diversity of power coalitions. In this opening chapter we first discuss some important institutional changes at the macro level that are conditioning current dilemmas in European city-regions. We explore the shift from European welfare states to a more varied and complex pattern. In the welfare state era, the national government in most European countries protected its national economies strongly and often also orchestrated the supply of public amenities in metropolitan areas. Strategies of spatial coordination in urban regions were backed by the proactive involvement of national governments. Since the early 1980s two crucial trends have produced dramatic institutional shifts: the globalisation of the new information-led economy and the liberalisation of economic markets on the one hand, and – almost simultaneously and to a considerable degree linked – the emergence of a new differentiation in intergovernmental relationships on the other. This latter trend had a major effect on the centrality of the former national 'welfare state' with shifts to both supranational and decentralised arenas. National governments still have a strong stake in metropolitan development, but the policy arena has turned into a 'multi-actor and multilevel game' (Hooghe and Marks, 2001). The challenge for metropolitan governance and spatial policy coordination is increasingly complicated under these dynamic and more open-ended circumstances.

Next, the internal dynamics of urban regions are analysed. The metropolitan arena is facing new, often paradoxical challenges in its institutional and spatial development. Devolution of governmental competencies has increased local

accountabilities and responsiveness but also feeds the rivalry between the municipalities within a nation. Local conditions in the metropolitan landscape usually
show strong differences and inequalities in social and economic composition and
these might hamper inter-municipal cooperation. On the other hand more regional
coordination and cooperation is needed in the face of increasing competition
between economic regions at the international scale. Regarding the spatial
dimension, many metropolitan regions are in a process of structural transformation.
The actual spatial processes and chains or networks of urbanisation have surpassed
almost everywhere the traditional city borders and are creating new and dynamic
patterns of urban space at metropolitan or regional levels. The 'morphological
city' and the 'material city' have become increasingly divergent. There are many
dilemmas and much incongruity in these processes of urban transformation. The
resulting differences in coordination strategies are at the heart of the comparative
investigation undertaken in this book.

Finally, reflecting the above-mentioned exogenous and endogenous conditions,
the central issue of the book is identified and operationalised. How could successful strategies of metropolitan coordination be formulated under such conflicting
conditions? What is to be learned from failures of coordination and what from
good practices? What is – in practical experience – the meaning of metropolitan
governance? There is good and inspiring theoretical debate on the issue of
metropolitan coordination – usually based on generalised assumptions – but
comparative lessons from different practices are relatively scarce. The analyses in
this book attempt to bridge the general theories and the different experiences of
practices in metropolitan governance, focusing on spatial policy. The basic elements
in the investigation are shown in figure 1.1.

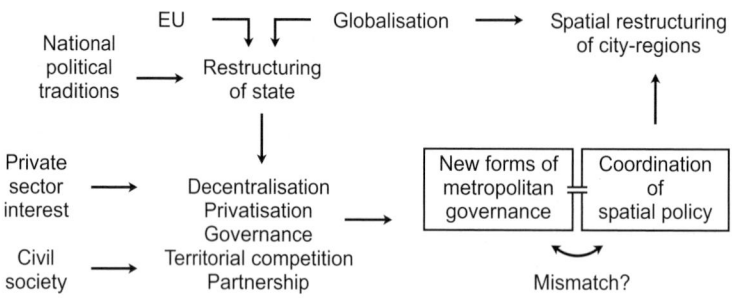

Figure 1.1 Some key elements in the analysis

Institutional shifts in European welfare states

National governments all over Europe took an active role in the post-war expansion of the welfare state, a process which dominated the political scene from the 1950s to the 1980s. This is not to say that institutional conditions were similar in all European states. On the contrary, the socio-economic patterns of European countries differed significantly, their intergovernmental structures were rooted in different national traditions and administrative cultures exhibited very different styles (see e.g. Esping-Andersen, 1996; Mény, 1990; Rowat, 1988). In some countries the political and socio-economic patterns were traditionally dominated by corporate relationships (e.g. the Netherlands), while in others national competencies were structured by regional federalism (Germany and, more recently, Belgium) and yet others had a tradition of unitary government. This last category contained many varieties from the Napoleonic region of southern Europe (the purest model being, of course, the French one), the communist regimes of Eastern Europe and the highly centralised British state. A key dimension of these differences relates to the way responsibilities and competencies have been distributed between layers of government. This will be a significant factor in determining the degree of autonomy held at the metropolitan scale. Where this autonomy is set out very precisely in a written constitution (e.g. in Germany) it is difficult to change whereas where no constitution exists at all (e.g. in Britain) it is possible to abolish the metropolitan level of government if national government so desires. The variation in the relationship between central and local government can be illustrated by comparing the 'fused' system of France, a coexistence of different layers of government operating in a given arena, with the 'agency' model in Britain where the two levels are very separate and local government delivers services within a policy framework already set out by central government. Such differences can also be exemplified by the contrast between the British concept of 'ultra vires' which limits the competence of local government to the activities set out by central government, and the doctrine in the rest of Europe of 'general competence' implying that the local level has a general power over the affairs of its locality (Norton, 1991). Thus it can be seen that institutional conditions in the European context are quite diverse (Newman and Thornley, 1996). Nevertheless the role of central government was strongly manifest in all these countries during the development of the national welfare state. Rising social expectations kept governments under pressure to produce results during this period and most followed a kind of social democratic consensus (Esping-Andersen, 1990). It was in this political environment that most national systems of town and country planning were born.

However, from the early 1980s a dramatic shift occurred in the position of national governments in Europe. The degree of change varied from one country to another, as did the detailed features of the new approach. These differences can be largely traced to the alternative traditions that existed within the general welfare state approach, as illustrated above (Batley, 1991). However the common features of change are sufficient to support the claim that the period from the 1980s brought an institutional transformation to all European cities. Three overlapping dimensions can be identified in this shift:

- A reduction in the government's proactive role in the economy and society.
- The diversification of decision-making throughout a wide range of organisations.
- The restructuring of intergovernmental relationships.

The first dimension of structural change refers to the receding of governments' proactive role in the economy and society. The opening up of national boundaries to allow the movement of persons and goods in most parts of Europe, the expansion of a common European market, the globalisation of new information-led economies and the resultant liberalisation of world markets, all contribute to the rise of new market-led societies and the new networks of international connectivity (Castells, 1996; Sassen, 1991). One of the most dramatic changes in the organisational structure of national economic systems in Europe has been the gradual abolition of national protectionism and other forms of economic regulation as a result of European economic legislation. Also the primacy of the national government in satisfying social and physical needs has changed. Clearly, we may observe here a similar variance of institutional patterns as that occurring earlier in the development of the various welfare states. Some governments were accustomed to providing many public amenities (some supplied health care, labour, housing, infrastructure and even automotive or airline companies), while other governments cooperated strongly with the nationally organised private sector, and yet others merely conditioned the supply and distribution of public amenities. Everywhere in Europe, though, national states were strongly involved in the provision of public goods; even private consumption goods were often treated as collective goods. In most sectors of public policy, however, processes of liberalisation and privatisation have become dominant in the last 20 years. Some countries, such as Britain, made the shift more abruptly; those that changed gradually usually had to continue the process of withdrawal or re-regulation over a longer period. Thus market-type approaches gradually became dominant in the economic organisation of European states. As most countries had based the provision of public goods on the institutional foundation of group organisation, the transition to a liberal or conditional economy was fundamental. Producers that used to be protected by rules and protective legislation now had to operate under the harsh conditions of international competitive markets and their structuration of powers. These processes are now evident in the provision of electricity, water, public housing, education, health, transportation, etc. In summary, all relevant spatial activities have been brought into a new institutional arena – one that gives greater privilege and status to the private sector.

The receding of government centrism occurred not only in the economic domain of society but also in the social one: the aspirations of the civil society have been revived during the last two decades (Putnam, 1993; Van Gunsteren, 1998). Before the Second World War and before the expansion of the welfare state regimes, most societies in Western Europe were organised in a more or less sociocratic way, relying strongly on the self-organising powers of individuals, social groups and local organisations. Some authors claim that the return to civil responsibilities in the aftermath of the welfare state resembles pre-war conditions between citizens and state. They consider the rise and fall of the national welfare state as an intermezzo (a sort of *Fremdkörper*) of modern history. As will be demonstrated later, this is actually not the case. However, it is important to conclude that the revival of citizenship, the tendencies towards the social organisation of public responsibilities and the new attempts 'to privatise the organisation of the public domain' are important signals of a transformation of the cultural and economical relationships that used to be so manifest in the construction of the national welfare state.

However, it could be argued that in more recent years a new political movement has been emerging in Europe, one that attempts to respond to new social trends, including the reassessment of the concept of citizenship and the forces of globalisation. Perhaps the most vigorous presentation of this approach has occurred in Britain with the 'Third Way' (Giddens, 1998; Blair, 1998). The rhetoric claims that a new form of politics is required to match the new conditions at the turn of the millennium. The basic essence of the Third Way is that it is possible to find a consensus and compromise to replace the conflictual politics between advocates of liberalisation and advocates of socialism. In this consensus the greater freedom the private sector has established over the last 20 years can be retained while at the same time overlaying this with positive policies towards such issues as the environment, social inclusion or the better universal provision of education and health facilities. This approach places a great deal of emphasis on consensus-building and coordination – central issues of this book. The Third Way came into existence in the US and Britain and was in many ways therefore a reaction to the previous neo-liberal rule. As a result, this specific exposition of the approach has been rejected by many European countries as giving too many concessions to the past. However, if one takes a rather broader definition of the new approach – as a rejection of the past left-right political alternatives and a search for a new way – then similar trends can be identified across many countries in Europe, though adopting different labels (Giddens, 2001).

We have described the second dimension of institutional change as the spreading of decision-making from within government to a wide range of different organisa-tions. This trend is often encapsulated in the idea of a shift from government to governance. It is clearly linked to the reduction of government described above with its greater emphasis on privatisation, and has given rise to a proliferation of *ad hoc* bodies and appointed organisations often termed quangos (quasi-autonomous non-governmental organisations). These practices of governance can take many forms and are characterised by the involvement of non-governmental representation such as voluntary organisations and the private sector. In the box below we outline some interpretations of the concept of governance. The increased emphasis on the 'enabling' role of government is part of this trend. Government seeks cooperation with other organisations who carry out the actual service delivery, and a whole range of new procedures are devised to regulate and monitor this relationship.

The final dimension to the structural shift in the institutional context of the national welfare state refers to relationships within the public sector. There is evidence of a strong tendency towards significant changes in intergovernmental relationships. Since the late 1970s, intergovernmental relationships have been characterised by simultaneous processes of internationalisation and decentralisation. There is a major debate in the literature on globalisation concerning the impact that global economic transformation is having on the structures of government (see Held *et al.*, 1999). Some writers claim that we are witnessing the decline of the nation-state (e.g. Ohmae, 1995) as national governments lose their bargaining power vis-à-vis transnational corporations. However, a more productive line of analysis sees a restructuring of intergovernmental relationships in which there is a transfer of powers and responsibilities between levels (e.g. Scholte, 2000; Brenner, 1999). Nation-states feel compelled to strengthen their international relationships as many economic and cultural activities cross national borders. In particular, in the framework of the EU, international decision-making and cooperation has increased strongly and has created a vast body of legislation at the European level. Often Member States still have a strong stake in European legislation, but the European authority has expanded considerably, especially with respect to legislation concerning the liberalisation of economic markets, which in turn intersects with all kinds of national policies. The basic idea of open borders and a common economic market in Europe has been institutionalised in a relatively short time.

At the same time, most national governments recognise the need for decentralisation as centrally determined policies concerning social and physical provisions (e.g. education, health policy, housing, infrastructure) become ineffective. Central policies have become too detailed and too slow to respond. Many allocative decisions would be handled far more efficiently at lower tiers of decision-making. Furthermore, national governments in Europe started a 'race to the bottom' with respect to their social expenditures in an effort to improve the competitiveness of their national economies. Thus, national governments relinquished many responsibilities which had accumulated during the growth of the welfare states. Some institutional constellations were more appropriate than others in responding

Table 1.1 The meaning of governance

Despite its widespread use, 'governance' remains a concept with different dimensions and applications. Gualini gives an in-depth overview of the diverse applications and defines its general meaning as follows (Gualini, 2001):

> 'Governance' is – in general terms – a notion that deals with the reframing of both 'formal' and 'working' relationships between ideal types of social order in realising governing effects:

	keywords
state	public interest, hierarchy, coercion, monopoly of legitimate violence, territorial sovereignty
market	private interest, competition, exchange, failure in producing collective goods
community	'commons', reciprocity, cooperation, trust, solidarity
firms	corporate interest, hierarchy, principal-agent relationships, instruction-based relations, vertical integration
associations	concertation of collective interests, collective self-regulation, 'private government'.

This outline gives a flavour of the range of possibly very different interpretations of the notions according to the perspective adopted. It may therefore be useful to distinguish this meaning according to a broad categorisation of approaches to 'governance' in the social sciences (Gualini, 2001):

A   Governance as a concept for the analysis of state action (governance as form of social self-regulation instead of hierarchical government);

B   Governance as a concept for the analysis of societal capacities 'beyond' government (no more dualism between state and market but direct interaction: 'bargaining', 'negotiation', 'enabling', 'facilitating', 'mediating', 'entrepreneurial policies');

C   Governance as a concept for the analysis of the social order of economic systems (social and institutional embeddedness of economic systems).

Although all interpretations fit with the general notion of governance and all are fed by the negative reference to unilateral forms of 'government', more specification of the concept is needed. For the sake of our analysis it is important to focus on a particular dimension: the *territorial* aspects of governance and its challenges to territorial government. Territorial or local governance pertains to forms of management of territorial resources at the regional and local scale increasingly involving trans-scalar and inter-jurisdictional dimensions which stress the limits of effectiveness of given geographical rationales for governmental and administrative activity (Gualini, 2001). This specification of governance stipulates the significance of practices and experiments that complement or substitute the monistic policies of territorial governments. As conceived in recent conceptions of multilevel governance the important questions of this analysis focus on the following dimensions:

- the extent to which decision-making has shifted away from formal authoritative institutions to public/private networks;
- the change in relationship between jurisdictional territories (e.g. mutual exclusivity or overlapping);
- the change in their scope and purpose (e.g. specialised or general purpose);
- the change in their statute and nature (e.g. stable or fluctuating) (Hooghe and Marks, 2001).

to the new societal pressure of decentralisation. The traditional Napoleonic regimes encountered problems in the early 1980s and underwent strong institutional changes (e.g. Belgium, France, Italy, Spain, Greece, Portugal and – ten years later – the states in Eastern Europe). In the meantime, previously criticised models of regional federalism (e.g. German federalism) became role models for governmental organisation. The jump from unitary systems to real federal constitutionalism appeared too great in most countries, but new forms of regional government have been established in former unitary states. The rise of meso-government has gone hand in hand with the Europeanisation of intergovernmental relationships (Mény, 1990; Sharpe, 1993). European programmes even endorsed the establishment of meso-government in Member States 'the regions of Europe'. Recently, doubts have been raised about the actual impact of the new regional dimension in the power game with, usually more strongly equipped, national and local tiers (Le Galès and Lequesne, 1998). Nevertheless – as the empirical case studies in this book demonstrate – the balance is far more differentiated than general statements allow.

To conclude this part of the institutional analysis, it may be stated that the government-centred structure of the state has given way to more complex relationships. Both global economic reorganisation and the transition to a civil society have put the government in a more distanced position. However, this retreat of the administrative state does not necessarily mean less commitment. The idealised concepts of a self-regulating society based on spontaneous action by its citizens and enterprises belong to the realms of Utopia. Both in economic and cultural terms, a strong commitment of the state is needed to enable social initiatives to take place in a fair way. Experiences with privatising public amenities without first organising the necessary conditions for liberalised markets have shown many times over that public monopolies can transform themselves into private monopo-lies. With respect to the production of public goods, the government does not necessarily have to supply these itself or even establish performance criteria, though it certainly has to guarantee the *parameters* of the private provision and the distribution of public responsibilities. Here, the role of 'government' shifts into that of 'governance in a multi-actor context'. The new differentiation in inter-governmental relationships has created more complexity, leading to a multilevel pattern of governmental competencies. Governmental programmes (e.g. relating to urban policy or the regional economy) are made at all levels of government (i.e. Europe, the national state, the regions, the municipalities and levels in between). There are of course many relationships and even interdependencies between the governmental agencies, but they are not structured according to a top-down model: the new multilevel game is quite complicated and evokes fascinating games of conflicting and cooperative coalitions of power (both within the governmental domain and outside it). The relationships between the Member States and Europe oscillate somewhere between voluntary association and a federal constitution. The governmental relationships within the Member States are even more diverse. As Brenner (1999) says, 'the nature of urban governance within world city-regions is therefore conditioned strongly by patterns of intergovernmental relations within their host states' (p.444).

Implications for metropolitan development

How have the above-mentioned institutional shifts affected the conditions for spatial development in metropolitan areas? Interrelationships between metropolitan regions have been strongly affected by the change in these conditions. Economic development may be guided but is certainly not controlled by governmental agencies. Governments face corporations that operate in international networks within the margins of their own functional markets. These corporations no longer behave as 'home entrepreneurs'; they are not involved in attempts to integrate territorial policies but act in functional networks and space of flows (Castells, 1996). This is not to say that corporations have become completely footloose – the literature on 'institutional embeddedness' makes it clear enough that the position of global players is not detached from regional institutions and conditions, such as labour market characteristics, the grid of particular suppliers and buyers, specialised experiences, etc. (Storper, 1997; Scott, 1997). Corporations make their choices within the margins of their own international networks but at the same time they require particular qualities in local conditions. They need their supporting infrastructure such as airports, motorways, suitably located land and skilled workforce. They will seek locations where these conditions can be supplied with speed and certainty. The local institutional framework, and its ability to create these conditions, is therefore a vital element in the equation. Swyngedouw created the term 'glocalisation' to express the 'combined process of globalisation and local-territorial reconfiguration' (1992, p.61). There has been much recent theoretical literature that develops this idea and explores the impact of globalisation on the structures of local governance (e.g. Swyngedouw and Baeten, 2001; Brenner, 1998, 1999). One element of this restructuring of governance is the developing practice of metropolitan regions to become more concerned about their competitive position vis-à-vis other metropolitan regions, especially in the framework of the EU (Hall and Hubbard, 1998; Jessop, 1998). It is felt that regional economies have become more dependent on their position in global networks than on the traditional powers and investments of local industries and local entrepreneurs. The loss of economic protection, the opening of national boundaries, and the international – particularly European – legislation regarding the liberalisation of economic markets has given regional economies strong incentives to become better positioned in the new global networks. Since the 1980s, the main public and private stakeholders of most metropolitan regions have attempted to improve cooperation within their region in order to strengthen the conditions for competitiveness in the external world. Marketing techniques have been extensively used to profile cities and regions (Kearns and Philo, 1993). For example the symbolic appeal of Silicon Valley has given birth to innumerable sons and daughters.

Most national governments in Europe support these new regional approaches. They recognise the national economic interest in strong, internationally connected regions and adapt their regional programmes accordingly. In the 1950s, 1960s and even 1970s, national governments used to support backward regions, but in the new, post-1980s competitive context they feel the need to place their bet on the strongest regional horses. Thus, a great deal has been invested in such infra-structure as airports, high-speed rail connections and urban terminals, the new 'smart infrastructure' of knowledge. In the Netherlands, for example, so-called mainport strategies were introduced in the mid-1980s to support the country's strongest economic regions. The British government abruptly withdrew support from the iron and coal industry, and other governments followed suit but at a more gradual pace. Almost all national governments endorse these new trends in regional economic policy. For electoral reasons, some are obliged to continue to give some support to backward regions, but their real concern remains the improvement of the strong regions. Surprisingly, European regional policy (although favouring the regions as such) ignores this trend and continues to give support to economically disadvantaged regions.

The relationships within the metropolitan regions of Europe have also been severely affected by the institutional transformation of the welfare state. The tendencies towards decentralisation and privatisation have led to the social and economic development (and via these the spatial development) whereby metro-politan regions are less dependent on decisions by higher government. The increasing share of income from local taxes and the decreasing size of central grants have made municipalities more receptive to strategies to increase local investments. This is nothing new to American cities, but municipalities on the European continent were in general more accustomed to receiving support from national programmes to deal with their problems. The tendency towards fiscal and financial decentralisation in almost all Western European nations has increased the accountability of municipalities. The cities particularly needed this growth of accountability, as their political programmes and political expectations were narrowly focused on the wishes of the urban electorate. Traditionally, urban politicians opted for social expenditures that would be reimbursed by national governments. This may explain the delayed response to the urban crisis in countries with a strong dependence on national government. The recent decentralisation of financial responsibilities has brought the principles of accountability and electoral response more into balance (Elkin, 1987; Kreukels and Salet, 1992).

As a consequence of the above-mentioned trends, there is an increasing sense of entrepreneurialism exhibited by both public and private local actors. During the welfare state regime, not only the municipalities were dependent on national arrangements, but so too were many local producers of public amenities, such as schools, housing associations, hospitals, public transportation agencies, and so on. Often these so-called non-profit organisations made a lot of profit without being entrepreneurial at all! They were just spending the subsidies provided by the central government. The change in institutional conditions has brought about a strong dynamism and new efficiency into these non-profit agencies. This has led to fascinating new experiences of private agencies fulfilling public tasks in entrepreneurial ways. In the Netherlands, for example, old lacklustre housing associations have now become very keen developers. Of course, a great deal of attention is being devoted to how commercial and social roles can be fulfilled simultaneously (Salet, 1999). A consequence of this new responsiveness of public and private local actors is a sharp increase in rivalry. As municipalities have become far more dependent on their own income (e.g. taxes and fees) they have to invest in fiscal and other financial sources in order to become more attractive than neighbouring municipalities. In particular, the trend of fiscal decentralisation has brought about more competition between local actors. There is a tension between this tendency and the above-mentioned need for regional cooperation with respect to the position of the region internationally. On the one hand, metropolitan areas need strong cooperative regional profiles, while on the other hand the old problem of metropolitan fragmentation has worsened under current institutional conditions. Cooperation in this frame means cooperation between rivals, or 'adversarial cooperation'. This kind of cooperation may seem paradoxical but is not at all unusual in market relations. Adversaries may share common interests and cooperate, or be brought into cooperation, if they come to understand their common interests. Rival municipalities, for instance, may share the profit derived from developing certain industrial sites. Or they may jointly develop new regional shopping centres or recreation areas instead of frustrating each another's attempts to do so. This approach may become more familiar in the coming years since the above-mentioned transition of institutional conditions has a strong tendency to engender more local responsiveness. The strategies for metropolitan coordination should not neglect the changing conditions but take advantage of them.

Finally, the institutional changes have brought new actors into the metropolitan arena, actors who are behaving in different market conditions and different power relations. The tendency towards privatisation has brought international private companies into the public domain. The metropolitan debate on institutional relationships was focused for many years on balancing central and decentralised competencies in intergovernmental relations. Now, completely new institutional issues are arising, but so far without effective answers. While governments were decentralising and privatising during the last 15 years, market processes in the private sector were heading in the opposite direction. Private producers of public goods are undergoing phenomenal enlargements of scale, creating new oligopolies of multinational corporations. Public utilities are a case in point. These used to be provided and directed by municipalities and higher tiers of government. Although the step towards privatisation might seem a technical matter, the institutional arena is changing dramatically as a result of this. It is expected that 90 per cent of the European electricity market will be in the hands of five or six multinational companies within the next five to ten years. It is very difficult to stop the process, as municipalities and provinces are eager to sell their utilities. They are also selling public transportation services, health services, housing, water services, and so on. As a result, local customers and municipalities are becoming increasingly dependent on powerful international players.

New challenges of spatial restructuring and policy coordination

European city-regions have undergone considerable physical change in recent years. The dynamics of development have taken on new and complex forms and these demand innovative responses if coordinated and comprehensive land-use strategies are to be achieved. The suburbanisation process during most of the twentieth century resulted in the geographical spread of residential areas. The central city generally continued to provide facilities for this wider population, placing considerable emphasis on transportation issues. However, more recently these facilities (e.g. commercial, retail and services) have begun to radiate outwards, and deprive city centres of their exclusive centrality. At present, a huge variety of new spatial configurations may be identified, including 'twin cities', *Zwischenstädte* (in-between cities), polycentric regions, urban corridors, converged cities and even perhaps new 'edge cities' (Garreau, 1992). Dramatic changes have also taken place within metropolitan areas, such as the more intensive development of financial districts, the regeneration of dockland and railway land, and the gentrification of inner cities (Graham and Marvin, 2001). These changes can be seen as a response to internal factors, such as changes in population structure, income levels and consumer values, and also to external pressures from economic globalisation.

Spatial policies for metropolitan areas have to respond to these changes. However, these policies have had to be formulated in a turbulent governmental world. The arrangements for making decisions about the development of cities have also been undergoing dramatic change. The mid-1980s witnessed the abolition of many metropolitan governments, such as those of London, Copenhagen, Rotterdam and Barcelona. However, in some cities the mood has shifted again and there is a return towards strengthening metropolitan government. For example, experiments with city mayors in Italy and England indicate a desire to create a more positive climate for city-wide policy. There is also a widespread trend towards strengthening the regional level of government across Europe. Thus there are many changes in the formal structures of government that affect the way in which cities can formulate strategic policies. In many cases the administrative jurisdictions of the various local and regional governments do not match the evolving spatial configurations and urban developments mentioned above. Thus spatial development and administrative boundaries do not necessarily correspond with one another. One response to this has been the formation of organisational arrangements to reflect the new functional interrelationships between local, local/regional and even between regional administrations. These evolving administrative patterns may be formal or informal. Thus spatial policy has to be formulated in a way that corresponds to the shift from government to governance and the changing, perhaps more limited role played by formal government. This requires a collaborative and negotiating approach to the creation of strategic policy over the metropolitan arena (Healey *et al.*, 1997). Coordination is a central theme in this fragmented institutional landscape.

One major trend towards inter-agency working has been the adoption of public-public and public-private partnerships. One interesting aspect of the investigation of a range of European cities is whether this shift to partnership has followed a similar pattern across Europe or whether different cities in different countries are experimenting with different approaches. For example, can *Communitées d'Agglomaration*, *Sociétées mixtes*, *Bezirke Kommunal Vereine* and City Pride Partnerships be considered as responses to a general pressure or as reflections of particular national circumstances? Such agencies of governance can potentially vary in their relationship with the formal structures of government and also in the degree to which they contain a local democratic input. Sometimes these arrangements might improve the potential for strategic coordination. However, the trend towards governance can also fragment the decision-making process and make it difficult to achieve an overall strategic approach. These changes in the patterns of metropolitan governance interact with the spatial reorganisation of social and economic markets. The question of how and in what way metropolitan governance and spatial policy can once again be brought into harmony is pressing in virtually all urban regions in Western Europe (Newman and Thornley, 1996).

It may be concluded that the arena of metropolitan development is becoming more complex in the post-welfare state era. On the one hand there is a need for a regional focus in multi-actor and multilevel cooperation, while on the other hand metropolitan fragmentation and competition between more autonomous local actors has increased. And while governments are decentralising and privatising, new hierarchies and international oligopolies and monopolies are emerging in the private sectors. The challenges for spatial development in metropolitan regions have to be addressed under these contradictory conditions. In most metropolitan regions the challenges for spatial policy include the following questions:

- How can regional economies be organised to meet the competitive conditions of international connectedness? This question includes the efficient spatial management of infrastructure, and public amenities such as the teaching of professional skills and labour services.

- How can environmental qualities be balanced in a regional context of institutional fragmentation? This question includes new themes such as the creation of new urban landscapes in the urban region, the multiple use of water and nature, and the variation and contrast of activities in regions.
- How can growing structural spatial inequality be prevented? Many metropolitan regions cope with the problem of growing inequalities between relatively poor central cities and flourishing suburban environments. This question includes the spatial differences in health, education, housing, and labour markets.
- How can cultural identities be established and re-established at the metropolitan scale under conditions of continuing spatial extension and detachment?

These challenges are not new to the spatial development of metropolitan regions in Europe. However, they are now manifest under institutional conditions that are very different from those of 20 years ago. Referring to the above-mentioned issues of spatial development in the metropolitan regions, the basic question is how public and private action can be coordinated in a context of institutional fragmentation and continuing spatial detachment (Salet and Faludi, 2000). These challenges have to be met by new strategies, which are being sought throughout Europe. Can strategies of governmental reorganisation help meet the challenges signalled above? Strategies of this kind certainly belong to the most tried and true options, but they are usually not completely satisfactory. Often too much is expected of governmental reorganisation – the need for social coordination cannot be fulfilled solely by governmental intervention, let alone by creating new forms of government. Governmental strategies will be more successful if they are backed by economic and cultural strategies. Moreover, it is extremely difficult to find adequate forms of government that are able to match the dynamic spatial development in metropolitan areas. Usually governmental reorganisation lags behind these spatial developments and it may be questioned whether it is prudent for governmental reorganisation to run continually after the newest spatial configurations. Sometimes, it may prove better to have sound and durable forms of government and to look for flexible policy responses of governance rather than to concoct new forms of organisation. Notwithstanding these remarks, it may still make sense to analyse the significance of governmental reorganisation – new forms of government could make a difference – in close relationship with the commitment to more flexible coalition formations and types of governance.

It is fascinating to see how these games are played in practice. In almost all European metropolitan areas, forms of government have been established which deviate in one way or another from the 'standard' nation-wide administrative systems. In fact, deviating forms of government are standard in metropolitan areas. They are often not very durable and their structures often reproduce the inequalities and the cultures of distrust and fragmentation. Most experimental forms focus on the highest tier of local government, as the regional level of meso-government is usually considered too large and distant to enable real regulatory powers. Sometimes new intermediary forms emerge. The significance of regional meso-government is usually more manifest in the establishment of strategic perspectives and in the role of governance (by connecting programmes of different tiers of government with each other). The policy centres of gravity, however, are usually sought at the highest levels of local government. Here, the major cities try to upgrade their responsibilities to higher levels of spatial scale. Attempts made in this vein include those intended to bridge social and economic differences and particularly attempts to smooth out the fiscal disparities between municipalities. The experiments in metropolitan government are often pushed forward by the major cities (taking the initiatives for governmental reorganisation, bringing in local entrepreneurs, soliciting funds from the central government) and the surrounding suburban municipalities are urged, willingly or not, to participate in metropolitan governance. European experiences demonstrate that fragmentation and conflicts are not easily overcome by this strategy, because the resultant forms of government are built upon a foundation of quicksand.

Fragmentation and competition may be conceived of as problems in themselves, but it makes a big difference whether these problems are conceived from a polycentric or a monocentric point of view. In the latter case, when fragmentation is seen from a city-centred view, all fragments have to be brought under a common denominator. In the former case, however, differences and polycentric responsibilities are accepted and the metropolitan area is not expected to operate unilaterally and without fragmented and rival powers. On the contrary, fragmentation and competition are considered beneficial because they enable innovative and dynamic development, and keep local agencies alert. From this point of view, metropolitan fragmentation and competition are only problematic insofar as they become dysfunctional. The levels of aspiration from these different approaches are quite different and they focus on different solutions. The first approach tries to force all different conditions of metropolitan development into a uniform framework (e.g. establishing equal fiscal conditions in the whole metropolitan area, or equal parking regulations for shopping centres, or equal conditions for attracting companies). The second approach acknowledges the existence and the significance of diversity, establishes limits where they threaten to become dysfunctional, and focuses its main attention on options for cooperation. In the following chapters, the use of these different strategies and their impact will be studied in the real-life experience of European city-regions.

Bibliography

Batley, R. (1991) 'Comparisons and lessons', in R. Batley and G. Stoker (eds) *Local Government in Europe: Trends and Development*, London: Macmillan.

Blair, T. (1998) *The Third Way: New Politics for the New Century*, London: Fabian Society.

Brenner, N. (1998) 'Global cities, glocal states: global city formation and state territorial restructuring in contemporary Europe', *Review of International Political Economy*, 5 (1) Spring 1998: 1–37.

Brenner, N. (1999) 'Globalisation as reterritorialisation: the rescaling of urban governance in the European Union', *Urban Studies*, 36 (3): 431–51.

Castells, M. (1996) *The Rise of the Network Society*, Oxford and Malden: Blackwell Publishers.

Dunford, M. and Kafkalas, G. (eds) (1992) *Cities and Regions in the New Europe*, New York: Belhaven Press.

Elkin, S.L. (1987) *City and Regime in the American Republic*, Chicago: University of Chicago Press.

Esping-Andersen, G. (1990) *The Three Worlds of Welfare Capitalism*, Cambridge: Polity Press.

Esping-Andersen, G. (ed.) (1996) *Welfare States in Transition*, London: Sage.

Garreau, J. (1992) *Edge City*, New York: Anchor Books.

Giddens, A. (1998) *The Third Way: The Renewal of Social Democracy*, Cambridge: Polity Press.

Giddens, A. (ed.) (2001) *The Global Third Way Debate*, Cambridge: Polity Press.

Graham, S. and Marvin, S. (2001) *Splintering Urbanism*, London and New York: Routledge.

Gualini, E. (2001) *Planning and the Intelligence of Institutions*, Aldershot: Ashgate.

Gunsteren, H.R. van (1998) *Theory of Citizenship*, New York: Westview Press.

Hall, T. and Hubbard, P. (eds) (1998) *The Entrepreneurial City*, Chichester: Wiley.

Healey, P., Khakee, A., Motte, A. and Needham, B. (eds) (1997) *Making Strategic Spatial Plans: Innovation in Europe*, London: UCL Press.

Held, D., McGrew, A., Goldblatt, D. and Perraton, J. (1999) *Global Transformations*, Cambridge: Polity Press.

Hooghe, L. and Marks, G. (2001) *Multi-level Governance and European Integration*, Lanham, MD: Rowman and Littlefield Publishers.

Jessop, B. (1998) 'The narrative of enterprise and the enterprise of narrative: place marketing and the entrepreneurial city', in T. Hall and P. Hubbard (eds) *The Entrepreneurial City*, Chichester: Wiley.

Kearns, G. and Philo, C. (1993) *Selling Places*, Oxford: Pergamon Press.

Kreukels, A.M.J. and Salet, W.G.M. (1992) *Debating Institutions and Cities*, WRR V 76, Den Haag: Sdu Uitgevers.

Le Galès, P. and Lequesne, Chr. (1998) *Regions in Europe*, New York: Routledge.

Mény, Y. (1990) *Government and Politics in Western Europe*, Oxford: Oxford University Press.

Newman, P. and Thornley, A. (1996) *Urban Planning in Europe: International Competition, National Systems and Planning Projects*, London: Routledge.

Norton, A. (1991) 'Western European local government in comparative perspective', in R. Batley and G. Stoker (eds) *Local Government in Europe: Trends and Developments*, London: Macmillan.

Norton, A. (1994) *International Handbook of Regional and Local Government*, Aldershot: Elgar.

Ohmae, K. (1995) *The End of the Nation State*, New York: Free Press.

Putnam, R.D. (1993) *Making Democracies Work: Civic Traditions in Modern Italy*, Princeton, NJ: Princeton University Press.

Rowat, D.C. (ed.) (1988) *Public Administration in Developed Democracies*, New York: Marcel Dekker.

Salet, W.G.M. (1999) 'Regime shifts in Dutch housing policy', *Housing Studies*, 14 (4): 547–57.

Salet, W.G.M. and Faludi, A. (eds) (2000) *The Revival of Strategic Spatial Planning*, Royal Dutch Academy of Arts and Sciences (KNAW), Amsterdam: KNAW Edita.

Sassen, S. (1991) *The Global City: New York, London and Tokyo*, Princeton, NJ: Princeton University Press.

Scholte, J.A. (2000) *Globalization: A Critical Introduction*, Basingstoke: Palgrave.

Scott, A. (ed.) (1997) *The Limits of Globalization*, London: Routledge.

Sharpe, L.J. (ed.) (1993) *The Rise of Meso-Government in Europe*, London: Sage.

Storper, M. (1997) *The Regional World. Territorial Development in a Global Economy*, New York: The Guilford Press.

Swyngedouw, E. (1992) 'The mammon quest: "glocalisation", interspatial competition and the monetary order – the construction of new scales', in M. Dunford and G. Kafkalas (eds) *Cities and Regions in the New Europe*, New York: Belhaven Press.

Swyngedouw, E. and Baeten, G. (2001) 'Scaling the city: the political economy of "glocal" development – Brussels' conundrum', *European Planning Studies*, 9 (7): 827–49.

2 Metropolitan regions in the face of the European dimension

Regimes, re-scaling or repositioning?

Stuart Wilks-Heeg, Beth Perry and
Alan Harding

Introduction

This chapter considers the significance of European integration as a factor influencing governance and spatial planning in the continent's major metropolitan regions. While the book as a whole is organised around the notion that national administrative traditions and policy frameworks are crucial to understanding observable variations in metropolitan planning and governance, it is critical that the European dimension is not overlooked. Indeed, there is now a widespread recognition among scholars and policy makers that the dynamics of European economic integration have significant spatial consequences, which have become apparent at a variety of geographical scales – national, regional, metropolitan and urban (Brunet, 1989; Dunford and Perrons, 1994; Brenner, 2000; Taylor and Hoyler, 2000). Similarly, growing attention has been paid to the role that European policies are playing in reshaping governance at the sub-national level, with a number of authors pointing to the possible 'Europeanisation' of local governance (John, 1996; Atkinson and Wilks-Heeg, 2000) or the emergence of forms of 'multilevel governance' that connect European, national, regional and city-based policy makers through complex networks (Marks, 1993; Hooghe, 1996). Furthermore, from a spatial planning perspective, the influences of European economic integration on metropolitan regions, as well as the requirement for governance at all levels to take steps to counterbalance the resultant polarisation in the urban system, have specifically been recognised in the European Spatial Development Perspective (ESDP, 1999).

Given this context, our aims in this chapter are twofold. First, we chart the economic processes operating at a European level that have spatial implications for metropolitan regions. Here, we focus our attention on the patterns of structural economic change associated with European integration and wider globalisation dynamics that are promoting enhanced inter-metropolitan competition within Europe. It is widely claimed that, as a result of economic restructuring, there has been a resultant reordering of national urban hierarchies, leading to the emergence of a new European urban system, dominated by a core axis of beneficiary cities. We critically assess the validity of such accounts of a new European metropolitan geography and consider the role of the ESDP as a policy response that is intended to promote a more balanced, polycentric system of European metropolitan development. Second, we seek to consider the key ways in which these European-wide dynamics may influence metropolitan policy responses and ask whether it is possible to identify any generic trends in European metropolitan governance arising as a result of these developments. We pay particular attention to three key ideas that have emerged in the recent literature on comparative metropolitan governance. The first is the notion of transition from the managerial city to an entrepreneurial city, a shift that is seen to be closely related to the growth of inter-metropolitan competition in Europe. The second is the suggestion that, as a result of such competition, European cities are seeing the emergence of urban regimes or growth coalitions which prioritise economic development as the key activity of urban governance. The third is the theory of state re-scaling, which suggests that new forms of metropolitan governance are emerging as specifically state-led, spatial responses to economic restructuring.

Metropolitan regions in an integrating Europe: hierarchies, geographies, policies

The dynamics of structural economic change associated with European integration impact on metropolitan regions in a complex variety of ways and there is no scope here to explore the full range of possible cause and effect relationships. Instead, we seek in this section to outline three key dimensions of the European influence on individual metropolitan regions. First, we discuss the extent to which European economic integration has contributed to a reordering of European metropolitan *hierarchies*, expressed most dramatically in the emergence of a relatively small number of metropolitan regions as the key economic centres in the European economy. Second, we assess whether this process of economic restructuring is also promoting a polarisation of metropolitan *geographies* within Europe, in which a select European metropolitan core has been able to develop at the expense of cities located towards the outer peripheries of the EU territory. Third, we note the way in which the EU has sought to respond to these perceived patterns of urban and regional change through the introduction of new *policies*, particularly following the publication of the European Spatial Development Perspective (ESDP).

There is now a vast literature on the process of economic restructuring that has taken place in Europe over the past three decades (see, *inter alia*, Amin, 1994; Castells, 1993; Amin and Thrift, 1994). While there are important differences in the theoretical perspectives underpinning such analyses (see, for example, the discussion of neo-Schumpetarian, regulationist and flexible specialisation accounts in Amin, 1994), the key elements of structural change in the European economy are widely accepted. In basic terms, structural economic change has involved a steep decline in employment in labour-intensive primary and secondary sectors, compensated for by a growing share of economic product and employment in services, particularly banking, insurance and other financial services, as well as in certain high-tech manufacturing. While accounts vary in the emphasis that they place on the precise balance of factors driving structural economic change, three key shifts tend to be highlighted throughout. First, there has been an emergence of a new international division of labour (cf. Fröbel *et al.*, 1980), whereby factory production, and hence employment, has increasingly moved from the advanced capitalist economies to countries with lower labour costs. Second, there has been a move towards the introduction of new, flexible production processes, involving the replacement of labour-intensive production processes with procedures based upon new technologies (it is in this particular context that the notion of a shift from Fordism to post-Fordism has most consistently been used). Both of these trends have led to a sharp decline in manufacturing employment in the advanced capitalist states. Third, the deregulation of a variety of global economic flows – such as trade, inward investment and finance capital – has enhanced employment in a number of service sectors, particularly those highlighted above. At the same time, the increasing integration of the international economy that has resulted from the enhancement of these global flows has intensified inter-firm competition, thus accelerating the introduction of cost-saving, flexible production methods and the shift of production to lower cost countries.

Hierarchies

The implications of structural economic changes for Europe's cities have been profound and highly uneven. Cities that grew and prospered as centres of manufacturing during the Industrial Revolution – such as Sheffield, Manchester and Dortmund – have generally experienced the most negative transition, resulting in high levels of business failure, unemployment and social exclusion. Conversely, those cities that have been able to adapt to or attract high-tech production methods have emerged as 'new industrial districts', with examples including Cambridge and Stuttgart. Finally a small number of cities have emerged as key economic nodes in this new economic order – constituting the most important concentrations of financial and business services and the favoured locations for the global and European headquarters of major multinational corporations. This elite group of cities includes the likes of London, Paris, Amsterdam and Frankfurt.

While the economic changes outlined above stem from wider global, rather than simply European dynamics, the process of European integration has played a lead role in shaping the character of structural change within Europe. Most fundamentally, European integration has been motivated by the goal of creating a single European economic space, in which there are no barriers to trade, inter-firm competition or movement of the mobile factors of production (capital and labour). The introduction of the Single European Market in 1992 and the Single European Currency (the euro) in 2002 have been key staging points in this hitherto unparalleled attempt to integrate national economies. As a result, the European Commission has directly introduced or promoted many of the supply-side interventions that have underpinned the acceleration of structural economic change, including privatisation, market deregulation and the removal of trade barriers. At the same time, the creation of the single market has greatly intensified competition for European market share between indigenous companies, and has prompted American and Japanese corporations to invest heavily in EU Member States in order to secure a foothold in the now vast European market, thereby further enhancing competition.

The trends outlined above have important implications for cities that, in the main, previously operated largely in the context of their respective national economies. While cities remain the key sites of business activity, enhanced inter-firm competition and capital mobility have meant that cities have increasingly found it necessary to introduce special measures to retain and attract businesses. As a result, there is a general agreement that, in addition to inter-firm competition, European integration has also unleashed powerful forces of *territorial competition* within the EU and, in particular, competition between its cities (Amin and Thrift, 1994; Bagnasco and Le Galès, 2000). As a result, an array of studies over the past 10–15 years have sought to analyse the changing role and status of Europe's cities. Within this literature, two broad types of study can be identified. A first group of studies has produced rankings of EU cities (Cheshire *et al.*, 1986; Cheshire, 1990, 1999; Lever, 1999). These accounts have largely been motivated by a concern to measure the significance of particular variables in affecting urban economic performance and have generally deployed regression analysis. The second set of studies, dominated by continental Europeans, have sought to capture how economic restructuring affects the overall system of cities and, based on this analysis, has produced typologies of cities based on functional hierarchies (Brunet, 1989; Cattan *et al.*, 1994; Kräkte, 1995. For English-language discussions of these works, see Dematteis, 2000 and Brenner, 2000). These accounts of changing functional hierarchies have frequently presented a more theoretical account of urban change, generally with reference to regulation theory or the literature on world cities (see Brenner, 2000).

Despite the fundamental differences of approach, there is a great deal of commonality in the conclusions reached by both sets of studies. In particular, it is suggested that the metropolitan areas that have been most successful in adjusting to the new economic order have been able to secure a growing concentration of higher-order corporate and financial functions, inward investment and advanced manufacturing and production, often at the direct expense of those cities and regions that continue to suffer ongoing industrial decline. Such studies persistently bracket cities such as Frankfurt, Paris, London, Brussels and Amsterdam among the winners of this inter-metropolitan competition and Naples, Liverpool, Duisburg, Le Harve and Liège among the losers. Consequently, it is claimed that a significant shift in urban hierarchies is taking place as a result of the intensification of inter-metropolitan competition within Europe.

Figure 2.1 provides one of the more sophisticated examples of such accounts. This typology, presented in Brenner (2000), identifies two key dimensions that are driving the reordering of the urban hierarchy within Europe: the shift from Fordist to flexible specialisation systems and the varying degrees to which cities exercise 'control capacity' (for instance, as financial centres or key locations for corporate headquarters) in the European economy. These two dimensions are then used to produce six tiers on the European urban hierarchy. At the pinnacle of this hierarchy are the 'global' cities of London, Paris and Frankfurt, followed by a number of 'European urban regions', including Amsterdam, Milan and Barcelona. At the bottom of the hierarchy we find those cities most marginalised in the contemporary European economy – the likes of Naples and Cottbus – and, just above these, those cities which have struggled particularly with the transition from Fordist production processes – such as Duisberg and Manchester. Sandwiched between these key sets of winners and losers are those cities that have emerged as national urban centres and those that have proved more successful in negotiating the shift to post-Fordist forms of production. To underline the fact that the European urban hierarchy is not simply the 'outcome' of the process of economic change outlined above, but a fluid and dynamic system of ongoing competition and change, the typology is structured around the assumption that cities will continually change positions in this hierarchy.

Such attempts to rank cities in a European hierarchy have not been without their critics. Some authors have suggested that, despite the realities of territorial competition, the notion of a shift from national urban hierarchies to a European system of cities is overstated. Dematteis (2000, p.58) suggests that the idea of a single system of European cities 'is a more or less implicit hypothesis' in the studies that have been referred to above and lacks firm empirical foundations. Likewise, in stark contrast to many recent accounts of the reordering of urban hierarchies in Europe, Bagnasco and Le Galès (2000a, p.10) suggest that the urban system in Europe has been relatively stable for several hundred years. According to this view, long-run historical evidence suggests that there has been relatively

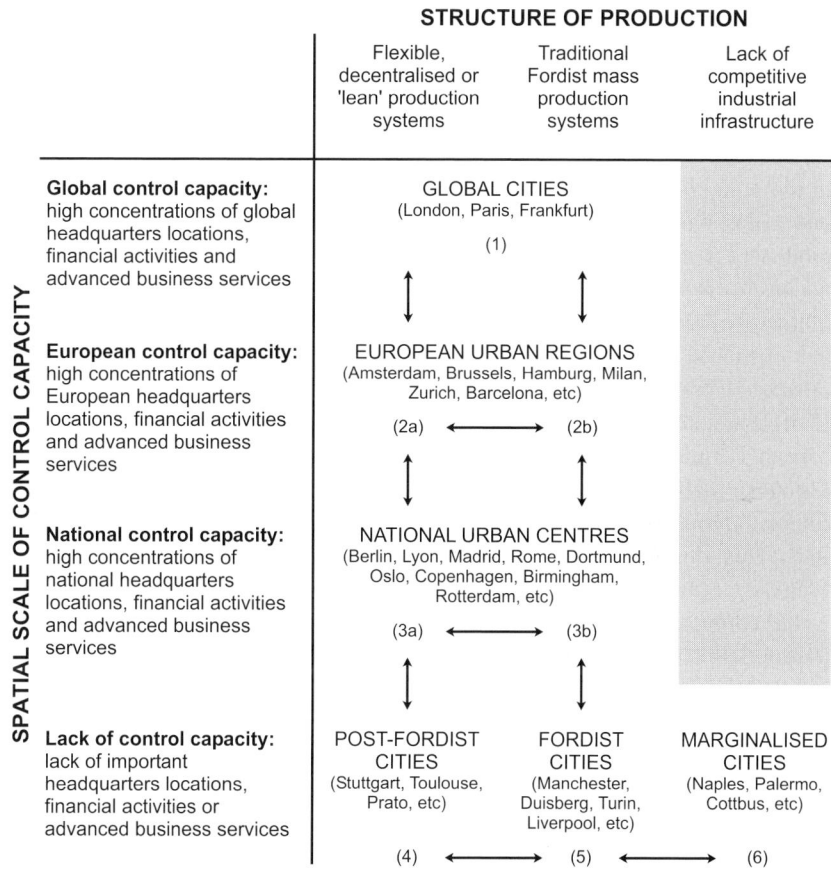

STRUCTURE OF PRODUCTION

Figure 2.1 The changing European urban hierarchy. *Source:* Brenner, 2000, p.61.

little change in the overall hierarchy of cities in Europe since the Middle Ages, even allowing for the upheaval of the Industrial Revolution. Rather than being a product of recent economic change, '...the hierarchy of European cities has taken centuries to come about' (Bagnasco and Le Galès, 2000a, p.10). Nonetheless, for our purposes, typologies such as that presented in figure 2.1 can be regarded as a useful heuristic device, in that they capture the uneven effects of recent economic change on Europe's key metropolitan regions. As such, they are a valuable means of identifying the diversity of policy challenges faced by metropolitan regions across Europe. Clearly, the priorities for governance and spatial planning in cities such as London or Frankfurt that have experienced rapid growth in a number of high value-added sectors as a result of their global city functions, will be very different from those pertaining in cities that continue to suffer adversely from large-scale industrial decline and concomitant job loss. Such diversities are demonstrated by the individual case study chapters in this volume.

Geographies

In the view of a number of analysts, the changing hierarchy of European cities outlined above is not merely the result of structural economic change, but also the product of an allied set of spatial processes. According to such accounts, European integration has been closely associated with the emergence of a distinctive pattern of metropolitan polarisation within the European economy. Here, the argument is that enhanced inter-metropolitan competition within Europe has shaped a new urban economic geography, whereby the 'winners' tend to be clustered in the European 'core' and the 'losers' in the European periphery. Portrayed as the 'blue banana' (Brunet, 1989) or 'Europe's vital axis' (Dunford and Perrons, 1994), the European metropolitan core is seen to stretch in an arc from the south-east of England through the Benelux countries, Germany, Switzerland and into northern Italy. This axis, which incorporates, *inter alia*, London, Amsterdam, Brussels, Frankfurt, Stuttgart, Geneva, Zurich and Milan, constitutes a 'vast urban corridor, whose components are tightly interlinked through advanced communications and transportation infrastructures' (Brenner, 2000, p.57). These features constitute key locational advantages for cities along this axis, which also boast significant concentrations of highly-skilled workers, leaving them well placed to attract further high-order activities (Dunford and Perrons, 1994). As a result, it is suggested that the process of European integration exhibits distinctively centripetal tendencies (cf. Brenner, 2000), generating the highest growth rates in and around this metropolitan core, which is immediately bounded by the majority of Europe's most advanced national economies and a number of additional cities of European importance (Barcelona, Copenhagen, Berlin). According to this representation, the remaining EU territory – constituting the Atlantic coast, the southern Mediterranean and Greece, and eastern Germany – forms 'an outer layer of relatively underdeveloped zones and peripheries' (Brenner, 2000, p.58).

There are numerous problems with such spatial depictions of the European metropolitan system. First, it has been widely noted that concepts such as the 'blue banana' have frequently been produced by particular national and regional planning authorities and may thus be driven more by particular geopolitical interests than by detailed empirical analysis (Kunzmann and Wegener, 1991; Taylor and Hoyler, 2000; Brenner, 2000). Thus, the original blue banana was produced for DATAR, the French regional planning authority, and can be read as an attempt to demonstrate the dominance of Paris within France (Kunzmann, 1992). Many subsequent variants were produced in other national or metropolitan contexts and were equally 'shaped by the desire to belong to the perceived European core area' (Taylor and Hoyler, 2000, p.179). Second, since there appears to be no clearly defined methodology guiding the production of such spatial images, it has been perfectly feasible – and no less legitimate – for an array of alternative depictions of European metropolitan geography to be produced. To date these include the image of the bunch of grapes (Kunzmann and Wegener, 1991), to stress the polycentric nature of the European urban system, the bowl of fruit salad (Goddard, 1995), evoking the notion of multiple inter-metropolitan systems and the red octopus (van der Meer, 1998), representing a more balanced urban system, through which the majority of Europe's cities are linked to the core via a set of longitudinal corridors. Third, spatial images such as the 'blue banana' have been criticised for their tendency to reduce complex sets of interactions to highly simplistic, and static, models of economic geography (Brenner, 2000). Indeed, the recent resurgence of cities apparently located on the European periphery – such as Manchester or Marseilles – points to dynamics that are not adequately captured by such models. Finally, some authors have questioned whether the emergence of a European metropolitan core is as closely bound up with the process of European economic integration as is often claimed. For instance, as Taylor and Hoyler (2000) demonstrate, there is a remarkable continuity between the 'blue banana' and the European spine of cities already identified by Rokkan (1970) as being of long-run historical importance.

These concerns notwithstanding, it is difficult to deny the importance of this central spine within Europe. Two recent studies underline the overwhelming significance of the cities making up the axis. First, Taylor and Hoyler (2000) use the world city concept to rank 53 European cities according to their importance as centres for advanced producer services. The resultant analysis underscores the importance of the vital European axis, which accounts for all four of Europe's 'alpha' world cities (London, Paris, Frankfurt and Milan) and two of its four 'beta' world cities (Zurich and Brussels). Second, Jönsson et al. (2000) analyse urban accessibility in Europe by calculating how many of Europe's inhabitants can reach each of its major cities for a one-day visit. This analysis, which highlights those cities that serve as the key transport and communication nodes in Europe, once again demonstrates a remarkable concentration of such 'hubs' along the central spine of cities. Finally, it is also important to note that the EU largely accepts the definitions of core and periphery sketched out above. This is demonstrated most clearly in the European Spatial Development Perspective (ESDP), which refers to a 'zone of global economic integration' made up of 'a pentagon defined by the metropolises of London, Paris, Milan, Munich and Hamburg' (ESDP, 1999, para. 68). It is to this 'policy' aspect of the European dimension that we now turn.

Policies

During the 1980s and 1990s a body of EU policies emerged that had significant, and to some extent contradictory, spatial impacts within the European territory.

On the one hand, policies such as the completion of the European Single Market and Economic and Monetary Union, as we noted above, have had highly uneven impacts on the European space economy. On the other hand, there are a string of EU initiatives (such as the European Regional Development Fund and the establishment of trans-European networks) that attempt to promote and manage the balanced development of the same territory. During the 1980s, EU spatial policy was thus criticised for being inherently 'reactive': as negative spatial impacts of EU policies became apparent, they were counteracted by further positive and targeted interventions. By the end of the 1980s, it became clear that a more thorough approach to the European spatial dimension was needed to make sense of the mosaic of spatial patterns developing within the EU. In 1989, informal meetings between ministers responsible for spatial planning began at Nantes. Ten years later, the Informal Council of Ministers for Spatial Planning formally agreed the ESDP at a meeting in Potsdam (ESDP, 1999).

The ESDP is premised on the assumption that in the context of progressive economic integration and related intergovernmental cooperation 'national spatial development policies of the Member States and sectoral policies of the EU require clear spatially transcendent development guidelines' (ESDP, 1999, p.7). It therefore seeks to lay out EU agreement on common objectives and concepts for the future development of the EU based on three key goals: economic and social cohesion; conservation and management of natural resources and cultural heritage; and more balanced competitiveness of the European territory (ESDP, 1999, p.10). In order to move towards these goals, the ESDP advocates three key policy guidelines:

- the development of a balanced and polycentric urban system and a new urban-rural relationship;
- securing parity of access to infrastructure and knowledge;
- sustainable development, prudent management and protection of nature and cultural heritage (ESDP, 1999, p.11).

Of particular significance for metropolitan regions in the EU is the document's vision of polycentric urban development, a direct response to the centripetal dynamics of European integration. While islands of isolated growth are seen to exist beyond the core pentagon of the 'global zone of integration', the regional disparities that are in evidence beyond this metropolitan core are seen to work against economic and social cohesion objectives and to damage the economic competitiveness of the EU as a whole. The ESDP (p.20) thus recommends that 'the creation of several dynamic zones of global economic integration, well distributed throughout the EU territory and comprising a network of internationally accessible metropolitan regions and their linked hinterland will play a key role in improving spatial balance in Europe'. At the same time, this polycentric development at the level of the EU should be balanced: the development of several cores of global economic integration should not weaken existing strong regions and should not be funded by outflows of resources to the periphery. Finally, principles of polycentric development are recommended not only at the EU level, but within countries and regions.

While the ESDP is seen to impact on three sets of actors – the institutions of the EU, the Member States and sub-national actors – it focuses primarily on the latter. It does not envisage the EU as having a vital role to play in implementing the priority measures it identifies. Rather, the EU role is to coordinate action and to establish a forum or mechanism for the intergovernmental exchange of experience. Similarly, while it is proposed that the application of the ESDP has various implications for the Member States (such as the continuation of project-oriented transnational cooperation within the framework of INTERREG – programme for promoting stronger inter-regional ties), few concrete actions for Member States are recommended. Instead, regional and local authorities are defined as the 'key players in European spatial development policy' (ESDP, 1999, p.42). Indeed, the majority of the ESDP's recommendations necessitate action on a city-region or region-wide scale and the sub-national level is deemed as the appropriate level of action with respect to most of the policy options contained within the ESDP.

Implications for metropolitan governance: the entrepreneurial city?

We have already hinted that the developments at the European scale outlined above have significant but highly diverse implications for metropolitan governance. A great deal of this diversity is captured in the individual case study chapters contained in this volume and there is no scope to present such empirical detail here. Instead, in order to try and capture more generic trends, we focus primarily on considering theoretical accounts, with potential for cross-national application, that provide a conceptual basis for understanding the influence of European integration on metropolitan governance and spatial planning. We begin by outlining the notion of the 'entrepreneurial city', which has been key to wider attempts to theorise the links between Europeanisation dynamics and change in metropolitan governance. We then critically assess the relevance of two bodies of work that have sought to develop this concept: (i) the literature on urban regimes and growth coalitions, and (ii) more recent theories of state re-scaling. This discussion highlights serious limitations with both sets of theories and we instead propose that analysis should focus on the way in which 'Europe' is used by different actors in the metropolitan policy process as a basis for mobilising forms of entrepreneurial governance.

Stuart Wilks-Heeg, Beth Perry and Alan Harding

The entrepreneurial city

While there are grounds to dispute the emergence of a pan-European system of cities, the intensification of inter-metropolitan competition within Europe has meant that major cities in Europe increasingly seek to measure their own economic performance against their counterparts throughout the EU. At the same time, the redefinition of cities' functional roles arising from wider patterns of structural change in the European economy has firmly established economic development as a key issue on all metropolitan policy agendas. Indeed, it is widely suggested that economic development activity has become perhaps the defining feature of contemporary urban politics (Keating, 1991; Newman and Thornley, 1996). In view of these trends, many authors have proposed that a paradigmatic shift has taken place in urban governance: the transition from urban managerialism to urban entrepreneurialism (cf. Harvey, 1989).

Urban managerialism evokes an era of urban governance that evolved in the context of post-war economic expansion and the growth of the welfare state. It is held that the key roles of city and metropolitan authorities in this period were to guide and regulate the location of economic activity through the planning system and to directly provide a range of services, such as education, housing and public transportation. In other words, urban managerialism was essentially concerned with issues of collective consumption (cf. Castells, 1977). By contrast, it is argued that the period of economic restructuring and welfare state retrenchment since the late 1970s has ushered in a new form of urban politics. Faced with large-scale job loss, city authorities have increasingly sought to develop more proactive forms of spatial planning, in which business expansion and inward investment are directly promoted, rather than responded to reactively. These efforts have been augmented by a range of other activities, such as city-marketing campaigns, bidding for major international sporting or cultural events, and investment in prestige projects designed to increase the attractiveness of the city to international investors and tourists. Meanwhile, it is suggested that in some European countries, but most notably in the UK, city authorities saw their role as providers of collective services go into enforced decline as a result of a combination of budget cuts, privatisation, contracting-out and institutional restructuring. In short, city governance is increasingly characterised by a focus on entrepreneurial activities concerned with economic development and issues of production, rather than a concern with the more managerial issues of social welfare and collective consumption.

The broad character of this shift from managerialist to entrepreneurial politics is particularly evident in Europe's larger cities, where its influence has been clearly discernible in patterns of institutional change as well as in the redefinition of spatial planning policies. While doctrines of urban managerialism favoured the creation of overarching metropolitan authorities with key roles in areas such as housing and transportation (e.g. the Greater London Council), such models were increasingly jettisoned from the 1980s. Instead, there was a shift towards a variety of new organisational arrangements, particularly semiautonomous, single-purpose agencies or public-private partnerships (PPPs), whose activities have focused on the development potential of particular districts, economic sectors or prestige projects rather than on strategic metropolitan coordination. Examples include the London Docklands Development Corporation, and the Schiphol Area Development Company in Amsterdam. In many cases, this increased emphasis on economic development activities has led directly to a greater involvement of corporate actors in the political process and there is now widespread evidence of the existence of PPPs in urban governance across Europe (Harding, 1997; Le Galès, 2000). Le Galès (2000) suggests that such developments in urban governance are a direct product of the increased economic competition and market exposure experienced by both cities and companies as a result of European integration and globalisation.

Urban regimes?

In light of this apparently generic emergence of the entrepreneurial city in Europe, two key theoretical accounts have emerged that offer the potential to understand how European integration is serving to reconfigure metropolitan governance. A first body of theory is provided by authors that have suggested that the proliferation of PPPs and other similar arrangements points to the emergence in Europe of the 'urban regimes' or 'urban growth coalitions' that have become the driving force in US urban politics (Axford and Pinch, 1994; Levine, 1994; Stoker and Mossberger, 1994). According to this archetypal model of the entrepreneurial city, city governments and local businesses are drawn into close cooperation arising from their mutual self-interest in the promotion of local economic development. City authorities, particularly those experiencing fiscal retrenchment, depend on development and growth to generate income, for instance through local business taxes. At the same time, there are powerful local, corporate actors whose commercial interests can only be furthered through local economic growth – such as landowners and property developers. Under these socio-economic conditions, there are strong mutual dependencies between public and private actors, which clearly favour cooperation as a means of achieving shared objectives (Stone, 1989). Crucially, European integration provides the conditions in which such mutual dependencies become evident. In particular, capital mobility and inter-urban competition may promote regime-type arrangements, since both city authorities and (parochial) capital share a common interest in promoting the local conditions that will help attract inward investment and corporate relocation (Mayer, 1994; Harding, 1997).

Despite the appeal of the growth coalition concept, considerable doubts have been expressed about the efficacy of interpreting PPPs in European cities as the emergence of US-style urban regimes or urban growth coalitions (Le Galès, 2000; Harding, 1997; Le Galès and Harding, 1998). Le Galès and Harding (1998) question whether the focus of activity in the majority of European cities has decisively shifted from social provision to economic development. Even in the British case, cities have retained many of their service delivery functions (Atkinson and Wilks-Heeg, 2000) and, elsewhere in Europe, cities have expanded their direct role in welfare provision as a result of state decentralisation programmes. In stark contrast to American cities, which depend critically on business taxes, European cities largely receive their income from a combination of central government grants and taxes paid by local residents. In other words, European city authorities are still overwhelmingly funded by taxpayers to provide collective services. Thus, even though the majority of European cities now engage in economic development activity 'it could hardly be said to be the single, overriding priority of those cities' (Le Galès and Harding, 1998, p.131). Furthermore, empirical research in European cities suggests that there are a number of key limitations to applying the regime/ growth coalition model to European cities (Harding, 1997). First, it would appear that development coalitions have nothing like the same degree of salience in European cities as they do in the US context. Second, where coalitions have emerged, they are much less likely to involve private sector landowners, since land available for development in European cities is often owned by public authorities. Third, the public sector tends to play the lead role in European urban development projects, where the private sector appears to be far more risk-adverse than in the American context. Finally, most large-scale development projects in major European cities have involved national governments as a major player.

State re-scaling?

The second account of the role that European integration has played in shaping the emergence of more entrepreneurial forms of metropolitan governance is provided by Brenner (1998, 1999, 2000). Rejecting the 'methodological localism' of regime accounts and drawing instead on regulation theory, Brenner argues that the globalisation of European economic space and the concomitant transformation of the European urban system have triggered a process of 'state re-scaling' in which the emergence of the entrepreneurial city plays a central role. Specifically, he suggests that, under conditions of intensifying global competition, large corporations become increasingly dependent upon localised agglomeration economies. This has, in turn, prompted nation-states to seek to compete in the global economy by mobilising 'place-specific economic assets' and promoting endogenous growth within major city regions. According to Brenner, the entrepreneurial city is not simply the product of local responses to globalisation dynamics, but a key element in the emerging spatial strategies employed by nation-states as a form of crisis management in the face of accelerating globalisation. Thus, in this view, urban entrepreneurialism represents the logical, if not inevitable, state-led response to European economic restructuring.

Brenner's account is consciously offered as a contribution to the literature based on a high level of theoretical abstraction and as a possible framework for cross-national empirical research. However, even existing knowledge would appear to highlight a number of key problems with Brenner's proposed theoretical framework. First, while nation-states have played an important role in shaping particular examples of urban entrepreneurialism, even the apparently paradigmatic British case suggests that other levels of governance are at least equally significant. As Atkinson and Wilks-Heeg (2000) note, British local authorities initially developed economic development strategies as a direct challenge to the highly centralising tendencies of the Thatcher governments in the 1980s. Moreover, the same authors catalogue that, in the case of 'entrepreneurial' cities such as Birmingham, major local development projects emerged as the result of British cities securing European structural funds, with national government often being bypassed in the process. Other examples emerge from recent EU-funded initiatives such as the Liverpool-Manchester Vision study. Initiated by the Regional Development Agency for North-West England, this study has resulted in a common economic strategy that directly seeks to improve the competitiveness of the two cities and the wider region in the global economy (Regeneris Consulting and SURF, 2001). This is to be achieved through a variety of collaborative projects that aim to create 'critical mass' across the Liverpool-Manchester conurbation. Although it offers a perfect example of a spatial re-scaling in response to enhanced global-isation and inter-urban competition, the Liverpool-Manchester Vision is far from constituting a spatial strategy employed by the British nation-state. Conversely, it is best interpreted as part of a wider attempt among England's provincial cities and regions to lobby the nation-state for large-scale investment outside the capital.

Second, it is far from clear that the entrepreneurial city is emerging as a common response to European economic change. Available evidence would already seem to suggest that it would be misleading to suggest that such tendencies can be identified in all, or even most, European metropolitan regions. It is clearly undeniable that the majority of European metropolitan regions have become increasingly engaged in economic development as a result of structural change in the European economy and enhanced territorial competition arising from European integration (Le Galès, 2000). The logic of this shift in metropolitan activity is not in doubt. However, it is far from evident that the structural forces favouring the emergence of the entrepreneurial city have enabled it to permeate all aspects of metropolitan governance, as Brenner seems to suggest. In the case of European cities, there are significant factors that act to constrain the extent to which economic development is permitted to dominate metropolitan governance. As a result, issues such as tackling social exclusion and promoting environmental sustainability remain high on many European policy agendas and are frequently invoked as challenges requiring a reconfiguration or re-scaling of metropolitan governance and spatial planning (Barlow, 1997; Roberts et al., 1999). Despite its growing salience, competitiveness is not the only discourse in metropolitan politics.

Europe as metaphor?

Indeed, it is possible that it is precisely because of such tensions that the Europe dimension is becoming an increasingly important element of metropolitan governance and spatial planning debates. Metropolitan actors seeking to advance more entrepreneurial forms of governance may increasingly appeal to the concepts outlined in the first half of this chapter in an attempt to influence policy and mobilise governance around a competitiveness agenda. Evidence of this more subtle form of 'Europeanisation' is provided by Healey's (1998) analysis of spatial planning policy in ten European cities. Healey (p.139) highlights the importance of Europe as a 'metaphor' in the policy discourses surrounding the 're-emergence of strategic spatial planning at the urban region scale'. Specifically, she proposes that the pressures arising from the process of European integration establish 'Europe' as a key issue for certain stakeholders within urban regions, primarily large companies and political elites.

While diverse interpretations of Europe emerge in different metropolitan contexts (see table 2.1), the uniting feature is the attempt to position or reposition the urban region in relation to the types of spatial images discussed above. Thus, strategic plans for Bergen and Lancashire define their urban regions as 'peripheral' and regard the upgrading of transport routes to an appropriate hub in the European core as a priority for the area. This interpretation is in keeping with the core/ periphery distinction implied by notions such as the 'blue banana' and the vital European axis. Likewise, in the case of Orestad (Copenhagen), 'Europe' was the driving force behind the construction of a fixed link across the Oresund between Copenhagen and Malmo, the aim of which was to 'transform the location of Copenhagen from a periphery to a European node' (p.146). Conversely, cities such as Lyons and Zurich have produced strategic plans that portray their regions as already being 'well-integrated in European territory', evoking a spatial image similar to Kunzmann's 'bunch of grapes'. On the basis of her analysis, Healey suggests that 'Europe' has become increasingly influential as a metaphorical concept in spatial planning but notes that, in such contexts, 'Europe' becomes an essentially local construct, generated by local political and institutional dynamics. As a result, she suggests that such developments should not be interpreted simply as the outcome of a shift towards more entrepreneurial forms of governance. Rather, they are as much a product of a need to mobilise stakeholders in metropolitan regions around a common economic development agenda.

The role of 'Europe' as a contested notion in metropolitan governance and spatial planning is likely to be further fostered by the ESDP. Given its ambitious remit, relatively ambiguous recommendations and proposed relevance to all tiers of government, there is clear scope for the ESDP to be used to underpin competing notions of metropolitan development. Evidence from the UK context, where take-up of the ESDP appears to be particularly advanced, suggests that its principles

Table 2.1 The metaphor of 'Europe': region, nation and European space

The nation in European territory:	Orestad
	(Bergen)
The city/region in European territory:	Bergen
	Lancashire
	Marks Kommun
The city/region in a Europe of the regions:	Lyon
	Zurich
	Lisbon
The city/region in the national territory:	Lyon
	Zurich
	Lisbon
	Bergen
	Lancashire
	Marks Kommun
The city/region in a global territory:	Lisbon
	(Lancashire)

Source: Healey, 1998, p.149.

have already begun to form the basis for contested metropolitan development scenarios. Bailey and Turok (2001) show how the notions of the polycentric urban region outlined in the ESDP are being applied in the context of central Scotland via a project funded by the European Commission under the INTERREG IIc programme. While the authors note that the study suggests that the polycentric urban region may have limited relevance to the central Scotland context, it has nonetheless provided the basis for greater collaboration between the area's two main cities – Glasgow and Edinburgh – and a strengthening of metropolitan planning arrangements. Elsewhere in the UK, the ESDP has been used as a basis for exploring the arguments favouring a polycentric development framework for the West Midlands, the metropolitan region surrounding Birmingham (ECOTEC, 2001). In another case, the ESDP was drawn upon extensively in objections to regional planning guidance raised by a major property developer in the north-west of England (David Lock and Associates, 2001). In short, although non-statutory, the concepts outlined in the ESDP are finding their way into UK planning discourses through a variety of routes.

Stuart Wilks-Heeg, Beth Perry and Alan Harding

Conclusion

This chapter has presented an overview of the complex and changing relationship between the European and metropolitan scales in spatial planning. Our principal conclusions arising from this discussion are threefold. First, although we have highlighted that there are important questions as to the true extent of the impact of European integration upon the European urban system, it is evident that change at the European level has an increasing influence on spatial planning in Europe's metropolitan regions. In particular, the dynamics of structural economic change and territorial competition unleashed by the process of European integration represent key challenges for metropolitan governance. Heightened awareness of these trends, and their possible spatial implications for the EU territory, is clearly found both in metropolitan planning policies and in European policy initiatives. However, the ways in which notions of 'Europe' are translated into local metropolitan contexts would appear to be highly diverse.

Second, because of this diversity, it seems unlikely that patterns of metropolitan change arising from European integration will have prompted convergent trends in metropolitan governance. The notion of the 'entrepreneurial city' is undoubtedly useful in that it captures some widespread trends across Europe's metropolitan regions. However, we would question the value of conceptions of the entrepreneurial city that suggest that it is a near-universal product of metropolitan governance adjusting to a new European economic order. Evidence of US-style urban regimes is scant and institutional responses to structural economic change are far more complex than is suggested by notions of state re-scaling.

Finally, we would propose that there is considerable value in seeking to apply the concept of 'multilevel governance' to the new forms of spatial planning that are emerging as the European level becomes an increasingly important variable in shaping metropolitan policy frameworks (see Chapter 5). Although multilevel governance is a concept that initially grew up around the complex, multilevel policy networks created by European regional policy, there is real scope to apply it to more general accounts of the changing nature of urban and regional governance in Europe. Such an approach would offer the potential to tease out causal linkages between European and metropolitan change, while also taking account of the highly diverse outcomes of such interaction.

Bibliography

Amin, A. (ed.) (1994) *Post-Fordism: A Reader*, Oxford: Basil Blackwell.
Amin, A. and Thrift, N. (eds) (1994) *Globalisation, Institutions and Regional Development in Europe*, Oxford: Oxford University Press.
Atkinson, H. and Wilks-Heeg, S. (2000) *Local Government from Thatcher to Blair: The Politics of Creative Autonomy*, Cambridge: Polity Press.
Axford, N. and Pinch, S. (1994) 'Growth coalitions and local economic development

strategy in southern England: a case study of the Hampshire development', *Political Geography*, 13 (4): 344–60.

Bagnasco, A. and Le Galès, P. (2000a) 'Introduction: European cities: local societies and collective actors?', in A. Bagansco and P. Le Galès (eds) *Cities in Contemporary Europe*, Cambridge: Cambridge University Press.

Bagnasco, A. and Le Galès, P. (eds) (2000b) *Cities in Contemporary Europe*, Cambridge: Cambridge University Press.

Bailey, N. and Turok, I. (2001) 'Central Scotland as a polycentric urban region: useful planning concept or chimera?', *Urban Studies*, 38 (4): 697–715.

Barlow, M. (1997) 'Administrative systems and metropolitan regions', *Environment and Planning C*, 15 (4): 399–411.

Brenner, N. (1998) 'Global cities, global states: global city formation and state territorial restructuring in contemporary Europe', *Review of International Political Economy*, 5 (1): 1–37.

Brenner, N. (1999) 'Globalisation as reterritorialisation: the re-scaling of urban governance in the European Union', *Urban Studies*, 36 (3): 431–51.

Brenner, N. (2000) 'Entrepreneurial cities, 'glocalizing' states and the new politics of scale: rethinking the political geographies of urban governance in western Europe', Working Paper #76a and #76b, Centre for European Studies, Harvard University.

Brunet, R. (1989) *Les Villes 'européennes'*, Paris: DATAR.

Castells, M. (1977) *The Urban Question*, London: Edward Arnold.

Castells, M. (1993) 'European cities, the informational society, and the global economy', *Tijdschrift voor Economische en Sociale Geografie*, 84 (1): 247–57.

Cattan, N., Pumain, C., Rozenblat, C. and Saint-Julien, T. (1994) *Le Système des villes européennes*, Paris: Anthropos.

Cheshire, P.C. (1990) 'Explaining the recent performance of the European Community's major urban regions', *Urban Studies*, 27 (3): 311–34.

Cheshire, P.C. (1999) 'Cities in competition: articulating the gains from integration', *Urban Studies*, 36 (5–6): 843–64.

Cheshire, P.C., Carbanaro, G. and Hay, D.G. (1986) 'Problems of decline and growth in EEC countries', *Urban Studies*, 23 (2):131–49.

David Lock and Associates (2001) Manchester Ship Canal Study, Milton Keynes: David Lock and Associates

Dematteis, G. (2000) 'Spatial images of European urbanisation', in A. Bagnasco and P. Le Galès, *Cities in Contemporary Europe*, Cambridge: Cambridge University Press.

Dunford, M. and Perrons, D. (1994) 'Regional inequality, regimes of accumulation and economic development in contemporary Europe', *Transactions of the Institute of British Geographers*, New Series, 19: 163–82.

ECOTEC (2001) *A Polycentric Framework for the West Midlands*, a final report to the West Midlands Local Government Association and the DETR, ECOTEC Research and Consulting Limited, Birmingham.

ESDP (European Spatial Development Perspective) (1999) *Towards a Balanced and Sustainable Development of the Territory of the EU*, Brussels: Committee on Spatial Development.

Fröbel, F., Heinrichs, J. and Kreye, O. (1980) *The New International Division of Labour*, Cambridge: Cambridge University Press.

Goddard, J. (1995) 'Information and communication technologies, corporate hierarchies and urban hierarchies in the New Europe', in J. Brotchie, M. Batty, E. Blakely, P. Hall and P. Newton (eds) *Cities in Competition: Productive and Sustainable Cities for the 21st Century*, Melbourne: Longman.

Harding, A. (1997) 'Urban regimes in a Europe of the cities?', *European Urban and Regional Studies*, 4 (4): 291–314.

Harvey, D. (1989) 'From managerialism to entrepreneurialism: the transformation of urban governance in late capitalism', *Geografiska Annaler*, 71b: 3–17.

Healey, P. (1998) 'The place of "Europe" in contemporary spatial strategy making', *European Urban and Regional Studies*, 5 (2): 139–53.

Hooghe, L. (ed.) (1996) *Cohesion Policy and European integration: Building Multi-Level Governance*, Oxford: Oxford University Press.

John, P. (1996) 'Europeanization in a centralizing state: multi-level governance in the UK', *Journal of Regional and Federal Studies*, 6 (3): 131–44.

Jönsson, C., Tägil, S. and Törnqvist, G. (2000) *Organising European Space*, London: Sage.

Keating, M. (1991) *Comparative Urban Politics*, Aldershot: Edward Elgar.

Kräkte, S. (1997) *Stadt – Raum – Ökonomie: Einführung in aktuelle Problemfelder der Stadtökonomie und Wirtschaftsgeographie*, Basil: Birkhäuser.

Kunzmann, K. (1992) 'Zur Entwicklung der Stadtsysteme in Europa', *Mitteilungen der Österreichischen Geographischen Gesellschaft*, 134: 25–50.

Kunzmann, K. and Wegener, M. (1991) 'The pattern of urbanisation in western Europe', *Ekistics,* 350: 282–91.

Le Galès, P. (2000) 'Private-sector interests and urban governance', in A. Bagnasco and P. Le Galès, *Cities in Contemporary Europe*, Cambridge: Cambridge University Press.

Le Galès, P. and Harding, A. (1998) 'Cities and states in Europe', *West European Politics*, 21 (3): 120–45.

Lever, W.F. (1999) 'Competitive cities in Europe', *Urban Studies*, 35 (5–6): 1029–44.

Levine, M.A. (1994) 'The transformation of urban politics in France: the roots of growth politics and urban regimes', *Urban Affairs Quarterly*, 29 (3): 383–410.

Marks, G. (1993) 'Structural policy and multilevel governance in the EC', in A.M. Sbragia (ed.) *Euro-politics*, Washington: The Brookings Institute.

Mayer, M. (1994) 'Post-Fordism in city politics', in A. Amin (ed.) *Post-Fordism: A Reader*, Oxford: Basil Blackwell.

Newman, P. and Thornley, A. (1996) *Urban Planning in Europe: International Competition, National Systems and Planning Projects*, London: Routledge.

Regeneris Consulting and SURF (2001) *Liverpool-Manchester Vision: Strategy and Action Plan*, Warrington: North West Development Agency.

Roberts, P., Thomas, K. and Williams, G. (1999) *Metropolitan Planning in Britain: A Comparative Study*, London: Jessica Kingsley/Regional Studies Association.

Rokkan, S. (1970) *Citizens, Elections, Parties,* New York: McKay.

Stoker, G. and Mossberger, K. (1994) 'Urban regime theory in comparative perspective', *Environment and Planning C: Government and Policy*, 12 (2): 195–212.

Stone, C.L. (1989) *Regime Politics: Governing Atlanta 1946–1988*, Lawrence, KS: University of Kansas Press.

Taylor, P.J. and Hoyler, M. (2000) 'The spatial order of European cities under conditions of contemporary globalisation', *Tijdschrift voor Economische en Sociale Geografie*, 91 (2): 176–89.

Van der Meer, L. (1998) 'Red octopus', in W. Blaas (ed.) *A New Perspective for European Spatial Development Policies*, Aldershot: Ashgate.

PART II

London, Birmingham, Cardiff/Wales, Stockholm

3 London

Institutional turbulence but enduring nation-state control

Andy Thornley

In exploring the relationship between strategic planning and governance in London over the last 20 years, two issues stand out. The first is the lack of any regional level of government. Here, region means the travel-to-work catchment area of the city – the south-east region – which covers an area within a 60-mile radius from the centre of the city and had in 2000 a population of 18.1 million people. The second issue has been the instability in the government of the metropolitan core, that is, the built-up area of the city within the green belt – usually referred to as Greater London – which contains 7.4 million people. This vacuum or uncertainty in governance at a strategic scale has led to the national government taking a dominant role in strategic planning for London. However, with the establishment of the Greater London Authority for the metropolitan area in 2000 a new era has begun. It might be hypothesised that this has brought about a shift in governmental control over planning from the nation-state to the metropolitan level. We will explore these themes in more detail.

The spatial economy of the London region

A brief historical review is necessary to explain the current spatial pattern of London's urban fabric. Past trends have created a city with relatively low-density, low-rise housing surrounded by a green belt that is mainly farmland with a few villages that existed before the ban on development, and which have been bought by the wealthy population. Beyond the green belt, the region contains a large population, many of whom commute into the city. The physical fabric of London was largely established during the nineteenth century. In 1800 the population of the city was about 1 million and this rose to 6.5 million by the end of the century. As the population of the city within the green belt is currently estimated to be 7.4 million, it can be seen that this nineteenth-century legacy has an important influence on the structure of the city. During the first part of the nineteenth century the population increase was largely established within a confined area with increasing densities. This was a period when there was much concern and publicity about the poor living conditions of the city's working population. From the middle of the century onwards the population spread into the surrounding areas with the provision of public transport, first as horse-drawn carriages then as trams and buses. The new suburbs were largely two-storey terraces built according to the new building 'bylaws' and this kind of housing still features in the inner suburbs of the city. The beginning of the twentieth century saw further suburbanisation with the building of the underground system. This later suburbanisation took the particular building form of the semi-detached family house. These were oriented towards the middle classes with finance available from the newly formed building societies. They were largely built by small speculative house-builders at about 12 houses per acre, using model designs from building manuals, and they still cover a large part of the city landscape. In 1939 Greater London reached its highest population figure of 8.6 million.

One of the most crucial factors influencing the spatial configuration of London was the establishment shortly after the war of the green belt. A band of several miles was established around the built-up area and no further development was allowed in this belt. This policy has been strictly applied and so further sprawl has been prevented. However, the population of the city continued to grow. This growth was now accommodated in the area beyond the green belt, some in new towns but mostly in private housing developments. In the first decade after the war these tended to be located up to 30 miles from London, but by the 1980s the distance had increased to about 60 miles. This trend was facilitated by the rapid increase in car ownership. The result was a decrease in the population of London, as defined by the area within the green belt, and an increase in the broader region, which increased by 1 million people in the 1950s and a further 800,000 in the 1960s. The decrease in London was to a great extent fuelled by the programmes to clear the poor housing areas and lower the densities in the crowded inner-city residential areas. Thus the population of London dropped to a low point of 6.8 million in 1983 while the population of the larger region of the south-east increased rapidly. The total population of the region, including London, reached about 17 million at this time.

In the 1990s the region outside London continued to grow. Meanwhile London's population decline stopped and there was a steady increase. There continued to be a flow of people moving out of the city into the surrounding regions. This particularly applied to young families seeking an affordable family home and good schools. However, there was also inward migration particularly from outside Britain, reflecting London's world city role. There has also been an increasing interest from wealthier people in returning to live in the centre of the city – typically older professional couples whose families have left home. So the population of London has risen to 7.4 million and is projected to continue to rise, reaching about 8 million within the next 20 years. This population increase within Greater London is supported by current policies at both the national and the Greater London level.

We will now turn to the economic structure of London. During the nineteenth century when London grew so rapidly, its major economic activities were oriented towards its trading and port functions and its administrative role as the centre for parliament and royalty. The city was the centre of a world-wide Empire and this generated economic prosperity and stimulated its trading and financial functions. The City of London – an area that emerged in medieval times as the commercial centre of the guild system – was the hub of this international activity. It has retained its special administrative autonomy that dates from this medieval period. Given the size of London, economic activity also included the servicing of this large population and contained a significant workshop and manufacturing sector. In the 1920s and 1930s, at the time of the suburban expansion, many new industrial estates, with factories mainly producing consumer goods, were built in these suburban areas. After the war, the emphasis was on decentralising the population from the city. This also applied to industry that now sought new factories in greenfield sites in the new towns and existing settlements beyond the green belt. The dispersal of these factories, together with the strong policies to attract industry to the more peripheral regions of the country, and Britain's general decline as a

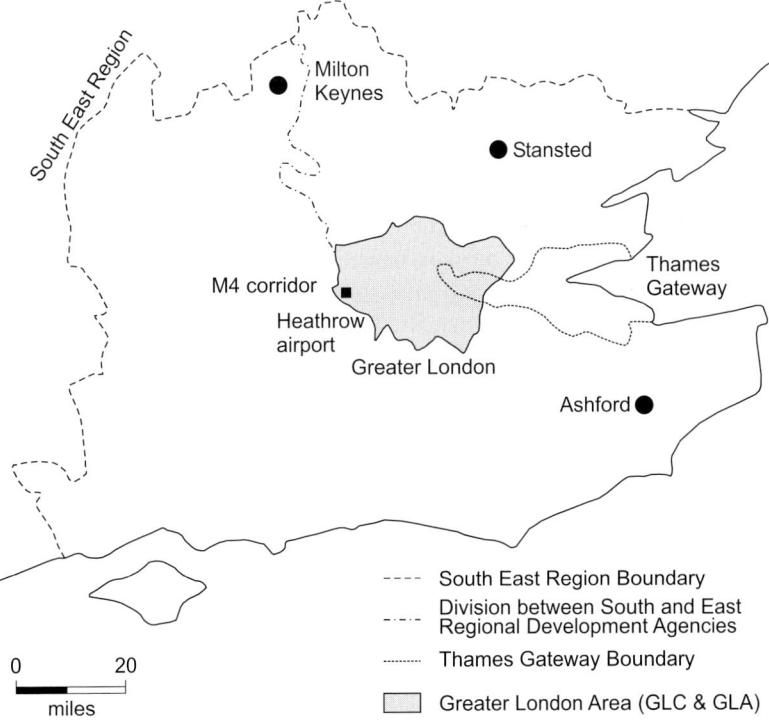

Figure 3.1 The London region

manufacturing nation, meant that one of the main trends in London in the post-war period was the decline in the manufacturing sector. In the middle of the twentieth century manufacturing jobs were held by about a third of the working population but this had shrunk to 17 per cent by 1981 and again fell sharply in the following decade to around 10 per cent. Meanwhile the business and financial services sector grew enormously and now account for a third of the employment and 40 per cent of London's wealth. Other major sectors of the London economy today are in culture, tourism, design, retailing and entertainment.

One of the features of this kind of urban economy is that it is highly concentrated in the central area. Many of the changes to London's built environment have been made in order to accommodate the need for office space for these expanding sectors. This need has extended beyond the central area to the development of a new office district a few miles east of the centre, in London Docklands. This area was the centre of the trade and port activities of the nineteenth century, but a modern port was constructed further down-river leaving behind a huge area of derelict land and docks. From the mid-1980s onwards this has been the major development area within the Greater London boundary. Apart from these office developments in the central area and in Docklands, the major areas of economic growth have been beyond the green belt. To the west, stimulated by the location of Heathrow Airport, the corridor along the M4 motorway has been described as Britain's Silicon Valley. This area has experienced a huge growth in high-tech industries and offices and associated demands for housing. A second growth area has centred on Cambridge and the new Stansted Airport in the north and contains many science parks and R&D developments with links to the University. Meanwhile the area to the east of London contains many deprived communities with high levels of unemployment and has found it harder to attract development. Some neighbour-hoods within London are also the most deprived in the whole country. Thus within the metropolitan area there are extremes of rich and poor. Having sketched out these population and economic trends we will now turn to an exploration of the institutional framework for policy development.

Navigating the maze of regional governance

Employment and residential activity has spread beyond the boundaries of Greater London. Thus the whole of the south-east region can be considered as a single 'functional region' containing linked residential and employment centres with regional patterns of journey-to-work movements. However, there has never been a political entity to match this region. Instead decision-making of a regional nature has taken place within central government, sometimes with the advice of *ad hoc* bodies comprising local authorities in the area. These local authorities are at two levels – the broader county level and the more local districts within them. To increase the complexity, reforms in the mid-1990s led to the creation of unitary authorities for some areas in which the functions of counties and districts were combined.

Since the early 1960s there has been the Standing Conference on South East Regional Planning (SERPLAN). This body comprises representatives from the county planning departments and prepares advice for central government on regional issues. At intervals, central government produces regional policy in the form of Regional Guidance for the South East. This Guidance covers the area called the South East Region and is roughly equivalent to the 'functional region'. The Guidance must be followed by all the local authorities and other bodies within the region. Central government determines policy on big regional issues such as airport location and regional transport. This Guidance also estimates the population increase in the region and the demands for new dwellings, and gives each county target figures for house-building. Recent Guidance was produced in 1994 and 2001 and, although central government changed from the Conservative government of Mr Major to the Labour government of Mr Blair, the regional policy guidance has been fairly consistent through this period. The major issues have been to promote the regional economy in the face of European competition while coping with problems of environmental sustainability and congestion. 'Overheating' of the region has been a strategic concern especially as a large part of the countryside is protected by conservation policies. Current population projections show an increasing demand for new housing, especially because of increasing household formation in the young and elderly population. Meanwhile using green land for development is a highly charged political issue. National government has therefore adopted a policy of increasing the amount of new development taking place within urban areas on brownfield sites. Only 40 per cent of the new demand is expected to take place on green land. A major thrust of central government policy is therefore directed at making towns and cities more attractive and increasing densities in new development. These policies are reflected in the Regional Guidance. Another element of this Guidance is to try and balance the location of new activity across the region. The Cambridge/Stansted area is viewed as able to accept more development and further expansions are planned in Milton Keynes New Town and Ashford near the Channel Tunnel entrance. However, a major aim of Regional Guidance for some time now has been to try and encourage development to the east of London. To this end an area has been designated as the Thames Gateway – this stretches from the centre of the city outwards along both banks of the Thames right out to its estuary. For this area special strategy documents, agencies to coordinate the different public authorities operating in the area, and promotional activity have been instigated. Regeneration grants and individual projects such as new river-crossings are proposed but essentially the approach is one of trying to stimulate the various agencies, including the private sector, to take more interest in the area.

In 1994 central government introduced the idea of Government Offices for the Regions. This was intended to improve the coordination of regional policy between the various national ministries that might be involved in regional policy issues. An office was set up in each region throughout the country with representation from each of the relevant ministries. They were staffed by civil servants and were accountable to central government. However, when the new Labour government came into office in 1997 these offices were overlaid with a further initiative – the Regional Development Agencies (RDAs). The aim of the new government was to make regional policy less centralised and more responsive to the local area. RDAs were intended to improve the problem of regional institutional fragmentation, and were given the remit to make their regions more competitive in the global economy. Thus they were primarily economic development agencies but also had the responsibility to coordinate the urban regeneration activity in their region. The RDAs are supervised by regional assemblies made up of representatives of local authorities, business and voluntary organisations from the area. They also have regional planning boards, and in the south-east the board has taken over the function of SERPLAN. However, the picture is complicated because in creating the RDAs the government has split the south-east region into three parts. The South East RDA covers the area to the west and south of London, while the East RDA covers the part to the north-east. There is then also a new development agency for Greater London – the London Development Agency (LDA). There is no mechanism for the coordination of these three parts of the region. The Government Offices for the Regions also continue to exist.

The result is that, whatever the government intention, the regional picture is now even more fragmented and still lacks accountability. There is no democratic political regional body but a complex interaction between various quangos and local authorities. Many of the regional quangos now only cover a part of the 'functional region'. In this interaction, central government continues to play a dominant role through providing the basic statutory framework of Regional Guidance. Thus, in contrast to other parts of the country such as Scotland or Wales, central government is still highly involved in the strategic regional issues for the capital.

The fragmentation of London governance after the abolition of the GLC

Although Britain has shown little interest in the development of government at the regional level, finding a suitable government for London has been a major preoccupation since the nineteenth century. As London grew to about 6 million towards the end of that century, the localised form of government was seen to be inadequate. After much debate a new form of government was set up in 1888 called the London County Council (LCC) and this covered the complete built-up area at that time. However, as we have already noted the central financial core district (of about a square mile) maintained its autonomy and medieval governmental form and continued to be administered by the City Corporation.

As suburbanisation developed, the city grew beyond its LCC boundaries, raising again the issue of appropriate government. So another reform of London government took place in 1963. This set up the Greater London Council (GLC) to be responsible for strategic issues and covering the whole metropolitan area within the green belt. The local tier of government under the GLC was reformed and 32 boroughs were created together with the City Corporation.

The next reform of London government took place in 1986. This time the motivation for the change was political rather than administrative efficiency. The GLC during the early 1980s, led by Ken Livingstone, was developing policies that were a direct challenge to the new central government led by Mrs Thatcher. For example, they were pursuing a cheap fares policy on London Underground, developing policies oriented towards women, disabled and ethnic minorities, and creating a community protection policy to safeguard neighbourhoods threatened by office expansion. Central government saw this as a threat to their own approach and decided to abolish the GLC altogether. The removal of this tier of government fitted into the political ideology of the period that stressed minimal intervention and market freedom. Some saw this as a welcome move that led to the strengthening of the lower-tier boroughs (Hebbert, 1992), or an opportunity for spontaneous innovation through the creation of more action-oriented, and financially efficient, *ad hoc* bodies. However, the new arrangement lacked a coordinated strategic perspective and this was to prove a problem over the following years.

After the abolition of the GLC there was no government for the whole of the metropolitan London area. The powers of the old GLC were reallocated to central government, the lower tier of the London boroughs or to some kind of joint body. The London Planning Advisory Committee (LPAC) was set up to discuss strategic city-wide planning issues. This committee, made up of representatives from the boroughs, prepared strategic planning reports but it was only an advisory body. It presented its ideas to central government, which now prepared the statutory Strategic Planning Guidance for the city. In tune with the non-interventionist ideology of the period, the guidance in 1989 was only a few pages long and simply set out the main parameters within which the local authorities should operate. So, as a result of the ideology of non-intervention and institutional fragmentation, very little strategic planning took place after the abolition of the GLC. LPAC produced its strategic policies but these had limited impact.

Eventually increasing concern was expressed from many quarters about the lack of an overall vision and leadership (Newman and Thornley, 1997) and from the late 1980s onwards there was increasing pressure for more concerted action. The City Corporation was active in commissioning reports and funding promotional bodies. LPAC also commissioned its own research on the needs of London as a centre of world business. These studies concluded that London was at a disadvantage in not having a single voice to promote the city. By the early 1990s central government had also accepted the view that more needed to be done to enhance London's competitive position and counteract its fragmented institutional structure. In 1992 central government set up the London Forum to promote the capital but the following year this was merged into London First, a similar body set up by the private sector. This pattern of private-sector leadership combined with central government backing dominated strategic thinking in London over the next five years.

In the same year another central government initiative was announced called City Pride. The idea was that central government would give some financial backing to its three major cities if they produced visions or strategies to show how they could make themselves more successful in the competition with other cities in the world. They were asked to prepare a prospectus of future priorities and action which coordinated the public, private and voluntary sectors. In London the job of orchestrating this exercise, through a document called the *London Pride Prospectus*, was given to the private-sector body London First. Meanwhile central government itself was becoming more and more involved in strategic planning for the city as the problems of fragmentation continued. It established a Minister for London, a Cabinet Sub-Committee for the capital, the Government Office for London with representation from the different ministries with interests in London policy, and produced a new enhanced Strategic Guidance for London. This time, illustrative of its greater importance, the guidance extended to 75 pages.

In 1995 the *London Pride Prospectus* was published and set the frame for strategic priorities. In its opening statement it said that its aim was to ensure London's position as the only world city in Europe. It sought to achieve this through three interrelated missions of a robust and sustainable economy drawing on a world-class workforce, greater social cohesion, and a high quality provision of infrastructure, services and good environment. Although it contains short sections on targets for affordable housing and policies to improve air quality, energy conservation and waste management, most of the prospectus was devoted to business growth, the development of skills and transport provision. Measures were set out to support business and attract inward investment such as adequate provision of good sites, telecommunication facilities, suitably trained labour market, promotional activity, improved access to the airports and better public transport. The priorities of the *Prospectus* then had a strong influence on central government thinking, for example as input into the revised and expanded Strategic Guidance for London. However, one of the features of this period was the proliferation of more and more organisations with complex interrelationships. They lacked any clear channels of accountability and created a confused network that made it difficult to identify who was responsible for decisions (Newman and Thornley, 1997). So the strategic policy vacuum was filled, not by a government for London, but by central government heavily influenced by representatives of the business sector.

The birth of the Greater London Authority

In 1997 a major change took place in British politics when the Labour Party under Tony Blair won the election after 18 years of Conservative rule. This was to have a significant effect on the institutional context for strategic planning in London. The Labour Party pledged itself to greater transparency in government, to tackle the issues of the proliferation of unaccountable *ad hoc* bodies and to devolve governmental power. They also indicated that they would give greater emphasis to issues such as social exclusion and environmental sustainability. Policy coordination or 'joined-up policy thinking' was also one of their new slogans. These procedural and policy priorities heralded a major change to the governance of London and the approach to strategic planning.

In their 1997 election manifesto, the Labour Party had included a commitment to an elected mayor of London. The mayor was conceived as having strong executive powers. Alongside the mayor an elected Assembly would have a scrutinising and checking role. It was hoped that the strong mayor would overcome the problem of lack of political leadership in the capital and that the electoral processes would introduce greater transparency and accountability into strategic decision-making. One of the major features of the new model was that it would be a streamlined authority. There was no intention of returning to the huge bureaucracy that was a feature of the old Greater London Council.

Having won the election in 1997 the Labour Party began the process of implementing the new political system and the Greater London Authority (GLA) Act was passed by parliament in November 1999. The Act sets out the powers to be allocated to the mayor. In principle these powers are for policies having a strategic impact on London as a whole. The lower tier of government – the 32 boroughs and the City Corporation – continue to exist and the GLA must not duplicate their responsibilities. Many of the powers of the GLA therefore arise from taking over existing quangos, with some devolution from central government. The GLA has responsibility for policing the city through a new organisation called the Metropolitan Police Authority, a role that was previously undertaken by central government. The GLA also has responsibility for three 'statutory organisations' (often referred to as the 'functional bodies'): Transport for London, the London Fire and Emergency Planning Authority, and the London Development Agency (LDA). In addition to having the responsibility for overseeing the operation of these bodies, the GLA will also have other strategic and coordinating functions.

Most of the executive powers of the GLA are vested in the mayor, who formulates policy, proposes a budget, coordinates all the different partners and makes appointments to the statutory bodies. A major task of the mayor is to develop strategies for the topics he or she has responsibility for. These have to be consistent with national policy. The mayor also has to produce an annual progress report followed by a 'State of London' debate and a twice-yearly 'People's Question Time'. The Assembly has 25 members of whom 14 are elected on an area or constituency basis and 11 on a London-wide basis. The role of the Assembly is to scrutinise the mayor's activity, make the appointments to the permanent executive and also appoint some members of the statutory bodies. The mayor reports to the Assembly each month and answers questions. The mayor's proposals and budget are reported to the Assembly for endorsement. If they have a two-thirds majority the Assembly can request that the mayor makes amendments. The Assembly has the power to set up committees of investigation into topics of their choice and draw upon outside experts to provide advice and information.

One of the important features to note about the new arrangement is that the mayor does not have much financial autonomy. The GLA will take over the central government grants that previously went to the various transport operators and these will be paid to Transport for London. However, this money can only be used for transport purposes. It will also inherit the existing public spending in London on police, fire, economic development and regeneration. The important aspect of these funding arrangements is that central government still has a controlling influence and the mayor cannot switch funds between the different statutory bodies. Central government retains a reserve power to set a minimum level for the police budget. There will also be a small annual general-purpose grant from central government to cover the operating costs of the GLA. A very small amount of local taxes will come from a precept on the boroughs. The GLA will also have access to a very limited amount of its own resources through new powers to impose congestion charging and workplace parking fees.

A major feature of the new arrangement is the attempt to combine all the old bodies responsible for different aspects of transport into a single body, although railways bringing in commuters from outside London will continue to be run by private companies. Reflecting the new coordinated objective, the mayor will produce an integrated transport strategy for London. The GLA will also have the duty to promote a sustainable approach to economic, social and environmental issues and this is reflected in the requirement to produce a number of environment strategies. These are an air quality strategy, a municipal waste management strategy, an ambient noise strategy, and a biodiversity action plan. The mayor will produce a report on the state of London's environment every four years. The mayor also has the duty to promote culture in London and produce a cultural strategy. As already mentioned, a new body called the London Development Agency has been created to promote economic development and regeneration, and produce the economic strategy.

As far as land-use planning is concerned the mayor will prepare a new kind of plan called the Spatial Development Strategy (SDS). This will give a strategic

Table 3.1 Responsibilities for governance and planning of the London region

Level	Organisation	Plans
National	Ministries	Strategic Guidance for South East (SE)
	Government Office for SE	Strategic Guidance for London
	Government Office for London	(until replaced by SDS)
Regional (appointed)	SERPLAN (until 2001)	Advisory Regional Strategy
	SE Regional Development Agency	SE Economic Development Strategy
	East Regional Development Agency	East Economic Development Strategy
Metropolitan (elected)	Greater London Authority (since 2000)	Spatial Development Strategy
		Transport Strategy
		Cultural Strategy
		Biodiversity Strategy
		Waste Strategy
		Noise Strategy
		Air Quality Strategy
	London Development Agency (since 2000)	Economic Development Strategy
Local (elected)	Counties	Structure Plans
	Districts	Local Plans
	Unitary Authorities and London boroughs	Unitary Development Plans

overview of planning in London and replace the Planning Guidance for London produced by central government. The London boroughs' own plans (Unitary Development Plans) will then have to conform to the new SDS. The detailed content of the SDS will be left to the mayor; however, central government expects it to cover transport, economic development, regeneration, housing, retail development, leisure and culture, environment, built heritage, waste management, use of energy and London's world city role. It can immediately be seen that this coverage overlaps the other strategies mentioned above. Coordination will therefore be a key requirement in the strategic policy work of the GLA. It has been suggested that the SDS could play a major role in this coordination by pulling together all the other strategies through their requirements and impact on land-use and development. However, the coordination of the different strategies has proved to be a fraught business during the first year of the GLA's existence. Some strategies were given greater political priority and were prepared in advance of others. The first to appear were the economic and transport strategies and these were used to reinforce the mayor's priorities to improve transport and promote London's economy in a climate of increasing global economic competition. The various environmental strategies were very slow to appear and therefore had to fit the parameters already set by the earlier strategies. The SDS has not yet been able to undertake its role as a vehicle for coordination. As a statutory document it takes longer to prepare and needs to go through a more formal consultation process. A draft was prepared in early 2001 by officials in the GLA, based upon work previously carried out by the LPAC, with considerable input from the boroughs. However, the mayor rejected this as not sufficiently reflecting his political priorities and requested more work – a new draft is due in 2002. Meanwhile he prepared his informal document *Towards the London Plan*, published in May 2001, with a heavy emphasis on developing London's world city activity.

According to the GLA Act, where applications for development have a strategic importance for London they have to be passed to the mayor by the boroughs who receive all applications. The mayor can give a direct refusal if the development does not conform to his strategies. The definition of which developments have strategic importance has been set out by central government in the new regulations. The definition is based on the floor-space and height of the proposed development, with variations between outer and central London and for areas adjacent to the Thames. The City Corporation lobbied the government strongly during the preparation of the regulations and managed to get special treatment for the City. As a result larger and higher buildings can be developed there without the need for the mayor to be involved. However, in the event, promoting tall buildings has been one of Livingstone's clear policies, linked to the promotion of London's world city role. Any development in London involving 500 or more houses is also considered strategic and will need to be referred to the mayor. He is using this power to insist on developments containing more affordable housing. The lack of suitable housing for key workers such as nurses, transport workers, teachers and police personnel is threatening the economic functioning of the city.

Discussion

The directly elected nature of the mayor is intended to provide a clear focus of accountability so that the citizens of London can hold the mayor responsible. There are also other methods of accountability proposed to supplement the electoral process. The Assembly is a forum for discussion and there are public hearings.

However, the election for mayor indicated that although Blair was keen on devolution he also wanted to keep control of the process. He did everything he could to stop the election of Ken Livingstone as he saw him as too independent and likely to develop his own policies rather than conform to central government. The obvious conclusion is that Blair was in favour of an elected mayor as long as the right person was in the post. This raises the issue of how much independence the mayor could, or should, have. Decentralisation can take a number of different forms depending on whether the devolution is one of responsibility, legal powers or financial independence. The form of devolution in the London case is clearly one limited to responsibility. The Act sets out these responsibilities which include the formulation and coordination of a number of strategic policies and the implementation of policies on such matters as transport and crime. However, central government retains control of law-making powers, sets the regulations and allocates most of the finance. Even though the mayor's powers are limited, he or she can use his or her electoral mandate to voice opinions and pressurise the government for more autonomy. This is precisely how Livingstone sees his role (Livingstone, 2000). His broad agenda is to increase the financial resources available to the mayor and also expand the policy topics under his control. He has said that he aims to turn the British regional government system into one that is similar to that of Germany.

One of the issues is how to combine two aspects of the new London government; that is, how to make London more accountable to its citizens while also allowing leadership and visions to project its competitive economic advantage. Citizens may not see such policies as in their interest, or at least not as their major priorities. This potential dilemma is tackled through the notion of consensus. This is now an all-pervading notion that is utilised by both central government and the new GLA. The idea is that all can be winners and that business interests and citizen interests can be brought together into a common approach. Policies are required to balance economic, environmental and social objectives. Central government has placed this consensus-building at the centre of its approach to government. During its first year in office the new government sought to develop an ideological framework in which to place the principles it had expounded during the election campaign. One of the major influences on Blair was Anthony Giddens, whose book *Beyond Left and Right* (1994) set out a new approach to politics. This was further developed in *The Third Way*, which was published in 1998. The new approach sought to extend beyond the previous political divisions of neo-liberalism and socialism and also to respond to contemporary trends in society, such as globalisation, increasing uncertainty and social diversification. The features of the approach included rethinking the welfare state using the principle of empowerment, more transparency in government utilising dialogue, and reconciling autonomy and interdependence in social life. These ideas influenced the new government, culminating in the Prime Minister's Fabian pamphlet entitled *The Third Way: New Politics for the New Century* (Blair, 1998). In the pamphlet Blair emphasises the need to reconcile views that appear to be in conflict and to build up consensus around a more coordinated approach. Such an approach was directly fed into the wording of the GLA Act of 1999. It therefore provides the framework expected from the new mayor who is indeed using the terminology in his draft policy

Andy Thornley

documents. These documents are being presented to the public for consultation with a view to 'building a consensus among the many groups and stakeholders in London' (GLA, 2001, p.vii). The experience of the first year of the GLA shows that there has been much activity around this idea of comprehensive involvement with a whole range of innovative approaches to participation. However, this involvement has lacked focus and has not been directly linked into the priority setting process. Meanwhile the business lobby has organised itself well, creating the London Business Board. This Board and representatives from the City of London have gained regular access to the Mayor's Office and with it the ability to input their priorities into the strategic policy agenda.

Finally, there is the question of how the experience of the new government in London might be related to the debates over globalisation and the restructuring of the nation-state. First let us note the way in which the mayor is using globalisation in his approach to the planning of London. His approach in *Towards the London Plan* makes it very clear that he sees the promotion of London as a world city as his primary role. His argument is that globalisation leads to increasing competition and that London must fight to retain its position. To do so it needs to grow economically and in population terms. He portrays the success of London as being necessary for the nation as a whole and therefore that central government should provide more resources for the development of the capital. Here then is a clear challenge to the national government, utilising the threat of competition between global cities. Livingstone writes that:

> London contributes over £19 billion net each year towards investment in the rest of the UK. As a result, demands placed on London by the rapid economic growth and population increase have not been adequately matched by increased supply of homes, improvements in transport, skills, office stock and other factors. This inadequate supply side response has had negative consequences for economic growth, competitiveness, living standards, quality of life and the environment. This is in sharp contrast to the experience of the capital cities and key economic centres in other nations that have more correctly understood the effects of globalisation. These include New York, Paris and Berlin. These cities either keep a far more substantial proportion of their GDP … or are actively subsidised by their national economies … this allows them potentially to improve their position in competition with London.
>
> (GLA, 2001, p.6)

There has been considerable discussion about the restructuring of the relationship between different levels of the state as a result of globalisation (e.g. Ohmae, 1995; Jessop, 1997; Friedmann, 1997; Brenner, 1999) and the London example is extremely interesting in this respect. The indications show that initially the nation-state, in the form of the New Labour government, saw the advantages of devolving

54

some responsibilities to the city. However, at the same time they expected to be able to keep a tight rein over the actions of its political leader and this has proved not to be the case. They are still able to maintain considerable control through setting the regulations for the new government, reserving certain powers to intervene if necessary, and keeping the financial power. Their unwillingness, even against popular opinion, to hand over financial control of the London Underground to the mayor, indicates the strength of their desire to maintain overall control. However, the mayor at the city level is using his newly acquired political and symbolic power to press for greater control and resources, claiming that this is required if both nation and city are to survive in the context of global competition. A new site of conflict is therefore unfolding.

The green belt has proved to be a very firm policy that has created a strong boundary around the metropolitan area. This has had implications in institutional terms. There tends to be a divorce between the governance of the metropolitan area and the governance of the broader region. It should be stressed again that the mayor's geographical area of responsibility only covers the area within the green belt. As noted above, many people travel into and out of this area for employment and leisure purposes and many London facilities such as Gatwick and Stansted Airports lie outside the mayor's area. Therefore there will need to be considerable cooperation between the strategies for London produced by the mayor and the work of surrounding local authorities and regional agencies. As yet the mechanisms for this coordination have not been developed in the context of the new GLA. In the broader region governance has became increasingly fragmented with a large number of different kinds of local authorities, the different RDAs, the Government Offices and *ad hoc* organisations such as Thames Gateway. In this landscape of organisational fragmentation it is central government that is continuing to provide the coordinating strategic policy role. Thus central government has retained its dominant role in the region but devolved some political and symbolic power to the mayor within the metropolitan area. However, even here they are reluctant to give up their controlling and monitoring ability. So as far as strategic coordination is concerned national government has made its job more difficult in the region through its new institutional structures, while the mayor is more interested in pushing his specific political priorities than ensuring coordination across the metropolitan strategies. As yet there is little attempt to coordinate between region and metropolis. This will prove ever more difficult as relations between mayor and central government become more conflictive.

Bibliography

Blair, T. (1998) *The Third Way: New Policies for the New Century*, London: Fabian Society.
Brenner, N. (1999) 'Globalisation as reterritorialisation: the re-scaling of urban governance in the European Union', *Urban Studies*, 36 (3): 431–51.

Friedmann, J. (1997) 'World city futures: the role of urban and regional policies', Paper presented to the 4th Asian Planning School Association Congress, Bandung, Indonesia, 2–4 September.

Giddens, A. (1994) *Beyond Left and Right*, Cambridge: Polity Press.

Giddens, A. (1998) *The Third Way*, Cambridge: Polity Press.

Greater London Authority (2001) *Towards the London Plan*, May, GLA, London.

Hebbert, M. (1992) 'Governing the capital', in A. Thornley (ed.) *The Crisis of London*, London: Routledge.

Jessop, B. (1997) 'A neo-Gramscian approach to the regulation of urban regimes: accumulation strategies, hegemonic projects, and governance', in M. Lauria (ed.) *Reconstructing Urban Regime Theory*, Thousand Oaks, CA and London: Sage.

Livingstone, K. (2000) Interview with Mayor conducted by the LSE ESRC project, 'Strategy co-ordination and interest representation under the GLA' (Grant No. 000223095).

Newman, P. and Thornley, A. (1997) 'Fragmentation and centralisation in the governance of London: influencing the urban policy and planning agenda', *Urban Studies*, 34 (7): 967–88.

Ohmae, K. (1995) *The End of the Nation State*, New York: Free Press.

4 The Birmingham case

Alan Murie, Mike Beazley and
Dave Carter

Introduction

After London, Birmingham is the biggest city in the United Kingdom. The city of Birmingham has a population of some 1 million and the size of the city contributes to its diversity. It includes affluent, high-status, suburban areas; older residential enclaves in the middle-ring and the inner-city which have high property values and environmental quality; areas of older working class housing dating from before 1919 with rows of high-density terraced housing; slum clearance council housing estates located in the inner-city; peripheral estates of 1960s council housing; and a mixed quality suburban residential zone in between. Birmingham is an industrial city based on manufacturing and has undergone major changes in the structure of its economy in the last 30 years. Issues of industrial dereliction, contaminated land and the reuse of old industrial premises are prominent ones. The city and region has an industrial and manufacturing history. While the city has successfully replaced jobs lost in declining sectors it remains at risk because of the continuing over-dependence on manufacturing and especially employment linked to the fragile automotive sector. Birmingham is a modern city of migration. Its principal and most rapid growth was associated with the Industrial Revolution and migration from rural to urban areas associated with expanding employment opportunities. Migration to the city has remained high and the diversity of population in terms of ethnicity, religion, culture and family history is significant. Birmingham has a large ethnic minority population, which is more mixed than in any other part of the UK, except London. The combination of residential and employment change has contributed to a hollowing out of the city with high concentrations of deprivation in the older inner core of the city and in areas of public sector housing.

The dominant competitiveness agenda of the city of Birmingham relates to its role as a regional centre and as an international city with a full range of business and cultural activities involving significant restructuring of the employment and economic base of the city away from manufacturing and towards the service sector and cultural industries. Some of the key issues for the city relate to whether the rest of the region perceives it as having this same future and whether the rest of the region is willing to contribute to its achieving this vision. The agenda also includes addressing the pattern of migration and social exclusion and attracting higher income households to live in and remain in the city. A major and successful transformation of the city centre over recent years has been partly associated with this but is also linked with a vision for the city as a modern international city attractive to visitors and to business.

The city and its region

The population of the West Midlands is 5.33 million (1999) with the seven metropolitan districts accounting for roughly half (2.63 million) within which the population density is around 3,000 people per sq. km. The remainder of the population is dispersed: Staffordshire (0.8m), Warwickshire (0.5m), Shropshire (0.3m), Worcestershire (0.5m) and the unitary authorities – Stoke-on-Trent (0.25m), Herefordshire (0.2m), and Telford and Wrekin (0.15m). The West Midlands accounts for just over 10 per cent of England's population and covers an area of just over 13,000 sq. km with an average population density of around 400 people per sq. km.

The region's population grew by 2.9 per cent between 1981 and 1999. This is approximately half the rate of increase for the UK (5.6 per cent) over the same period. With the exception of Solihull and Dudley, the populations of the metropolitan districts have declined. In much of the rest of the region there were increases in population, by as much as 23.6 per cent in Worcester. This pattern is associated with both natural increase and migration. There is a longstanding trend whereby Birmingham residents have sought housing opportunities in the wider region. Many of those who have moved out of the city have retained employment within it, contributing to the substantial increase in commuting (particularly by car) over recent decades. There is a further pattern of moves out from the more suburban parts of the conurbation into the shire counties.

This fits the 'cascade' pattern of migration between districts in different positions in the urban hierarchy (Champion, 2000). The work carried out by Champion indicated that the net outflow per thousand of the population from the West Midlands conurbation was greater than for other major conurbations in England and that a high proportion of outmigration from the West Midlands conurbation was to surrounding shire counties rather than longer distance. The gross flows out of the city are substantial – around 5 per cent of all households per annum, and 7 per cent of the 30–64 age group, or a quarter to a third of all households over a five year period. At the same time the inflows of households to the city are also substantial with a net outflow of only 1,000 households in 2001. As the types of household moving out of the city (average size 2.2) are larger than those moving in (average size 1.9), migration results in less net loss of households than of population. As a result, the net level of new household formation from the existing population is also relatively small. The most notable impact of this pattern of migration has been a decline in the level of economic participation within the

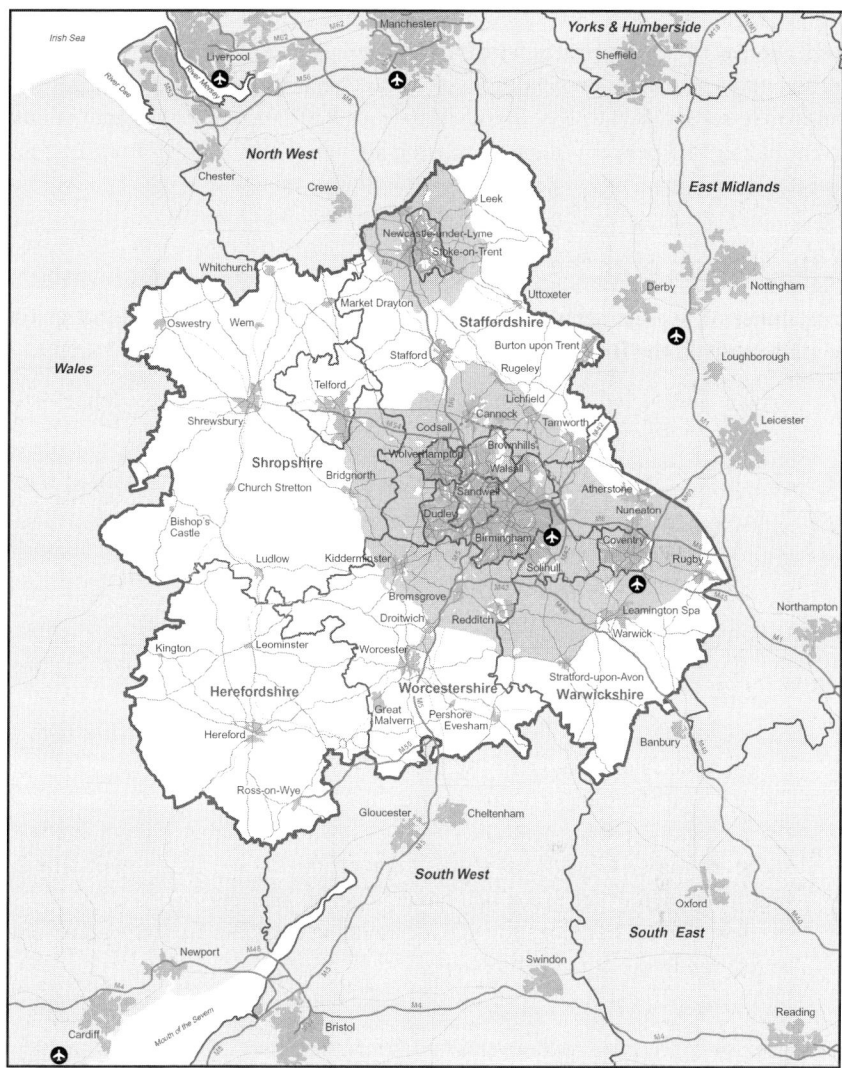

Figure 4.1 The West Midlands region. *Source:* Birmingham City Council Planning Department, produced using Brussels UrbIS®©

population remaining in the city, especially amongst men, and hence a rise in hidden unemployment. The inevitable outcome of these processes has been increased social polarisation as outmigrants have disproportionately included the more prosperous. This identification of an issue associated with differential migration and the hollowing out of the centre of the city is a recurrent theme in policy discussions and in making the city a more attractive place to live in for higher income groups.

Alan Murie, Mike Beazley and Dave Carter

The region has the second highest regional percentage of ethnic minority people (8.2 per cent). (This compares with the UK average of 5.5 per cent.) The majority of the ethnic minority population lives in the West Midlands metropolitan area and to a lesser extent in Rugby, Warwick and East Staffordshire. In the metropolitan conurbation 14.5 per cent of the population are non-white, ranging from 23.2 per cent in Birmingham to 2.8 per cent in Solihull.

Urbanisation over the last 20 years

A number of key elements have been involved in urbanisation and the spatial configuration in the Birmingham city region over the last 20 years:

- Private-sector-led decentralisation of employment and residence with increasing commuting and transport by road;
- industrial restructuring and manufacturing decline;
- polarisation in the city and the region reflected in patterns of residence and employment and property values;
- relocation of retail activity to out-of-city shopping centre;
- the further development of road systems and the motorway network with Birmingham in a crucial national position in relation to these;
- the development of Birmingham International Airport as a major regional resource;
- the decline of some smaller towns and older manufacturing areas in the region, for example, Stoke-on-Trent and the Black Country boroughs;
- the revival of Birmingham city centre;
- the continuation of the green belt as a key restraint on urban growth, but with scope for minor adjustments without compromising key issues built into the original design of the green belt having been exhausted;
- the development of innovation and regeneration corridors presenting problems in relation to the green belt policy;
- lack of investment in infrastructure: existing roads, railway systems, and public works;
- the impact of major regeneration initiatives such as Dudley Enterprise Zone, the Heartland's Urban Development Corporation, Newtown/South Aston City Challenge, several Single Regeneration Budget projects and Kings Norton New Deal for Communities.

Over the past two decades or so, where development has taken place infrastructure provision has tended to be funded by the private sector through planning agreements. Public sector infrastructure no longer leads the pattern of development. Where growth should occur is strongly led by private initiative and there is a lack of clear decisions about the distribution of growth; consequently, growth is widely spread around (for example, with small extensions to different villages

60

rather than big strategic decisions about expansion). In the past there has been a reticence in the wider region for Birmingham to be recognised as the regional centre and a world city; however, the new Regional Planning Guidance that is emerging promotes Birmingham as a world city. The rest of the region has not recognised the importance of Birmingham in the way that the north-west region has recognised the importance of Manchester. However, it may be that greater acceptance is emerging.

The formal structure of government

Because of the fragmentation of London government, Birmingham is the largest municipality in the UK. The administrative boundaries of the city come closer to meaning that there is a city council, which has a spatial remit that corresponds to that of some key functions of the city. Nevertheless, administrative boundaries mean that other local authorities are involved in decisions which have a fundamental impact on the city and the city region. Administrative boundaries still bear little relation to the workings of the city or regional economy. There have been a number of formal changes in the structure of government and some changes in practice.

The most obvious change in the structure of government was the abolition in 1986 of the old West Midlands County Council (WMCC) and the establishment of new unitary authorities in parts of the West Midlands region. The city of Birmingham itself has retained its integrity and status throughout this period but changes in other parts of the region have had an impact. The WMCC had been established in 1974 and related to the metropolitan area (Birmingham, Coventry, Dudley, Sandwell, Solihull, Walsall, and Wolverhampton). The abolition of the WMCC involved the formal loss of the strategic role in planning and transport which was carried out by WMCC. Birmingham and other English cities were left without any form of elected metropolitan government. This problem has been mitigated by the adoption of effective joint working processes. Ironically, it may be that the rivalry between different levels of government has been removed and a more collaborative approach between authorities with the same powers has emerged from this. The West Midlands Planning and Transportation Sub-committee which has taken on the coordination of these issues at a metropolitan level, arguably works as effectively as the old metropolitan county. Although there is still an argument that there should be a strategic authority, it would be more logical if this functioned at a city region level – perhaps for the whole West Midlands region rather than at a metropolitan level. There is some confusion at a regional level with some unitary authorities and some two-tier structures. However, it is not clear that this presents enormous problems and the mechanisms for coordination and collaboration can be effective.

The establishment of the Government Office West Midlands (GOWM) in 1994 was designed to better integrate the activities of different central government departments operating through a regional office. GOWM was accountable to the Department of the Environment, Transport and the Regions (DETR) and designed to ensure more coherent leadership and coordination of central government in the region. Following the general election of 2001, regional government offices have come under the remit of the Cabinet Office rather than a service department.

The third important formal development affecting the West Midlands, and other regions of England, was the establishment in 1999 of the Regional Development Agency for the West Midlands (Advantage West Midlands) and the Regional Chamber to guide it. These new regional bodies have emerged as part of the regional programme of the Labour government elected in 1997 and have yet to settle down. They are appointed rather than elected bodies and in the light of this are faced with a difficult task of winning the support of different stakeholders in the region. Local authorities in the region have a long tradition of cooperative work to solve regional and sub-regional issues and have often pioneered new approaches and techniques to this end. For example, in the 1990s the West Midlands was the first region to hold a conference before an independent chairman prior to submitting advice on Regional Planning Guidance (RPG) to the Secretary of State. The metropolitan authorities pioneered the 'package' approach to transport that resulted in a major shift in the allocation of the Transport Supplementary Grant. This cooperative approach has been carried through into the current RPG review process. The West Midlands Local Government Association (WMLGA) is the designated regional planning body for RPG purposes. The governance of the city and region in 2001, after these changes, is shown in table 4.1.

The operation of regional government

In considering how regional governance operates in practice it is appropriate again to refer first to the size and national importance of the city of Birmingham. Because of this it has not always been a good regional player. It will go its own way and go directly to central government and to ministers rather than feeling that it has to build a coalition with its neighbours before developing proposals. The city council has a tradition of strong leadership established over more than 100 years. While the mayor has formal and ceremonial duties and holds office for a year, the leader of the council is elected by the majority party on the council and is re-elected periodically. It is the leader, working within a strong system of party discipline, who drives policy. Under recently introduced arrangements, the leader works with a cabinet elected from among other councillors in the controlling group. The cabinet members have portfolio responsibilities with other councillors involved in scrutiny committees. In general, over the last decade and longer the city council's competitiveness and city centre revitalisation strategies have gone ahead with little contribution from the rest of the region. European funding has played a vital role along with support from central government. The process of building regional

Table 4.1 The governance of the city and region in 2001

UK government	Executive formed by and accountable to Parliament Elected on the basis of one member representing a geographical constituency. Co-ordination of government activity through Government Office West Midlands.	Raises income and other taxes and revenues and controls local taxation. Distributes funds to lower levels of government. For local government funds allocated according to negotiated formulae related to assessment of spending needs.	Framework of legislation and finance for national, regional and local strategies and policies, including those related to planning, economic development and public services. Bargains with autonomous system of local government.
West Midlands region	No elected bodies. Bodies appointed by central government (including the Regional Development Agency - Advantage West Midlands - and advisory Regional Chamber) have specific tasks. Local authorities support co-ordination bodies, e.g. WMLGA.	Funding mainly from central government. Local government meets costs of joint bodies designed to deal with matters of common interest inclusing planning.	Specific tasks. No body tasked with regional government. WMLGA designated regional planning body for RPG. AWM responsible for the regional economic strategy.
Metropolitan or Conurbation area	Local authorities consult and coordinate their Independent activities.	Local government meets costs of joint bodies designed to deal with matters of common interest.	No body tasked with metropolitan government.
City of Birmingham	Elected local authority with 3 members representing a ward.	Heavily dependent on central grant funding but responsible for own budget and, within the framework set by central government, levies a local tax (council tax) linked to property value and generates some other revenue.	Responsible for the full range of public services in the city and for the planning matters including the Unitary Development Plan.
Wards and neighbourhoods	Ward level structures established by the city council to achieve stronger local participation.	Limited specific budget from the city council.	Providing advice and a consultation mechanism for the city council.

Table 4.1 The governance of the City and Region in 2001

coalitions and, more recently, involving the Regional Development Agency involves delays and uncertainties. The policies pursued in relation to the city centre, regeneration and inward investment, are, however, developed with strong support from the business community – with joint ventures between the city and private sector a consistent feature of development.

The agenda for the appointed Regional Development Agency (Advantage West Midlands) is predominantly concerned with economic competitiveness and policy and as a new body is still feeling its way. By channelling funding through AWM it has a key role in regeneration and in coordinating concerns about the inadequate transport and public transport infrastructure. Leaving aside the general debate about regional government there are other issues about regional definition. The framework for the present regional structure arises from the administrative divisions, which were adopted by central government to serve a different administrative agenda. But the West/East Midlands division has little other logic – there is no natural geographical fault line such as that which divides the North of England

and the transport systems and economies of the two parts of the Midlands are intertwined. A larger Midlands region would possibly punch harder in political debates and resource allocation at a national level – although it could be more difficult to hold a larger region together without divisions emerging more strongly and limiting the effectiveness of the regional lobby.

One of the spatial planning issues which has aroused considerable controversy in recent years illustrates another dimension of changing governance. Enterprise zones and Urban Development Corporations established under Conservative governments after 1979 took particular parts of the region outside the normal planning and governance system. The most obvious example of this in the West Midlands is the Merry Hill development. Merry Hill has developed into a massive retail centre. It was built on the site of the Round Oak Steel Works that closed in the early 1980s and its establishment as an enterprise zone was recognition of the severe impact that the closure of this steel works had on the locality. The intention in establishing an enterprise zone was to create a different environment that would encourage enterprise, but it was not intended that it would enable a large retail development. The aim was to free the area from red tape and provide fiscal advantages that would enable an area affected by industrial decline to recover. In practice the developers spotted a loophole in thinking around this and developed the site as a mainly retail development. This was strongly resisted at the time – unsuccessfully. Subsequently the local planning authority, Dudley, has been supporting further development of Merry Hill through the Brierley Hill Area Development framework – proposing the redefinition of Merry Hill as part of a new town centre and so avoiding the block on out-of-town shopping centres. There continues to be conflict over the nature and speed of further growth of Merry Hill as a town centre. The crucial issue here is really about the removal of spatial planning decisions from local control. The concerns about a large retail development on the edge of the conurbation undermining existing retailing, including Birmingham city centre, were real and have contributed to some of the fight-back by the city and other towns in the region, such as Wolverhampton.

All these elements in changes in the structure of governance and the formal arrangements of government have occurred against the background of a significant shift in the relationship between central and local government with a centralisation of decision-making and a closer control of finance. The amount that local authorities have been able to spend has been cut and central government has a greater degree of control over transport and planning issues for example. In the last two or three years there has been some relaxation and the development of regional institutions has brought about some changes in this situation. However, at this stage, it is quite difficult to assess the impact of this change. The establishment of the Government Office for the West Midlands in 1994 preceded the establishment of Advantage West Midlands. It was not always clear when the Government Office was championing the region and when it was acting as an agent of central government. The general view was that they act principally as an agent of central government and this view is reinforced by the switch to Cabinet Office account-ability in 2001. There is a view that the central administration, even under Labour in 2001, continues to be dominated by a centralisation tendency. Central govern-ment's concern for different regions and for the standing of London as a world city crucial to the UK economic performance is sometimes argued to affect the way that it considers certain issues. Some West Midlands enthusiasts would point to the experience of the Millennium Dome and the initial competition related to building a new national football stadium as examples where London is preferred despite its inability to propose and deliver effective developments.

These issues might lend themselves to regional paranoia and an exaggeration of the centralised and colonialist tendencies of the Whitehall mandarin. However, they should not be completely dismissed. At the same time it is clear that some of the problems with Birmingham and the West Midlands proposing major national facilities can be caused by a lack of coordination at a local level. Birmingham's initial bid for the national football stadium was undermined by opposition to its development in the green belt. It is interesting to note, however, that these differences can be negotiated and, for example, with the reopening of the national football stadium question following the failure of the agreed London proposal, Birmingham and Solihull successfully collaborated to produce the most effective new proposal. There was also a bid from Coventry, but there is a strong feeling by some in the region that London will remain the preferred option regardless of the quality of alternative bids. Beyond these formal changes there have been a number of other significant shifts in power. In relation to the region as a whole, Birmingham is no longer as dominant as it was. Decentralisation has resulted in population decline in the city and a rise in the population elsewhere in the region. However, the way the politics of the region work remains unclear, with relationships between the city of Birmingham and the region, and the metropolitan authorities and the region being important. But the way in which representation is organised (for example, in the Regional Chamber) also involves some prior compromises to give stronger representation to smaller authorities, for example.

Strategic policies

In the West Midlands region, with the current drafting of a revised RPG, the recently agreed 'Agenda for Action' to deliver the WMES (West Midlands Economic Strategy), new strategies for transport and culture, and the Regional Sustainability Action Framework, there is a more active debate about regional strategies than in the past. The major elements of this can be set out briefly.

Regional planning guidance

The main purpose of RPG, incorporating a regional transport strategy, is to provide a regional spatial strategy within which local authority development plans and local transport plans can be prepared. It should provide a broad development strategy for the region over a 15- to 20-year period and identify the scale and distribution of provision for new housing and priorities for the environment, transport, infrastructure, economic development, agriculture, minerals, and waste treatment and disposal. By virtue of being a spatial strategy it also informs other strategies and programmes. In particular it should also provide the longer term planning framework for the Regional Development Agencies' (RDAs') regional economic strategies.

The RPG for the West Midlands is currently being reviewed, in line with national guidance (Planning Policy Guidance Note 11 on Regional Planning (October 2000), PPG11) for 'new style' RPG. It will place a greater emphasis on a spatial strategy for the region, which integrates the regional transport strategy and which recognises strategic objectives for sustainable development, the WMES and other regional strategies and plans. The new spatial strategy for the West Midlands is based on two key pillars:

- The need for a step change in efforts to regenerate the major urban areas (MUAs)[1] of the region;
- A strengthened commitment to rural renaissance.

This in turn means that the spatial strategy will provide a framework that seeks to:

- adopt positive measures to address the relative decline in the regional economy;
- reverse the movement of people and jobs away from the MUAs and ensure there is a greater equality of opportunity for all;
- tackle road and rail congestion;
- achieve a more balanced and sustainable pattern of development, including rural areas.

The previous strategy sought to address the needs of the urban areas, in part, by providing for new development, especially housing, beyond their boundaries. The current review suggests that this approach is driving an unsustainable outward dispersal of people and jobs from these areas, resulting in little improvement of the overall quality of life within the region, whether within the MUAs, the overspill areas or the remoter parts of the region. The Regional Planning Body (RPB) therefore proposes that the spatial strategy for the region should be redirected to focus on the following key policy principles:

- concentrating development and investment within the MUAs so that they can increasingly meet their own economic and social needs;

- modernising and diversifying the region's economy but ensuring that opportunities for growth are linked to meeting needs and help reduce social exclusion;
- promoting urban renaissance;
- tackling rural deprivation;
- modernising the transport infrastructure of the region.

The RPB recognises that this strategy will require a step change in investment and action. Programmes for urban and rural regeneration, in particular, will require a better integrated policy approach with packages of policies covering economic development, environment, education, health, housing, transport and other services, as well as community development and action. In order to articulate the above principles, eleven interrelated headline objectives have been defined. Together, these form the Spatial Strategy for the West Midlands Region. The objectives are:

1 To promote sustainable development;
2 To support the modernisation and diversification of the regional economy;
3 To address the needs of disadvantaged and vulnerable areas;
4 To improve significantly the region's transport systems to a quality comparable to that of competitor regions;
5 To make the MUAs increasingly attractive places where more people will choose to live, work and invest;
6 To promote Birmingham as a world city;
7 To retain the green belt but to allow an adjustment of boundaries where this is necessary to support urban regeneration;
8 To support the other cities and towns of the region to meet their local and sub-regional development needs;
9 To support the regeneration of the rural areas of the region;
10 To ensure the quality of the environment is conserved and enhanced across all parts of the region;
11 To create a 'joined up' multi-centred regional structure in which all areas have distinct roles to play.

Regional economic strategy

The WMES prepared by Advantage West Midlands (AWM) has now progressed to the stage of publishing an Agenda for Action (AfA) which sets out more of the detail behind the broad goals. The AfA sets out three mechanisms to contribute to the delivery of the WMES:

- *Regeneration Zones* – which seek to target regeneration resources at the areas of greatest need, at the same time linking these areas to areas of opportunity in the context of the improved coordination of regeneration activity in each zone (table 4.2 describes the six zones).

- *Clusters* – the development of linked sectors (either through supply chains or indirect research and education links). Ten clusters have been identified which will receive attention in terms of mapping (spatial and economic), market research and foresight exercises and the development of business networks (table 4.3 indicates the ten clusters). Although not fundamentally a regionally or locally defined set of relationships, there are some spatial concentrations of the selected clusters that will allow some cross-reference to the spatial dimension of the regional economic strategy.
- *High Technology Corridors* – areas where business development activity will be focused to build on the strength of opportunity to foster clusters and high technology business. Three corridors have been identified. A strategy has been developed for each one, along with specified projects. The projects are a mix of property-based ones and those which aim to improve the interface between universities, research establishments and firms (table 4.4 presents the High Technology Corridors).

These mechanisms have a number of common features: first, they require active partnerships, especially in support of cross-boundary collaboration between authorities; second, they have a spatial dimension, but with the clear purpose of benefiting the whole region; and third, they seek to direct the benefits from exploiting opportunities for growth to deprived communities.

The boundaries of the corridors are not clearly defined. Corridor 'partnerships' have been established in each case.

Other regional strategies

There are a number of other important regional strategies. These include:

- *Regional Sustainability Action Framework* – this provides a series of targets directed to improving the sustainability of the region. These targets are largely specified in relation to changes from 2000 (the base year) and 2010, with some interim targets specified for 2005. The targets provide a clear guide for the development of regional strategies.
- *Regional Transport Strategy* – this emphasises the need to support the RPG in its aspirations for urban and rural renaissance. A key element is to improve public transport and to reduce the need for travel. By improving the accessibility of existing settlements and areas within the conurbation, the strategy will contribute to ensuring sufficient access to work, shops, schools, health services, and leisure and recreation facilities. By supporting and enhancing housing choice in the conurbation, a relative reduction in travel distances will be achieved. It is now a requirement that the Regional Transport

Table 4.2 Regeneration zones

Six regeneration zones have been identified which cover a third of the population and two-thirds of the long-term unemployed:

- *Marches* (population: 283,000) – remote rural area, covers most of the rural parts of the Objective 2 area,
- *East Birmingham/North Solihull* (424,000) – extends eastwards from Birmingham centre,
- *North Black Country/South Staffordshire* (292,000) – covers parts of Wolverhampton and Walsall,
- *North Staffordshire* (255,000) – Potteries and parts of Stoke and Newcastle-under-Lyme,
- *Coventry/Nuneaton* (205,000) – extends northwards from Coventry,
- *West Birmingham/South Black Country* (441,000) – extends westwards from Birmingham into parts of Dudley and Sandwell.

Table 4.3 The ten clusters in the WMES

Clusters in WMES:

1. Transport technologies	7. Specialist business and professional services
2. Building technologies	
3. Food and drink	8. Environmental technologies
4. Tourism and leisure	9. Interactive media for education and entertainment
5. High value consumer products	
6. Information and communication technology	10. Medical technologies

---

Table 4.4 High technology corridors

The high technology corridors cover:

- The A38 technology corridor from the centre of Birmingham, past Birmingham University and Longbridge out through Worcestershire to Malvern,
- The Wolverhampton/Telford technology corridor running along the M54 axis,
- The Coventry, Solihull, Warwick area.

Strategy has to be incorporated into the RPG and therefore be fully integrated into the whole spatial strategy for the region.

- *Regional Cultural Strategy* – In January 2001 West Midlands Life[2] published 'The Vision and Aims of the Regional Cultural Strategy 2001–2006', which aims to make the West Midlands: 'A very special place … offering the best you can find anywhere … with the widest range of choices … to the greatest number of people … contributing to prosperity for all ... and making a lasting difference'. It is intended to bring together sectoral and local strategies at the regional level and to add value across cultural sectors. Key strategic priorities articulated in the subsequent Call for Action that are relevant to an emerging Regional Cultural Strategy include: 'to ensure that distinctive sub-regional and local cultural identity within the West Midlands is celebrated; and, to contribute to better social inclusion by encouraging the targeting of resources, outreach and promotional activity at those that are currently excluded …'.

A number of comments can be made about regional approaches in recent years. Some people would argue that the region's ability to promote a more coherent approach to investments in transport infrastructure, for example, has been hampered by a lack of resources from central government. A good example of this is the recent 10-year plan from the Strategic Rail Authority (SRA) that in terms of earmarked resources for the region threatens to undermine the transport strategy that is contained in the RPG. There is a lot of regional support for improved infrastructure, which appears to be undermined by central government and its agencies. There are those who believe that the West Midlands region contributes much to the national economy and feel strongly that it is not unreasonable to expect a larger slice of national resources. There is the concern alluded to above about the skew of resources to London.

A further comment relates to the emphasis placed on markets and enterprise, which again has been touched upon. This element has been most evident in approaches to commercial, retail and industrial development and the encouragement of inward investment, yet is also apparent in residential policy. The sustained emphasis upon encouraging the private sector and home ownership and enabling the market to operate has meant an encouragement of private speculative building in locations where – broadly speaking – builders want to build and build the type of property they consider most appropriate. The strength of the regional policy input into these debates has been rather weak – there has never been a regional housing strategy, for example – although new proposals will change this. Local authorities in areas where developers see opportunities for profitable private sector development have been inclined to take advantage of this and have either been unable or unenthusiastic about taking their share of affordable housing provision. Local authorities in areas where builders do not see a great demand for executive and high-priced property have had a disproportionate role in the provision of rented housing and low-priced home ownership. There is some argument that this has contributed towards the emergence of a segregated housing market with relatively limited interaction between an edge-of-city market and the market in the older, inner areas of the conurbation.

There are important elements in the strategies of the city of Birmingham, and other individual authorities, to counter urban decline through the revival of city centres and the attraction of new residential accommodation into the city centre. This is part of an attempt to create a housing market and promote the whole concept of city living, but the units built tend to be at the higher end of the market. There is now a recognition of the need to retain those people with higher incomes who would otherwise move out of the city or perhaps choose not to come. It is important, however, to see this as part of a broader approach which sees the encouragement of greater housing choice for all income groups. There have also been major inputs into industrial restructuring and policies to deal with the decline of manufacturing industry. These include staving off the closure of businesses, employment replacement, the development of infrastructure that would make inward investment and employment replacement easier, spine roads, regeneration corridors, developing new uses for old sites and reusing former industrial sites for other purposes, considerations about rethinking the hierarchy of settlements within the region, notions of a polycentric city and, within Birmingham, notions of series of villages and quarters. Development around transport corridors has also been emphasised.

There may be a question about how these approaches represent genuine strategic policies formulated for the metropolitan region or for the West Midlands region. The Planning and Transportation Sub-committee of the Metropolitan Authorities does involve regional thinking at the metropolitan level, for example the Regional Planning Guidance acceptance of the importance of Birmingham as a regional centre. However, this is a relatively recent development and its impact is not yet clear. The setting up of the West Midlands Roundtable for Sustainable Development is an example of more positive regional thinking. The National and Regional Planning Guidance framework for all local authorities in the region ensures that there is some coincidence of priorities, but the Single Regeneration Budget, New Deal for Communities and the National Strategy for Neighbourhood Renewal are not based on regional or metropolitan strategic thinking. The Regional Development Authority is beginning to develop an approach to economic development and inward investment, which has a regional remit.

A key element in emerging approaches relates to partnership. The current fascination with stakeholder politics in Britain and with joined-up thinking suggests partnership as a rational response designed to deal with the failings of policies which are developed with inadequate communication between different organisations and agencies working in the same context. However, at another level, partnerships are the hard reality of the situation where there is inadequate power or resources for local authorities to develop responses commensurate with the scale of problems that they face. As the denigration of public sector provision has increased and it has failed to respond (for example, through maintaining infrastructure), so the reputation of the public sector has been damaged and the arguments for partnership have become stronger.

There is a genuine attempt currently to develop Regional Planning Guidance through effective stakeholder consultation in order to involve partners at an earlier stage in plan-making processes. This involves giving away some power at this stage, but the hope is that it will produce a more powerful plan with fewer challenges to it. Against this is the risk of producing a plan which relates to the lowest common denominator and involves inadequate democratic accountability with no regional elected body, no consultation with stakeholders and ignores the role of the Regional Development Agency and the Regional Chamber raise questions. One of the key issues for the future is whether Regional Chambers will develop into elected bodies and whether they might be given tax-raising powers.

Coordination problems

Birmingham is a large city with unified administration. Its governance is not initially affected by the fragmentation of local government associated with other European cities of its size or, for example, with London. Nevertheless, boundary problems are present and affect strategic issues at a metropolitan and regional level. What has been described above involves some processes – which have increased the fragmentation and lack of coherence of policy approaches – and some developments, especially informal and partnership developments, which have strengthened the coordination of policy. At the present time there is more emphasis upon these issues of coordination than at any other time and the emergence of regional bodies is important. However, there are important tensions remaining. Reference has been made to those between the city of Birmingham and some of its neighbouring authorities. There are tensions between the older, urban areas in the region and rural areas. Within Birmingham there are tensions between the high quality suburbs such as Sutton Coldfield and the dilapidated inner city areas. There are rivalries then at almost every level: within authority, within the metropolitan area and within the region. The West Midlands is a large and diverse region and the rivalries are endemic. Cross-boundary working arises as a response to this and is likely to continue to do so on a relatively *ad hoc* or issue-specific basis rather than underpinning the approach to policy. If we were to identify a model of the approach being adopted, it is probably appropriate to refer to diversity and complexity. Partnership approaches are strong, but rivalries and contested positions are also apparent. There is a continuous process of bargaining and negotiation around certain issues, including residential and economic development, while transport is subject to a greater degree of agreement.

Some of the effective partnerships and cooperative mechanisms are not regional or metropolitan in their scope. Sub-regional partnerships, for example between Coventry and Warwickshire, could be seen to involve a degree of rivalry with other parts of the region. Groups such as the Black Country Joint Advisory Group and the Black Country Consortium are about cross-boundary working within the Black Country but may be seen partly as a defence mechanism against Birmingham's dominance. The RDA has a genuine regional remit and its proposed regeneration corridors go from the metropolitan core to the rural heartland of the region. But the politics of the RDA may leave it a hostage to rival stakeholders and deferential, as a non-elected body, to elected local government. There are public and private partnerships in relation to a range of different elements, especially within individual local authorities and the voluntary sector is involved in partnerships, especially in connection with regeneration. The Regional Planning Guidance has been developed in conjunction with stakeholders from all sectors. Neighbourhood-level initiatives place most emphasis upon the involvement of the local community. Hence there are examples of different kinds of partnership and association at different levels, but it is difficult to typify the approach at all levels.

Evaluation

At present the mechanisms for implementing plans are assisted by the state of the national economy and the capacity to negotiate arrangements with developers to finance or provide infrastructure or other planning gains. However, this may be seen as a positive feature associated with the economic cycle, and one which will come into question in the event of economic downturn. The system, perhaps because of this, is also marked by uneven capacity. Planning gains are associated with new development but there is much less capacity to deliver in relation to social exclusion and regeneration. Increasing affluence and rising property values pose challenges to the development of the region, which may be as great as those associated with social exclusion and deprivation. In either case there is little evidence of a coherent strategy towards affordable housing or residential development.

The stated objectives of new Regional Planning Guidance relate to reversing outward migration, the quality of life in urban areas, modernising and diversifying the regional economy, challenging social exclusion, promoting sustainable urban renaissance and rural renewal, and modernising transport strategy. However, more specific objectives related to particular places remain unclear. It may be that we have a general system which can agree on the big picture, but which comes up against objections and local rivalries when the implications arise for any particular locality. In this context the planning system has an important role to play in terms of providing the framework in which urban and rural development can take place. Where there is a coincidence between the thinking of government and the private sector, there are effective partnerships. Where such coincidences do not exist, and especially where the private sector is not engaged, the likelihood of major new development is very limited.

Some of the key issues affecting the region and the degree of coordination in metropolitan government and spatial strategies reflect the weakness of these elements in the past. The emphasis on the market and enterprise, the failure to maintain the infrastructure of the region and the lack of a coherent strategy in relation to residence continues to have an important impact on the development of the region and its metropolitan core. However, the immediate environment is one in which there is much more discussion of regional strategies and one in which regional government is stronger. The informal mechanisms, which have in some cases proved relatively successful, are being replaced by more formal mechanisms and there is a stronger commitment by government to these elements. At the same time the partnership approach is one which is widely accepted for a variety of reasons. It remains the situation that central government is remarkably inter-ventionist in relation to key decisions: for example, major factory developments or office developments within the region are likely to be referred to the Secretary of State for a decision. There is no logic to this in terms of spatial planning or regional strategies except that local people often oppose such major developments. What is good for the region is often not seen to be good for the immediate neigh-bourhood. In itself it may be that this reflects the lack of an agreed and accepted framework for regional and metropolitan development – hence any major proposal arouses short-term local opposition. While there is support from the business community and professional groups the regional agenda is still treated with some suspicion by local government and those concerned with local services. Perhaps the suspicion that regional agendas are driven by central government and business interests is exacerbated by the unelected nature of regional bodies and a change in this would change the perception of the regional agenda.

In general, the increasing emphasis upon regional strategies and partnership approaches and the emphasis upon the need to collaborate across administrative boundaries and to involve different stakeholders is seen as an improvement in the situation which has applied in the past. However, some of the fundamental weaknesses associated with the earlier phase of development still apply. These in particular relate to public sector resources. A strong, sustained commitment of funds for developing transport and public transport to enable Birmingham and the region to develop the kind of infrastructure associated with similar and smaller cities in Europe would demonstrate that the regional agenda was about modernisation and change rather than political control and management.

Conclusion

What general conclusion can we draw from all of this? The scale and diversity of the region make it a complex area to manage effectively. Birmingham is the largest local authority in the country, and operates as an entity in its own right. While the city does not suffer from the fragmentation of administration that affects some large European cities, the surrounding administrative boundaries mean that other local authorities have a major impact on the city and the region. Administrative boundaries bear little relation to the workings of the city or the regional economy. The process of working across these boundaries inevitably involves tensions and difficulties, but the positive news is that it appears that the region is getting better at this. There is evidence that more genuine strategic frameworks are emerging. The major obstacle may be how these frameworks can move things forward in light of the dominant role played by central government, particularly over issues such as land-use planning and transport. The key issue for the future relates to finding mechanisms that enable the region to fully realise its potential in the centralised nature of British governance in terms of both policy development and access to resources. Much will depend on how the regionalism agenda evolves in the near future.

Notes

1 The MUAs are defined as Birmingham, Black Country, Coventry and the North Staffordshire conurbation.
2 West Midlands Life is one of eight Regional Cultural Consortiums set up by the Department for Culture, Media and Sport across England.

Bibliography

Advantage West Midlands (1999) *Creating Advantage: West Midlands Economic Strategy*, Advantage West Midlands.

Birmingham City Council (1993) *The Birmingham Plan: Birmingham Unitary Development Plan 1993*, Birmingham City Council.

Birmingham City Council (2001) *The Birmingham Plan: Alterations and Environmental Appraisal Deposit Draft 2001*, Birmingham City Council.

Champion, T. (2000) 'Flight from the cities?', in R. Bate, R. Best and A. Holmans (eds) *On the Move: The Housing Consequences of Migration*, York: York Publishing Services Ltd.

Department of the Environment, Transport and the Regions (1992) 'Planning policy guidance: housing', *PPG3*, London: HMSO.

Department of the Environment, Transport and the Regions (1998) 'Planning and affordable housing', *Circular 6/98*, London: DETR.

Department of the Environment, Transport and the Regions (2000) 'Quality and choice: a decent home for all', *The Housing Green Paper*, London: TSO.

Department of the Environment, Transport and the Regions (2000) 'Planning policy guidance', *Note 3 Housing*, London: DETR.

Government Office for the West Midlands (1995) *Regional Planning Guidance for the West Midlands Region*, London, HMSO.

Holmans, A. (2000) 'Estimates of future housing need and demand', in S. Monk and C. Whitehead (eds) *Restructuring Housing Systems*, York: York Publishing Services Ltd.

Monk, S. and Whitehead, C. (2000) (eds) *Restructuring Housing Systems*, York: York Publishing Services Ltd.

West Midlands Local Government Association (2001) *Draft Regional Planning Guidance, November 2001*, Birmingham: West Midlands Local Government Association.

Whitehead, C. and Crook, A. (2000) 'The achievement of affordable housing through the planning system', in S. Monk and C. Whitehead (eds) *Restructuring Housing Systems*, York: York Publishing Services Ltd.

5 The experience of Cardiff and Wales

Jeremy Alden

Spatial patterns of development within Wales

Whilst Cardiff is one of Europe's smallest capital cities, with a 1998 population of 321,000, the Cardiff metropolitan region has a population of 1.8 million and accounts for 62.1 per cent of the total population of Wales (2.9 million in 1998). The population of the individual unitary authorities within the metropolitan region is shown in table 5.1, and the location of the 22 unitary authorities in Wales in figure 5.1.

Table 5.1 Population of the 12 new Unitary Authorities comprising Cardiff and its metropolitan region

Unitary Authority	Population (1998) (thousands)
Cardiff	320.9
Rhondda Cynon Taff	240.4
Swansea	229.5
Caerphilly	169.6
Newport	139.2
Neath and Port Talbot	138.8
Bridgend	131.4
The Vale of Glamorgan	121.3
Torfaen	90.2
Monmouthshire	86.3
Blaenau Gwent	72.0
Merthyr Tydfil	57.0
Metropolitan Region	1,796.6

Source: Compiled by the author from Digest of Welsh Local Area Statistics 2000, The National Assembly for Wales, 2001

Cardiff was granted city status in 1905, and was confirmed as the capital city of Wales in 1955. It has experienced rapid growth. The first census of population in 1801 revealed a figure of 1,018 for Cardiff, a figure which a century later had grown to 200,000, with the city becoming the greatest coal-exporting port in the world. Cardiff's growth was due to the development of the coal and steel industries in South Wales and its links with the valley communities remain an important component of the city region.

Over the past 20 years the city of Cardiff and the regional economy have undergone considerable economic restructuring. Cardiff itself has become increasingly dominant at the centre of what has developed into a south-east Wales urban metropolis. The special needs and potential of Cardiff and its region were recognised in 1987 with the creation of the Cardiff Bay Development Corporation. The stated objective of the Urban Development Corporation (UDC) was to put Cardiff on the international map as a 'superlative maritime city'. The UDC has been significant in terms of both resources and size. From its inception, the impact of the Cardiff Bay UDC was seen as being regional rather than just local. The powers and operation of the Cardiff Bay UDC have now been transferred to both the National Assembly for Wales (NAW) and Cardiff City Council.

In its City Centre Strategy (1998–2002), Cardiff City Council (2000) confirmed its commitment to promoting Cardiff in Europe and on the international stage. The Strategy provides a framework for the future of the city centre. It also demonstrates an integrated approach to the city centre, bringing together the aspirations of business interests, public sector organisations and local communities. The City Centre Strategy is supported by the recent Cardiff Unitary Development Plan 1996–2016 (2001). The City Council is required by legislation to prepare a Unitary Development Plan (UDP) to replace existing structure and local plans. The Draft 2001 UDP was agreed by the city council in January 2001 and was subject to public consultation until June 2001. The UDP seeks to support Cardiff's development as a thriving European capital and regional centre. It also seeks to enhance the quality of life in Cardiff and is strongly driven by issues of economic growth, sustainable development, social inclusion and equal opportunities.

Nowhere in the UK has interest in spatial planning and multilevel governance been greater than in Wales. This interest has been increased by constitutional reform in the UK in devolving decision-making and governance to the regional level.

The impacts of devolution on multilevel governance for Wales and spatial planning has seen the UK make a significant shift away from its longstanding profile as the classic unitary state model. This has led to Wales and its capital city – Cardiff – together with the other local authorities, reviewing their relationship with governments and policies at both the UK and the EU level. Cardiff and its metropolitan region, and indeed all 22 local authorities in Wales, have increasingly recognised and emphasised the importance of the European context for issues of spatial planning and governance. The ESDP and EU Structural Funds probably

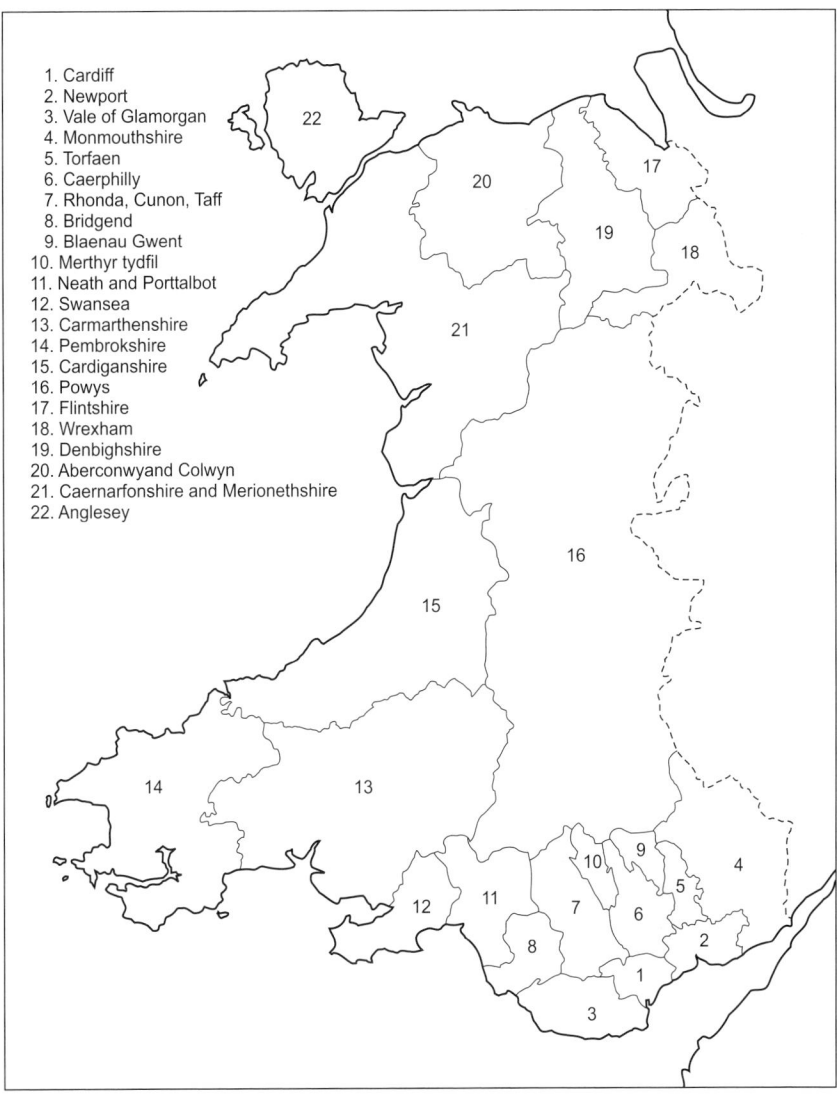

1. Cardiff
2. Newport
3. Vale of Glamorgan
4. Monmouthshire
5. Torfaen
6. Caerphilly
7. Rhonda, Cunon, Taff
8. Bridgend
9. Blaenau Gwent
10. Merthyr tydfil
11. Neath and Porttalbot
12. Swansea
13. Carmarthenshire
14. Pembrokshire
15. Cardiganshire
16. Powys
17. Flintshire
18. Wrexham
19. Denbighshire
20. Aberconwyand Colwyn
21. Caernarfonshire and Merionethshire
22. Anglesey

Figure 5.1 The location of the 22 Unitary Authorities in Wales

have a greater role to play for areas in Wales like the Cardiff metropolitan region than elsewhere in the EU. Why is this the case? The answer lies largely with the designation of the South Wales Valley Communities (10 of the 12 local authorities in the Cardiff metropolitan region) as Objective 1 areas within the EU Structural Funds programme for 2000–2006. Cardiff and its metropolitan region is also very aware of its need to maintain its competitive position on the European scene, particularly in relation to spatial development strategies contained in the ESDP (1999) and Interreg IIc Community Initiative (2000) (see figure 5.2).

Although these EU documents have no formal status in terms of statutory planning, they have nevertheless had a significant impact on spatial planning in

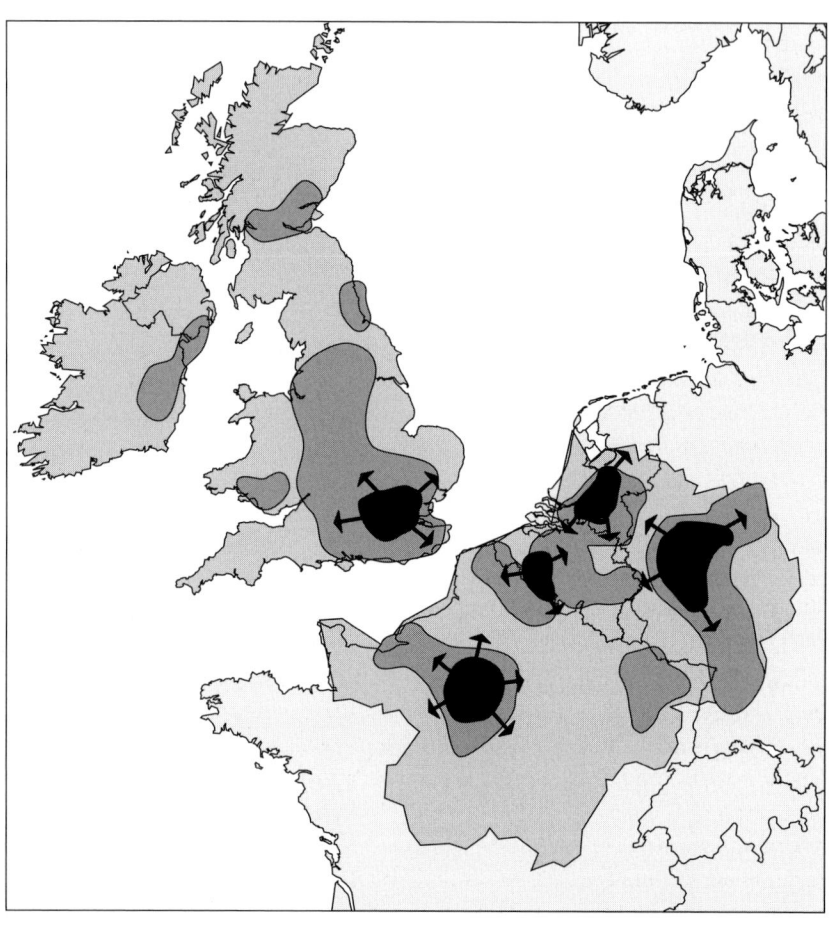

Relatively sparsely populated and lower access to urban services and functions

Concentration of global economic functions and high level of urban services

Urban spread reinforcing polarisation of space

Growth opportunities arising from deconcentration of economic functions

Figure 5.2 Spatial pattern of North-west Europe. Compiled by the author from 'A spatial vision for north-west Europe', INTERREG IIc Community Initiativ, 2000

the UK and particularly in Wales. Of particular importance to the Cardiff metropolitan region has been the ESDP concepts of polycentric development, corridors of growth, and more balanced competitiveness of the European territory. Wales as a whole is the poorest region in Britain, with a GDP per capita only 79.4 per cent of the national average. One of the most difficult issues facing the NAW is how to address the increasing concentration of economic gravity on the successful South-East economic corridor (focused on the M4 motorway) in the Cardiff metropolitan region and the need to provide economic growth to other poorer areas in Wales.

Changes in multilevel government and governance

Nowhere in the UK have shifts in the structures of government been more marked than in Wales and for its capital city of Cardiff. These have led to changes in the relationship between levels of government at national, regional, metropolitan and local levels. These changes have been in terms of both territorial organisation and functional specialisation. As Albrechts *et al.* (2001) have shown, the changing institutional landscape of planning has been a marked feature of many EU countries, and nowhere more so than in Wales and the UK.

Whilst Wales continues to share planning legislation with England, it has produced its own Planning Policy Guidance since 1996. Wales now has a comprehensive planning framework, both in terms of spatial and functional issues, led by its National Assembly. In 2001, the NAW was responsible for approximately half of all public expenditure in Wales, and had a budget of some £9 billion a year.

The NAW has 60 elected Assembly Members, and is responsible for planning policy, economic development, housing, education, environment, transport and local government. The NAW was specifically created not only to devolve power and decision-making to the 'regional' level but also to provide a strategic approach to policy issues at an all-Wales level which the new unitary planning system of 22 local authorities could not provide. The NAW was also created to provide more impetus to improve the economic performance of Wales. The NAW has a committee structure which includes its important Environment, Planning and Transport Committee, chaired by a cabinet minister (currently Mrs S. Essex). However, the committees cover an all-Wales basis rather than sub-regional groupings such as the Cardiff metropolitan region.

It is still very early days in the life of the NAW and the new formal structures of government at all spatial levels. The challenge of devolution for multilevel governance and spatial planning in Wales (and the UK regions) was discussed at an international conference held in Cardiff in October 2000. The contributions have been published in a special issue of *International Planning Studies* (Alden, 2001). Tensions and conflicts have arisen over powers and policies between the NAW and Cardiff City Council. For example, when the mayor of Cardiff attempted to raise the financial allowances of its principal members, these increases were blocked by the National Assembly as being unreasonable. There have also been questions posed as to whether Wales has too many levels of government, e.g. election of MPs to the UK Parliament, members to the National Assembly, members to local government, and also members to the European Parliament.

As pointed out by Alden and Essex (1999), although Wales has developed a fairly unique and comprehensive institutional framework for the operation of both statutory and non-statutory planning at a variety of spatial levels in recent years, this has not included a metropolitan structure in terms of local government. At present, Cardiff City Council is one of 12 local authorities which comprise the Cardiff metropolitan region. Whilst the mayor of Cardiff may like to see a reorganisation of local government to create a metropolitan (local) government, the National Assembly would see this as being too big and powerful, containing over 60 per cent of the population of Wales. There is clearly a tension between the relative powerfulness of the mayor of Cardiff (a capital city) and the first minister of the National Assembly (comparable in a way to that between the mayor of London and UK government ministers). However, the NAW has encouraged local planning authorities to engage in voluntary joint working arrangements, i.e. collaborative planning to prepare common strategic objectives and policies where appropriate. Within Wales, four sub-regional strategic planning groups have been established, for each of South East Wales, North Wales, Mid and East Wales, and South West Wales. The strategic policies formulated for the Cardiff metropolitan region in south-east Wales are examined below, identifying the actors initiating these policies and the interests involved.

Strategic policies formulated for Cardiff and its metropolitan region

Strategic policies formulated for the Cardiff metropolitan region over recent years have come from three main sources: (i) Strategic Planning Guidance for South East Wales prepared by the South East Wales Strategic Planning Group (SEWSPG) of local planning authorities in 2000; (ii) the new Unitary Development Plan for the City (and County as it is often referred to) of Cardiff prepared by the City Council's Planning Department, and (iii) the spatial development concepts and vision contained in European documents such as the ESDP (1999) and INTERREG IIc (2000).

In addition to these three strategic policy initiatives for Cardiff and its region, the new NAW is now progressing its Spatial Plan for Wales which it is committed to produce by 2003. One of the key issues to be addressed by the NAW is how to reconcile the twin objectives of (a) developing the potential of the Cardiff metropolitan region as the 'engine' of economic growth for Wales, and (b) promoting a more even or balanced spatial distribution of economic prosperity throughout

Wales. Moreover, within the Cardiff metropolitan region there continues to be a similar debate on how to meet the needs of the lagging valley communities in the former South Wales coalfield (now a designated Objective 1 area) and at the same time continue to promote and develop Cardiff and its expanding coastal belt. With the 'winding up' of the Cardiff Bay UDC after its 13-year life, both the City Council and the NAW have a key role to play in resolving these difficult and politically contentious issues.

Local planning authorities have been encouraged to collaborate in setting strategic objectives and policies establishing, as appropriate, voluntary working arrangements to achieve this. The local planning authorities in the Cardiff metropolitan region have taken common action in preparing strategic planning guidance for their region, i.e. south-east Wales. This guidance has been prepared by the unitary local authorities in the region through the Strategic Planning Group (SEWSPG). The SEWSPG holds meetings on a regular basis attended by members and officers of the respective authorities. The SEWSPG produced its Strategic Planning Guidance for South East Wales in 2000. It was prepared in accordance with advice from the NAW and the Welsh Local Government Association, i.e. joint collaboration between the national/regional/local levels of government/ governance.

This Strategic Planning Guidance serves the following purposes:

(i)   to identify strategic objectives for the metropolitan region;
(ii)   to provide strategic policy advice and guidance;
(iii)   to provide a strategic context for the preparation, consideration and review of Unitary Development Plans (UDPs);
(iv)   to minimise delays and conflicts between planning authorities at the public inquiry stage of plan preparation;
(v)   to identify areas of agreement on common issues and facilitate the development of common policy approaches;
(vi)   to identify strategic policy issues that may need resolution and identify the mechanisms for resolving them;
(vii)   to advise Welsh Assembly policy;
(viii) to provide agreed regional statistical information to inform UDP policies;
(ix)   to provide an opportunity for interested organisations to contribute to the regional planning process for the Cardiff metropolitan region.

The Strategic Planning Group for the metropolitan region has addressed a wide range of issues facing the area. These include population and housing, transportation, retail development, employment, land reclamation, green belts and green wedges, land and nature conservation, and urban regeneration. Many of these issues contain controversial aspects for planning policies, and no more so than in the case of green belts and green wedges. Green belts and wedges have been used extensively in the UK to prevent the continued growth of urban sprawl. At present, there are no statutory green belts designated in Wales. Does this indicate a lack of development pressure even in the Cardiff metropolitan region? In fact, Welsh local planning authorities have, to date, achieved similar objectives to green belts by utilising a package of alternative mechanisms such as 'green wedges' and settlement boundaries which, when taken together, perform similar functions to those of a green belt. Discussion within the Strategic Planning Group has indicated that the regional importance of Cardiff requires the strategic protection of a green belt but that other designations are more appropriate elsewhere in the metropolitan region. A package approach to anti-coalescence of towns and landscape protection policies has therefore been put forward. Areas of local importance are designated as green wedges or Special Landscape Areas, and areas of strategic importance are designated as green belt. The primary purposes of the Cardiff Green Belt will be to prevent the coalescence of Cardiff and Newport, the two largest urban settlements in the metropolitan region.

Cardiff City Council is committed to promoting Cardiff in Europe. Its City Centre Strategy (2000) has the principal task of developing a united approach to the established city centre and its extension to the Inner Harbour in Cardiff Bay. This is also the location of the offices of the NAW. One of the main aims of the strategy is to develop Cardiff as a leading European regional shopping centre and office location whilst also fulfilling a more local role.

Some mention should be made here of the lead taken by the capital city of Cardiff to host international events, which will generate benefits throughout the city and its region, and indeed for other areas in Wales. Cardiff City Council, like many other cities in Europe (and world-wide), has sought to attract flagship sporting/cultural events to the city. In 1999 Cardiff hosted the Rugby World Cup. In 2001 a range of football events were held in Cardiff's Millennium Stadium, including Britain's FA Cup, watched by over 200 million people throughout the world. Cardiff is bidding to be designated the European City of Culture in 2008, and is hosting the International Festival of Music Theatre. In October 2001 Cardiff was announced as the venue for the European Ryder Golf Tournament, the third largest world sports event after the Olympic Games and Football World Cup. All the local authorities in the metropolitan region support these initiatives, led by Cardiff City Council, and including both public and private sector development agencies.

The Cardiff Unitary Development Plan (UDP) 1996–2016 provides a long-term strategic view for Cardiff. There is a legal requirement for the city council to prepare a UDP, and to consider land-use issues over a 15- to 20-year period. Policies and proposals in plans must relate to land-use matters but also have regard to economic, social and environmental circumstances. The UDP will, therefore, provide the land-use policies and proposals necessary to enable the city council to pursue its overall policy priorities.

The population of Cardiff, at over 320,000, is growing, as the result of natural increase and the draw of people to an attractive and prosperous city. This has brought a requirement for more homes, jobs, and community and recreation facilities. However, many people and communities within the city suffer from poverty and social exclusion. Many neighbourhoods, both in inner city and outer city housing estates, remain in need of regeneration and renewal. There is also concern within the Cardiff metropolitan region of south-east Wales that the continued success of the area has been (and is continuing) at the expense of the poorer valley communities located in the former South Wales coalfield.

The development strategy of the UDP is based on a number of principles, including:

- controlling the rate and size of Cardiff's expansion;
- locating development where it will cause least harm to the environment;
- establishing areas of green belt to protect the city and prevent it from merging with adjacent urban centres;
- promoting development on brownfield rather than greenfield sites;
- promoting the regeneration of run-down urban areas;
- promoting opportunities for inward investment focused on high quality development and jobs;
- promoting development where it minimises the need for car travel;
- promoting greater integration of land-uses;
- promoting development and improvements to the public realm that are both safe and attractive to users;
- locating development where good infrastructure facilities exist. This strategy is also underpinned by locational principles which are contained in the NAW's Draft Planning Policy Wales document (2001).

In addition to strategic policies formulated for Cardiff and its region by collaboration between local planning authorities, EU initiatives, and the Cardiff Unitary Development Plan itself, which have been discussed above, the NAW has published its new Draft Planning Policy Wales (2001). This guidance is for all unitary planning authorities in Wales and addresses a wide range of planning issues. There is, therefore, a fairly well-integrated system of strategic and spatial planning within multilevels of governance for Cardiff and its metropolitan region.

Problems of institutional and spatial coordination

As Alden (1999) has illustrated, there are a number of alternative scenarios for the future of the planning system in the UK. How far will the recent focus on 'regions' and 'Europe' be taken? The UK adopted a new planning system in 2001 which has moved significantly away from the previous classic example of a unitary state-led system to one of devolving more power to the regions and more towards an example of a regionalised unitary state. Wales, Scotland, Northern Ireland and London now have their own elected governments and responsibility for spatial policies.

Within Wales there has been established a more comprehensive institutional framework for planning and spatial policy with the creation of a NAW and 22 new unitary local authorities and collaborative planning between them at a regional level, as illustrated above by the example of the South East Wales Strategic Planning Group (for the Cardiff metropolitan region). The European dimension to this pattern of changing levels of governance and spatial policy has become more prominent with the influence of both the ESDP (1999) and INTERREG IIc (2000) in promoting the global role of metropolitan regions.

A particularly exciting development in the UK planning system was the government's announcement in November 1999 that the planning system will, for the first time, be required to take on a wider role than just land management, and become more closely linked or 'joined up' with national, regional and local economic development policies. A new feature of governance and spatial policy in Wales has been the integration of policies to address thematic issues such as economic prosperity, social exclusion, sustainability, urban regeneration and vitality of rural areas.

The NAW has also structured its committees and policies on a regional basis. The four regional groups of local authorities in Wales who are collaborating on strategic planning at a regional level also interact with four Regional Economic Forums, one of which is focused on south-east Wales.

The NAW has also introduced targets to be achieved in terms of its major policies and their spatial impact. In terms of its National Economic Development Strategy (1999) and its Strategic Plan Better Wales (2000), specific targets have been set on GDP per capita and job creation for certain areas, with particular reference to the Objective 1 area of the Valley Communities within the Cardiff metropolitan region.

Planning for the future of metropolitan regions like Cardiff and its region has now extended well beyond the confines of the statutory planning system to embrace a wide range of economic, social and environmental policies operated at a national level in Wales, but which have important regional dimensions. For example, in 2001 the NAW created a new National Council for Education and Training for Wales. It will be the lead body for post-16 knowledge and skills development in Wales, with an annual budget of £400 million. It will help to promote the economic competitiveness of Wales and the prosperity of its regions. Again, four Regional Committees have been established, one covering south-east Wales, to help operate the new council. The Regional Committee will also be responsible for developing links with other networks in the region, including the Regional Economic Forum, sector groups, and business networks with the aim of informing the regional statement of needs. The area-based approaches adopted by the national policies of the NAW represent a significant component of spatial policy and planning for the Cardiff metropolitan region.

Another exciting development in terms of governance and spatial policy in Wales, and particularly the Cardiff metropolitan region, is the willingness of the NAW to address in a robust way the 'difficult issues' (sometimes referred to as the 'wicked issues') which have been left unresolved, often for many years. In terms of regional focus, the NAW has stressed the importance of spreading prosperity to west and north-west Wales and the Valley Communities of south-east Wales, all of which is designated an Objective 1 area. However, should the spatial strategy of the NAW be to discourage fast growth in the 'hot spots' of south-east and north-east Wales? Furthermore, any strategy that focuses resources spatially – whether those of ESDP/INTERREG IIc and IIIb, or NAW – is likely to involve risks and create both winners and losers in terms of localities.

For the first time, the debate on which areas to promote, bearing in mind the need to raise GDP per capita for Wales as a whole as well as for its poorer areas, has faced difficult choices in an explicit way. The nature of the public/private sector relationship is critical here. The Confederation of British Industry in Wales (CBI Wales) has itself established a Planning Policy Panel for Wales to address spatial development issues. The CBI has become a major actor in the development process at both a regional and a local level, because the role played in development by the private sector is just as important as that played by the public sector. In the past, spatial planning was largely public-sector driven, but more recently the promotion of economic development and regeneration has focused on private/public sector partnerships. The private sector, represented in Wales by the CBI, has become as key a regional stakeholder as the public sector. The private sector has had to be actively engaged in spatial planning for the Cardiff metropolitan region.

The NAW has established a priority to attract economic development to the Objective 1 area, and especially the poorer Valley Communities within the Cardiff metropolitan region. It is generally recognised that these localities are amongst the poorest communities within the EU. Whilst Objective 1 funding seeks to lever private-sector monies, its emphasis is on public-sector funding. In contrast, the CBI represents the private sector. The developers in the private sector wish to focus investment in the more prosperous coastal belt within the Cardiff metropolitan region. Private-sector investment seeks the highest rate of return in areas with the greatest potential, rather than supporting initiatives in areas with the greatest need. Whilst public/private partnership is a hallmark of current development in both urban and rural areas, the public and private sectors clearly have different interests to pursue.

Evaluating the changing relationship between multilevel governance and spatial policy for the Cardiff metropolitan region

Interest in spatial policy and multilevel governance has never been greater than at the present time in the UK, Wales and the Cardiff metropolitan region itself. The encouragement given by the UK government to devolution and the creation of city mayors has heightened the institutional and political dimensions of planning at the regional level. The newly-created regional government of Wales is on a steep and fast-moving learning curve, and has only just begun. This new 'national' government has sought to engage all stakeholders in the region, in public, private and voluntary sectors, to help achieve national, regional and local policy objectives in Wales.

Figure 5.3 illustrates the widening and comprehensive nature of the relationship between the new forms of metropolitan governance and the coordination of spatial policy for Cardiff and its region. It might seem rather remarkable that although there is no metropolitan level of local government for Cardiff and its region, there is developing very rapidly a wide range of spatial policies focused at the metro-politan regional level. These spatial policies have emanated from both the EU global and UK national levels (i.e. top down) as well as from the national Wales and regional/local levels (i.e. bottom up) within Wales. They have not only, or mainly, been a product of action by local government itself, and certainly not just by individual local governments even if they are capital cities like Cardiff. However, just as there are benefits from London having a role as a world city, so there is a consensus in Wales and the Cardiff metropolitan region that both benefit from Cardiff's growing role as a capital city within Wales, but also within the EU context of capital cities. Examples cited above have shown that both statutory planning and collaborative planning have operated alongside each other to deliver economic and social benefits to the whole of the Cardiff metropolitan region.

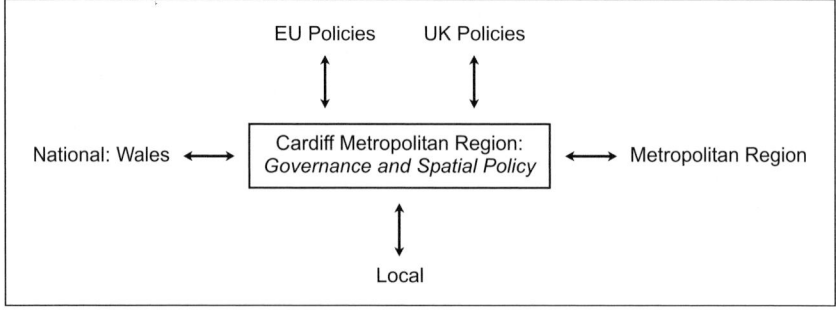

Figure 5.3 The relationship of Cardiff with other actors

The positive aspect of this relationship between new forms of metropolitan governance and spatial policy has certainly been an increased focus on addressing hitherto difficult issues. Debate on these issues has been brought into the public arena much more explicitly than in the past. Stakeholders throughout Wales and the Cardiff metropolitan region have engaged in this debate as they have sought and been offered some ownership on key strategic issues. The closer integration of policies at all spatial levels has also helped to ensure that spatial elements of all policies are working in the same direction and not in competition with one another.

One of the possible negative outcomes of this new pattern of governance and spatial policy in Wales might focus on the future role of local government itself, and in the case of Cardiff, its city council. Hitherto, one of the main features of planning in Britain has been its strong base in local government. This has certainly been the case in Wales. Central government has also had a strong role to play in preparing national guidance to be taken into account by local planning authorities in preparing development plans and in decisions on individual planning applications. All this has changed in recent years. The UK central government has provided legislative devolution down to regions at a time when sovereignty has also been moving upwards to Brussels. The new national government of Wales attaches the highest priority to improving the level of prosperity in Wales as a whole and its regions/localities. The metropolitan regional level of governance and spatial policy has acquired an increasingly more important place within the new spatial hierarchy. Just as regional government has come to Wales in the form of devolution, if Wales was to undergo a reorganisation of local government in the future, then pressures and opportunities at the metropolitan regional level might also see local government focused on this model. For the foreseeable future, however, local governments within the Cardiff metropolitan region are likely to continue to work together, and alongside the NAW, and EU and UK governments, to enhance their position within the global and European economy.

Bibliography

Albrechts, L., Alden, J.D. and Rosa Pires, A. (2001) *The Changing Institutional Landscape of Planning*, London: Ashgate Publishers.

Alden, J.D. (1999) 'Scenarios for the future of the British planning system: the need for a national spatial planning framework', *Town Planning Review*, 70 (3): 385–407.

Alden, J.D. (2001) 'Devolution since Kilbrandon and scenarios for the future of spatial planning in the United Kingdom and European Union', *International Planning Studies*, 6 (2): 117–32. This is a special issue of the journal devoted to multilevel governance and spatial planning.

Alden, J.D. and Essex, S. (1999) 'The Cardiff metropolitan region', in P. Roberts, K. Thomas and G. Williams (eds) *Metropolitan Planning in Britain: A Comparative Study*, London: Jessica Kingsley Publishers.

Cardiff City Council (2000) *City Centre Strategy 1998–2002*, Cardiff.

Jeremy Alden

Cardiff City Council (2001) *Cardiff Unitary Development Plan 1996–2016: Outline Proposals for Consultation*, Cardiff.
Cardiff University (2001) *Welsh Spatial Planning Framework: Comparative Spatial Planning Methodologies Research Study*. Final Report to National Assembly for Wales. Department of City and Regional Planning, Cardiff University (with ECOTEC Research and Consulting Limited), February 2001.
European Commission (1999) 'European spatial development perspective', final draft, *Towards a balanced and sustainable development of the territory of the EU*, Luxembourg: Office for Official Publications of the European Communities.
National Assembly for Wales (1999) *National Economic Development Strategy.*
National Assembly for Wales (2000a) *A Better Wales* (the first strategic plan of the NAW).
National Assembly for Wales (2000b) *Digest of Welsh Local Area Statistics*.
National Assembly for Wales (2001) *Draft Planning Policy Wales* (Public Consultation).
National Statistics (2000) *Regional Trends: UK, 2000*, Edition No. 35.
North West Metropolitan Area (2000) INTERREG IIc Programme, *A Spatial Vision for North-West Europe*, North West Metropolitan Area INTERREG IIc Secretariat, London.
South East Wales Strategic Planning Group (2000) *Strategic Planning Guidance for South East Wales*, Volume 1, January 2000, Volume 2, June 2000.
South Glamorgan County Council (1994) *Cardiff – Towards a Euro-Capital*.

6 The Stockholm region

Metropolitan governance and spatial policy

Björn Hårsman and
Amy Rader Olsson

Stockholm – like the rest of Sweden – suffered from a severe recession at the beginning of the 1990s, but since then its economy has been expanding steadily. Its infrastructure is of a high standard and well maintained, recreational opportunities abound and its environment is healthy. However, Stockholm's popularity has strained its resources and has exacerbated inherent spatial challenges. Every year, 15,000 more people move to the Stockholm region and most want to live in the inner city, which has an acute housing shortage. Major transport corridors are jammed with traffic during peak hours and the region's northern and southern halves are becoming increasingly segregated. This chapter describes the current regional policies and challenges in the Stockholm region, as well as recent attempts to unite the metropolitan region's municipalities in a new municipal association. The first section describes the region's structure, economy and land use. The second section reviews the current government structure. The third and fourth sections describe the nature and coordination of policies shaping the region's current and future spatial structure. The fifth section discusses the pros and cons of various metropolitan governance institutions in terms of addressing regional goals. The final sections offer reflections on the future governance of the region and how to meet its challenges.

The Stockholm region

Up until about the mid-1970s, the Stockholm metropolitan region roughly corresponded to the area covered by the 26 municipalities comprising Stockholm County. However, the functional labour market region is rapidly spreading into surrounding county council areas to the north, west and south and now comprises almost the entire Mälar River Valley (Mälardalen). The region includes both dense urban settlements and rural communities, including much of the Stockholm archipelago. Water is Stockholm's greatest natural resource but is also a spatial planning challenge; linking all but the closest islands with bridges or tunnels is expensive and harms unique natural habitats.

Table 6.1 Government in the Stockholm region

Level	Political	Financial	Responsibilities, including planning
National	Election	Redistribution of income to poorer municipalities and regions; Investment in national roads, rail	National sector plans for transport, housing, health care, education, etc.
Provincial Administrative Boards*	Appointed by national goverment	Administers some national funds for sector development, regional development	Regional economic planning, 'growth contracts' for regional development
County Councils*	Election	County income taxes, plus/minus redistribution grants/contributions to other countries	Prepares with health care, regional strategy (advisory only); and public transport
Municipalities	Election	Municipal income taxes plus/minus redistribution grants/contributions to other municipalities	Local land use planning (binding); strategies for local sector development (environment, energy, etc.)

Source: Inregia AB

* Note that the Provincial Administrative Boards and the County Councils cover the same geographic area. There is no official government authority corresponding to the metropolitan region's land area and population.

The Stockholm metropolitan region – also referred to in this chapter as the functional region – is home to about 2.1 million people. This region represents the commuting, housing and labour market region but does not have a corresponding public authority. The population of Stockholm County is about 1.8 million and the city itself has about 750,000 inhabitants.

Stockholm's location makes it relatively isolated compared to other European capitals. European business leaders recently ranked Stockholm nineteenth out of 29 European cities in terms of transport links with other cities and internationally (Healy and Baker, 2000). On the other hand, many see developments in the former Soviet Union and its satellite states as a major opportunity for Stockholm to act as a gateway between developed and developing European economies.

Land use

Stockholm County has a relatively dense urban core surrounded by smaller cities built along radial corridors, a legacy of planning in the 1960s. About 40 per cent of workplaces and 25 per cent of the population are in the central urban core. However, this monocentric structure has weakened slightly in recent years, as population growth has increased most in outer areas. This is partly due to the provision of improved road and rail infrastructure outside the urban core. Housing is more spread out than workplaces, and follows a predictable pattern of multi-family apartment houses in the core, villas in surrounding communities and vacation homes on the outskirts and throughout the archipelago. Much of the Stockholm metropolitan region is still forested and sparsely populated. The expansion of land use for dwellings and workplaces was much slower in the 1990s than in earlier decades.

Economic growth

Between 1985 and 2000, Stockholm was responsible for 40 per cent of Sweden's growth, and a similar pattern is expected for the coming 15-year period. The economy of the Stockholm metropolitan region is much larger and more diversified than that of other Swedish regions. Stockholm's size and diversity has been a chief competitive advantage relative to other Swedish markets. Over the past 50 years, Stockholm, like other European cities, has almost abandoned its manufacturing and production sectors in favour of service-related industries, capitalising on Sweden's research and development capacity and strong knowledge orientation. Four out of five Stockholmers have a job in the service-related sectors, particularly those related to biotechnology and information technology. The telecom industry has experienced particularly rapid growth. About one-third of the employed population works within the public sector.

Björn Hårsman and Amy Rader Olsson

An expanding spatial territory and population

Continued growth has pressured municipalities to allocate more land for housing and real estate. The labour market region has also expanded significantly, both by increasing density and by geographical expansion. The metropolitan region has grown by 1.1 million people in the past 50 years. The geographical expansion has mainly been caused by better and faster transport facilities along corridors radiating from the central core. At the same time, the sprawl has increased the demand for transportation infrastructure linking suburban areas.

The current regional plan anticipates that the growth of Stockholm's functional labour market region will continue over the next 30 years, though perhaps not at the current rate. The commuting region is expected to eventually encompass the entire Mälar Valley when planned high speed regional rail corridors linking the region to other cities in the Mälar Valley are realised.

The north–south divide

Stockholm's economic prosperity is not evenly distributed across its municipalities. Most northern municipalities enjoy low unemployment and steady growth, while many southern municipalities have lagged behind. An economic downturn at the beginning of the 1990s widened the chasm between north and south, which ultimately disadvantages the entire region. Plans for the coming 30-year period therefore focus heavily on the integration of these two regional halves, in part by increasing educational opportunities in the south and providing new north-south road and rail links.

Government structure

Sweden has been described as both highly centralised and highly decentralised. In theory, much power is devolved to the municipal level – which provides a broad range of public services – and the Swedish Constitution gives municipalities and counties the right to finance their own activities by imposing a local income tax. Swedish municipalities enjoy a higher local tax revenue as a percentage of GNP than those in any other OECD country (Andersson *et al.*, 1997). However, much of the power to govern the country rests with the central government. The national government has a redistributive policy compelling richer municipalities and counties to compensate the poorer ones. Stockholm County and the municipalities within its borders, as some of the country's richest, contribute about 700 Euro per capita and year to other regions.

Sweden has a national parliament, national ministries and national central agencies, provincial administrative boards (*länsstyrelse*), 23 county councils (*landsting*) and 289 municipal governments (*kommuner*). Provincial administrative boards and county councils have the same territorial borders. Compared to other EU Member States, Sweden has some of the largest municipalities and smallest counties. The parliament, county council and municipal governments are popularly elected. The governor of each provincial administrative board (*landshövding*) is appointed by the state. Most power rests with the national and municipal governments and far less with the county councils at the regional level. The county councils are mainly responsible for the provision of health care and regional transportation, functions with clear scale economies at the regional level. The provincial administrative boards are regional representatives of the central government but have little authority to govern the region in practice. In addition, there are sector representatives for large national government authorities, such as the national road and rail authorities. There are also both institutionalised and *ad hoc* inter-municipal agreements and cooperation on a range of issues such as air quality and watershed management, and the provision of some public services.

In table 6.1 a range of regional and sector planning structures are briefly described. In most cases, the various government levels attempt to ensure that plans are consistent with each other through ongoing interactive communication and consensus processes. However, there are a few rules that require harmonisation of local plans with overarching general policy. For example, municipal land-use plans are not subject to regional or national approval in a formal sense. Rather, planning at all levels attempts to incorporate the goals and plans at other levels. The exception to this is the right of the national government to impose constraints on local planning by defining natural or cultural sites of national importance.

Regional development planning

In 1971, a unique Swedish law granted the Stockholm County Council respon-sibility for regional planning. Stockholm's is in fact the only county council that produces a combined regional land-use and transportation plan. The plan suggests principles for the use of land and water areas as well as guidelines for the location of development and infrastructure, but does not have the force of law. The Council's Office of Regional Planning and Urban Transportation produces regional plans and conducts research on various regional development issues. The importance of the regional plans should not be underestimated just because they are optional. The process of producing the regional plan (about every ten years) is exhaustive and includes input from municipalities, interest groups and the general public. It is also critical to the planning of transportation infrastructure and services under the control of the county council. Even the national sector authorities for road and rail use the forecasts in Stockholm's regional plan as a basis for their own trans-portation planning for infrastructure within the region. The regional plan represents a consensus view among municipalities in the Stockholm region as to long-term development goals.

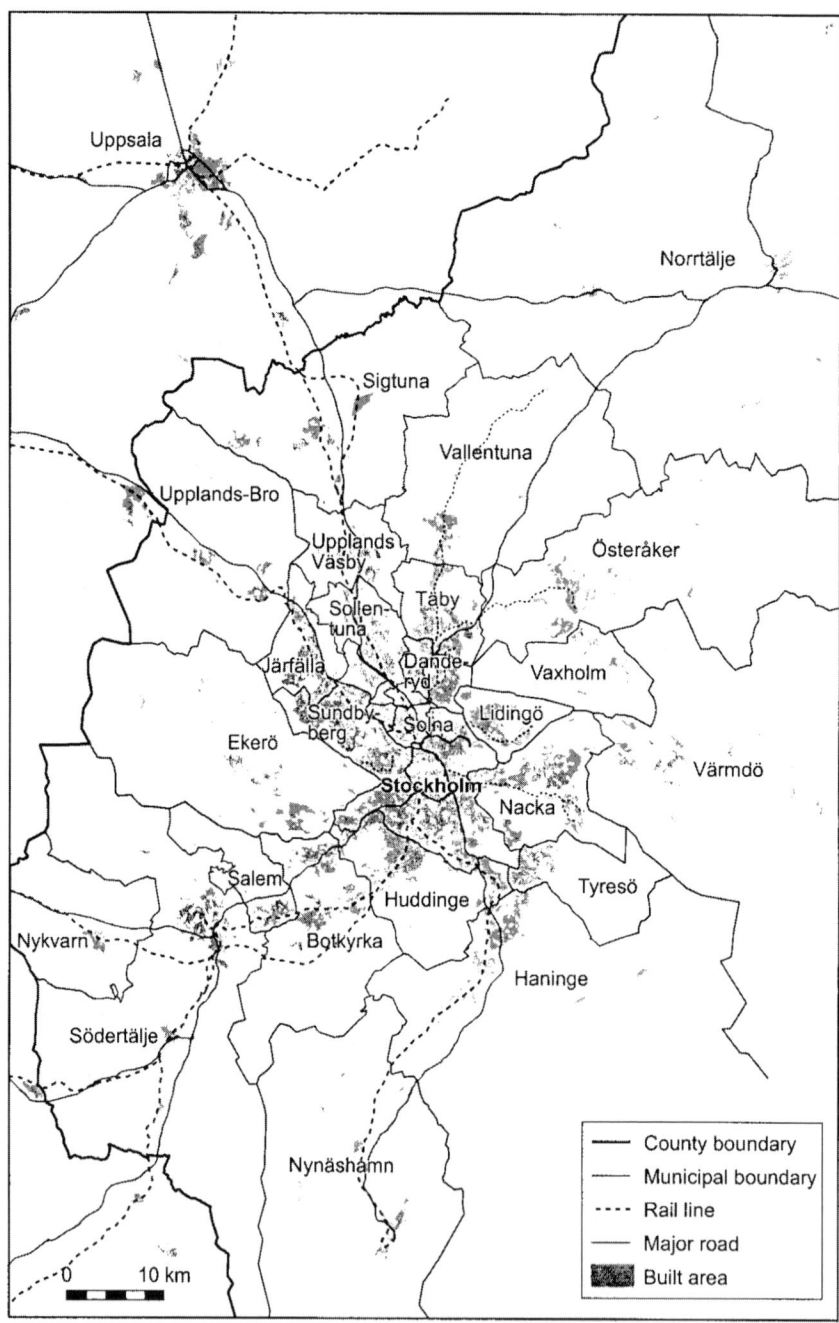

Figure 6.1 The Stockholm region. *Source:* Inregia AB and LMV, 2000

Until recently, the regional plan focused on the physical planning of land use, especially for housing and sensitive natural areas. However, the national law does not specifically limit the scope of regional planning. Recently, the regional plan has included plans and strategies for economic and social development as well. In other words, Stockholm's County Council has considerably expanded its functional role without being requested by the national government to do so.

The Stockholm Provincial Administrative Board is technically responsible for planning regional economic development. Under a recent central government initiative, 'growth contracts' detailing strategies for regional development are drawn up between the provincial administrative boards and the Ministry of Commerce, based on an EU model meant to promote cooperation among government levels and with the private sector. Although the county council and municipalities are consulted in this process, they have no direct authority to influence plans. As noted, the county council and most municipalities also produce studies and statistics on economic development issues, and produce their own economic development strategies. These activities are not formally linked to the 'growth contracts'.

Transportation planning

Sweden is unique among EU countries in that it has a nation-wide system of public transport authorities (PTAs) for the provision of all public transport modes within a county, as stipulated by a 1978 national law. The Stockholm County Council is also the public transport authority for Stockholm County, providing bus, light rail and subway services. Since the deregulation of Swedish public transport in 1989, Stockholm's PTA (*Stockholms lokaltransport–SL*) purchases bus and subway services on the open market through competitive tendering. Roads and related infrastructure are classified as municipal or national, with corresponding responsibilities for planning, financing, building and maintenance.

A variety of actors are involved in the planning and funding of roads, rail and related infrastructure. National road and rail administration representatives represent the government in regional transport planning and infrastructure investment negotiations. Technically, the provincial administrative boards are responsible for coordinating all the activities of the national government at the regional level, ensuring a balance between goals for improved mobility and environmental protection, for example. In Stockholm, this authority also disburses a modest annual budget (about EUR 33 million) to support transportation projects within the county. However, in practice sector authorities or ministries often choose to negotiate directly with county councils or municipalities when large investments are being negotiated.

A national commission is currently reviewing large-scale infrastructure needs for the Stockholm region in preparation for future investment negotiations. This process is a good example of the extent to which the national government has a direct role in determining key infrastructure investments in the transportation infrastructure of the Stockholm region. Although municipalities and the county council suggest investment priorities, it is ultimately the national government that decides what to support.

Land-use planning

Sweden's land-use planning is highly decentralised, with the 1987 Planning and Building Act granting municipalities the right to include both publicly and privately owned land in their 'comprehensive plans' and 'detailed plans', to outline proposed land and water use, new developments, and changes to existing development and conservation areas. Only the detailed plans are legally binding. There is no national spatial plan in Sweden, but municipal plans must be consistent with national sector plans and laws concerning environmental protection, cultural heritage and other national land-use interests. As noted, land-use plans are typically the result of an ongoing, interactive dialogue between regional and municipal planners.

Coordination among planning and governance institutions

Regional vs sector planning

As noted, the metropolitan region of Stockholm is in acute need of new housing and transportation infrastructure, to serve new and anticipated demand and to relieve existing road and rail bottlenecks in the central city. However, the regional plan only serves as a guide recommending new transport infrastructure. Not even the county's own public transport authority is obliged to follow this plan, though it is consulted during the planning process. Sector plans for road and rail that intersect the Stockholm region are in most cases consistent with the regional plan. However, the national government has the final say when it comes to implementing and financing infrastructure. During the 1980s, Stockholm's share of the national budget for investment in transport infrastructure was much lower than what was needed to implement the regional plan. In many cases this created serious problems, for instance in the inner city where commuter trains must share tracks with interregional trains. National roads also carry transit traffic through the heart of Stockholm.

Coordination of regional and sector plans is made somewhat more difficult by the fact that national sector authority boundaries are not congruent with those of the Stockholm region. The rail authority's 'Stockholm region' includes parts of two other counties, and the road authority includes the island of Gotland.

Public vs private planning

In determining the efficiency of the metropolitan planning and governance process, it is important not to underestimate the role of the private sector in shaping the region's spatial structure. Some argue that planning has become a meaningless bureaucratic exercise given the privatisation of public services and the inextricable ties of the region's economy to a global market. Investments in Stockholm's southern suburbs illustrate this. The national government, the county and municipalities poured money into large infrastructure investments in a regional commuter rail station, a new university and a new biotechnology centre near a major hospital. However, economic development here is still marginal, because firms prefer to locate in or near existing technology clusters or other attractive areas. Aside from contact through local chambers of commerce, the private sector is not involved in regional planning.

Regional association

The Stockholm metropolitan region has already outgrown its county borders, and this process will accelerate once new trains are purchased that can utilise high-speed interregional rail lines. An association of the counties and municipalities in the Mälar Region was formed in 1992 to coordinate some of the planning activities of municipalities and the four counties surrounding Mälar Lake (*Mälardalsrådet*). The idea to form the association was partly based upon the growth of Stockholm's commuting region. Many municipalities also believed that closer links with the growth engine of Stockholm would spill over to them and that the association would result in more money from the national government for investments in transport infrastructure. Most municipalities felt that it was important for the functional region to 'speak with one voice' as to the priorities for the region. This, it was argued, would help to strengthen the region's position relative to other parts of Sweden and also help it compete with other powerful European regions.

The association's focus has been on promoting consensus among the municipalities in the entire functional region in areas such as transportation investments, lobbying the national government and cooperating with the private sector. The large territory was seen as an advantage in representing the common interests of the region within the EU and in negotiations with the national government. The formation of the association was seen as a proactive step in preparing the region for an expected future in which the relative strength of the national level will diminish and that of EU authorities and regional and local agencies will increase.

However, this association has no formal authority and so far has mostly served as a forum for the exchange of ideas and as a clearing house for regional statistics and reports. As the mayor of Stockholm recently stated: '[The association] is only a promoting forum. The work within the council can be a catalyst. In its operations, the work of the association gives other actors the strength to act' (press release,

Mälardalsrådet, 2001; authors' translation). The association comprises municipalities from four counties. In three of these counties, almost all of the municipalities have joined the association. However, only about half of Stockholm County's municipalities have joined.

Managing conflict and cooperation within the region

In general, municipalities and county councils within the functional Stockholm region enjoy a close and stable relationship. There are both institutions for broad cooperation – such as the norms and rules used in the production of the regional plan – as well as a host of smaller bilateral or multilateral agreements among neighbouring municipalities. Although municipalities are not obligated to follow the land-use guidelines in the regional plan, most do. This is due to an extensive consensus process in the creation of the plan itself. The county council is considered by most municipalities to be sensitive to local concerns and there is broad agreement as to general development goals for the region.

However, this generally cooperative relationship is not immune to conflict. Plans to restrain employment growth in certain attractive areas are especially difficult to implement by municipalities interested in supporting local economic development. In those few cases in which municipal land-use decisions have come in direct conflict with the regional plan, municipalities have pursued exploitation plans despite regional protests.

Spatial policies in Stockholm County

Regional plans 1960–2000

Regional plans focus on long-term strategies for land-use, infrastructure, economic development and – more recently – environmental protection. The first regional plan for Stockholm County was presented in 1958. Over the past several decades, the main goals stressed in planning documents have remained similar although the focus has varied:

- In the 1960s, the economy grew rapidly and there was strong pressure to 'build away' housing shortages. The focus was on meeting the needs of rapid population growth, particularly measures to secure the supply of land for new transport links and for large new public housing and real estate developments. Manufacturing employment peaked during this decade and had started to decline by its end.
- The 1970s have been called the 'green wave' because inhabitants left the county for more rural parts of Sweden and the economy slowed down. Employment opportunities in the public sector expanded rapidly, especially outside Stockholm, encouraging outmigration from Stockholm. Planners

called for the need to integrate social, economic and physical plans and for small-scale development. Planning ideals reflected a decreasing market orientation. Social welfare issues and the decentralisation of workplaces were in focus. Suddenly, the large-scale housing estates built in the 1960s had become 'problem areas'.

- In the 1980s, the focus was on balancing the needs of business with the need to protect the environment. A decade of slow economic growth had convinced many planners to support regional growth proactively rather than to simply match its pace. Large-scale infrastructure was planned to sustain economic growth and to support a more even socio-economic balance between north and south. Between the 1970s and the mid-1980s, belief in the Swedish tradition of social engineering, which had marked planning in the 1950s and 1960s, slowly vanished and was replaced by a market orientation.
- The 1990s began with a severe recession followed by strong growth. The current regional plan reflects this situation.

Current regional plan

A new regional plan was outlined in 2000 and accepted in 2001. The stated overall objectives are international competitiveness, good and equal living standards, and a sustainable living environment in the long term. The plan includes transportation and physical planning strategies as well as strategies for economic development and environmental protection. Key aspects of the plan are reviewed below.

New regional centres

The new regional plan focuses on the transition from a monocentric to a polycentric structure, though the central core of Stockholm will still be far larger than any sub-centre. New regional centres will help focus suburban growth and link the Stockholm region to other regions. New transverse links will connect regional centres to each other.

Increase regional density

Continued population increases will exacerbate the already acute housing shortage. However, the plan seeks to preserve areas of cultural, recreational and natural value while making effective use of energy and transportation systems. Therefore, new built areas will be concentrated in existing urban and suburban cores.

Support the south

The north–south divide keeps poorer southern suburbs from developing and denies both employers and employees in the north access to the entire labour market. New roads ringing the inner city and a western orbital will connect north and south, and new rail links will increase the capacity of existing north-south routes and provide cross-suburban links as well. A new airport and more university positions are also planned to help improve the competitive position of the south.

Governing an expanding region

The transition from an industrial society to a service- and knowledge-based society, as well as the increased globalisation of national economies, are important structural forces behind Sweden's experimentation with regional governments. The knowledge orientation of the economy is clearly related to decentralisation trends. When only a small fraction of the population received a higher education, it was quite natural to organise activities hierarchically. However, such organisational principles have become successively obsolete as a result of a larger and more even distribution of knowledge capital.

Decentralisation, like globalisation, is also related to decreased costs of transport and communication. When these costs decrease, production activities can in principle be located more freely. One consequence is that the competition between metropolitan regions has increased. Firms seem increasingly interested in finding locations with good accessibility to transport, a well-educated labour force, high-quality universities and research institutes, and a liveable environment. International location hunting by firms and international city marketing are concrete manifestations of this.

These changes have also spurred employment and population growth in many metropolitan regions. By way of example, IT developments seem to have resulted in faster growth in large than in small metropolitan regions in Sweden as well as in the US. The growth and geographical expansion of the Stockholm region has increased the demand for coordinated regional planning and for support from the national government. The most common motives for a stronger planning coordination are that it would make decision-making concerning transport infrastructure easier, would strengthen the negotiation power of the region vis-à-vis the national government, and would make the region more competitive internationally. This seems to call for a strong regional authority. On the other hand, many municipalities have grown substantially and have widened their scope of responsibility and administrative apparatus. There are therefore strong arguments for continued decentralisation of power to the municipal level.

There is broad agreement as to the major challenges facing the Stockholm region: the critical need for new housing and transportation infrastructure in particular. There is also consensus that the current diversity of regional actors has led to a fragmented and uncoordinated system of regional governance. Stockholm's County Council and the municipalities in the region have expressed the need for a stable structure for regional cooperation. However, the municipalities within the region have not been able to agree on a new metropolitan governance institution that could effectively address current problems and strengthen the region's competitive position. This conflict between interests, and attempts to reach a common understanding among Stockholm's municipalities and between them and the county council, are described in the sections below.

Regional governance in Sweden

For many years, a debate has been ongoing in Sweden as to the benefits and disadvantages of various alternatives for regional governance. Many feel that the current county borders are too small and that health care planning and provision dominates their agendas, leaving little room for comprehensive regional development planning. Others argue that the regional planning process in Stockholm County already operates successfully within a county council structure dominated by health care issues. Debate has centred on two basic alternatives: a regional parliament or a municipal association. A regional parliament would have the legitimacy of being directly elected, but could lack the planning competence and experience of municipalities. A municipal association would include members with planning competence but lack the authority to enforce regional plans.

The Swedish Association of County Councils supports the establishment of either alternative but particularly a regional parliament. The national government has rejected this alternative for decades, but pressure from counties and municipalities led to a national government initiative to 'experiment' with both alternative forms for regional governance in several counties beginning in 1999. The stated goal of this initiative is to devolve authority for regional development planning to a local level. In practice this means that the county provincial boards in these regions have a more restricted role in development planning; they serve only to represent the interests of the national government rather than to produce plans themselves. Therefore, responsibility both for development planning and for the structure of the new institutions is decentralised from the central to the regional/local level.

The national government implemented alternative structures in different regions in order to learn more about the relative advantages and disadvantages of various forms of regional governance. A regional parliament was established in Skåne (marrying two counties and including the city of Malmö) and West Götaland (comprising an area somewhat larger than the greater Gothenburg region). A municipal association was established in Kalmar County. Several other regions are eager to participate in these state-sanctioned experiments, and the 'experiment' regions hope to formalise their new associations. However, there are indications that the national government would rather see more direct state control of local issues. In September 2001, the national government decided to extend the trial period for another four years but did not allow the 'experiment' regions the authority to make their new associations permanent.

Meanwhile, the national government has proposed the creation of additional municipal associations (*kommunala samverkansorgan*). These new bodies must include all municipalities in a given region and may include the county council. They would have responsibility for producing a development plan for the county and for coordinating all local initiatives used to meet this plan's goals. This would include the 'growth contracts' as well as plans for regional infrastructure and proposals for funding from the EU's structural development funds. The same proposition extends the responsibility of the provincial administration boards as regards the overseeing of state interests at the regional level. Sweden's Vice Minister of Finance summarised the proposal, saying:

> There is a need for a long-term evaluation of the division of responsibility between state, municipality and county council. We will initiate such an evaluation based on the goals of broad independent powers for municipalities within the framework of a strong national responsibility for citizens' welfare in the entire country.
> (Press release, Swedish Ministry of Finance, 2001, authors' translation)

The conspicuous absence of the county council's role from the Finance Minister's description of national priorities is not insignificant. The current national government is a coalition led by the Social Democrats. Their ambitions for income redistribution tend to make them stress the role of the national government in regional affairs. The next largest party – the Conservatives – advocates fewer government levels, with county councils replaced by municipal associations for regional planning. Therefore, the current proposition seems to be constructed so as to give the impression of more direct municipal influence while also reasserting more direct state control. Both come at the expense of the county council, despite the fact that the proposition has been heralded by the Swedish state as 'increasing regional influence for the entire country'.

Implications for Stockholm County

As noted, the Stockholm County Council has been granted special authority to develop regional plans for the Stockholm region. Therefore, the new proposition is not likely to affect this county role. If the political majority in the national government believes that a strong Stockholm region is critical for growth across Sweden, then the provincial administrative board and the county council for

Stockholm may find new ways to cooperate. If the political majority reasons that a strong Stockholm region could drain resources from the rest of the country, then the provincial administrative board and the county council may be at odds. The 2002 elections may prove decisive for the relationship between the national and county governments in the Stockholm region.

Will the municipalities in Stockholm County form a municipal cooperation organisation as allowed by the new proposition? In the near future at least, probably not. First of all, the county council already has both a special law and a tradition of producing regional plans, and most municipalities seem fairly satisfied with this arrangement. Indeed, most municipalities would be loath to spread already thin local resources to include contributions to another municipal organisation.

In addition, a recent proposal to form a new regional association of municipalities received only mixed support. A few years ago, the county council and the Association of Stockholm County Municipalities (*kommunförbundet i Stockholms län*) discussed the formation of a new regional association with responsibility for planning regional spatial development, infrastructure, economic growth, environmental protection and higher education. A proposal for such an institution was sent for comment to all of the municipalities in Stockholm County in February 2000. This proposal calls for the new authority to comprise 149 voting members, of which 49 would be appointed by the county council, 25 by the city of Stockholm and 75 by other municipalities. This would give the majority to 25 smaller municipalities that are each between 1 and 10 per cent of the size of the city of Stockholm, which together can out-vote both the city and the county council. Twenty municipalities were positive about the proposal, five were negative, and one did not comment. The city of Stockholm, representing some 41 per cent of the population in the region, was among those that opposed the regional association.

In the county council, the two largest political parties (the Social Democrats and the Conservatives) favoured the initiative, but the other parties opposed it, mainly because they prefer a directly elected authority. However, the two largest political parties probably have different reasons for supporting the municipal authority initiative. The Conservatives (who lead coalitions controlling both the city and county governments) advocate decentralising regional and transportation planning authority to municipal associations; the Social Democrats agree on the competence of the municipalities, but in contrast, see the new authority as an important complement to existing governance institutions. As noted, they probably also fear that powerful municipal associations or regional parliaments would make it more difficult for the central government to pursue redistributive goals.

Efficiency implications of a metropolitan association

The output of an association or parliament can be considered a public good that every member can enjoy. The larger the number of potential members that would benefit from the association, the more difficult it is to form due to the free-rider problem. If 50 municipalities expect to gain substantial national support for infrastructure investments by working closely together in an association, it will take considerable time and effort for them to agree on the use of this expected but uncertain budget increase. If on the other hand, three municipalities can expect the same amount by cooperating in the same way it will be much less costly for them to come to an agreement. This difficulty in forming larger associations is witnessed by the fact that many municipalities have decided not to be members of the Mälar region association.

Free-rider problems can be expected whether the association is formed freely or by a national government decision compelling all municipalities in a region to be members. Since planning services (e.g. a regional plan) may be characterised as a public good, every member will benefit from the input of other members. When determining their own level of input (by e.g. voting on member fees), each member will tend to consider their own benefits and costs but disregard the benefit their contributions create for others. As a result, each will contribute less than what would be optimal from the perspective of the whole association. The difference between the actual and optimal activity level will hence be positively associated with the size of the association membership: the larger the association, the larger the efficiency gap. The cost of negotiations contributes to the problems of reaching an efficient activity level in any association. This cost tends to grow exponentially rather than linearly with the number of members. Therefore, benefits must be far larger in order to make negotiations worthwhile in large as compared to small associations.

This efficiency drawback will also tend to be larger the more 'equal' the members are. If one member gains considerably more than others from a common action, it is likely that he will make substantial input irrespective of the input of others. However, the members that gain the least from a common activity can also abuse the situation, refusing to contribute to common actions. In a municipal association, one would hence expect a tendency for small municipalities to exploit the larger ones. This might well explain why the city of Stockholm was negative to the proposed planning association in the Stockholm region.

Since the rich municipalities and counties of Sweden are forced to contribute part of their tax income to poorer municipalities and counties, the equity aspect is not an issue at the regional level when metropolitan governance is discussed in the Stockholm region. However, it might explain why the national government so far has been rather negative to a stronger planning authority in the Stockholm region. A strong regional government in Stockholm and other major metropolitan areas may be considered a threat to the national policy ambitions to support all parts of Sweden. Probably it is also difficult for a national government dominated by Social Democrats to devolve power to the Stockholm region, a stronghold of the Conservatives.

Another aspect related to metropolitan governance relates to what can be called dynamic efficiency. To control both land-use and transport planning and have a budget to implement plans and to finance other economic growth and welfare initiatives is probably the dream of many planners at the metropolitan or regional level. However, it is not obvious that such a concentration of power in one authority would be efficient in the long run. There are not only market failures but also government failures. A concentration of power that causes all actors to move in the same direction may be positive in the short run. But if the surrounding world changes in an unexpected direction, these short-term benefits can turn into much higher long-term costs. As Ostrom (2001) argues, 'polycentric' governance systems, which include a certain amount of redundancy and overlap in institutional responsibilities across many levels, may make systems less vulnerable to external shocks or internal malfunctions. Furthermore, the presence of many actors in the metropolitan planning arena may foster creativity and better analysis of alternative proposals and initiatives. In a way it seems a contradiction to argue for a strongly concentrated metropolitan planning power when growing diversity seems to be a main feature of metropolitan regions.

Conclusions

The functional labour market region in Stockholm already comprises 2.1 million people and by 2030 could grow by another million inhabitants. This growth has put pressure on the region's infrastructure: housing is in short supply and both road and rail infrastructure are overburdened. In addition, there is a risk that the region will become more spatially and economically segregated as high-income families and private investment flock to the inner city and northern suburbs while poorer southern municipalities languish.

Within Stockholm County, regional planning is based on a generally stable and accepted process led by the county council with significant input from implementing municipalities. However, there is no regional authority with any formal power representing the successively growing functional region, currently comprising Stockholm County and four surrounding counties. Recent discussions in Stockholm indicate that the region lacks the unanimous support needed for the creation of a municipal association for regional planning. Small municipalities support any measure that increases their influence relative to the mighty city of Stockholm, but the city has little incentive to join any organisation that could allow smaller municipalities to affect city policy. In addition, the national government is unlikely to support the creation of a large municipal association comprising the entire functional region because it could give the already powerful Stockholm region even more influence over national policy.

The current institutional structure for regional governance constrains the functional region's ability to utilise its full potential, particularly the mismatch between county borders and those of the functional region. However, it is not clear that the creation of a single governing structure is desirable either. Rather, the following initiatives may be more effective and more politically feasible:

More cooperation with the private sector: The current regional plan includes measures to improve the amount and quality of information about regional priorities for land-use and infrastructure given to companies, primarily through electronic access to planning documents, maps and so on. In addition the regional chapter of the chamber of commerce is allowed to comment on the draft plan. However, in general planners rely on land-use planning and new infrastructure to spur private investment rather than involving private sector representatives directly in planning negotiations. Closer cooperation with the private sector could encourage developers and firms to actively work together with municipalities and the county to develop struggling areas while meeting the needs of private investors. Such cooperation could include a more formal role for the private sector in developing regional plans as well as public/private joint initiatives to develop/redevelop target areas.

Flexible planning institutions at a variety of levels: The national government's plan to promote municipal associations may work well in other Swedish regions, but in Stockholm it will not serve the needs of a region that has outgrown its county borders. However, the county council has over time developed a fairly successful, comprehensive regional planning process in coordination with municipalities within the county. Conscious or not, the increasing tendency of the county council to include a broad range of regional development issues in its regional plan rather than focusing solely on land-use may have increased its legitimacy and its prospects for retaining a role as planning coordinator for the region. The council could work more closely with other municipalities and municipal associations outside the county but within the functional region. The most effective form of governance might be a complex web of interrelated, even overlapping, formal and informal institutions that can respond to political shifts, economic cycles and labour market expansion.

Public orators have often compared large cities to forceful machines, engines for national and economic growth. Nowadays, the machine metaphor looks somewhat outdated when applied to the knowledge society and the biological 'revolution'. Perhaps metaphors from life sciences are more useful. A city is more like a body than a machine. It is complex and dynamic with many interacting and counteracting parts and processes only partly known and understood. Understanding these processes and building institutions to support them should be an essential part of making our metropolitan regions better places to live in.

Bibliography

Andersson, A., Hårsman, B. and Quigley, J. (1997) *Government for the Future: Unification, Fragmentation and Regionalism*, Amsterdam: Elsevier.

Christoferson, Inger (ed.) (2001) *Swedish Planning in Times of Diversity*, Gävle: Strålins.

Healy and Baker (2000) European Cities Monitor, October.

Olson, Mancur (1965) *The Logic of Collective Action: Public Goods and the Theory of Groups,* Cambridge, Massachusetts: Harvard University Press.

Ostrom, Elinor (2001) 'Vulnerability and polycentric governance systems', *Newsletter of the International Human Dimensions Programme on Global Environmental Change*, Bonn: IHDP.

Regionplane- och Trafikkontoret (2001) *Regional utvecklingsplan 2001 för Stockholms-regionen*, Stockholm: Rtk.

Regionplane- och Trafikkontoret (2001) *Scenarier för Stockholms län 2030*, Stockholm: Rtk.

Regionplane- och Trafikkontoret (2001) *Regionkärnor – Vision och strategiska möjligheter*, Stockholm: Rtk.

Regionplane- och Trafikkontoret (2000) *Stockholmsregionens framtid, en långsiktig strategi*, Stockholm: Rtk.

Regionplane- och Trafikkontoret (2000) *Regionplan 2000*, Stockholm: Rtk.

Regionplane- och Trafikkontoret (1996) *Det regionala arvet: Förpliktelser och möjligheter för planeringen i Stockholmsregionen*, Stockholm: Rtk.

PART III

Berlin, Frankfurt, Hanover, Stuttgart, Amsterdam, Rotterdam

7 Berlin

Hartmut Häussermann

Introduction

Between 1949 and 1989, the city of Berlin and its surrounding districts were separated from each other. The Wall completely interrupted earlier economic and commuter relations between 1961 and 1989; in fact, it isolated West Berlin completely. In 1990, the developments characteristic of urban development in the Western world also started in the Berlin-Brandenburg region: deindustrialisation, suburbanisation and decentralisation. Soon after unification, joint efforts by the political authorities of the city and the surrounding state of Brandenburg started to control regional development and prevent the destruction of the landscape by urban sprawl. The main focus of this chapter is on the organisational arrangement of joint planning in a region embracing areas belonging to different states. This is an exceptional experiment in Germany, caused by the failure of the referendum on the unification of the city-state of Berlin and the state of Brandenburg.

History: an exceptional case

Until the Second World War, Berlin was the capital of the Prussian state and of the whole country. Because Germany's national government was in favour of the development of its capital city – which had undergone a period of rapid and immense growth between 1870 and 1914 – there was a historically exceptional chance to reform its administrative boundaries. In 1920 an administrative reform (by law of the Prussian State) created the new area of Berlin, in the form it is today. This reform meant the incorporation of the surrounding municipalities (which had already reached the size of big cities) into *Gross-Berlin* (Big Berlin). Since then, Berlin has consisted of a large area, including lakes and forests – a much larger area than that ever covered by any other big city in Germany. In fact, at the time the new *Gross-Berlin* was more of a region than a city.

Between 1945 and 1990 there was no cooperation in regional development or planning between Berlin and its suburban surroundings, because the Iron Curtain divided this metropolitan region in two. The only sphere of cooperation, which began in the late 1970s, concerned the disposal of waste. Because of the spatial limitation of West Berlin, it was not possible to dispose of all the waste produced by such an affluent society. For East Germany this provided a good opportunity to acquire West German currency. But this deal did not include any regional development aspects. Communication and negotiation between Western and Eastern administrative units was only possible on the national level of state governments, and so there was no cooperation (except on some technical issues, such as grey water disposal).

The situation was exceptional up to 1990. The process of suburbanisation was frozen at the 1939 level: for West Berliners it was not possible to move to the suburban regions because West Berlin was totally enclosed by the Wall, and in East Berlin spatial development and housing was under the strict control of the central state. Private ownership was not allowed in the German Democratic Republic (GDR), and because land had been nationalised no private initiative could occur. The aim of the socialist urban policy was a compact city, consisting of high-rise buildings – implemented as large housing estates on the edge of the city. As a consequence, there is still a sharp distinction between the city and the surrounding areas: the high density of the city area as opposed to the very low density of the adjoining area, which remained rural in a period when in all Western metropolitan areas booming suburbanisation had changed the urban landscape.

Since unification, the situation has been changing quickly. Facing the then expected large growth of economic activities and population in the region, the conditions for expansion into the outer area were provided by the numerous small municipalities in the suburban ring. After reunification in October 1990, there was in fact no administrative unit for the control of municipal planning. Because the administration of the newly created states in the area of the GDR still had to be established, the municipalities acted in a certain sense in a lawless environment. Immediately after it had become clear that the Eastern regions would be incorporated into the economic system of the West, private developers visited the mayors, who did not know their duties or their powers, and persuaded them to grant a lot of planning permits for retail centres and new housing estates. By this uncoordinated process of competition between the municipalities freed from the patronising centralist system and the 'big neighbour' Berlin, all courses were set for the spatial development the experts had warned of. After the fall of the Wall, real estate developers and speculators from West Germany had persuaded the inexperienced new local administrations to provide them with green land on which to develop retail centres and housing estates. Until 1993 there was virtually no control over local planning by a higher level, because the administration of the new states had still to be settled.

Already in 1990 a planning group, including administrators from Berlin and Brandenburg, proposed a regulated and concentrated spatial development in order to prevent urban sprawl, which was expected as a consequence of the expected growth. Although this group recommended planning principles and designed a preliminary regional plan, the plan had the status of a non-binding statement. After the formation of the state of Brandenburg in 1990, the government and the administration were mainly concerned with clarifying their own interests. Before coming to terms with cooperating with the city-state of Berlin, in 1994 a new planning system comprising five planning regions was established in Brandenburg, which feared being dominated by the big core city. Because of its historical origins, Berlin formed an island in the middle of Brandenburg after the Second World War, and the representatives of the Brandenburg state were mainly concerned with a concentration process around Berlin. Thus planning regions stretching from the border of Berlin to the peripheral borders of Brandenburg were designed, motivated by the aim to bind together the peripheral and the more central areas. These planning units were shaped like pieces of pie around the central area.

A formal joint planning organisation of the two states – the Joint Spatial Development Department (JSDD) – was finally formed in 1996. The JSDD was created in anticipation of the formal unification of the two states, upon which the governments had agreed to restructure the situation to what it was before the war. In the face of the starting process of suburbanisation, the governments and parliaments wanted to avoid the disadvantageous consequences, which were known from the situation of Hamburg and Bremen, both of which were also city-states. In these regions the more affluent households had been leaving the city-area for many years, and in consequence the financial power of the city-states was constantly declining. Because there is no internal financial equalisation scheme within the urban region, but only between the states as a whole, there is always competition for taxpayers, in the form of economic activities or inhabitants. The central cities usually suffer from losing their high-income households and rising per capita costs for transport, schools and cultural facilities, which are also used by the inhabitants of the suburban region.

According to German constitutional law, changes to the boundaries of states have to be confirmed by majorities in a referendum in the states affected. A referendum on the unification of the two states was held in 1996: the Berliners said yes, the Brandenburgers no. At the time, the post-Communist party (*Partei des Demokratischen Sozialismus*) rejected unification of the two states by enforcing the fears of the Brandenburgers of domination by the city of Berlin – even though Potsdam (the capital of Brandenburg) was to be the capital of the new Berlin-Brandenburg state. Some months before the referendum, the JSDD was formed as a visible sign of the seriousness of the purpose to form one state. But because the referendum failed, today there is the strange situation that the spatial planning units of two states are joint, demanding special processes of decision-making.

Initial situation: project area

The Berlin-Brandenburg region has a total area of 30,365 km^2, approximately 6 million inhabitants and exists as a heterogeneous spatial structure. Berlin is a high-density centre but around it, in the Immediate Sphere of Influence (the immediate suburban area) in Brandenburg, are a number of small and medium-sized towns with extensive settlement spaces and areas characterised by agriculture with numerous natural areas.

Since 1990 and the fall of the Wall, there has been a tendency to suburbanise these direct surroundings. The Immediate Sphere of Influence (ISI) profits from the establishment of businesses and the influx of families from Berlin. The number of inhabitants and workplaces continues to grow in this ISI, while in Berlin the consequent decrease in the number of inhabitants and workplaces is not being compensated for by a population influx from other parts of the federal region. Some issues have been defined as being of predominant common interest: the construction of a new international airport in Brandenburg but next to Berlin, the preservation of natural areas as environmental resources and as opportunities for recreation and leisure, and the coordination of the reconstruction of the transport system in the region as a whole.

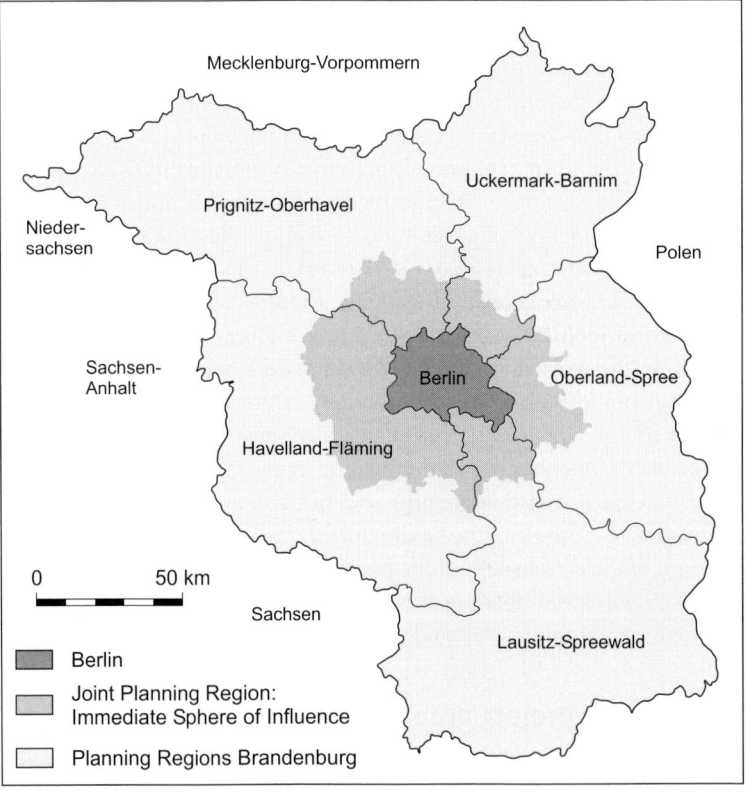

Figure 7.1 Regional planning units in Berlin-Brandenburg

Within the ISI, the uncontrolled suburbanisation of households and businesses (especially those engaged in retail trade) is seen as dangerous in that the clearly defined settlement structure with its open spaces will be destroyed and the unique existence of natural regeneration areas with their associated relaxation qualities will be threatened. The peripheral regions of the state of Brandenburg contain, on the other hand, the most thinly populated areas of the Federal German Republic. Since 1990, these areas have seen a severe drop in the number of workplaces, especially in the industrial sector, as well as a severe population decrease following migration into the Berlin surroundings as well as an acute drop in the birth rate. These areas are now classified as underdeveloped.

Table 7.1 shows the suburbanisation process that started in 1990. In that year, about 81.4 per cent of the region's population lived in the core city; by 1999, the share had declined to 78.7 per cent. Because of the overall slow growth of the population this share is expected to remain stable for the next 10 years – an optimistic assumption. However, it might be justified, because in 1999 the number of persons migrating from Berlin to the suburbs was smaller than the year before, for the first time since 1990. The bad economic situation of Berlin and the stagnation in the development of the population has reduced housing demand, and since 1998 there have been many empty dwellings both in the city and in the suburbs. This allows affluent households to obtain larger, better-equipped apartments within the city of Berlin, and thus the outward stream has slowed.

Objectives

The object of the JSDD is to provide plans for the development of the joint planning area of Berlin-Brandenburg which transcend ministries and are supra-regional and integrated. The JSDD looks after those tasks of spatial and regional planning of the Berlin Senate Department for Urban Development as well as the Brandenburg Ministry for Agriculture, Environmental Protection and Spatial Planning. The target is the balanced use of development potentials and distribution of the development possibilities.

Table 7.1 Population in 1990, 1999 and 2010 (estimated), in thousands

	1990	1999	2010	Change 1990–2010
Berlin	3,433	3,386	3,617	+ 5%
Close sphere of influence	784	916	983	+ 25%
Joint Planning Area	4,217	4,302	4,600	+ 9%

Sources: Übersichten 2000 (for 1990 and 1999); Strategy Report (for 2010), (own calculations)

Hartmut Häussermann

The protection and preservation of the natural resources in accordance with the principle of sustainability should contribute to this goal, in that the joint planning space exists within the competing European regions. The binding basis for regional planning and development in Berlin and Brandenburg is made up of the Joint Spatial Development Programme and the Joint Spatial Development Plans, which evolved from this programme, and from which the development targets for functionality or spatial parts of the region will be established. The responsibilities of the JSDD include:

- Drawing up, organising, modifying and continuing the joint regional development programmes and the regional development plans;
- Guaranteeing the compatibility of the regional planning communities' regional plans with the aims of spatial planning;
- Implementing regional policy harmonisation procedures (*Raumordnungs-verfahren*). This method is applied to find favourable routes and suitable locations for planning objects with supra-regional importance, to coordinate them with other projects within the scope of regional planning policy at an early stage and to limit intervention in areas worthy of preservation (e.g. in the case of Berlin-Brandenburg International Airport and retail centres);
- Ensuring the conformity of municipal building plans with the aims of spatial and regional planning, especially in Berlin;
- Coordinating and representing the joint planning interest on a federal level;
- Coordinating cooperation on an international level, especially reinforcing and intensifying cooperation with the Polish Republic and other immediate eastern neighbours.

The JSDD of the states of Berlin and Brandenburg has the task to coordinate and summarise the individual plans of Berlin and its districts as well as the municipalities, districts and regional planning communities of the state of Brandenburg in terms of their spatial, economic, infrastructure and settlement structures. These tasks were set up in order to establish joint economic and spatial development and to stop undesirable trends of land consumption and urban sprawl. A further goal is to create joint awareness between the citizens and the municipal decisions as the region of Berlin-Brandenburg is further adopted as a joint development space.

In February 1992, the states of Berlin and Brandenburg decided to implement the Joint Spatial Development Programme and the Joint Spatial Development Plan for the ISI. When the regional planning treaty between Berlin and Brandenburg came into effect on 1 January 1995, the formation of the JSDD was agreed upon and it started work exactly a year later. The JSDD took overall charge by elaborating the Joint Spatial Development Programme, which came into effect on 1 March 1998 after assent was given by both state parliaments, and the fundamental development outlines were proposed.

Organisation

The leadership of the JSDD is the duty of both the State of Berlin Senate Department for Urban Development and the State of Brandenburg Ministry for Agriculture, Environmental Protection and Spatial Planning. The head of the JSDD must come from the State of Brandenburg, and there must be a representative from the State of Berlin.

This joint regional planning for two federal states is unique in Germany. In order to ensure its effectiveness, the Joint Regional Planning Authority has been given direct political power to enforce its decisions. Furthermore, a Joint Regional Planning Conference is convened if significant problems pertinent to the principle of agreement between Berlin and Brandenburg cannot be solved either internally or by the permanent secretary and the heads of departments (ministers). Procedures for joint spatial planning are envisaged for spatially significant projects which have regional relevance (e.g. large retail trading estates, route planning of regional roads).

Decisions of the JSDD can only be made by mutual agreement. Those questions that remain in contention are brought to notice through a consensus procedure at different levels of the administration until agreement is reached. These 'consensual steps' are taken at the state secretariat level but if an agreement is not reached here, the minister/senator level will attempt to come to an understanding. If there is still disagreement, a state planning conference is summoned, consisting of the Prime Minister of the State of Brandenburg, the mayor of Berlin, the responsible senator and minister for spatial planning, heads of the Chancelleries, and four other ministers and senators from both state governments.

A further level of planning has been established with planning regions. Here, responsibility is usually placed on either the subordinate authority, the land district or municipal associations. Regional planning in Brandenburg is the responsibility of five regional planning communities (*Planungsgemeinschaften*). Cooperation between Berlin and Brandenburg as far as regional planning is concerned, is carried out within the framework of a regional planning conference. Such a conference is formed by the mayors of the communities located in the respective area.

In Berlin, responsibility for development planning is divided between the senate administrations with overall territorial responsibility and the district offices (*Bezirke*). The district authorities have the right to design building plans for their area, but these plans have to be approved by the senate administration (state level). Spatial decisions of major importance (concerning e.g. main transport routes, central places or issues of major importance, such as the national government district) can be discussed by the senate and finally decided upon. There is no clear distinction between planning on the local level (i.e. districts) and planning on the city or state level (i.e. senate), and very often there are conflicts between these administrative levels. For example, the response to the need to invest in the infrastructure of the eastern part of the city after unification was not a coordinated decision by the districts, but was made only by the senate. The budget of the districts is distributed by the senator of finances (secretary of state) at the state level, and as a consequence the districts are a sort of local administration with very limited room for their own decisions. A key role in integrating the various planning levels is played by the principle of mutual consideration (*Gegenstromprinzip*) as it stipulates top-down planning control by bottom-up participation. This means, for example, that every municipality that draws up or alters a local development plan has to inform the JSDD, and that the targets of the regional plan for these spaces must be evaluated. Only after the joint regional planning statement has been considered by the municipalities can the plan be approved. Experience shows that while two out of three submitted plans are approved (possibly with conditions attached), only one reaches the implementation phase. Through bottom-up participation, the municipalities contribute to the approval process of the regional plans based on their own local development plans.

Instruments of realisation: financing

JSDD employees are provided jointly by Brandenburg and Berlin, and both states finance the JSDD with equal rights. This is a process of mutual adjustment and negotiation. Because the land-use plan for the state leaves room for interpretation, the final decision on the acceptance by the state administration is made during a process of reciprocal adjustment; however, the final decision is up to the state. The usual problem is that the localities want to build as many houses as possible, in order to attract more inhabitants. But in the end this would mean that no control over the spatial development would be possible.

The instruments for implementing the joint regional planning are the spatial development programme and the spatial development plans, which are binding on the subordinate administrations. The decisions of the JSDD related to the regional policy harmonisation procedure for large projects and the coordination of the local development planning with the targets and tasks of the spatial and regional planning have a legally binding character and have a lasting effect on the choice of location for infrastructure provision and the land-use on a municipal level.

The central task of the JSDD is defining the principal targets for the regional planning and to found a common interest to guarantee the adjustment of the local development plans to these regional intentions as well as the choice of location from large projects corresponding to specific targets. The JSDD, therefore, is in the position to guide and coordinate those partially diverging interests of the economy, the municipalities (with their planning sovereignty) and the population in such a way that sustainable development is ensured.

The state-transcending joint regional planning department is aiming to provide sustainable, long-term protection of open spaces as well as a balanced development and allocation of the growth potential in the sense of creating equal living standards and infrastructure in all parts of the states.

The overall aim agreed upon by both states is the sustainable development of the region; that is, to preserve and protect natural resources, to perform cautious scalable settlement activities and to concentrate available settlement cores. To achieve this, the JSDD prepares a Joint State Development Plan for the whole area of the two states, and a Joint Spatial Development Plan for the ISI, which covers the area of the city of Berlin and the suburban region.

The coordination of infrastructure investments is demanded by the aims formulated in the Joint State Development Plan, but does not belong to the duties of the JSDD. This task has to be realised by the responsible departments or regional associations of both states. Also the transport system is not under the direct responsibility of the JSDD; it is planned and operated by various institutions on various spatial levels: the Deutsche Bahn (German Railway), which is a national company, the private owners of the bus transport facilities, and by the states, land districts and municipalities, which have to contribute to the costs of the system. Associations of local transport providers set the prices, the routes and the frequencies of the public transport system – very often during controversial discussions and negotiations.

The JSDD sets the spatial framework for settlement activities and the details are decided upon by the municipalities, although the final plan has to be approved by the JSDD. But this framework has to be filled with investments by public and private investors. Also various forms of communication and advice provision have been established to encourage and coordinate this process.

Joint Spatial Development Programme

This programme is an interdisciplinary and spatially related planning strategy for the future development of the metropolitan region of Berlin/Brandenburg. The representatives of the municipal and regional planning departments participate in the discussion of the plans and have the duty to implement these actions (counterpoint principle).

Joint Spatial Development Plans

Joint Spatial Development Plans are used to establish more concrete spatial targets and enhance the thematic and spatial focus of the Joint Spatial Development Programme. Such plans include:

- Joint Spatial Development Plan for Decentralised Concentration (in force); decentralised concentration has been the basic concept of the regional plan. It aims at the decentralisation of spatial development but in a controlled way: the number of municipalities designated as growth areas should remain limited

– and not only those municipalities located next to Berlin should benefit from the suburbanisation process.
- Joint Spatial Development Plan for the ISI (in force).
- Joint Spatial Development Plan for International Airport Schonefeld (in the process of decision: regional policy harmonisation procedure).
- Joint Spatial Development Plan for General Development within the ISI (in the process of elaboration).

These plans were adopted via a process of discussion and in adherence to requirements of participation of municipal and regional planning representatives.

Technical planning (e.g. infrastructure)

Spatially significant regional plans and planning intentions are coordinated within the framework of spatial planning actions and measured against the requirements of spatial and regional planning. Spatial planning procedures are initiated by those directly responsible or are introduced on the initiative of relevant agencies and, if necessary, integrated into an environmental impact assessment (EIA). An EIA is especially important where technical infrastructure is involved, such as motorways, the international Berlin/Brandenburg airport, waste disposal sites, large retail estates (factory outlets) and large recreation complexes. Through the EIA process, locations are confirmed in terms of their space compatibility, land-use conflicts, physical space requirements and logistical considerations.

Informal or motivating projects

Besides these formal frameworks of joint regional planning, the authorities have been strengthening their involvement to expedite plan implementation through subordinate authorities and/or within the framework of informal inter-municipal working groups. The joint regional planning authority understands that its task is not over when the plans are agreed upon and adopted: it must continue to actively promote the acceptance and implementation of the plans by initiating inter-municipal cooperation and motivating projects. An example of this is the formation of cooperative regional park projects in the ISI (in order to balance spatial demands) as well as the acquisition of INTERREG IIc projects for international cooperation. In addition, the joint regional planning authority itself participates in organising discussions in municipalities and partial areas (e.g. Stadtforum Berlin, Brandenburg Forum) and also acts as the contact for initiatives (also involving NGOs).

The following graph provides an overview of the various levels and organisational forms of regional planning in the area; the land-use plan of the city of Berlin is detailed and legally binding for the area of the city. A Joint State Development Programme was elaborated by the JSDD and agreed upon by the parliaments of both states, as well as the Joint Spatial Development Plan for the ISI. Berlin's land-use plan is part of this plan.

The planning regions of Brandenburg prepare regional plans, partially overlapping the ISI, constituted by the city of Berlin and the joint land districts. Below these levels are four inter-municipal neighbourhood forums, formed by the peripheral districts of Berlin and nearby located municipalities of Brandenburg. These forums provide an opportunity to exchange information, to coordinate and to discuss the aims of and controversies surrounding the ongoing spatial development.

Evaluation

Thus, the process of coordination and decision-making is very complex. The need to organise such a complex process of joint planning is the consequence of the historically contingent division of the metropolitan area, the inner part of which now forms the city-state of Berlin, and the outer part of which belongs to the state of Brandenburg. The organisational problems could be reduced by unifying the two states; another referendum on this issue is provisionally scheduled for 2006.

But unifying the two states would not reduce the competition between the municipalities, as the examples of other metropolitan areas in Germany show. The pressure would not be so high in the Berlin-Brandenburg region because there is a lot of formally determined space for new settlement within the existing framework. The strongest instrument of regional planning – granting permission to develop new building areas – comes into effect only when new plans are prepared. Because of the uncontrolled planning in Brandenburg in the period 1990–4, many municipalities now have big reserves of permitted land-use plans, allowing them to act locally not in total accordance with the regional planning schemes, which have since come into effect.

Table 7.2 Partial areas covered by various plans in the Berlin-Brandenburg region

Spatial areas	Berlin	Brandenburg State	
	City of Berlin	Suburban area	Peripheral areas
Legally binding plans	Land-use plan		
	Joint Spatial Development Plan for the Immediate Sphere of Influence (JSDPISI)		
	Joint State Development Programme		
Formal and informal cooperation / communication		Planning Regions Brandenburg	
	Inter-Municipal Neighbourhood Forums		

Hartmut Häussermann

The weakness of the planning system lies in the fact that the other technical departments of the state governments have not built up formal or informal mechanisms of cooperation parallel to those of the joint regional planning authority. Consequently, planning remains merely the instrument of area management. During the establishment of joint agendas for economic development and location development/tourism as well as for science, research and development, the general development targets of regional planning have not found commensurate consideration. Conflicts resulting from the fiscal consequences of the new spatial division of labour within the region also remain an area of tension between the two states. For instance, in competition for the attraction of new businesses the city of Berlin and the municipalities in Brandenburg are used to offering enterprises subventions. These cases cannot be controlled by the JSDD in detail, because it has no right to intervene in such everyday business matters.

The demand for new sites for large retail centres outside but near Berlin has declined because of saturation and the stagnation of the purchasing power of the region's population over the last three years. The economic crisis of Berlin has in the same way reduced the expansion of economic activities, and thus the process of suburbanisation of workplaces has slowed down. As a consequence, at present the conflicts between the city and the Brandenburg municipalities have been smoothed over. However, this does not mean that conflicts cannot become serious again in the near future, and then the regional planning system will be tested.

Bibliography

Gemeinsam planen für Berlin und Brandenburg. Gemeinsames Landesentwickelungsprogramm der Länder Berlin und Brandenburg (1998) ed. by Senatsverwaltung für Stadtentwickelung, Umweltschutz und Technologie, Minseterium für Umwelt, Naturschutz und Raumordnung des Landes Brandenburg, Potsdam.
Regional parks in Brandenburg and Berlin (2000) ed. by Senate Administration for Urban Development of the State of Berlin, and Ministry for Agriculture, Environmental Protection and Regional Planning of the State of Brandenburg, Potsdam.
Sinz, M. (1998) 'Metropolenraum im Gleichgewicht?', in *Nachhaltige Raumentwicklung: Szenarien und Perspektiven für Berlin-Brandenburg*, Akademie für Raumforschung und Landesplanung. Hanover: ARL (Forschungs- und Sitzungsberichte, Akademie für Raumforschung und Landesplanung.
Strategy Report. Metropolitan Region Berlin-Brandenburg (1999) ed. by Ministerium für Landwirtschaft, Umweltschutz und Raumordnung des Landes Brandenburg, und Senatsverwaltung für Stadtentwickelung des Landes Berlin, Potsdam.

8 The Frankfurt Rhine-Main region

Bodo Freund

Rhine-Main: a polycentric city region favoured by post-war conditions

Frankfurt is beyond doubt the dominant city in a highly urbanised polycentric region currently called the Rhine-Main region, which includes Wiesbaden, Mainz, Darmstadt, Offenbach and many smaller towns with fewer than 100,000 inhabitants. The densely populated area is mainly constituted by the southern part of the federal state of Hessen, but includes parts of Rhineland-Palatinate (Mainz, Bingen) and a corner of Bavaria (Aschaffenburg). It extends approximately 100 km from east to west (Aschaffenburg–Bingen) and 80 km from north (Bad Nauheim) to south (Heppenheim), where there is a transition to the Rhine-Neckar region (Heidelberg, Mannheim, Ludwigshafen).

From the late nineteenth century until the 1950s, regional economic growth was mainly based on rather diversified manufacturing, the leading sectors being the chemical and pharmaceutical, automotive, mechanical and electrical appliances industries. Also, there was a tradition in financial services, transport and communications (Frankfurt), high-ranking administration (Darmstadt, Wiesbaden) and spas (Wiesbaden, Bad Homburg, etc.).

As a consequence of the post-war division of Germany, enterprises and central government institutions were transferred to the newly created Federal Republic, especially from Berlin and Leipzig. One should mention the central bank and the headquarters of the other leading banks, the headquarters of the state railways, the headquarters of industrial enterprises (Wella, Schott; former AEG), several insurance companies, department store corporations, publishers, national associations, the incipient producer services (accountancy, advertising, market research, engineering) and important fairs. This meant strengthening and diversification of the regional economy.

In Western Germany, the region was now in a central position and offered good accessibility by all means of transport. Foremost, it was linked to the world by a large-scale and modern airport, which the American forces had enlarged. Due to its excellent economic performance, the Rhine-Main region saw an outstanding

Bodo Freund

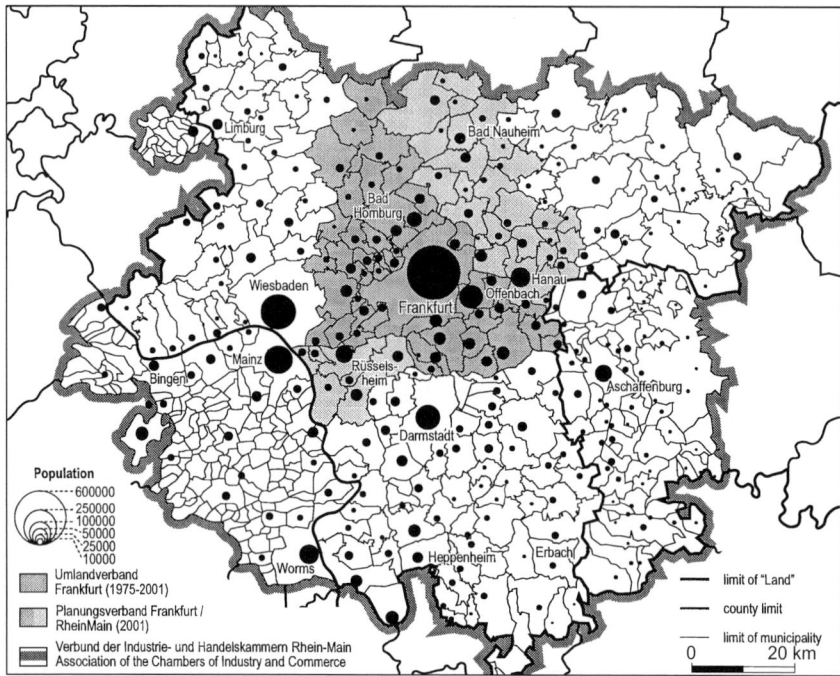

Figure 8.1 Population, administrative and institutional limits for regional planning and organisation in the Rhine-Main area

increase in population as a result of internal migration (1947–65) and proved to be very attractive to immigrants during the period of Mediterranean guest worker contracts (1955–73).

The late 1940s and the 1950s were an epoch not only of urban reconstruction, but also of rapid motorisation as a precondition for suburbanisation. Therefore, the maximum population of the big cities was attained rather early (Frankfurt 1963), whereas suburbanisation boomed until the mid-1970s and thereafter continued at a lower rate.

As city governments generally restricted low-density housing and were rather eager to use means for high-density social housing, the population distribution gradually changed and the income gradient tipped over. Today, the surrounding municipalities (*Gemeinden*) and even whole counties (*Kreise*) have wealthier inhabitants. Considering the German income mean as a basis of reference (=100), Frankfurt in 2000 scores only 112, whereas two neighbouring counties score 149 and 132, respectively. In addition, the rates of unemployment and welfare dependency are generally higher among the city's residents. The Rhine-Main region was also the German pacemaker in the suburbanisation of industrial plants (late 1950s), office buildings for headquarters (1962), shopping malls (1964), wholesale agglomerations (1965), hotels (1967) and a wide variety of other businesses including leisure and entertainment facilities.

Compared to residential suburbanisation, which is limited by a lack of building land, the locational mobility of business establishments has remained astonishingly strong for the last 20 years. Manufacturing plants have been scattered in nearly all directions up to about 75 km, and normally this was taken as an opportunity to improve production techniques and reduce the number of personnel. In contrast, industrial headquarters – particularly those of foreign-based enterprises without local production – were relocated to the close north-western environs of Frankfurt.

Table 8.1 The Frankfurt Rhine-Main region

Planning authority association Frankfurt Rhine-Main Region	Council of the Region	Inter-communal cooperation
Chamber of the association Representatives from all cities and municipal units: 75 members with 93 votes altogether. Number of votes in the chamber: Frankfurt 12 Offenbach a.M. 4 Hanau 3 Rüsselsheim 2 Bad Homburg 2 70 cities and municipal units 70	**Composition** • Two representatives for each town which constitutes an administrative district in its own right (*kreisfreie Stadt*); two representatives per municipal unit with at least 50,000 inhabitants plus three representa-tives per administrative district (*Landkreis*). • Mayors (*Oberbürgermeister*) and heads of the administrative districts (*Landräte*) are members due to the position they hold. • Founding chair of the council is held by the city mayor of Frankfurt; chair is elected afterwards.	**Principle** • Task-oriented cooperation between cities, municipalities and administrative districts through regional associations and companies. • On principle, voluntary nature of cooperation. • State government may order obligatory and binding associations.

Shared branch office

Tasks	Tasks	Tasks
• Creation of regional land-use plan in cooperation with the Regional Assembly of Southern Hessia. • Creation of landscape-plan. • Participation in inter-communal cooperation.	• Put forward principles for a common tackling of tasks. • Communal conferences. • Obligatory reports on communal cooperation. • Improve a common image for the region. • Cooperation with neighbouring local authorities and communal associations.	• Supra-local cultural institutions • Locational marketing. • Regional park Rhine-Main. • Regional transport planning and transport management. • Supra-local sports and recreational facilities. • Waste disposal and waste management. • Civil and industrial water supplies. • Supra-local sewage disposal.

Source: Gesetz zur Stärkung der kommunalen Zusammenarbeit und Planung in der Region Rhein-Main vom 19. Dezember 2000, in *Gesetz- und Verordnungsblatt für das Land Hessen*, 29 (1), 27 December 2000.

Bodo Freund

This is the direction of the preferred residential areas with good access to the city centre and to all transport facilities including the airport. The same area was chosen for the headquarters of other economic sectors (tour operators, car rental, telephone corporations, international haulage contractors, airlines, federal agencies). Big accountancy firms moved in this direction as well, but preferred to remain inside Frankfurt's city limits. The back offices of banks did not show a directional bias since new locations were normally chosen in office parks close to the city's periphery. The result of many relocations and local evolutions is a general shift of workplaces from Frankfurt and the other big towns to surrounding municipalities.

Currently, we may roughly describe the local and regional specialisations in the following way: Frankfurt is a European centre for banking and stock exchange, air traffic and fairs (automobile, books, consumer goods); in the national context, it has an outstanding position for law firms, accountancy, real estate agencies, telecommunication, foreign-based insurance companies, foreign economic and tourist representations, incoming tourism, advertising and business conventions. Wiesbaden is the capital of the federal state of Hessen and the location of two big federal offices (statistics, police); in addition, it is a centre for insurance and engineering companies and has important chemical and mechanical industries

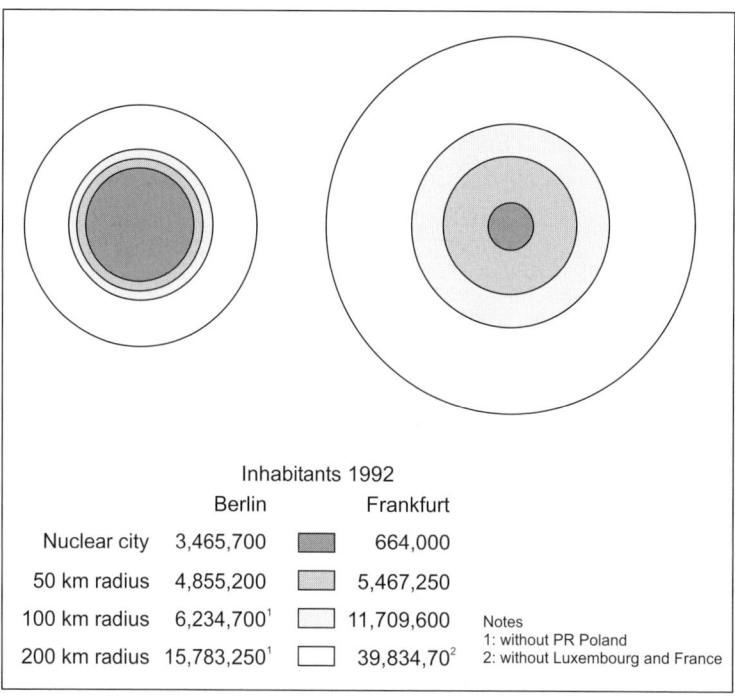

Inhabitants 1992		
	Berlin	Frankfurt
Nuclear city	3,465,700	664,000
50 km radius	4,855,200	5,467,250
100 km radius	6,234,700[1]	11,709,600
200 km radius	15,783,250[1]	39,834,70[2]

Notes
1: without PR Poland
2: without Luxembourg and France

Figure 8.2 Populations of Berlin versus Frankfurt regions in 1992

(Linde). Mainz, the neighbouring capital of Rhineland Palatinate just on the other side of the Rhine, is known for television and radio and has a highly specialised glass industry (Schott). Darmstadt is the location of the district government (*Regierungspräsidium*) for southern Hessen including Frankfurt and Wiesbaden. It is important for telecommunications (T-online), cosmetics industry (Wella), pharmaceutical, chemical (Merck, Röhm) and mechanical industries, software producers and its technical university. Hanau is specialised in less known high-tech industries which rely on the precious materials (Degussa, Heraeus) used in many branches. The airport should be mentioned separately because it has profoundly influenced neighbouring and even more distant municipalities with industrial areas (*Gewerbegebiete*) directly accessible by highway junctions. It is a strong factor for the location of distribution depots (computer hardware, pharmaceuticals, garments, etc.), often combined with the service and training centres of importers.

Due to the economic specialisation there is a tendency towards large-scale intra-regional social segregation. In the sector north-west of Frankfurt, well-off residents including highly skilled expatriates live in the municipalities on the slopes of the Taunus Mountains, extending from Wiesbaden to Bad Nauheim. Generally speaking, the opposite south-eastern half of the area is less prosperous. High percentages of immigrant population can be found in the corridor of early indus-trialisation along the Main river and in noise-polluted municipalities around the airport.

Table 8.2 Rhine-Main region: the labour market employees in the compulsory social security system* according to workplace in core cities and environs, 1980–99

Area of employment exchange	Sum 1980	Sum 1999	Index (1980 = 100)
Frankfurt	434,652	450,888	103.74
Wiesbaden	113,551	119,977	105.66
Darmstadt	114,698	119,168	103.90
Offenbach	78,732	72,731	92.38
Hanau	72,459	60,345	83.28
Rüsselsheim	66,038	59,363	89.89
Sum core cities	880,130	882,472	100.27
Sum environs	347,056	411,998	118.71
Sum total	1,336,505	1,421,114	106.33

Source: Landesarbeitsamt Frankfurt, 2000.

* The social security system covers 75–80 per cent of all gainfully employed persons. Not included are civil servants, self-employed and a very few employees with high income. Data include only employees in the parts of the region belonging to Hessen.

As a consequence of intensive suburbanisation of households and establishments from several cities, the built-up area of former villages has expanded enormously. Typically, the Rhine-Main region has been taken as the example of a region where city and suburbs form a continuum (*Zwischenstadt/Sieverts*). In this respect, and not only for high-rise office towers in downtown Frankfurt, Rhine-Main is the most 'Americanised' region of Germany. Currently, an extremely controversial regional problem is the projected expansion of the airport because costs and benefits are unequally distributed. The municipalities around the airport form a league of protesters, and demanding people further away also feel vexed about the recent redistribution of flight corridors. On the other hand, the European and inter-continental connectivity is undoubtedly a strong factor contributing to the prosperity of the whole region by reducing transaction costs.

Another very long-standing problem is the lack of inter-municipal cooperation. Frankfurt is a dwarf global city (650,000 inhabitants), drawing its strength from economic activities in suburban municipalities and even from other towns in the region. Evidently, prosperity of the suburbs is based on the transfers of high-income groups and enterprises from the core city. Frankfurt politicians tend to claim financial compensation for the infrastructural burden of regional relevance. On the other hand, mayors of surrounding municipalities defend a rather comfort-able situation. And the big towns of the region do all they can to prevent acquiring a subordinate role.

The history of metropolitan government: the first round

Ideas and concrete political preparations for regional planning in the emerging metropolitan region date back to the beginning of the twentieth century. In 1912, the Greater Berlin Joint Authority (*Zweckverband Groß-Berlin*) was created as an intermediate step towards the formation of a single city in 1920. In the same year, the Ruhr area had been tied together by a special purpose Ruhr Area Association for Settlement Development (*Siedlungsverband Ruhrkohlebezirk*, 1920), and the city of Hamburg struggled for territorial expansion (1915/19–37). But the Frankfurt initiative of 1929 was blocked by Prussian veto in Berlin, and afterwards the Nazi regime was likewise not favourable to this town.

After the Second World War, outline development planning (*Bauleitplanung*) in the newly created federal state of Hessen was first (1948) attributed to the county (*Kreis*), and by federal law of 1960 it was transferred to the municipality (*Gemeinde*), at that time mostly made up of villages. The position of the mayor in these villages was usually part-time and honorary. As local revenues in Western Germany were extremely dependent on business tax (*Gewerbesteuer*), mayors tried everything to attract investors, which is one reason for the scattering of non-agricultural activities even in rural areas. At the same time, local parliaments promoted the development of agricultural land into building land, especially in peri-urban municipalities with many commuters and structurally weak part-time agriculture. Evidently, the regulation system and the socio-economic conditions gave way to a spatially uncoordinated evolution, especially in prospering regions. For this reason, initiatives for regional planning in highly urbanised areas came up again.

In order to avoid defective evolution, the 1962 Hessian State Regional Planning Act (*Hessisches Landesplanungsgesetz*) offered the possibility to create regional planning associations. In the Frankfurt area, the Regional Planning Association for the Lower Main Region (*Regionale Planungsgemeinschaft Untermain/RPU*) was founded in 1965. Based on the assumption that the population would continue to increase, planners provided a lot of land for settlement purposes. Initially, they only focused on a concentrated settlement development, and four criteria were considered essential for the locations: availability of open space to prevent the reduction of woodland, poor soils in agricultural terms, accessibility by existing or projected arteries of mass transport and no noise pollution caused by airport activities. Later, additional targets were included in the regional plan, namely local combination of living and working in the settlement nuclei, transformation of the radial road structure into a net, and definition of a green belt (*regionaler Grünzug*) in order to limit expansion of settlement land.

After acceptance by parliament (*Planungsversammlung*) and the Chamber of Local Authorities (*Gemeindekammer*) of the planning association, the regional plan was enacted in 1972.

Unfortunately, the RPU had three deficiencies:

- Its planning region was very restricted and did not cover the whole commuter catchment area dominated by Frankfurt. It did not even include the municipalities around the airport, which extends beyond the southern limits of the town. Hence, these neighbouring industrialised and commuter munici-palities felt free to continue the land development of poor soils, irrespective of long-term damages to their own growing populations and to the Rhine-Main region as a whole.
- Until 1972 it was commonly believed that demographic expansion would continue unrestricted although the birth rate had slumped since 1965, internal migration had dropped and beginning economic crises would lead to the immigration ban in 1973. Consequently, the long-lasting freedom enjoyed by a host of little municipalities and the erroneous assumption for regional planning resulted in the offer of much more land for settlement expansions than could be absorbed in the medium term. Thus, not only was the regional plan enacted too late but also its capability to trigger further evolution turned out to be rather weak.
- The RPU lacked the capacity to impose a will of its own because of internal and external conflicts. Internally, Frankfurt was not inclined to cooperate and

even tended to adopt blocking positions because it was convinced that the small municipalities had been given too much political weight. Externally, the RPU had entered into a dispute with the government of Hessen because in addition to its planning activity it claimed the entitlement to order, control and enforce what had been planned. Evidently there was reason for discontent.

As early as 1971, the mayor of Frankfurt suggested substituting the RPU with another organisation that should be spatially smaller but stronger in political and administrative terms. He proposed a two-tier model of a 'regional city' (*Regionalstadt*), as was put into practice in West Berlin and Hamburg. The central city would incorporate a lot of peri-urban municipalities and the whole should be divided into five boroughs (*Bezirke*) with their own parliaments for local affairs. Thus, Frankfurt would become a really big city in demographic and spatial terms, get more freedom for development planning and more revenue for the costly infrastructure. But politicians of the municipalities and counties made strong protests, arguing that this reform would undermine decentralised local self-government. Of course, they perceived that incorporation would imply the loss of proper tax revenues and no substantial profits. It was remembered that municipalities incorporated half a century ago by Frankfurt (like Höchst) had seemingly been neglected by the city government as peripheral parts.

It must be mentioned that in the period under discussion, a territorial reorganisation of local government (*Gebietsreform*, 1968–76) in Hessen was fundamentally changing municipalities and counties by creating bigger units. On average, newly created municipalities were constituted by mergers of six to seven of their predecessors. Under these circumstances, local politicians saw promoting municipal integration as a priority. They were gaining self-confidence, struggling for power and did not feel inclined to devolve municipal competencies. Consequently, they proposed the alternative model of an urban county (*Stadtkreis*) with similar area but preserved independence for the municipalities.

The second round: Umlandverband Frankfurt (1975–2001)

Nobody denied that regional planning should be more comprehensive and powerful. But neither of the two models was adopted, and there remain doubts whether the Land government would have been willing to accept an extremely powerful city. Instead, in order to create an organisation to succeed the RPU, most of its area was taken to form a new mandatory multipurpose association, the *Umlandverband Frankfurt/UVF*, which started its activities in the beginning of 1975. This association of Frankfurt and peri-urban municipalities was composed of 43 units with 1.5 million inhabitants.

Meanwhile, the perception of the future had changed, and this was reflected in planning guidelines. As population increase was no longer assumed and economic growth seemed doubtful or even undesirable, future decisions had to help to manage structural change instead of facilitating expansion. Environmental protection came to the fore, as did nature-related leisure activities. The joint authority had the following entitlements provided by special law of the federal state:

- Preparation of a land-use plan for the whole planning region;
- Acquisition of land in order to build up a proper stock;
- Preparation of a comprehensive traffic plan;
- Coordination of technical planning, such as
  - public transport systems;
  - energy provision;
  - water supply;
  - sewage treatment;
  - refuse disposal;
- Landscape planning;
- Construction and management of leisure facilities of supra-local dimension.

Undoubtedly, all tasks were urgent and could best be carried out on a regional level in order to reduce costs and create synergies. Actually, however, the performance of the UVF was extremely diverse in its fields of official entitlement.

The best result was the preparation of the most extensive land-use plan of the old Federal Republic. This very detailed plan was elaborated by interacting with about 200 representatives of public interest (*Träger öffentlicher Belange*) and negotiating with many municipalities with divergent interests. With the year 2000 as a horizon, it was accomplished in 1985 entirely on a digital basis and enacted in 1987. In the West German planner community, this output gave widespread prestige to the joint authority.

In addition, the UVF became eminent among experts for its promotion of sophisticated research on local climates and the application of these findings in regional planning, e.g. by keeping open the strips where cool fresh air enters the densely built-up lower parts of the planning area.

As to the construction and management of facilities for leisure, the joint authority invested mainly in landscaping and equipping quasi-natural settings like frequented hilltops, the beaches of artificial lakes, sites for public barbecues, and shelters for hikers in the green belt and more distant recreation areas. In this respect, the UVF gained merits that were acknowledged by a larger public especially in the 1990s. But the association failed to bring together its members for costly and spectacular projects (like a stadium) that might have attracted general attention and become a symbol of unity to the regional population. Water supply and sewage treatment, being among the UVF's official duties, effectively resulted in monitoring using its own laboratory.

In the preparation of a comprehensive traffic plan, results were rather deceiving for the association. Calculations and projections could be made and maps designed, but investment by the monopolist railway corporation *Deutsche Bahn* and the Land agency for road building could hardly be influenced. In these realms decisions were taken according to available budgets, technical aspects and political influences of other agencies. Thus, the coordinated development of settlement areas and mass transit facilities that had already been projected in the early 1960s could never be realised, resulting in negative consequences, especially for the populations living to the east and south of Frankfurt.

As to the coordination of public transport, a combined transport authority (*Frankfurter Verkehrsverbund, FVV*) completely independent from the UVF was founded in 1974. In 1995, it was replaced by a much bigger organisation – the *Rhein-Main Verkehrsverbund* (*RMV*) – which covers not only the whole Hessian part of the Rhine-Main region and the adjacent Mainz area but also embraces the vast central part of the Land. Although not all promises as to service have been fulfilled, the two successive combined transport authorities have proved to be powerful organisations giving some coherence to a vast region. The RMV is present in the everyday life of much of the population, and for this reason has probably become better known than the planning association.

The most controversial issue was refuse removal, but – strangely enough – not the question of its treatment or disposal. There were two incinerators and two dumps for rubble in the area of jurisdiction. One of each was handed over to the association because the owning counties could thus get rid of financial burdens. The others were held on to because they were profitable. Decreasing regional amounts of waste and rubble – combined with the possibility to export it legally to other regions at lower costs – led to a reduced use of the environmentally friendly regional facilities and an increase in financial liabilities for each municipality. For this reason, many municipalities were unwilling to support them at all. In this situation of prolonged internal conflicts, the Land government was unwilling to support the position of the UVF joint authority and to enforce its own special law against municipalities which resisted. In search for a solution, a majority in the association's parliament voted in 1997 to eliminate the waste and rubble disposal from the UVF jurisdiction, and the Land parliament agreed to abolish this entitlement by amending the relevant law. What was intended to be an appeasing solution, however, turned out to be the first step towards the dissolution of the association.

In 1995, a former minister for development of the Land Hessen (a member of the ruling party at the time) had already proposed a radical reform for the southern part of this federal state by abolishing the corresponding administrative district (*Regierungsbezirk*), its counties and the UVF association. Instead, two enormous 'regional counties' (*Regionalkreise*) should be created, one consisting of Frankfurt, Offenbach, Wiesbaden and the hitherto adjacent counties, the other comprising Darmstadt and its hinterland. By this incisive reform, tiers would be suppressed and administrative procedures accelerated without any loss of quality. Since then, discussions about a completely new regional organisation have become intense, and did not end with the new conditions established in 2001.

Table 8.3 The planning region Frankfurt/Rhine-Main

Municipalities	75
Area in km²	2,459
Population (31/12/1999)	2,151,000
Non-Germans in %	17.4
Inhabitants per km²	875
Employees in the mandatory social security system, mid-1998	940,822
Employed persons in % of Hessen	44.7
Total tax revenues in % of Hessen, 1995	54.6
Taxable revenue per capita in relation to Hessian (mean = 100)	144
Taxable salaries and wages per capita in relation to Hessian (mean = 100)	109
Land occupancy in % of area	
Settlements (14.8) + enterprises (0.5)	15.3
Recreation	1.9
Traffic	8.8
Agriculture	39.4
Forestry	32.2
Water	1.5
Others	0.8

Source: Compiled on the basis of Grün, Günther (2001) 'Ballungsraum Frankfurt/Rhein-Main aus statistischer Sicht', in Hessisches Statistisches Landesamt (eds) *Staat und Wirtschaft in Hessen*, 5/01: pp. 158–68, Wiesbaden.

Changing organisations, lasting problems

The creation of a joint authority implies the devolution of power from the municipal and county level. Evidently, local politicians cannot be interested in reducing their own power. Especially the county presidents (*Landräte*), who administer supra-municipal affairs, have always been the fiercest enemies of joint authorities. The Land governments, irrespective of their political composition, have never been interested in a strong regional association in the Rhine-Main region. Since the creation of this federal state, population and economic output in Hessen have been unequally distributed, and this disequilibrium has continued to increase. Among the three districts, the southern *Regierungsbezirk* Darmstadt is dominant; it has 61.6 per cent of the population (2000) and is responsible for about 70 per cent of the gross domestic product.

The creation of a powerful association in the economic heartland is perceived as a virtual challenge to the Land government. The situation is aggravated by the fact that in the Land governments, northern and central regions of this state were over-represented until 2000 – that is, for more than half a century. In the Rhine-

Main region, *Führungskräfte* – executives and leaders – preferred to be 'in the banks or in Bonn/Berlin'. Thus there was always a political bias to give preferential treatment to the less successful parts of Hessen. For this purpose, even restrictions to expansion in the Rhine-Main region seemed justifiable with ecological arguments, as could be detected in the 1995 Regional Policy Plan (*Regionaler Raumordnungsplan*) for the Darmstadt District. This aroused protests from nearly all political parties and economic associations in the region because there was much more fear of losing investments to competing regions in Europe than a belief in the spill-over effects on the less prosperous parts of the Land.

The association of municipalities with extremely different dimensions in terms of demographics, economy, infrastructure, etc. (e.g. Frankfurt and a distant rural *Gemeinde*) implies not only varying and even antagonistic interests, but also differences in self-image and attitudes towards each other. These distinct positions could not be neutralised by the number of members in the association's parliament. Besides, as land-use planning is an unalienable entitlement of German municipalities, it was necessary to have a chamber of local authorities (*Gemeindekammer*) with one representative for each municipality. The unsatisfactory output of the two successive joint authorities is largely due to obvious disinterest on the part of Frankfurt to cooperate under these conditions.

In Germany, there is generalised competition between municipalities, since local revenue is largely influenced by the proceeds from business tax, wages and income tax, and consequently by the location of enterprises and people with a good income. It will be virtually impossible to overcome such a rivalrous mentality until municipalities receive compensation for unused opportunity.

The authority territories have never been tailored in an appropriate dimension and form. In this respect, one may distinguish two levels: first, even for a small solution solely centred on Frankfurt the planning regions of both the RPU and the UVF have been too restricted and rather strangely shaped. Of course local political acceptance of associations played a major role. The result may seem incredible: on the one hand, a municipality having common borders with the core city and even participating in the airport area with its own territory was never an associate in the joint authority; on the other hand, a remote rural municipality could be influential by its vote. Evidently, the results can be deficient or even harmful for the region's development at large.

Second, over the course of time a much larger area should have been organised by a joint authority. Already in the late 1980s, the discussion about the Single European Market and the Europe of (competing) regions made the inadequate dimension obvious, not to mention globalisation and positioning in a world economy.

The tasks of the two successive joint authorities have not been suitable to attract publicity. Although inhabitants of the planning region voted every four years – simultaneously with local elections – for the deputies in the association's parliament, their interest in the authority's task remained low. It was probably a fault of the joint authority and its large staff (up to about 150) to consider the delegated tasks in a merely technocratic way. For an extremely long time they were satisfied with good professional work and nation-wide esteem or even admiration of colleagues. Rather late the joint authorities realised that there was a lack of support by the public at large. In fact, this became obvious only when leisure facilities – although rather modest – attracted interest in the media, thus leading to a positive feedback.

As early as in the 1980s it was stated with regret that there is a lack of regional identity or emotional coherence. Generally, this is attributed to history since the Rhine-Main region had for centuries been fragmented into tiny territories. Until 1866 and 1933, respectively, Wiesbaden and Darmstadt had been capitals of medium states. Frankfurt – *Freie Reichsstadt* up to the annexation by Prussia in 1866 and then hindered from increasing its administrative power – had always followed supra-regional economic interests. But this is only a part of the explanation. Since the late nineteenth century, other cities in the region (e.g. Rüsselsheim) have grown, gaining importance as centres for commuters and customers and thus creating their own areas of influence. Furthermore, a large part of the regional population is not of regional origin and has always been rather mobile with exterior and interior exchange, a factor reducing identity. Last but not least, people in leading positions have a wide activity space and a lack of time for regional political engagement.

Towards new forms of regional organisation

The shift from the conventional, multipurpose regional association to a set of more flexible, single-purpose associations was promoted by economic agents and journalists rather than by politicians. In 1989, business associations ordered an investigation into the economic prospects of the region under conditions of a completed common European market (1992). It considered the interrelation between parts of the extended region and the nine chambers of industry and commerce (*Industrie- und Handelskammer*) joined together in 1990 in an alliance covering not only southern Hessen, but also including neighbouring parts of Rhineland-Palatinate (Mainz) and Bavaria (Aschaffenburg). This economic region (*Wirtschaftsraum Rhein-Main*) is home to 4.8 million inhabitants with a purchasing power approximately 20 per cent above the national average and a gross regional product per capita of nearly 50 per cent above the mean. The chambers demanded land development for settlement, business and leisure facilities and pleaded for task-oriented cooperation, e.g. in transportation or waste disposal. In the following years, the associations organised public conferences and workshops, and the area of its member associations was increasingly considered the most adequate definition of the actual Rhine-Main region. Even the UVF agreed to publish statistical data on the region using this much larger demarcation than its own jurisdiction.

In the mid-1990s, the two leading newspapers of nation-wide influence (*Frankfurter Rundschau* and *Frankfurter Allgemeine Zeitung*) published a series of articles on the metropolitan organisation in their regional supplements, thus stimulating public discussion. At virtually the same time, the division for economic promotion of the UVF merged into the spatially much larger Economic Promotion Board Frankfurt/RhineMain (*Wirtschaftsförderung Frankfurt/RheinMain*), with many territorial authorities, public institutions and publicly owned enterprises (e.g. Fraport, Frankfurt Airport Inc) as members. A year later, big private enterprises in the region founded the Economic Initiative Frankfurt/RhineMain (*Wirtschaft-initiative Frankfurt/RheinMain*).

In contrast, the performance of the politico-administrative side was dis-appointing. The state-led regional planning for the *Regierungsbezirk* Darmstadt, which was institutionalised in 1981, notably refrained from making projections for economic development. In 1991, the mayors of the big towns (*Oberbürger-meister*) declared their willingness to cooperate and to create working groups; during the following ten years, however, the results were very meagre. Instead of developing new strategies for common development, claims for more funds were made. A convention organised by the Land government in 1994 had no tangible consequences. This was after all highly due to the fact that in the then leading Social Democratic Party (SDP) there were antagonistic ideas separating the state-level from the party-organisations in the region. There, the party dominantly spoke out in favour of a radical administrative reform by the merger of four urban and ten rural counties (*Stadtkreis*, *Landkreis*) into two enormous regional counties (*Regionalkreise*) vested with the accumulated competencies of the county and the district level. The government, however, insisted for years that it would not accept this at all.

Meanwhile, the UVF was unable to increase its power; rather, there were signs of erosion, taking into consideration the 'outsourcing' or creation of new organisa-tions such as the Economic Promotion Board and the Rhine-Main Transportation Organisation, both of which started operations in 1995. Later, waste disposal and landscaping were organised in several private limited companies. After the oppo-sition had won the 1999 Land elections and a new government was based on the coalition of Christian Democrats (CDU) and Liberals (FDP), a new metropolitan organisation of the Rhine-Main region was put on the agenda.

The coalition of Conservatives and Liberals based its legislation on the following assumptions and ideas: radical alterations of subdivisions on the municipal and county levels are politically impossible, especially incorporations into Frankfurt. Central cities, however, bear special burdens in social, cultural, medical and other respects and have to face decreasing revenues from business and income taxes. On the other hand, suburban municipalities are profiting from the infrastructure offered by central cities and can expect their financial situation to improve. If municipal autonomy should be preserved, the creation of special purpose associations is considered the sole viable solution in order to organise more adequate financial equation between cities and suburban municipalities. The organisation of the metropolitan region must cover a larger area than before, but it would be extremely risky or even impossible to impose membership in the new planning board upon big cities like Wiesbaden and Darmstadt. Even without these cities, the newly defined region considered here is polycentric and its inhabitants continue to preserve very local identities. For this reason it is necessary to combine a sense of belonging to a global city and the feeling of local identity. Despite the complexity of the region, the name of the dominant city is absolutely necessary for the far-flung propagation of an image.

The compulsory multipurpose association *Umlandverband Frankfurt* was dissolved in March 2001 and a new law became effective from the following April. The Land government has delimited an enlarged *Ballungsraum Frankfurt/ RheinMain*. For this area, a mere planning association has been installed, the *Planungsverband Ballungsraum Frankfurt/RheinMain* which is the legal successor to the *Umlandverband Frankfurt/UVF*, though with extremely restricted assignments. It is instructed to make the land-use plan in cooperation with the assembly of municipal representatives (*Regionalversammlung*) for the surrounding Darmstadt district and to make the landscape plan for its enlarged area (2,459 km^2 as opposed to 1,427 km^2 of the UVF). As respective plans had already been enacted for the areas of the former UVF and the newly included municipalities, this actually meant the integration of existing plans into a larger whole and its future continuation. In addition, the planning association may help to resolve assignments of inter-municipal cooperation. As land-use planning is an unalienable privilege of German municipalities, all the 75 urban and rural municipalities (*Städte und Gemeinden*) in the planning area must be represented in a chamber of the association (*Verbandskammer*). Towns with at least 50,000 inhabitants have more than one vote, with a maximum of 12 in the case of Frankfurt.

The second institution for the *Ballungsraum Frankfurt/RheinMain* is the Council of the Region (*Rat der Region*) composed by representatives of the big cities or urban counties (*kreisfreie Städte, Stadtkreise*), the so-called rural counties (*Landkreise*) and the towns belonging to these rural counties but having more than 50,000 inhabitants. Some of these representatives are members due to the position they hold as mayor of big independent cities (*Oberbürgermeister*) or head of a rural county (*Landrat*), while others are elected by parliaments on the municipal level (*Stadtverordnetenversammlung, Gemeinderat*) and the county level (*Kreistag*). The Council of the Region can be considered as a steering committee. It puts forward the principles of managing common assignments for all local authorities and calls for conferences of municipalities of the region. In cases of

Table 8.4 Population data for the Planungsverband Frankfurt/RhineMain (PFRM) and the Rhine-Main region, 1950–2000

Area	1950	1961	1970	1980	1990	2000
Total PFRM	1,306,404	1,667,663	1,940,382	2,010,934	2,076,735	2,155,982
Frankfurt	546,800	701,816	699,305	629,375	644,865	645,079
Surroundings	759,604	965,847	1,241,077	1,381,559	1,431,870	1,510,903
Surroundings in %	58.1	57.9	64.0	68.7	68.9	70.1
Total region	3,520,696	4,123,000	4,667,854	4,898,684	5,073,965	5,383,710
Core cities	1,177,689	1,502,641	1,530,653	1,473,285	1,479,165	1,503,275
'Rural' counties	2,343,007	2,620,359	3,137,201	3,425,399	3,594,800	3,880,431
'Rural' counties in %	66.5	63.6	67.2	69.9	70.8	72.1

Sources: Planungsverband RheinMain, Hessische Gemeindestatistik Statistisches Landesamt Bayern, Statistisches Landesamt Rheinland Pfalz. Compilation and calculation, Bodo Freund.

activities exceeding the limits of the region, it organises the participation of neighbouring authorities.

Most of the assignments of the former Umlandverband (UVF) are now supposed to be carried out by voluntary inter-municipal cooperations that may be organised in various legal forms, such as registered association (*eingetragener Verein, e.V.*) or private company (*Gesellschaft mit beschränkter Haftung, GmbH; Ltd./Inc.*). Corresponding special purpose areas must not coincide with the delimitation of the planning region. Evidently, there already are formalised organisations for various tasks such as economic promotion, water supply, sewage disposal, waste management, rubble disposal and the creation and management of the 'Regionalpark', an equipped green network throughout the agglomeration. The publicising of cultural institutions and programmes in the region has already begun. As to common investment in big regional sports and recreational facilities and their management, nothing has been realised up to now.

As financial flows between municipalities are necessary to compensate for profits and burdens, it will be difficult to reach an agreement on the creation of inter-municipal bodies for some necessary tasks. Under certain conditions, the Land government can declare a task mentioned in the law as indispensable. If municipalities in the planning region do not join forces to create an appropriate executive body in the course of one year, the *Landesregierung* is entitled to enforce a compulsory association. The decree can only be rejected by unanimous vote of the Council of the Region. Thus the government is equipped with a lever to influence reluctant municipalities. Out of respect for municipal autonomy, however, compulsory associations are seen only as the second-best way to cooperation.

On the whole, the new legislation aims at a set of voluntary associations instead of one compulsory multipurpose association. In the past, often a special regional tier with a political basis of its own was considered a comprehensive means of cooperation. Now, however, it has been deliberately rejected out of respect for municipal rights and with reference to the many forces that are willing to hamper its functioning, as experience has shown. In this respect it is an approach for a more flexible organisation of the metropolitan region, as is generally preferred in the United States. For such a type of solution it is no longer necessary to have a regional parliament with directly elected members. The new 'legislation on strengthening inter-municipal cooperation in the Rhine-Main conurbation' is valid for the restricted period of six years, an indicator that it has to a certain extent a preliminary and experimental character.

The model has been criticised by academics such as Bördlein (2000) as a step backwards. In her view, metropolitan organising capacity and the democratic basis for the envisaged institutions have been weakened. The multipurpose association *Umlandverband Frankfurt* with a parliament of its own has been substituted by a weak planning authority on one side and an undefined number of single-purpose associations based on inter-municipal contracts on the other, thus partly withdrawing from democratic control. The council of the region is mainly a team for proposals, discussions and organisation with a deficit in democratic legitimacy (since members are not explicitly elected for regional affairs) and a lack of executive powers. It may deteriorate into a 'party' of chatterers. None of the academic critics, however, has mentioned that the new organisational framework is largely the factual conclusion of the progressive dismantling of the former *Umlandverband Frankfurt* by its own constituting municipalities. The new law results from the insight into what has turned out to be politically feasible and the understanding of what should at least be realised.

Open end

During 2001, politicians did not use the new legal framework for innovative activities. On the contrary, as soon as 32 additional municipalities had been included in the enlarged planning area, some of them prepared legal action against this incorporation.

At the end of the year, local parliaments in 20 of the newly included municipalities decided to support a suit at the State Court of Hessen. Most of the complaining municipalities as well as the legal representative of their judicial party are led by Social Democratic mayors. Formerly subliminal tensions between the planning authority and regional Social Democratic Party representatives on the one side and the Land government on the other side have now turned into a partisan regional opposition to a disliked Land government. The arguments put forward are:

- Municipalities are threatened by a reduction of the autonomy guaranteed by basic law;
- For the solution of regional tasks, the newly delimited area of the Planning Association Frankfurt/Rhine-Main is inadequate as it does not include Wiesbaden and Darmstadt;
- Towns with fewer than 50,000 inhabitants and other municipalities have no individual representation on the Council of the Region; they should have the right to be individually involved;
- Municipalities must fear future financial participation in infrastructure of supra-local relevance which is generally located in big cities, as it applies to the zoo or municipal theatres in Frankfurt. As there already is an intercommunal financial equation system, this would imply an unjustified additional transfer.

On the level of metropolitan institutions, activities were no more productive. By a decision of the Green Party in Frankfurt, the Social Democrats and this small party rather unexpectedly formed a majority in the Chamber of the Association. Furthermore, both parties agreed to nominate a Social Democrat for the post of director of the Planning Association and a member of the Greens as his substitute

(*Erster Beigeordneter*). As the Greens had been expected to form a coalition with the leading Christian Democrats in a new Frankfurt government, their decision was perceived as an act of disloyalty. Because insufficient attention was paid to the standing orders of municipal parliaments, however, the plan on the metropolitan level could be put into practice only in January 2002. To the general public interested in politics, it must seem strange that political parties fight for the leadership of an institution the existence of which they fight against in court.

These two-way actions on the local and the regional level and some public remarks indicate that the narrow majority considers metropolitan institutions and politics as instruments of opposition against the *Landesregierung* and – also – the mayor of Frankfurt. Certainly, neither the city of Frankfurt nor the Land governments have been known for having an especially beneficial attitude towards metropolitan organisation. On the other hand, it is new to consider metropolitan policies as a means of opposition to federal state government. At the end of 2001, there was still no new initiative for regional cooperation nor a suggestion for a better organisation; relations with the government and inside the region had deteriorated – which was not a good start.

During the course of 2001, regional chambers of commerce and big enterprises created *Metropolitana Frankfurt/RheinMain* – a non-profit organisation aimed at invigorating the feeling of regional identity and improving the regional image abroad, given the challenging interdependence of globalisation and regionalisation. The main emphasis is on presenting Rhine-Main as a region of competitiveness, urbane lifestyle, hospitality and zest for life, which offers a wide choice of cultural and scientific resources. Big projects might be promoted for stronger regional identification, infrastructural improvements and intensified international attention, e.g. applications for European cultural capital in 2010, football championships, Olympic Games in 2012 or an international exhibition of architecture and town planning ('*Regionale*'). In fact, economic agents have remained leaders in handling metropolitan issues. It is striking that, compared with the activities of economic agents, there is nothing which would be worth mentioning in terms of social and cultural non-profit organisations.

It is certainly impossible to give a comprehensive explanation for the bad performance of the political agents. There is a widespread opinion that the hitherto good economic situation in the region has not yet engendered a sense of vulnerability and the need for common action, as in the cases of Hanover and Stuttgart.

Bibliography

Blotevogel, H.H. (2000) 'Zur Konjunktur der Regionaldiskurse', *Information zur Raumentwicklung*, 9 (10): 491–506.

Bördlein, R. (2000) 'Die neue Institutionalisierung der Region. Das Beispiel Rhein-Main', *Informationen zur Raumentwicklung*, 9/10: 537–48.

Bodo Freund

Grün, G. (2001) 'Ballungsraum Frankfurt/Rhein-Main aus statistischer Sicht', *Staat und Wirtschaft in Hessen*, 56 (5): 158–68.

Heinz, W. (1997) 'Ansätze interkommunaler Kooperation. Frankfurt und das Rhein-Main-Gebiet', *Archiv für Kommunalwissenschaften*, 36: 73–97.

Heinz, W. (ed.) (2000) *Stadt und Region. Kooperation oder Koordination? Ein internationaler Vergleich* (Schriften des Deutschen Instituts für Urbanisitik, Bd.93) Stuttgart, Berlin.

Rautenstrauch, L. (1990) 'Region Rhein-Main: Frankfurt und sein Umland. Planung, Politik und Perspektiven im Bereich des Umlandverbandes Frankfurt', in M. Streit and H.-A. Haasis (eds) *Verdichtungsräume im Umbruch*, Baden-Baden: Nomos.

Scheller, J.P. (1997) *Rhein-Main. Eine Region auf dem Weg zur politischen Existenz Materalien*, 25 (Institut für Kulturgeographie, Stadt- und Regionalforschung , Universität Frankfurt), Frankfurt.

Sturm, P. (2000) 'Region Frankfurt/RheinMain', *Informationen zur Raumentwicklung*, 11/12: 705–12.

9 The Hanover metropolitan region

Dietrich Fürst and Ansgar Rudolph

Introduction

Hanover, the capital of the State of Lower Saxony, is situated in the north of Germany at the crossing point of some of Europe's most important railway and motorway connections. The city of Hanover has about half a million inhabitants. It is best known for having the biggest fairground in the world, where the world exhibition EXPO 2000 was held, and where the world's biggest fairs (e.g. CeBit and Hanover Messe Industrie) and many other events attract millions of visitors each year.

Besides its important administrative functions, Hanover was characterised in the past by its strong industries, such as the production of cars and railway vehicles, arms, building machines, chemical products and food. As a result of dramatic structural change in the second half of the twentieth century, the industrial sector has lost much of its importance for the regional economy. Evaluating such potentials as centrality and physical and scientific infrastructure, some experts consider the Hanover region to be one of the best business locations in Europe; however, compared to other metropolitan regions in Germany, its economic performance is only average.

The Hanover metropolitan area has a long tradition in spatial planning. Regional cooperation has been institutionalised in the Greater Hanover Association, a multipurpose district consisting of the city of Hanover and the surrounding county with 20 municipalities, representing altogether about 1.1 million inhabitants (figure 9.1). Its role in regional governance and the political activities to reform its legal constitution will be explained later. With the transfer of some county-level responsibilities to an above-county level, the administrative structure in the Hanover region differs from the normal administrative structure in Lower Saxony (see table 9.1). Administrative responsibilities, especially for spatial planning, vary in the German federal system.

Considerable statistical material on such regional trends as suburbanisation, traffic and the economy have been collected on this spatial level. However, in recent years it has become obvious that the interdependencies between the city of

Table 9.1 The German administrative and planning system – the case of Lower Saxony

Level	Political	Financial	Responsibilities, incl. planning
Federal/National	Election 2 chambers: 'Bundestag'; 'Bundesrat' (represents 'Länder')	Raises all income tax and most other taxes (VAT, mineral, oil, tobacco, etc.) and redistributes to lower levels	National guidance for spatial planning ('Raumordnungspolitischer Orientierungsrahmen'); non-obligatory
Lower Saxony ('Land', pl. 'Länder')	Election 'Landtag'	Grants from the Federation according to a redistribution key	Spatial planning scheme 'Landesraum ordnungsprogramm'; obligatory for public institutions
County (some large municipalities have county status, too)	Election 'Kreistag'	Contributions from the municipalities; grants from the 'Land' and from the Federation	Regional plan ('Regionales Raumordnungsprogramm'); obligatory for public institutions
Municipalities	Election 'Stadtrat' or 'Gemeinderat'	16% from the residents' income tax, business and other (minor) taxes, grants from the 'Land' and the Federation	Preparatory ('Flächennützungsplan') and legally binding ('Bebauungsplan') land-use plans, obligatory for private and public
Hanover region	Special administrative structure in the Hanover region: see text.		

Hanover and its surrounding communities affect an area much larger than that of the Greater Hanover Association.

Trends of urbanisation and spatial configuration

In the last 20 years, the Hanover region has experienced a very moderate population growth. The trend was negative in the 1970s and 1980s, but in the 1990s German reunification and immigration from abroad, mainly from eastern Europe and the former Yugoslavia, more than compensated for these slight losses. At the same time, growing wealth and changing individual lifestyles led to a decrease in the size of households and, consequently, to a higher demand for more and larger individual dwellings. There was a considerable shortage of dwellings in the first half of the 1990s which stimulated the efforts of both the city and the district to enable the creation of more units in the district.

Like most city regions, the Hanover region has undergone a strong process of suburbanisation: while the city of Hanover had almost 20 per cent more inhabitants than the district in 1970, today the ratio is nearly the other way round (figure 9.2). Especially those municipalities that are direct neighbours of the core city profited

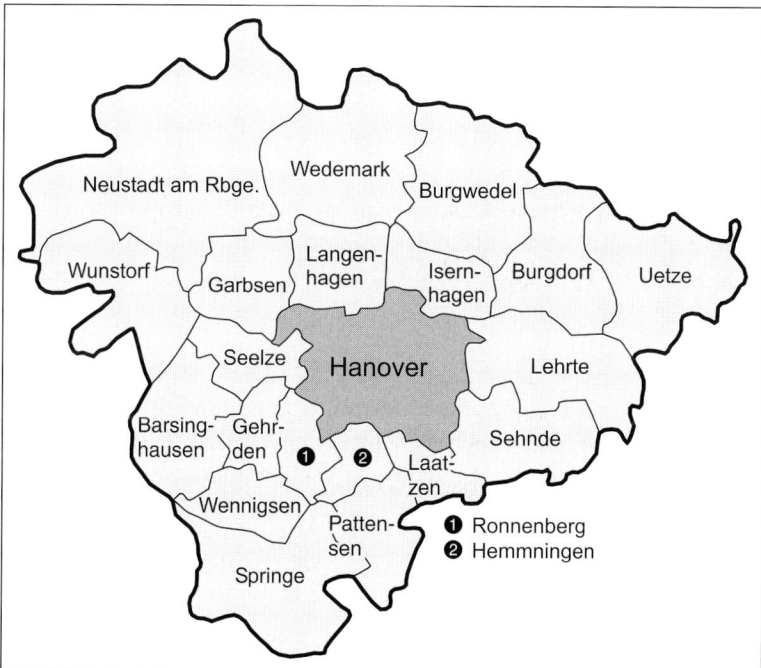

Figure 9.1 The Greater Hanover Region, consisting of Hanover City (dark) and the surrounding Hanover county

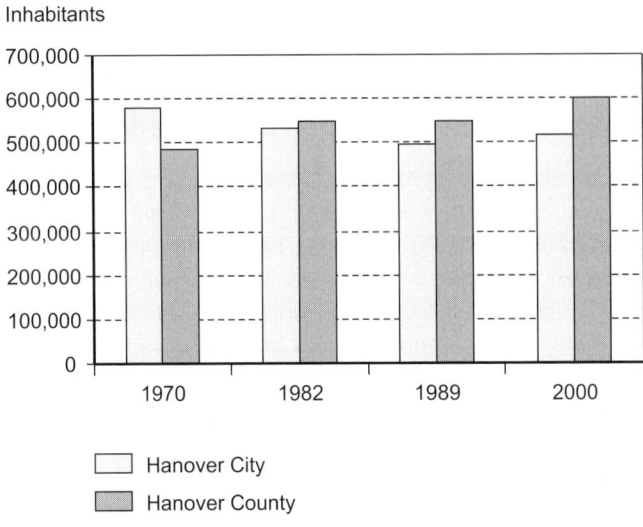

Inhabitants

Hanover City
Hanover County

Figure 9.2 The development of population in Hanover City and Hanover county. *Source:* Landeshauptstadt Hanover

from suburbanisation, but the more peripheral places grew as well. In general, two tendencies of migration can be found in the region: people from abroad and university students move to the core city, and people with higher incomes and especially families with children move into the suburbs and the partially rural outer parts of the district. Migration into and within the region is a crucial factor for regional development, and its consequences can be seen in various fields, concerning ecological, social and financial aspects.

Transport

With more and more people living in suburban and peripheral areas, the role of public transport has declined in the last decades despite an offensive policy with uniform pricing and the construction of a light railway system that is internationally renowned for its efficiency. The number of cars grew dramatically from about 388,000 in 1980 to about 536,000 in 1999, 60 per cent of them being registered in the district. Intensive transit traffic passing through the region aggravates the nuisance caused by vehicles.

Consumption of open space

The urban sprawl leads to a continuous demand for open space, which is a limited resource. By the beginning of 2000, nearly half (49.6 per cent) of the surface of the city of Hanover was covered by buildings or transport infrastructure – an increase of more than 16 per cent since 1979. Recent figures for the district are not available, but it can be assumed that the tendency is more or less the same, though on a lower level.

Social housing and social welfare

Social segregation is a side-effect of suburbanisation: people in precarious social situations – e.g. the unemployed, single persons with children or persons with a drug problem – stay or even move into the core city where they integrate more easily into a greater variety of social structures. On the other hand the core city loses wealthy, socially stable people who make their dream of 'a little house in the country' a reality. The rising number of underprivileged people in Germany during the last two decades is mainly a problem of the core cities. Several neighbourhoods in Hanover have serious social problems, and the city will have to expand its programme for social assistance and regeneration. Social assistance, financed by the municipalities, has become a major part of the city's expenditures. The total today is nearly four times as high as it was 20 years ago, with the gap between it and the district municipalities ever widening (figure 9.3).

Municipal budgets

The costs of social welfare are not the only expenditures the city of Hanover has to cover due to its central role in the region. It also has to pay for theatres, museums, hospitals, schools, sports facilities and other central city functions. On the other hand, the city's income is affected by suburbanisation. In the last two decades, the city's overall tax revenue grew more slowly than that of the surrounding muni-cipalities. A major reason for this is the local revenue system. Financial law says that 16 per cent of the income taxes must be redistributed from the Federation to the municipalities according to the number of employed and differentiated as to income levels. The suburban cities profit from their wealthy inhabitants. Although the county municipalities' per capita tax revenue is generally much smaller than that of Hanover itself, their revenues from income tax are larger (figure 9.4). The city could not completely compensate for this with its higher dynamics in business tax.

Economic development

More than suburbanisation, economic development is a heavily discussed topic in the Hanover region. As mentioned, the region is endowed with considerable economic potential. In 1996, the German consultancy company Empirica together with a renowned German business magazine identified and examined the strengths

Dietrich Fürst and Ansgar Rudolph

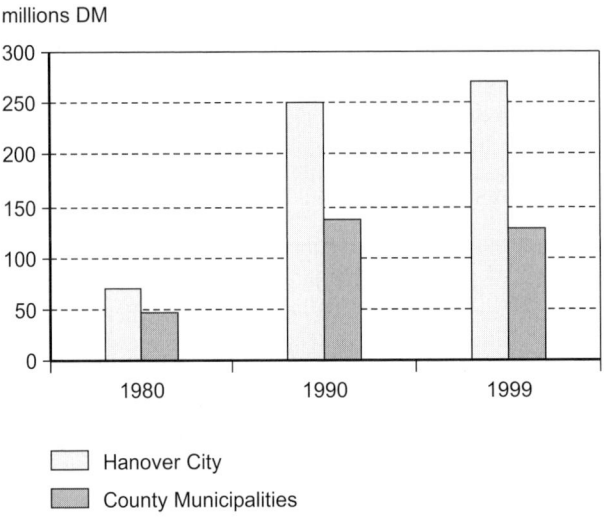

Figure 9.3 Expenditure on social welfare in Hanover City and the municipalities of Hanover county. *Source:* Landeshauptstadt Hanover

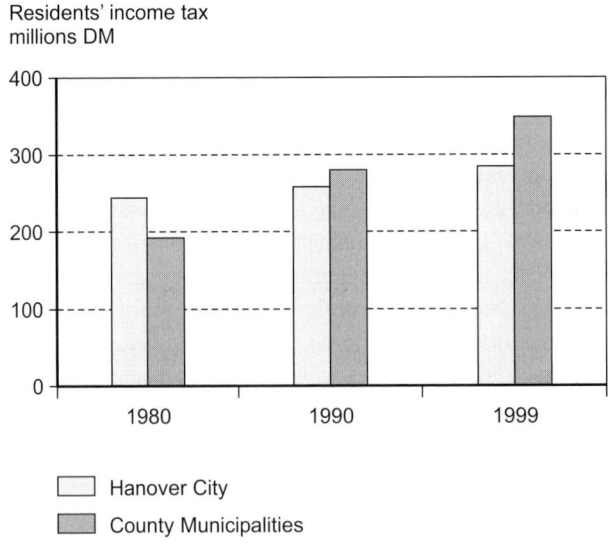

Figure 9.4 The revenues from the residents' income tax. Hanover City and county municipalities. *Source:* Landeshauptstadt Hanover

and weaknesses of the 267 NUTS II[1] regions in the EU on the basis of five indices (qualification potential, patterns of economic growth, quality of life, transport/ contact, communication benefits). The Hanover region was second to the Dutch province of Gelderland, due to special strengths in transport links and qualification potentials. From Hanover, about half of the EU population can be reached by road haulage vehicles within eight hours, and the links to Eastern Europe are excellent, too. Apparently, however, the region cannot harness its potentials:

- After a temporary rise in the early 1990s, economic development has lost its dynamics. Holding fourteenth place in terms of population among the German city regions, its ranking in GDP per capita is only slightly higher (thirteenth).
- The per capita gross income in the Hanover region is only 16 per cent above the German average, compared to 71 per cent in Munich, 42 per cent in Frankfurt and 23 per cent in Hamburg and Stuttgart (Jung et al., 2000).
- The unemployment rate in the Hanover region is slightly above the average in Germany. Although the population has grown in the last two decades, the number of employees included in the social security system is now smaller than it was in 1982 (figure 9.5).
- A migration of workplaces from the core city into the surrounding county is occurring. The city is losing its central role as the location of workplaces: today, the rate of employees per capita in some of the neighbouring munici- palities is nearly as high as in the city. Especially Langenhagen, a town with 50,000 inhabitants to the north of Hanover, is performing very well: it is the location of the airport and of one of the most important motorway crossings in the country.

The Hanover region suffers from the typical problems of all city regions, although many are not as distinct as in other regions. Regional governance in the Hanover region has three main factors to deal with:

Conflicts between the core city and the surrounding municipalities

Functional disparities between the core city and its periphery could be reduced by closer cooperation in many fields, such as housing, transport, central infrastructures, waste disposal, recreation, ecological compensation. Discussion on a functional level does not always take place with the necessary intensity, and very often there is not enough clarity about the role and competence of the Greater Hanover District, the county and the municipalities. But more than on the functional level, financial conflicts between the municipalities are virulent, as Hanover and several county municipalities are in a precarious financial situation.

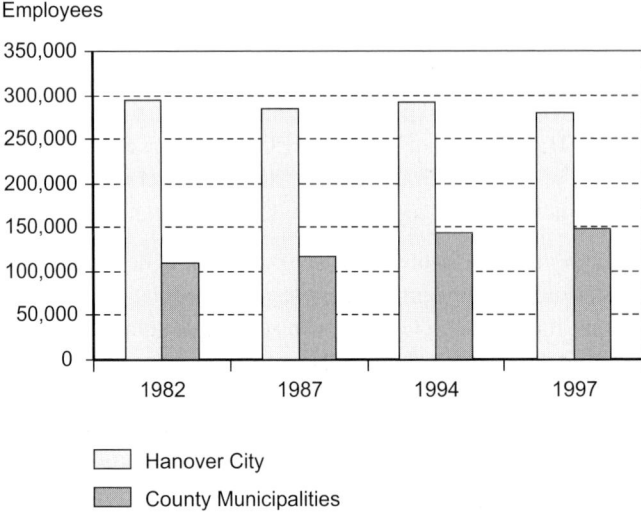

Employees

Figure 9.5 Employees included in the social security system. *Source:* Gerlach/
Lehmann, 1998

Efficiency

The region's administrative structure has not always been able to cope with the
problems to be faced. However, strong endeavours have been made to introduce
'new public management' concepts not only in the central city but also in the
suburban municipalities and in the county. In addition the region is about to
reorganise its government structure (see below).

Sustainability

Although the region has launched some very innovative programmes to save natural
resources (e.g. the use of wind energy and improving the energy-efficiency of
public buildings), regional and local planning has not prevented the continuation
of the ecologically critical trends of increasing traffic or the consumption of open
space, but compared to other city regions the quality of the environment in the
Hanover region is still quite good. However, a growing problem of sustainability
could become the social component of the concept (balance between economic,
ecological and social stability): in particular the core city is confronted with growing
problems of maintaining social cohesion in and between its neighbourhoods. This
has already prompted civic leaders to improve the situation, following the Anglo-
Saxon concept of a citizen's foundation that collects money from the business
sector and from wealthier citizens to promote projects for the disadvantaged.

Changes in the structure of government and governance

The Greater Hanover Association (*Kommunalverband Großraum Hanover*) was founded in 1962–3 on the initiative of the city of Hanover (in cooperation with Lower Saxony) as a special district. The goal was to control the increasing inter-relationship between central city and suburbs by means of spatial planning devices. In the beginning, the district had only the competence of planning, an auxiliary for annexing the neighbouring communities which at the time was no longer an option. In 1969 the district enlarged its competence when it received the authority over public transportation after Hanover's public transport system met stiff resistance from the public due to a misled pricing policy. In the wake of the territorial reform of the 1970s the number of communities within the region was reduced to 21, the number of counties to just one and the district was transformed into a 'multipurpose district' with directly elected representatives: it then consisted of the central city, 20 surrounding communities and the county of Hanover (which comprises the 20 surrounding communities). And the tasks of the new association were greatly extended to include waste disposal, provision of hospitals, promotion of social housing, etc.

In 1976 a political power change took place on the Land level (from Social Democrats to Christian Democrats), partly due to the voters' general frustration with the results of the territorial reform. Spurred by the communities which – now enlarged and strengthened by the territorial reform – resisted strong regional governments, a reorganisation of the region came into force in 1980 accompanied by a reorientation of the planning system: Lower Saxony reduced the 'multipurpose district' to a mere special district and required regional planners to withdraw from interfering in local planning. In 1992 the district was legally transformed into a regional association (*Kommunalverband*), which meant enlarged competencies, but the real effects were unimportant.

In 1996 an initiative (the 'Hanover Region' project) was launched by the association, the county and the central city of Hanover with the aim of reorganising the region by combining the county, the association and the central city into one new two-tier system in the form of a 'regional county'. In addition, some of the licensing functions of the regional prefect (*Bezirksregierung*) were also to be transferred to the regional county. The 20 hitherto county-dependent communities should in general remain unchanged and become members of the new regional county. Within less than four years the project was finalised and the new regional county came into existence on 1 November 2001. The dominant motives driving that change were: a) strengthening the competitiveness of the region; b) regional institutionalisation of regional common tasks (waste disposal, regional economic development, etc.); and c) improving the inter-community fiscal relations (by transferring the authority on social assistance from the local to the regional level and making the communities pay for it via contributions).

The 'political opportunity structures' (Maloney *et al.*, 2000) for the initiative were exceptionally good: all the three chief executive officers were about to leave office; the general elections for Lower Saxony had brought the Social Democrats back to power (and they were more open to reform); and the increased interregional competition, intensified by the European Common Market, and lessons drawn from other regions (Frankfurt, Stuttgart, Copenhagen and others) had spurred decision-making. Even preparations for the Hanover EXPO 2000 supported the reform project. But most important was that the project seemed to produce an all-winners game: the county of Hanover wanted to get rid of the regional association; the central city wanted to relieve its fiscal stress by burden-sharing with the region; the county-dependent communities hoped for more local autonomy within the greater regional county; and the association intended to get revalued by combining its forces with those of the county.

Strategic policies for the metropolitan region

Changes of strategic patterns

The special district of 1962–3, although initiated by the central city, very quickly changed into an association of the surrounding communities against the city. In reaction, the central city withdrew its cooperation even though it remained financially and politically involved: the central city contributed half of the district's fiscal resources and sent 50 per cent of the representatives to the district assembly.

What made the district strong was the take-over of public transportation: thus the district not only gained more financial and personal resources but became more visible to the general public. Due to the regional system of public transportation, regional integration and regional identity increased considerably.

Since the district is based on a special law and any major alteration of its organisational structure needs a change of law, the district tried to outflank the tedious legal procedures by using 'soft law': instead of structural reforms it chose procedural reforms, informal regulations and even the outsourcing of functions to private organisations. In particular, outsourcing became a strong instrument because by doing so it developed its own operational basis (which hitherto had not existed, since the district was mainly confined to planning). Outsourced tasks were regional economic development, real estate policy and supplementary transportation tasks (together there are now more than nine private organisations belonging wholly or partly to the association). Despite the fact that the former 'multipurpose association' of the 1970s was reduced to a mere district in 1980, the institution grew considerably (from 81 posts in 1981 to 140 posts in 2000). In the 1980s and 1990s the district adopted more flexible planning devices which supplemented the traditional regional planning: regional conferences, patterns of 'cognitive framing' via seminars, workshops, exhibitions and scenarios, as well as extended networking with local authorities and finally the approach to develop the regional plan of 1996 out of a process of a collectively designed *Leitbild* (commonly agreed upon vision) for the region.

Changes of strategic policies

With regards to planning, from the beginning the district pursued a concept which a) closely related the settlement structure to public transportation, b) was based on 'decentralised concentration' and c) gave highest priority to open space conservation and development. In the 1980s open space policy became dominant, first because the green movement became strong and, second, because the Land government (led by the Christian Democrats) strictly forbade spatial planners to intervene in local planning. The district used the potential of restrictive planning inherent in the open space conservation by creating an open space concept in collaboration with landscape planners. The new concept introduced green belts (hitherto not used in Hanover) and devices to extensify the agriculture (in the northern parts of the region) as well as to define a regional concept of raw material extraction. In particular, much attention was drawn to the rural parts of the region (conservation of old villages, improving the landscape as a 'soft locational factor').

In addition, the increased interrelatedness of the communities led to a new planning approach: regional planning should be governed by a collective process of developing a regional Leitbild. The new Leitbild substituted the traditional centre-suburb hierarchy with a concept of inter-linked communication structures. The Leitbild was drafted by an external consultant but developed in consultation with leading actors of the region. In addition, cross-community solutions responding to pressing problems like wind energy, major shopping areas, etc. were developed. As mentioned, the development of the 1990s led institutionally to the reorganisation of the region into a regional county: the new Hanover region will have all the authorities of a German county plus the competencies of the former Hanover Association (i.e. regional planning, coordination of public transport, regional marketing, support and development of recreational facilities). In fact, the new region will be a great county with an annual budget of more than EUR 1 billion and an integrated authority to develop the region economically as well as ecologically based on a strong political decision-making power: the president of the region will be directly elected as will the 84 representatives of the regional assembly.

Problems of institutional and spatial coordination and reactions of the regional organisations

The most important institutional cleavages of the Hanover region are hardly different from those in other regions:

- *Between the district and local authorities:* Basically the problem has to do with conflicts over local autonomy. But in Germany this conflict is overshadowed and intensified by the cleavage just mentioned.
  Reaction of the district: The district tried to develop cooperative and constructive approaches to open-space planning instead of interfering in local plan making. Hence the emphasis given to the 'open space concept', the 'concept for raw material extraction', the 'concept for defining spaces suitable for the use of wind energy', concepts to create inter-municipal industrial areas, etc.
- *Between central city and surrounding communities:* Due to the increasing competition of the surrounding communities (relocation of the higher-income households, business relocation, large-scale retail centres, growing fiscal stress of the central city).
  Reaction of the association: Intercommunal integration strategies like regular talks with local authorities, the creation of a common Leitbild, the regional retail concept, the Hanover Region project.
- *Between restrictive ordering functions and cooperative developing functions*
  The German spatial planning system is based on an ordering concept (restrictive rules to use the space). Only those plan objectives intended to structure land-use may become binding. Planning thus has restrictive effects and subsequently prompts conflicts with those concerned. In contrast, the developing function is based on regional cooperation but its objectives have only indicative quality – recommendations, advice, supporting guidelines. The more restrictive the district becomes in its ordering functions, the less cooperation it arouses in its developing functions (regional planning is then regarded as 'impeding activities').
  Reaction of the association: Although the association is legally bound to the ordering function, its aim is to change regional planning into a process of common interest of the stakeholders. Instruments to obtain that goal are: creation of a communicative climate by intensifying the talks with local authorities and 'framing' via seminars, workshops, conferences, publications, etc.
- *Between regional common tasks and local autonomy:* Since in Germany local autonomy is regarded as a constitutional legal good of the highest importance, the cleavage is programmed for: whenever the district declares an activity a regional common task it is attacked by the local authorities on the grounds that they fear a loss of sovereignty.
  Reaction of the district: As above (talks with local authorities, paradigmatic steering, etc.).
- *Between the functional and the territorial logic of action:* Regional planning and local authorities follow a *territorial logic* of action. Their ordering concepts are bound to the territory. In contrast, the economy and sectoral policies follow a *functional logic* of action. The ensuing cleavage is based on the fact that the

functional logic is flexible, project-driven, network-based and territorially unbound while the territorial logic is more inflexible, based on the region and bound to regional institutions with a strong tendency towards hierarchical governance.

Reaction of the district: Leaning more heavily on approaches of the functional logic of action by making use of a) the *spatial impact assessment* (*Raumordnungsverfahren*) where deals can be struck with the project owner, b) sectoral regional concepts which are developed in close cooperation with sectoral politicians (like wind energy concept, concept on raw material extraction, etc.), c) outsourcing activities to privatised agencies, and finally d) of models of public-private partnerships.

• *Between the public and the private sector:* Regional development and regional planning are considered as public goods to be provided by local and regional governments with the private sector reluctantly joining force. What is needed is a closer cooperation between the two sectors.

Reaction: The Hanover Association was about to break the ground for closer cooperation between the two sectors on the base of public–private partnerships – recently done by initiating work groups comprising high-ranking private and public officers to define lead projects for the regional economic and ecological development. Whether the cooperative mood will last once the Hanover Region is operational is open to question, since the private sector tends to withdraw when public-administrative competencies are firmly established.

• *Between region and Land level:* The new Hanover region will be a powerful entity within Lower Saxony. It will comprise about 15 per cent of the inhabitants, 18 per cent of the employees and 20 per cent of gross domestic product. The new regional president will become a political figure challenging the politics of the Land. In addition, should the Hanover region turn out to be economically successful it will trigger repercussions in other parts of Lower Saxony and eventually lead to full-fledged territorial reform (which presently is politically an unwanted issue).

Evaluation

Territorial reorganisations have changed from top-down approaches (of the Land) towards bottom-up initiatives of local/regional actors. The Lands are very reluctant to take up the issue of territorial reform after the traumatic experiences of the 1970s. But to mobilise bottom-up initiatives, there must be external pressures for local authorities to engage in that issue – the institutional own interests of preserving the local autonomy far outweighs the benefits of regional cooperation. External pressure stems from the need to become regionally competitive, to save costs by jointly producing regional common goods and to organise new regional tasks more efficiently. Yet, the pressure is seldom reinforced by either the mass media or the private sector. There are only a few regions with private engagement in regional development whose processes of regional reorganisation were or are strongly influenced by the private sector (e.g. Frankfurt, Kassel, Stuttgart). The Hanover region does not belong to that group. Why is that? The research on that question is still very weak. It could be assumed that it has to do with the German tradition of the public law which clearly separated the private and the public sector and tried to keep the public sector clear of any private entanglement (cf. Bossong, 2001). In the case of Hanover it also might be due to the fact that the number of headquarters of firms is very small in contrast to the number of branches of firms which are much less engaged in regional issues. Apart from that, Hanover enjoyed a very singular situation when initiating its regional reform movement (CEOs leaving their jobs, just one county, one association, one central city, heavy pressure to become more competitive). Hence, private engagement was not very necessary.

Being a bottom-up approach and initiated by the CEOs (Chief Executive Officers) of local governments, party politics did not play a big role. Certainly, parties reinforced the cleavages but since there were opponents and supporters in all the various parties it was very difficult for them to define party positions. The main conflicts thus ran along different institutional interests with the smaller county-dependent communities rather more opposed than in favour of the reform. But eventually, the process turned out to be not so different from other issues of regional innovation, with some actors taking the lead and others opposing the change at the beginning but supporting it later on.

Due to the private restraints, organising regions is an issue of local government, at least in Germany. Hence, there is a strong tendency to organise metropolitan associations which least interfere with local autonomy. But metropolitan associations (districts) tend to support centrifugal powers to the detriment of the hitherto centripetal orientation of the region: the surrounding communities are strengthened while the central city gets more restricted in favour of the regional organisation. In addition, the association tends to attract more functions to the detriment of local authorities by inventing and defining new regional common tasks. Even though the Hanover association was legally restricted in doing so it managed to appropriate new issues or to outsource those issues to newly created dependent units.

In their daily routine, associations tend to depoliticise their tasks by reducing the scope for decision-making to 'professional constraints'. Outsourcing to autonomous units, adopting informal action, etc. are also modes of depoliticisation. If associations want to modify their problem-solving capacity by new devices or innovative solutions they very much depend on 'political opportunity structures' (Maloney *et al.*, 2000). Opportunity structures are a) supporting paradigm shifts (in particular *Zeitgeist*), b) a situational reduction of transaction costs of changes, and c) external pressures to act. But most important are the promoters.

In the case of the Hanover region the *promoters* were the CEOs of the county, the central city and the association. Their motives differed but they were supported by a common *paradigm shift* in favour of a strong, competitive region reinforced by the regionalisation strategies of the EU and the German state. The *transaction costs of change* were situationally reduced due to the retirement of the CEOs and a parallel majority of Social Democrats at the local and the Land level. The *external pressures* to act came from the growing fiscal crisis of the central city and the increased interregional competition marked by organisational changes in Stuttgart, intensive discussions on reorganisation in the Frankfurt region and EXPO 2000.

To adopt changes is a learning process. The obstacles primarily stem from mental reticence to adopt a new philosophy of cooperation (normative side). Here, learning is hampered by status quo oriented core beliefs. Changes in core beliefs need stronger external pressures or paradigm shifts. In the case of Hanover, the pressure was felt and converted into reform action by political actors. Interestingly, local economic actors or civic leaders did not play any role at all. When it finally comes to choosing the 'right' solution (instrumental side) much depends on lesson drawing. In the case of Hanover the lesson was drawn from the Saarbrücken region where a similar model had already existed for over 20 years.

What the 'right' organisational structure for metropolitan regions should be cannot be determined by scientific research. Rather, organisational structures are one element of a system of regional governance. What their influence is can only be judged intuitively. Thus, the choice of organisational structures largely depends on the dominant organisational paradigm shared by the majority of decision makers. In Germany decision makers tend towards 'strong'[2] organisational structures. The reasons are (Fürst, 1999) that a) the German political culture is still strongly legalistically oriented; b) lawyers tend to prefer 'strong' structures, because they are regarded as necessary for decision-making, conflict resolution, etc.; c) since 'strong' institutions are less dependent on persons they are considered more reliable and easier to control; and d) as to 'intermediaries' between the strong local and state governments, the general opinion is that they also must be 'strong organisations' in order to countervail their partners. Conversely, social scientists prefer 'weak'[3] structures and networks of actors.

Formal organisational reforms on the regional level in Germany have very high transaction costs: they need legal approval from the Land parliament and arouse the resistance of other counties and even the regional prefects since changes in one region have repercussions in the institutional fabric of other regions. Consequently, the reaction of the German Association of Counties was harsh and hostile, the dominant motive being fear of new attempts to redraw county jurisdictions (Henneke, 2000).

Apparently, in Germany all metropolitan regions tend towards a combination of 'strong' and 'weak' organisational structures. Basic ingredients are an organisational core which has resources and a minimum of decision-making power. It is usually supported by network-like structures of cooperation.

The structure of the Stuttgart region could become a model: the organisational core is the directly elected regional parliament and its executive branch has but a limited number of competencies. But the association is open to new tasks of which they makes much use by drawing on 'weak' organisational forms of cooperation and networking (Knieling *et al.*, 1999). How far 'strong' institutions could be substituted or overlaid by 'weak' ones also depends to a large extent on the regional cooperative climate, the region's political culture and learning processes which already started in the past.

Changes in regional governance come about in various ways. Some regions implement changes gradually, while others do so only under strong external pressure. But typically, marked changes require a stimulus, a window of opportunity, an alliance of promoters (leadership) and an idea of what the 'right' new governance structure should be. The final response differs widely between the regions. It depends on the type of regional actors, the regional actors' constellation, the institutional framework and – in particular – the dominant organisational paradigm.

Note

1 NUTS II – regional delimination used by the European Statistical Office and refers to the second layer below that of member state level. In the case of Germany: NUTS I is the Land level; NUTS II is the level of established regions.
2 Strong refers to institutional devices which contain a well-defined assignation of competences, resources and powers to decide.
3 Weak, however, refers to organisations, which mainly consist of networks of actors and hardly have any power to decide.

Bibliography

Bossong, H. (2001) 'Der Sozialstaat am Runden Tisch. Entrechtlichung durch Verfahren', *Die Verwaltung*, 34 (2000): 145–60.

Droste, H., Fiedler, J. and Schmidt, V. (1997) 'Region Hanover. Entwicklung neuer Organisationsstrukturen für die Wahrnehmung regionaler Verwaltungsaufgaben in der Region Hanover vom 07.10.1996', in Akademie für Raumforschung und Landesplanung/ Kommunalverband Großraum Hanover (ed.) *Hanover Region 2001, Hanover 1997* (Beiträge zur Regionalen Entwicklung H.59), annex.

Fürst, D. (1992) 'Regionen in Europa – Herausforderungen für die kommunale Zusammenarbeit', in Beate Kohler-Koch, Hg., *Staat und Demokratie in Europa*, Opladen: Leske und Budrich.

Fürst, D. (1993) 'Kooperationshemmnisse und ihre Überwindung in der Region Hanover', in *Die Produktion von Stadt-Land-Schaft II* (Loccumer Protokolle 58/92), Loccum.

Fürst, D. (1994) 'Stadt und Region', in H. Mäding (ed.) *Stadtperspektiven. Difu-Symposium 1993*, Berlin (Difu-Beiträge zur Stadtforschung Bd.10), 41–55.

Fürst, D. (1996) 'The regional districts in search of a new role', in A. Benz and K. Goetz (eds) *A New German Public Sector? Reform, Adaptation and Stability*, Aldershot, UK: Dartmouth.

Fürst, D. (1997a) 'Der Wandel raumplanerischer Leitbilder – Wandel raumplanerischen Denkens', in H. Monheim and Chr. Zöpel (eds) *Raum für Zukunft. Zur Innovationsfähigkeit von Stadtentwicklungs- und Verkehrspolitik*, Festschrift für Karl Ganser, Essen: Klartext.

Fürst, D. (1997b) '"Weiche" versus "harte" Kommunalverbände: Gibt es Gründe für eine "härtere" Institutionalisierung der regionalen Kooperation?', in G. Seiler (ed.) *Gelebte Demokratie*, Festschrift für Manfred Rommel, Stuttgart: Kohlhammer.

Fürst, D. (1997c) 'Region Hanover – Aufbruch zu neuen Ufern?', in Kommunalverband Großraum Hanover, Hg., *Hanover Region 2001. Vorschläge zur Entwicklung neuer Organisationsstrukturen für die Wahrnehmung regionaler Verwaltungsaufgaben*, Hanover 1997 (Beiträge zur regionalen Entwicklung, Bd.59), 59–64.

Fürst, D. (1997e) 'Regionalverbände – Organisationen zwischen kommunalem Egoismus und regionaler Vernunft vor neuen Aufgaben', in M. Bose (ed.) *Die unaufhaltsame Auflösung der Stadt in die Region?*, Harburg (Harburger Berichte zur Stadtplanung Bd.9), 119–36.

Fürst, D. (1999a) '"Weiche Kooperationsstrukturen" – eine ausreichende Antwort auf den Kooperationsbedarf in Stadtregionen?', in *Informationen zur Raumentwicklung*, 9/10: 609–16.

Fürst, D. and Kilper, H. (1995) 'The innovative power of regional networks: a comparison of two approaches to political modernization in North Rhine-Westphalia', *European Planning Studies*, 3: 287–304.

Fürst, D., Blanke, B., Löb, St., Plass, St. and Schridde, H. (1997d) *StadtForum Hanover. 5. Fachforum: Eine Region Hanover im Jahr 2001?*, Hanover: University of Hanover.

Fürst, D., Klinger, W., Knieling, J., Mönnecke, M. and Zeck, H. (1990) *Regionalverbände im Vergleich: Entwicklungssteuerung in Verdichtungsräumen*, Baden-Baden: NOMOS.

Fürst, D. et al. (1999) *Interkommunale und regionale Kooperation. Variablen ihrer Funktionsfähigkeit*, Hanover: Akademie für Raumforschung und Landesplanung (ARL-Arbeitsmaterialien H.244).

Gerlach, K. and Lehmann, K. (1998) *Beschäftigtenentwicklung im Großraum Hanover VI* (Beiträge zur Regionalen Entwicklung, Kommunalverband Großraum Hanover, 72), Hanover.

Henneke, H.-G. (2000) 'Region Hanover – Experimentierfeld ohne Fernwirkungen oder Keimzelle einer neuen Gebiets- und Funktionalreform?', *Der Landkreis* 12 (2000): 790–94.

Jung, H.-U., Brandt, A., Franck, M., Weber, K. and Wieja, J. (1998) *Wirtschaftsreport Hanover Region 1998: Der Wirtschaftsraum Hanover im überregionalen Wettbewerb* (Beiträge zur Regionalen Entwicklung, Kommunalverband Großraum Hanover, 60), Hanover.

Jung, H.-U., Brandt, A., Franck, M., Weber, K. and Wieja, J. (2000) *Wirtschaftsstandort Hanover Region: Regionalreport 2000* (Beiträge zur Regionalen Entwicklung, Kommunalverband Großraum Hanover, 78), Hanover.

Knieling, J., Fürst, D. and Danielzyk, R. (1999) 'Kooperative Handlungsformen in der Regionalplanung. Konzeptionelle Überlegungen zur Analyse der Planungspraxis', *Raumforschung u. Raumordnung*, 57: 195–200.

Kommunalverband Großraum Hanover (1996) *Regionales Raumordnungsprogramm 1996*, Hanover.

Dietrich Fürst and Ansgar Rudolph

Kommunalverband Großraum Hanover (ed.) (1999) *Karten zur Regionalstatistik: Groß-raum Hanover, angrenzende Landkreise und Städtenetz EXPO-Region* (Beiträge zur Regionalen Entwicklung, Kommunalverband Großraum Hanover, 72), Hanover.

Landeshauptstadt Hanover (1980) *Statistischer Vierteljahresbericht Hanover*, Jahres-übersicht 1980, Hanover.

Landeshauptstadt Hanover (1990) *Statistischer Vierteljahresbericht Hanover*, Jahres-übersicht 1990, Hanover.

Landeshauptstadt Hanover (1999) *Statistischer Vierteljahresbericht Hanover*, Jahres-übersicht 1999, Hanover.

Landeshauptstadt Hanover (2000) *Statistischer Vierteljahresbericht Hanover*, Volumes 1–3, Hanover.

Maloney, W., Smith, G. and Stoker, G. (2000) 'Social capital and urban governance: adding a more contextual "top-down" perspective', *Political Studies*, 48: 802–20.

Wagener, F. (1974) 'Modelle der Stadt-Umland-Verwaltung', in H. Schneider and V. Götz, Hg., *Im Dienst an Recht und Staat*, Berlin: Festschrift für Werner Weber.

Zweckverband Großraum Hanover (1990) *Regionales Raumordnungsprogramm 1990*, Hanover.

Law on the Dissolution of the Verband Großraum Hanover (as of 24 March 1980) (Nds. GVBl. 1980, p.65).

10 Governance in the Stuttgart metropolitan region

Susanne Heeg

Introduction

The Stuttgart metropolitan region is part of the federal state of Baden-Württemberg (south-western Germany) and consists of the administrative counties[1] Ludwigsburg, Rems-Murr, Göppingen, Esslingen, Böblingen and the city of Stuttgart at its centre (see figure 10.1). Thinking in terms of a Stuttgart metropolitan region – and not only in terms of different administrative counties and municipalities – is a rather new phenomenon: it dates back only to the early 1990s when the term was coined in the context of the reorientation of spatial planning policy in Germany and Baden-Württemberg. Since then, such metropolitan regions as Stuttgart, Rhine-Main, Hamburg and Berlin are seen as motors of socio-economic development in the process of European integration. The hope is that the Stuttgart metropolitan region will act as a catalyst for economic competitiveness and foster the integration of other regions in Baden-Württemberg into the European economy. To support this goal, an institutionalisation in the form of the Association of the Stuttgart Region has taken place in order to let the economic region – as regional actors emphasise – speak with one political voice.

The Stuttgart metropolitan region and its Association of the Stuttgart Region (*Verband Region Stuttgart*, VRS) are an example for the reorganisation of inherited political boundaries in response to the challenges of the economic restructuring and regionalisation of socio-economic relations. In that sense, the VRS is an example of the new institutional and governance structures created to complement and improve traditional forms of politico-spatial organisation. The VRS should be seen as an attempt to innovate and increase the effectiveness of politico-administrative and planning structures in order to mobilise regional potentials in the context of locational competition for investments and jobs.

In the following sections, I will sketch the trends in the Stuttgart metropolitan region in recent decades. I will then describe the paradigm shift which made possible the institutionalisation of the VRS and the establishment of new governance structures. Third, I will analyse the forms of governance by looking at important policy fields of the VRS. Finally, I will analyse changes in governance in a theoretical perspective.

Trends in regional development

As in many other European city regions, the Stuttgart metropolitan region is characterised by a strong process of suburbanisation of economic growth, population and industries. Those municipalities which border on the city of Stuttgart have gained most from suburbanisation in the last 20 to 30 years. Whereas the city of Stuttgart lost 56,300 inhabitants between 1961 and 1999 (–10 per cent), the whole region[2] gained 577,600 inhabitants (+ 28.6 per cent). Similar tendencies can be seen in the development of employment.[3] While the decrease in employment in the city was 8.1 per cent between 1975 and 1998, the region underwent an 8.6 per cent increase. Particularly households with higher incomes and families with children left the city, while households with lower incomes and lower qualifications remained in the city. This created massive social and financial problems for the city of Stuttgart, while prosperous municipalities in the urban fringe developed into self-confident and autonomous cities and communities. Besides the financial problems for the city, this development led to an increase in the population density in the whole region. The settlement area in the urban fringe increased by 43 per cent between 1968 and 1985 (Hecking *et al.*, 1988: p.31). Many municipalities wanted to profit from economic prosperity despite its regional consequences. Consequences of this rapid and – from the perspective of the metropolitan region – scarcely controlled development were an increase in the consumption of natural resources and an intensified use of existing infrastructure:

- Increase in traffic; whereas the use of private cars increased strongly, the development of the public transport network has fallen behind partly due to the financial problems of the member municipalities but mostly due to difficulties in regional coordination;
- Increasing land utilisation and consumption of open space;
- Increasing ecological problems due to intensified use of natural resources;
- Trend towards social segregation; while poor households stay overwhelmingly in the core city, particularly prosperous households are in search of 'green surroundings' in the urban fringe.

While occupying only 10 per cent of the total area of Baden-Württemberg, in 1995 the Stuttgart region accommodated 25 per cent of the population and 28 per cent of the jobs. In 1996, 36.3 per cent of all jobs in financial services, 35.7 per cent of those in producer services and 34.1 per cent of those in knowledge intensive industries (e.g. mechanical engineering, computers, automobile industry) in Baden-Württemberg were located in the Stuttgart metropolitan region. As many

Figure 10.1 Map of Baden-Württemburg. Source: The Department of Trade and Industry (WBW, 1995: p.18)

165

as 27.6 per cent of all jobs in traditional industries (e.g. electrical engineering, clothing, textile and furniture industry) in Baden-Württemberg were located in the metropolitan region. Another indicator which shows the economic strength of the region is that 29.3 per cent of the gross value added of Baden-Württemberg in 1996 was produced in the Stuttgart metropolitan region. These trends are evidence that the Stuttgart metropolitan region is a socially and economically integrated region.[4] Whereas service industries dominate the inner city, production and R&D activities are predominantly located in the urban fringe.

However, from 1990 onwards, the metropolitan region experienced an economic downturn. Although the recession was a nation-wide phenomenon, it affected particularly the metropolitan region. Export intensive industries which were strongly hit by the economic recession (e.g. the automobile industry, and mechanical and electrical engineering) are highly concentrated in the region. As a consequence, the unemployment rate increased from 3.1 per cent in 1990 to 7 per cent in 1998. While the city of Stuttgart lost 35,645 jobs in manufacturing between 1990 and 1997 (–27.7 per cent), the total region of Stuttgart lost 112,681 jobs (–21.6 per cent) (see Batz, 1998: p.69). From 1992 till the end of the 1990s, the Stuttgart region lost in all branches a total of over 117,000 jobs (Steinacher, 2000: p.18).

This negative economic, social, infrastructural and spatial development triggered the fear that the economic motor of Baden-Württemberg would lose its power and dynamic. At the same time the negative tendencies made possible attempts to reform the regional institutional structure. An increased locational competition due to European integration and German reunification fostered the perception that the metropolitan region might lose locational advantages. Due to these pressures it seemed necessary to build up regional coherence and improve regional attractiveness.

Changes in the regional *Leitbilder*

In order to discuss consequences and develop solutions to the economic downturn in the Stuttgart metropolitan region, at the beginning of the 1990s the government of Baden-Württemberg established an advisory board. It formulated the challenge that 'the government of Baden-Württemberg as well as the municipal level had to establish an urban space with European radiation as a point of identification and orientation in the context of European integration (Greater Stuttgart)' (Oppermann, 1992: p.2; author's translation).

This advice triggered a 'locational debate' concerning the Stuttgart metropolitan region. According to many political, planning and scientific contributions, the economic success of Baden-Württemberg was and is dependent on the locational conditions in the Stuttgart metropolitan region. An example of this perception is a publication of the Robert Bosch foundation, in which it is claimed that: 'Whatever the long-term consequences of German reunification and enlargement of the

European Union will be on the German south-west, the Stuttgart region will face intensified competition from German and European regions' (Müller, 1994, preface). In a publication of the Friedrich Ebert foundation (Forschungsinstitut der Friedrich-Ebert-Stiftung, 1994), it is asked whether the economic changes will have negative consequences in the Stuttgart metropolitan region, and in a publication of the German Institute of Urban Affairs (DIFU) the mayor of the city of Ludwigsburg, Hans Jochen Henke, says he is looking for appropriate forms of cooperation in order to cope with locational challenges in the Stuttgart metropolitan region (Henke, 1993).

These questions and ideas imply a changed perception of problems: the spatial and economic competitiveness of the Stuttgart metropolitan region is a decisive precondition for the competitiveness of Baden-Württemberg. The Stuttgart metropolitan region not only has to compete with German cities (let alone cities in Baden-Württemberg) but also has to find its place in the national and international urban hierarchy; the region has to test its strength against other European agglomerations. Political actors in Baden-Württemberg and in the metropolitan region understood the economic problems of the metropolitan region as in fact being the central problems of Baden-Württemberg, since the Stuttgart metropolitan region has been the motor of Baden-Württemberg's spatial economy. This discussion indicates the shift in the regional approach: in order to mobilise regional potentials, it was no longer sufficient to organise the metropolitan region through spatial planning. Rather, it seemed necessary to develop proactive policy instruments for the region. An agreement was developed to overcome the regional patchwork situation and represent the region through one institution.

As a result of the debate, an unprecedented reformulation of political forms and institutions took place. In 1973, 12 public corporations responsible for spatial planning were established in Baden-Württemberg. The central tasks of these public corporations included putting forward and adjusting regional plans for corresponding regions, and participating in the continuation of the spatial developmental plan and subject-specific plans of Baden-Württemberg (Dispan, 1996: p.43). Responsible for these tasks in the Stuttgart metropolitan region was the Neckar Regional Association. In 1992, the Association was renamed the Stuttgart Regional Association (*Regionalverband Stuttgart*, RVS). The RVS should work as a forum, in which representatives of different municipalities could communicate with each other (Dispan, 1996: p.69). A weakness of this institution was that it lacked financial and decision-making competencies.

However, particularly in the context of debating the 'economic location Stuttgart', limited competencies did not seem appropriate to face the challenges. The economic and population growth within the administrative districts around the city of Stuttgart triggered considerable developmental pressure leading to a disordered development of the Stuttgart metropolitan region with regard to the structure of settlements and economic and transport infrastructure. According to

Jürgen Dispan (1996), pronounced discrepancies between important planning goals and the factual population and settlement growth showed up.

This is the background to the first regional conference in 1991 at which the government of Baden-Württemberg formulated goals and requirements for the Stuttgart metropolitan region: a 'European region Stuttgart' should be established in order to work as a model for identification and representation for investors not only in Baden-Württemberg or in Germany, but in Europe and world-wide (Dispan, 1996). For this goal, important political and economic actors supported the idea of a reform of the various associations and joint bodies (e.g. public transport, waste disposal) in the region. Most important was the government, and in particular the Ministry of Trade and Commerce, which used its power to reform the institutional infrastructure. According to Spöri, the former Minister of Trade and Commerce:

> it is necessary to strengthen the core region of Baden-Württemberg in the European and world-wide locational competition, to achieve an effective cooperation by the establishment of the Association of the Region Stuttgart. The approaches in favour of a constructive collaboration – which, without doubt, already exist – should be protected against particularistic interests. The economic development of the whole federal state is dependent upon an offensive infrastructural empowerment in order to trigger the dynamic of the core region. The motor of the federal state must go on.
>
> (Spöri, 1994: p.121; author's translation)

The aim was to build up only one institution with a broad array of tasks and decision-making capacity as well as capabilities to push decisions through. This aim was concretised after the 1992 elections when the Christian Democrats (CDU) and the Labour Party (SPD) made an agreement concerning their government coalition. Part of this agreement was the commitment that the government of Baden-Württemberg would establish structures and institutions which make it possible to find solutions for the regional level and in particular for the highly urbanised regions of the federal state. In February 1994, the state parliament (*Landtag*) passed the 'law concerning the improvement of cooperation in the Stuttgart region'. The law is the expression of the will to strengthen the position of Stuttgart in the face of European and international competition. When the law came into force in October 1994, the various joint bodies which were separately seeking solutions for the regions were brought together into the Association of the Stuttgart Region (*Verband Region Stuttgart*, VRS). Important tasks of the VRS are regional planning, regional transport planning, waste disposal, economic development, job training, locational marketing and marketing of regional tourism. Contrary to other regional associations in Germany and previous/present ones in Baden-Württemberg, the members of the VRS are elected by the regional population. This increases the political legitimation and improves the representation of the association in the region. In other regional associations in Baden-Württemberg, it is still common for the state parliament to elect the members of the assembly.

The aim of establishing the VRS is made clear in a publication of Stuttgart's Chamber of Commerce and Industry (Industrie- und Handelskammer, IHK):

> Similar to other regions, it is a commonly shared understanding in the Stuttgart region that the regional forces need to be concentrated in order to make the location perceptible and attractive and in order to solve regional problems on a regional level. By establishing the Association of the Stuttgart Region in October 1994, a regional political authority with a directly elected parliament was founded, which is up to now unique in Germany ... Against the background of regional competition, to optimise economic efficiency in space is a necessary survival strategy of the Stuttgart region as an economic location.
>
> (IHK Stuttgart/VRS, 1998: p.18; author's translation)

The VRS itself gives – in its journal which works as a 'spokesman' for its goals, plans and self-image – a similar justification for establishing the association. The following citation is interesting because it shows that in order to translate the aims of the VRS into action, it was seen as necessary to use new forms of governance rather than formal government mechanisms:

> Confronted with competing locations, regionalisation is the appropriate answer to economic globalisation. Whereas transnational companies think globally and act globally, locations have to think globally, too, but they can act only locally or regionally, respectively. This applies to public corporations which are responsible for particular locations, and also to small and medium size enterprises and even to the factory management of transnational companies. It means that all actors which, contrary to so-called global players, are locally/ regionally strongly embedded have to find a common base for their activities. A far-reaching network of business, science and politics in regions creates competency and attractiveness. Such networks for the support of new technologies as biotechnology, mobility technology as well as start-ups are an answer to globalisation. These networks can work effectively only on a regional level since individual municipalities cannot manage economic change and international competition on their own. Globalisation and regionalisation are not contradictions. However, globalisation has increased the significance of regions – as autonomous actors and not only as objects of analysis.
>
> (Region Stuttgart Aktuell, 4/99: p.6
> 'Regionales Handeln als Konzept für Europa'; author's translation)

This citation shows that a central goal of the VRS is to bring together and mediate between important political, economic and civil actors. To achieve this, administrative work and political activities have to switch from formal, imperative decision-making to new policy styles which imply networking, mediating, managing and communicating.

Regional policy and governance

Confronted with economic globalisation and intensified regional competition, a task of overriding importance in the understanding of the VRS is to shape the Stuttgart metropolitan region into an attractive location. To do so, the VRS voted for an innovative concept to combine spatial planning with economic development. In order to realise these plans, an economic development agency (*Wirtschafts-förderungsgesellschaft Region Stuttgart*, WRS) was established to work as a public-private partnership of local municipalities, enterprises, chambers of commerce, trade unions and various associations. The WRS is engaged in locational marketing, management of regional commercial/industrial areas, support of existing enterprises, acquisition of investors, labour market policy, etc. The main emphasis is on fostering and developing industrial areas, and on regional economic development.

Development of industrial areas

By adopting a regional integral approach in planning, the VRS attempts to eliminate regional bottlenecks in the planning of commercial/industrial areas, settlements, traffic and other regionally important infrastructure (e.g. fairs). An important task is to establish inter-local industrial areas (*interkommunale Gewerbegebiete*) as 'centres of gravity' in the region. Hope is that these 'centres of gravity' will generate positive economic effects beyond its regional borders. The realisation of inter-local industrial areas, as well as fixing its usage causes conflicts between the VRS and the municipalities. Spatial planners and mayors of municipalities very often see inter-local industrial areas as restricting their decision-making powers. However, the showcase for highlighting interest conflicts between the VRS and the municipalities is the planning of factory outlet centres (FOCs). According to Bernd Steinacher, the head of the VRS: '… all cities and municipalities share the view that the inner cities should be protected from being bled white. However, equally shared is the view that this is mostly a task of the neighbouring municipalities' (Steinacher, 2000, p.20).

Many local municipalities and/or administrative districts try to attract investors for FOCs by offering attractive land outside city centres and quite often close to adjoining municipalities or administrative districts. For the VRS this involves a disregard of regional plans and a threat to inner cities.[5] To manage and mediate the different interests of municipalities – which would like to maximise their tax income and create jobs – and the VRS – which would like to realise regionally integrated planning – the two parties agreed to develop an agenda in which points of overriding importance would be formulated (*Region Stuttgart Aktuell 2/2000 Spielregeln für Einzelhandelsriesen*). This agenda is an example of the advantage gained by including municipalities in planning questions early on. Generally, when guidelines are developed communication, mediation and discussion are high on the agenda for the VRS in order to increase the acceptance of future policy measures.

On the other hand, the VRS has also the power to use negative sanctions. The VRS can formulate a planning rule (*Planungsgebot*) and instruct the municipalities to fix inter-local industrial areas in their urban land-use planning (*Bauleitplanung*). If a municipality ignores the planning rule, the VRS can now sue the municipality. However, the VRS sees this as the last resort which should be avoided by holding discussions between municipalities, administrative districts and the VRS.

Economic development

In the 'law concerning the improvement of cooperation in the Stuttgart region', the task of coordinating regional economic development was fixed as obligatory for the VRS. Until August 1995 – when the economic development agency WRS was founded – central regional actors discussed its organisational structure and future tasks. The agreement included the following areas of responsibility: locational promotion, attraction of investors, management of commercial areas, advice for newly established firms, organisation of foreign trade relations, management of the project 'media region Stuttgart', promotion of innovations, support for environmental technology, computer services, Internet and establishing a regional job training agency. The VRS is still responsible for economic development in order to interlink spatial planning and economic policy. Not only the combining of these two jobs but also the emphasis on supporting existing firms and the attention paid to economic inter-local industrial areas show the innovative character of the VRS and the WRS. Particularly the establishment of a job training agency (Regionale Beschäftigungsagentur, REBAG) as a project of the WRS proves that there are attempts to break down the artificial separation of economic policy and job training (and spatial planning). Also the *Standortdialog Fahrzeugbau* (locational dialogue about the automobile industry) shows the attempt to organise the economic potentials through dialogue and information exchange (Region Stuttgart Aktuell 3/2000 WRS started *Standortdialog Fahrzeugbau*). Behind all the projects of the VRS and WRS are efforts to concentrate central forces and actors in various projects and teams in order to trigger innovation. The aim is for actors to acquire the competence to develop and realise projects and to develop the capacity for cooperation and networking.

Two projects of central interest – 'Stuttgart 21' and the new fair – show the VRS as an autonomous institutional actor (Steinacher, 2000) which applies new governance forms. Together with the federal state Baden-Württemberg and the city of Stuttgart, the VRS is involved in planning the new, EUR 50 million fair. The VRS is in overall charge in mediating between the various parties, particularly the affected municipalities. In the EUR 2.5 billion project to remodel the main railway station ('Stuttgart 21'), the VRS is a partner in the outline plan. The aim is to create vacant land for housing and services in order to establish an attractive European city.

To sum up, the government of Baden-Württemberg established with the VRS an institution whose task is to mobilise the productive potentials of the region by optimising the infrastructural and institutional preconditions and by supporting networks of actors. Far beyond traditional tasks and a sectorally working administration, the aim of the VRS is the integral valorisation (*Inwertsetzung*) of the region in order to gain a favourable position in the competition between regions.

Conclusion: from government to governance

In the Stuttgart metropolitan region, the application of new policy styles indicates a shift away from the central role of official state apparatuses in securing political hegemony and social and economic projects, towards a focus on various forms of partnership between a broad array of actors. This development involves a movement away from imperative coordination imposed from above by the sovereign state and its actors (government, i.e. forms of formal and hierarchical intervention and decision-making) to an emphasis on interdependence and the division of knowledge, on reflexive negotiation and mutual learning (governance). Governance includes an emphasis on promoting and/or steering the self-organisation of inter-organisational relations, and by that it involves a movement away from the taken for granted primacy of state apparatuses towards the need for quite varied forms of partnerships between official, parastatal and non-government organisations in the management of economic, political and social relations (Jessop, 1997).

However, one should not confuse the efforts of the VRS to mediate between different parties and to expand the range of networks and partnerships with a loss of political power: the VRS is still the institution where decision-making takes place, but before decisions are made, a variety of actors are included in the decision process. According to Beate Kohler-Koch, it is necessary that:

> different more or less autonomous actors, which are connected in a complex system of mutual dependencies, are committed towards a jointly decided aim. Governing has to be understood as a process of consent finding with important social actors, as a mutual mobilisation of problem-solving capacity, as an agreement on self-regulation in special fields and as legal standardisation and

financial steering by the government. In that sense, the change in the dimensions and quality of political activities in regional reform projects like the VRS has its basis in a change in the patterns of political activities, which can be characterised as forms of 'cooperative governing'.

(Kohler-Koch, 1998b: p.238)

This process increases the challenges regarding the 'governing' or management of new tasks. The former institutions of the local state and its sectorally working administration as well as its political representatives legitimised by parliament no longer seem to be capable of managing the complex challenges resulting from economic and social restructuring and the pressure towards locational promotion. It is necessary to include more actors and institutions which control important economic, political and social resources in order to make policy work. A plurality of interdependent but autonomous organisations need to coordinate their actions to produce a joint outcome which is deemed mutually beneficial. This includes the need to find and develop new institutional arrangements which make it possible to work together and focus resources and skills. In so far, governing in the Stuttgart metropolitan region goes beyond formal-rational legal sanctions and actions legitimised by parliament, and nowadays includes coordinating a multitude of actors on horizontal levels.

Notes

1 In Germany, administrative counties (*Landkreise*) join together municipalities in order to guarantee the provision of a broad array of public services. The spatial dimension of administrative counties is chosen so that public services are accessible to every citizen within an acceptable time and distance. Municipalities are, besides the level of the federal and the national state, the most important political level in Germany. Municipalities enjoy local autonomy which is guaranteed in the Common Law. This implies the autonomy to engage in economic development and spatial planning, i.e. to plan and develop their own territory. However, the municipalities also have to bear a large part of the costs of social welfare. The most important financial resources are the income and trade tax which are raised locally but divided between the municipalities and the federal and national state.
2 As a result of a reform of the administrative borders at the beginning of the 1970s, the area of the Stuttgart region before and after that time is not exactly congruent. In 1961 the area comprised 4,023 km^2 and had 2,016,800 inhabitants; in 1999, the region comprised only 3,654 km^2 and had 2,594,400 inhabitants.
3 In the following, data about employment refer only to those employees who are included in the national insurance system (*sozialversicherungspflichtige Beschäftigung*). Source of the data is the Department of Statistics of the federal state of Baden-Württemberg.
4 This does not mean that the region is in social and economic respects a coherent region.
5 For the VRS, problems and threats are as follows: loss of attractiveness and service functions in inner cities, deterioration of service supply close to residential areas, increase in car traffic and increase in land consumption.

Susanne Heeg

Bibliography

Batz, U. (1998) 'Zur wirtschaftlichen und beschäftigungspolitischen Lage in der Region Stuttgart', *Strukturbericht 1997/98*, Verband Region Stuttgart, IHK Region Stuttgart, IG Metall Region Stuttgart, Stuttgart/Tübingen.

Dispan, J. (1996) 'Neue Formen der räumlichen Planung in der Region Stuttgart'. Master thesis at the Geographisches Institut der Eberhard-Karls-Universität Tübingen, Tübingen.

Forschungsinstitut der Friedrich-Ebert-Stiftung (1994) *Eine Region im Umbruch. Perspektiven für Beschäftigung, Wachstum und Strukturpolitik im Raum*, Stuttgart Reihe Wirtschaftspolitische Diskurse 62, Bonn.

Hecking, G., Mikulicz, S. and Sättele, A. (1988) *Bevölkerungsentwicklung und Siedlungsflächenexpansion. Entwicklungstrends, Planungsprobleme und Perspektiven am Beispiel der Region Mittlerer Neckar*, Stuttgart.

Heeg, S. (2001) *Politische Regulation des Raums. Metropolen, Regionen, Nationalstaat*, Berlin.

Henke, H.J. (1993) *Aufgabenfelder der Region am Beispiel Stuttgart*, Berlin: Deutsches Institut für Urbanistik.

IHK Region Stuttgart/Verband Region Stuttgart (1998) *Die Region Stuttgart im Standortwettbewerb. Ein Vergleich von Regionen in Deutschland und Europa*, Stuttgart.

Jessop, B. (1997) 'Die Zukunft des Nationalstaates – Erosion oder Reorganisation? Grundsätzliche Überlegungen zu Westeuropa', in S. Becker and T. Sablowski (eds) *Jenseits der Nationalökonomie? Weltwirtschaft und Nationalstaat zwischen Globalisierung und Regionalisierung*, Hamburg.

Kohler-Koch, B. (1998a) 'Europäisierung der Regionen: Institutioneller Wandel als sozialer Prozeß', in Kohler-Koch, B. (ed.) *Interaktive Politik in Europa. Regionen im Netzwerk der Integration*, Opladen.

Kohler-Koch, B. (1998b) 'Leitbilder und Realität der Europäisierung der Regionen', in B. Kohler-Koch (ed.) *Interaktive Politik in Europa. Regionen im Netzwerk der Integration*, Opladen.

Müller, R. (1994) *Die Region Stuttgart: Leistungsfähigkeit und Entwicklungschancen im Vergleich*, Gerlingen.

Oppermann, T. (1992) *Hauptstadt und Region Stuttgart: Wieviel Einheit – wieviel Vielfalt?*, Tübingen.

Spöri, D. (1994) 'Wirtschaftliche Chancen der Region Stuttgart durch die neue Regionalorganisation', *Baden-Württembergische Verwaltungspraxis*, 21 (6): 121–2.

Steinacher, B. (2000) 'Zukunftsperspektiven für die Region Stuttgart', *Standort*, 2: 18–24.

11 Amsterdam and the north wing of the Randstad

Willem Salet

Introduction

Back in the mid-1950s, Peter Hall labelled the west of the Netherlands a 'greenheart metropolis'. The region was then renamed the Randstad in subsequent National Reports on Spatial Planning. Recently, in the Fifth National Report, the Delta metropolis metaphor was introduced to describe the area (Hall, 1984; Dieleman and Musterd, 1992; Faludi and Van der Valk, 1994; Ministry of Housing, Spatial Planning and Environment, 2001). Nonetheless, the west of the Netherlands has yet to become a coherent, urban area. Although the metaphors suggest strong cohesion and metropolitan unity, it is in fact a vast but fragmented green area of wetlands. Inside this area, around the cities of Amsterdam, Rotterdam, The Hague, Utrecht and a few smaller conurbations (such as the Gooi – comprising Hilversum, Naarden and Bussum – the Drecht towns and around several smaller towns) distinct patterns of urbanisation have emerged. The significance of these planning metaphors has been a constant subject of debate (Van Eeten, 1999; Salet and Faludi, 2000; Zonneveld and Hajer, 2000). While ties between the separate urban settlements have intensified in the past two decades, most people continue to commute short distances (45 minutes maximum) to work. This mobility is the most intense within the radius of the urban conurbation (Cortie and Ostendorf, 1986; Bontje, 2001). The job and housing markets of Rotterdam and The Hague are starting to overlap in the south wing of the Randstad. In the north wing functional business networks are emerging between the various metropolitan districts. Leiden, Haarlem, Schiphol (Haarlemmermeer), Amsterdam South, the centre of Amsterdam, Almere, Utrecht and Amersfoort are important nodes in these economic networks in the north wing. Ties between the north and south wings of the Randstad, however, remain very tenuous. Besides the considerable distance between them, the economic structure of the north wing (airport-related services, specialised service sectors, and finance, banking and insurance) differs strongly from that of the south wing (seaport, distribution and transportation industries, government centre The Hague). In this chapter I explore the north wing of the Randstad (especially Amsterdam and Utrecht). In the following chapter, Anton Kreukels examines changes in spatial planning and governance in the south wing (especially in Rotterdam and The Hague).

Trends in urbanisation and spatial configuration

In the past two decades patterns of urbanisation around both Amsterdam and Utrecht have undergone major changes that reflect the transition from a centrally located city as the obvious node for the surrounding conurbation, to a regional metropolis containing various urban centres linked through functional networks.

The transition from the central city to the regional metropolis reflects the growing importance of new, peripherally located nodes with a typically urban concentration of social and economic activity and the fact that the new nodes no longer rely unilaterally on the central city to operate. Fishman has described the

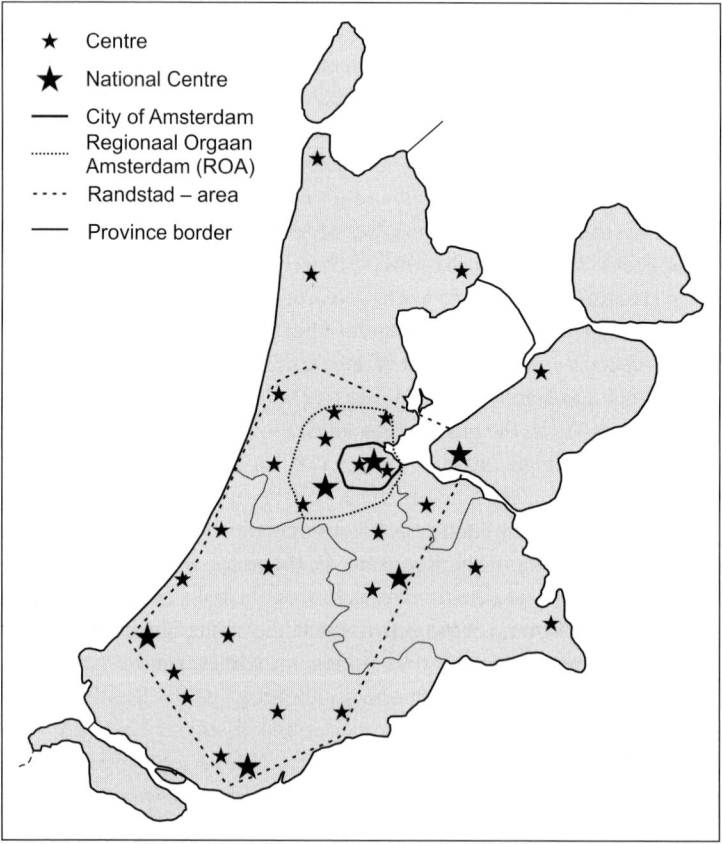

Figure 11.1 The city of Amsterdam and the wider metropolitan region. Compiled by J. Molenaar, 2002

structural aspect of this transition in North American metropolitan areas (Fishman, 1987; Salet, 1996). The new nodes in urban surroundings have experienced such robust growth that they have become nerve centres of urban interaction as well. In this context, the new regional metropolis has yet to establish its boundaries. Urban development is extremely dynamic. Urban activities occur increasingly in separate functional environments that do not coincide with the territorial boundaries of the city and are not symmetric. The regional markets for rental housing are distinct from those for owner-occupied properties in different areas, and thus each forms its own geography (Bertolini, 2000). As will be explained below, the authorities of such 'borderless regions' constantly need to mediate between these levels of scale. First we will take a closer look at the spatial trends in the north wing during the last two decades.

Back in 1980 Amsterdam was the epicentre of urban development. At the time, the inner city (including the nineteenth-century ring) was the most important area of employment in the Netherlands. While industries had moved away, the job supply had grown considerably in financial services, the commercial services sector and the typical urban economy with its cultural attributes (knowledge, culture, tourism, retailing). In 1980 the services sector (financial and business services) shifted only very gradually from the inner city towards the ring road. Amsterdam's central railway station was still the hierarchical node for public transport, and cars continued to enter the city via the narrow radial access roads. Around 1980 substantial investments were made in housing construction in Amsterdam, where the need has always been great. As the population and housing figures may illustrate, Amsterdam managed to stabilise the size of the urban population between 1980 and 2000 by realising a vigorous construction programme. The surrounding urban conurbation (the ROA (Regionaal Orgaan Amsterdam) – Regional Authority of Amsterdam) grew considerably in the same period. For the past 20 years the city has countered the urban exodus by implementing a vibrant urban construction programme. Moreover, the urban renovation policy demands additional housing. Outside the city much of the new construction is concentrated in the 'new town' of Almere, which has expanded into a city of 150,000 and will have 300,000 residents by 2025. The disadvantage of the substantial construction work in Amsterdam is that the migrations of households and businesses have been selective: in the 1970s and 1980s most of the construction in Amsterdam consisted of rental housing, while in the surrounding areas (e.g. in Almere) most properties were owner-occupied. Middle-class households (defined in terms of income and family composition) continued to leave the inner city, as did many firms: those that were expanding fled the urban congestion and settled on the periphery. In the early 1980s this growth started along Schiphol's access roads and truly got under way in the 1990s.

By around 1980, the 'daily urban system Amsterdam' seemed to have stabilised. Immediately afterwards, however, the international economy suddenly deteriorated.

Willem Salet

Table 11.1 Data of Amsterdam versus city-region ROA

11.1a Population of Amsterdam and of the city-region ROA (excluding Amsterdam)

Population (× 1000)	1980	1990	2000
Amsterdam	717	695	731
ROA	433*	580	717

*Excluding population of Almere and Zeevang.

11.1b Number of dwellings in Amsterdam and in the city-region ROA (excluding Amsterdam)

Dwellings (×1000)	1980	1990	2000
Amsterdam	302	337	369
ROA	141*	220	293

*Excluding population of Almere and Zeevang.

11.1c Rental and private houses on the housing market in Amsterdam and in the city-region ROA (excluding Amsterdam)

Rental/private (% of total housing stock)	1990	2000
Amsterdam	92/8	86/14
ROA	–	58/42

11.1d Registered unemployment in Amsterdam and in the city-region ROA (excluding Amsterdam)

Unemployment	1980	1990	2000
Amsterdam	20,870	65,309	23,100
ROA	–	–	10,500

Sources: Jaarboek 1980 (1980) dienst Bestuursinformatie, afdeling statistiek, Amsterdam. Amsterdam in Cijfers, jaarboek O+S 1990 (1990) Deel 1 Stad en regio, Het Amsterdams Bureau voor Onderzoek en Statistiek, Amsterdam. Amsterdam in Cijfers, jaarboek O+S 2000 (2000), Het Amsterdams Bureau voor Onderzoek en Statistiek, Amsterdam.

The Dutch government had to cut spending on facilities, including education, infrastructure and low-income rental housing. Unemployment skyrocketed (more than tripling in the first half of the 1980s), and programmes for creating jobs topped the political agenda. Around this time the selective composition of the urban population began to cause problems, as the economic recession was worst in the cities. In the new economic growth sectors at the edge of the city, demand for skilled labour persisted, but in the cities jobs were unavailable for the poorly skilled masses. The problem was described as the city's dual economy. Cities and their surroundings appeared to be adopting contradictory positions (Netherlands Scientific Council for Government Policy, 1992). Central cities and their surroundings appeared to differ substantially in social and economic respects as well. The selective migrations to and from the city had brought about huge differences between the city and the surrounding areas in all fields – from education to healthcare, and from the housing market to the job market. As I will explain below, this asymmetric pattern has deeply influenced the effort to reform metropolitan governance, which at last got under way around 1990.

By 1990 the international economy had recovered. Economic internationalisation and the growing importance of the knowledge infrastructure boosted the 'new' economy. After a decade of austerity, the Netherlands returned to the international arena in the new period of economic growth. Amsterdam and the surrounding areas had recovered, and the concentration of problems in the cities began to diminish thanks to the economic prosperity. The outside of the city continued to grow as well. Amsterdam is fortunate that the urban ring road lies within the city limits. This situation has enabled part of the economic boom along the urban periphery to take place inside urban territory, although the outward drive remains strong. The failure of the effort to establish a central business district in the city on the shores of the river IJ (the biggest river in Amsterdam) doomed the corporate economy of the inner city and augured the complete transition to a cultural economy in that historical part of the city. Amsterdam's central railway station lost its hierarchical supremacy, and the banks and leading offices for business services moved away in the 1990s. Firms flocked to Amsterdam's ring road, while new employment concentrations emerged also outside Amsterdam. Traffic congestion moved from the inner city to the surrounding areas, and Schiphol became the region's largest mega-hub and a primary stop for international trains, with connections to all national and regional railway lines. Both in industry and as a transport node, Schiphol has ascended to the top of the economic hierarchy. Amsterdam South (the renowned South Axis growth zone) now ranks second and aspires to become the second mega-hub for public and road transport. The centre of Amsterdam remains very desirable for housing and the cultural economy but has ceased to be the region's economic and infrastructure node that it was throughout the century. Various regionally significant subsidiary centres have emerged in the area around Amsterdam. Central Utrecht remains an important node for both economic affairs and transport. However, economic subsidiary centres continue to grow at the edge of this city, while the expansion of the centre of Utrecht has elicited serious resistance. In the future, Utrecht will probably experience the same outward drive that is already under way in Amsterdam.

Willem Salet

Changes in the structure of government

The Dutch administration is constituted as a 'decentralised unitary state'. This principle means that the central state in some respects relies on the relatively autonomous responsibilities of the provinces and – in particular – of the municipalities. In the Dutch constitution, all (i.e. about 600) municipalities are the same: there is no differentiation between urban and rural municipalities. The same applies to the 12 provinces. The structure of the constitution dates back to before the nineteenth century. Thus the position of provinces and municipalities is strongly institutionalised. Attempts to change the system – in particular in urbanised parts of the country – have been made since the early 1910s, but none has been successful (Netherlands Scientific Council for Government Policy, 1992).

During the last two decades, there were two main considerations behind the attempts to change the traditional structure of government in the urban conurbations. First, the core cities were in trouble, while their immediate surroundings were thriving. In the 1980s the urban situation became increasingly grim. In the Netherlands the international economic recession hit the cities especially hard because of the uneven composition of the population. Many people in the cities had been out of work for a long time, and many incoming migrants were poorly educated and not qualified for the jobs in the new economy. The need for austerity had begun to force the state to reduce support for the social provisions to which the cities (more than other municipalities) had grown accustomed in the welfare state. The resulting need to mitigate the discrepancies within the region led the cities to favour administrative reform. The growing importance of internationalisation was the second reason for the attempts to reorganise the regional administration. The cities realised that internationalisation of the economy and the government structure would increase interregional competition in Europe (Commissie Grote Steden/Montijn, 1989). Close collaboration within the region was necessary to ensure an edge in the external competition. Regional partnerships were the key here.

These dynamics led to the elaboration of a powerful strategy for combining spatial planning and government structure during the 1980s. This two-pronged strategy consisted of a successful cooperation between the four major cities and the state (the ministries of Spatial Planning and the Interior). The spatial planning strategy was to maintain a compact urban conurbation. This policy was designed to stop the forces of the city from draining away by encouraging them to remain within the metropolitan district. The idea was to situate both housing construction and industries within the city and along the edge. The outlying areas were cordoned off with 'green buffers', and urban expansion was prohibited beyond these limits. Major urban development projects appeared on the agenda at the same time, such as the IJ river project in Amsterdam and a mega-project for the centre of Utrecht. While not all these ambitions were achieved, they provided a sound foundation for spatial planning. The effort to introduce city provinces was the administrative counterpart to this programme. After all, the compact urban conurbation required an administrative framework (larger than the existing municipalities and smaller than the provinces) with the power to implement strategic decisions.

The planned change of the government structure was to serve a twofold mission: to reduce the differences between rich and poor in the region, and to give the region the strength to prevail in the domestic and international interregional competition. The first motive (equalisation) was obviously difficult to reconcile with the second motive (collaboration) – and this is the main reason why the reform failed. The model for government reform was a unique design that was to be introduced in seven urban regions in the Netherlands (in our case, in Amsterdam and Utrecht). It deviated considerably from the administrative relationships elsewhere in the Netherlands. The idea was for the desired city province to take over the provincial areas of authority (thus depriving the remaining provinces of North Holland and Utrecht of their urban heart). The new city province would also assume the strategic areas of authority of the municipalities within its limits (thereby relegating these municipalities to second-class status). The municipalities would continue to exist but would have less authority. The course for implementing the government reform – which had never succeeded in the past – was designed with great circumspection and flexibility: the minister did not have a blueprint detailing the desired ultimate situation. She allowed the municipalities to negotiate the specific details of their city province. The state rewarded successful reform with substantial grants.

However, the effort to reorganise the government failed. Too many compromises were required. The central cities wanted a powerful city province in order to realise regional equalisation and solid regional development programmes. Amsterdam anticipated this objective by dividing the city into 16 neighbourhoods, with the expectation that the city province would become inevitable as a result. The surrounding municipalities, however, were willing to work together but not to be equalised. They also feared the development policy of strong city provinces (where urban interests would prevail). The municipality of Almere (which is located between Amsterdam and Utrecht) dropped out of the negotiations before the final agreement was reached. The compromise that resulted from these tedious negotiations was rife with inconsistencies, was subject to many protests and had a deplorable lack of support. When the outcome was submitted for approval to the population of Amsterdam in a referendum in 1994, it was rejected without even a serious attempt to defend it.

Despite its failure, government reform left behind a trail of complexities, especially in Amsterdam: the central city administration had been partly devolved into 16 neighbourhoods each with an elected government (recently, the number of neighbourhoods was increased to 17). The neighbourhoods, in turn, cannot vie with other municipalities. They do not levy taxes and depend on transfers from the central city; the central city is also entitled to withdraw strategic projects from the neighbourhoods; finally, the neighbourhoods do not have the discretionary authority to collaborate with other municipalities. As for the urban conurbation, the city province was never established, but a partnership arrangement was established and still exists: the Regional Authority of Amsterdam (ROA). This association continues to manage some state subsidies but has little policy jurisdiction in other respects and lacks the population's support. The failure to reorganise the government has thus complexified the already complex situation.

Meanwhile, spatial planning has continued at the upper echelons (above the level of the urban conurbation) and has led to a search for new government strategies. During the booming 1990s, spatial trends expanded beyond the confines of the compact urban conurbation. Politicians did their best but were unable to keep up with the reality. The efforts to halt the outward urban expansion clashed with all social forces. The rising standard of living made the increased use of space by people and businesses impossible to restrain. Hoping to recapture the initiative, the province of North Holland is currently preparing a new strategic spatial plan for the whole region in close collaboration with the preparation of the new structure plan of Amsterdam. Simultaneously, the four major cities (Amsterdam, Rotterdam, The Hague, Utrecht) joined forces to create a new strategy for the western part of the country. They formed a coalition with surrounding municipalities, the provinces and the national state – this time with the ministries of Spatial Planning and of Transport, Public Works and Water Management. The new spatial planning theme was a design for urban networks, which applies throughout the Randstad (now the Delta metropolis). On the Delta metropolis agenda will be new ecological guidelines (water storage in the green buffer to ensure a stronger barrier against urban expansion, integral extension of the coast and strengthening of the ecological green structure), new infrastructure policy (a separate public transport link between the four big cities, known as the 'Randstad circuit') and new development projects.

The urban lobby appears to be headed for success once again. While the major projects on the wish list have yet to be approved by the state, the minister has adopted the urban networks concept in the first section of the fifth report on national spatial planning (2001). This report has also cautiously introduced a new category of government networks. The underlying idea is for municipal and provincial authorities throughout the Randstad to establish joint administrative coordination of all strategic spatial policy issues. The area of operations concerns four provinces and dozens of municipalities. The new strategy therefore appears unlikely to resolve the serious issue of administrative complexity. At the moment, 'governing in networks' appears to be even more complicated.

Strategic policies: 'dancing on the volcano of spatial scale'

In the sections above I have explained that trends in spatial use have become harder for the authorities to control, because this practice involves individual, capricious networks and is becoming ever less likely to coincide with the territorial borders of the public government. Many of the typical urban activities have left the cities. Outside the cities such activities acquire an autonomy that makes their changes progressively less attributable to the course of events within. The new metropolitan region that is emerging has abundant functional network relations, but the borders of the new metropolis remain undefined. They shift continuously, along with the whims that affect the functional networks of labour markets, housing markets and various markets of industry. At the metropolitan level, new asymmetric processes of spatial selection have necessitated coordinated administration. These processes include the disproportionate part of low-income rental housing markets within the city limits and the equally unilateral growth of owner-occupied homes outside; the emergence of new urban centres at intersections of motorways that are poorly accessible by public transport; competition between municipalities which may cause fragmentation of sites of economic activity; disintegration of green structures which eliminates opportunities for leisure and enjoyment of nature. Many metropolitan issues desperately need government coordination, but no administrative solution is available.

The north wing of the Randstad abounds with new government networks. In addition to official government institutions (municipalities, provinces and – of course – the urban and regional policy departments of the domestic and European policy institutions), many unofficial partnerships have arisen at intermediate levels. We have reviewed the neighbourhoods within Amsterdam (with an elected government but without officially independent municipalities) as well as the district partnerships between municipalities in the ROA that originally were intended as the new city province. There is also a very informal but influential consultative association of municipalities in the north wing of the Randstad (mediated by the province of North Holland). For the Randstad as a whole, a strong new lobby association has emerged to represent the major cities and the other municipalities in the area (the Delta metropolis). Its influence on national policy is considerable. In addition to these territorial structures, there are powerful functional associations, such as the parties on the labour market, the housing market and the transport markets. These functional associations often transect the territorial demarcations. Finally, major private and semi-private organisations are operating in the region, including NV Schiphol, large financiers and project developers (e.g. ING Real Estate and ABN-AMRO Bank), and auctioneers. This arena accommodates a broad variety of players.

Many public–public coalitions have emerged. The authorities wear many hats, with the city of Amsterdam participating in all sorts of coalition. The neighbourhoods, the municipality, the district and the north wing fit together like the trunk, branches and twigs of a tree, if the harmonious indications in the memoranda are to be believed. In reality, however, the various coalitions compete with and displace each other. Large public transport projects, for example, cannot be carried out for the Randstad, the north wing of the Randstad, the ROA region or the city at the same time. Priorities need to be set (Bertolini *et al.*, 2001). The competition for new regional nodes and corresponding locations of offices is particularly intense.

The incipient shifts in the balance of power are particularly fascinating in the north wing. Until recently, Amsterdam was the undisputed champion of the entire north wing. Amsterdam set policy within its metropolitan region (the strategic spatial perspectives for the inter-municipal ROA association were drafted at the city hall in Amsterdam) and diverted the influence of the provincial authorities from the urban area to North Holland's remaining agricultural regions. And Amsterdam had direct access to several state ministries. Not surprisingly, the above two-pronged strategy of the compact urban conurbation and the city province was developed in the early 1990s by the major cities and implemented in consultation with the state. The provinces lost out, as did the smaller municipalities adjacent to the big cities.

The intended regional development was closely centred on the cities. The failure of this two-pronged strategy – which was conceived in the 1970s but introduced only in the early 1990s – illustrates its obsolescence. It might have worked in the 1970s, but now too many urban nodes have formed outside the city limits to implement the city-centred strategies successfully in the north wing. The suburbs are becoming 'emancipated'. Almere has withdrawn from the inter-municipal regional association ROA. Since Almere can expand either towards Amsterdam or towards Utrecht, the town has started flirting with both. Haarlemmermeer (Schiphol) is growing more dynamically than anywhere else in the north wing and is willing to enter into partnerships but not to be subordinated. Expansion is taking place in all directions at and around Schiphol, sometimes irrespective of the course of the public coalitions. The edges around Utrecht are starting to go through the same process. Another fascinating turn of events in the public coalitions is the return of the province of North Holland to the urban development scene in search of opportunities for effective regional networks between old and new urban nodes instead of concentric expansions of the major cities, which were so dominant until recently. Finally, unlike the metropolitan trends in some other European countries, EU considerations hardly figure in the regional public coalitions in the north wing of the Randstad. The state government is more concerned with Europe than any of the other authorities.

As for the influence of the private institutions in policy coalitions, Schiphol is deeply involved in improving accessibility, transportation and the flow of traffic. At the airport new industries and retail outlets are popping out of the ground like mushrooms, thereby thwarting the accessibility objective. The major project developers are remarkably active as well. Recently a consortium of banks told the state that it would guarantee tens of billions of euros of investment in Amsterdam's South Axis for 30 years, if the Ministry of Transportation, Public Works and Water Management provided one billion euros for infrastructure there. In the Dutch situation, such investments amount to a mega-project. Nonetheless, these same banks have already staked out land at sites outside Amsterdam. The large financiers have adopted this ambiguous position because on the one hand they have many interests in the current urban environment that require constant infusions of investment, while on the other hand the new nodes outside the urban environment abound with development opportunities. Basically, the major financiers have not yet played out their hand.

Conclusion: dilemmas of spatial and institutional coordination

How should the authorities respond to the increasing fragmentation, displacement and uncoordinated decision-making by public and private parties in the new metropolis? Theoretically, several options are available to provide the coordination needed, and they merit exploration from different perspectives. First, strategic options should be arranged along a continuum from 'unitary' to 'dual' structures of metropolitan government, ranging from hierarchical to collaborational methods of metropolitan coordination. Second, 'integration-oriented' types of organisations should be distinguished from 'functional' (sector-specific) ones. And third, whether metropolitan coordination or collective regional action should be arranged by private organisation (social integration or market integration) (Ostrom, 1990; Putnam *et al*., 1992). This last form may occur with organised citizenship, as well as with an active orientation of parties in the economic market, as in the above example of the consortium of financiers. Often these will be *ad hoc* methods of project organisation.

The dilemmas will be discussed very briefly here. Although the issue of fragmentation is the stumbling block in all debates on administrative reform in Dutch urban regions, the option of unitary metropolitan government has not seriously been raised. It most probably would not prove to be effective. After all, the administration would become even more detached from a highly dynamic urban reality. Further, mismatches with all kinds of location-based policy allocation would become very likely. Also internationally, this method is rarely fully applied in practice. There are, however, types of unitary government in which only strategic decisions are made at the central metropolitan level; other policy is relegated to lower echelons. This method reflects a plan for a general framework and is essentially a mitigated top-down model. It is often tried in practice. One of the crucial political problems is that urban government is then directed by higher metropolitan authorities, which causes much policy friction within government circles. In the

Willem Salet

Netherlands, major cities are not in favour of controlling provinces. However, their own attempts to build strategic metropolitan guidance (via 'urban provinces') failed. The opposite option does not claim hierarchical coordination but relies on collaboration. The 'partnerships between different municipalities' option presumes a willingness to work together. The advantage of this option is that it generates a wealth of solutions, although Nimby-type issues may cause a deadlock because of the disproportionate distribution of costs and benefits. Cooperative models may nonetheless be complemented in such issues by entrusting these areas of authority to a higher administration. This combination is commonplace. The option of inter-municipal cooperation fits very well with an 'intermediate' rather than a 'hierar-chical' position for the provincial meso-government.

The above organisational options may be focused on integration or arranged by functional lines (by sectors). Unitary forms of functional organisation are very common, especially when the organisation of a certain service or task needs to be withheld from competing parties in order to operate effectively (for instance, functional organisations created to arrange regional public transport). These functional organisations may also be constituted on partnership arrangements.

Finally, regional project organisation and private associations exist in many different forms and often support the options described above. A regional board that is not covered by a density of social organisations and private projects usually lacks the 'institutional thickness' to be truly effective (Putnam *et al.*, 1992). In a period of oscillating levels of spatial scale the absence of such a support base is often a problem.

Rethinking metropolitan governance for Amsterdam and the north wing of the Randstad, I believe the following suggestions might be useful:

- Distinguish the structural pattern of universal layers of government (i.e. the provinces and the municipalities) from the need for flexible, *ad hoc* associa-tions. While both are necessary, do not try to have the structural institution match the dynamics of spatial trends. Specifically: no elected governments in the neighbourhoods that are actually pseudo-municipalities, no pseudo-city provinces but real municipalities and provinces that function as territorial government bodies through universal areas of authority. Develop a series of flexible administrative responses constituted by these structural tiers of governance (flexible in terms of scale and duration, as well as sphere of operation; for example, focused on cooperation between municipalities or on timely functional organisation).
- Recognise the institutional significance of the provinces as 'intermediate' and the municipalities as 'developmental' government. The institutional role of the provinces in the Dutch system is to link higher and lower tiers of govern-ment (in both directions) by developing strategic perspectives, and to coordinate the fragmented decision-making at local levels. Development policy is primarily a community affair and occurs in conjunction with private sector

initiatives. The province should figure here only very selectively, in special projects. The role of intermediate government is to solve local stalemates, to stimulate and to act as catalyst. Further, also some distributive policies and Nimby-type policy considerations are primarily the concern of higher authorities (i.e. at provincial or state levels).

- Do not use the central city as the centric axis for organising inter-municipal governance. Acknowledge the emergence of new regional nodes and strengthen their position in terms of governmental competencies (for instance by merging suburban municipalities) to create a fruitful basis for cooperation with the cities.

- Social support is indispensable for all aspects of governance. This support used to exist at the urban level but has eroded without the emergence of new social associations at metropolitan levels. Investments in new metropolitan identity are an important cultural mission.

Bibliography

Bertolini, L. (2000) 'The borderless city', *Town Planning Review*, 71 (4): 455–75.

Bertolini, L., Salet, W.G.M. and Milikowski, F. (2001) *Stedelijkheid in het Structuurplan van Amsterdam*, Amsterdam: Amsterdam Studycentre for the Metropolitan Environment.

Bontje, M. (2001), 'Dealing with deconcentration: population deconcentration and planning response in poly-nucleated regions in north-west Europe', *Urban Studies* 38 (4): 769–87.

Commissie Grote Steden (Committee Montijn) (1989) *Grote Steden, Grote Kansen*, The Hague: Ministerie van Binnenlandse Zaken.

Cortie, C. and Ostendorf, W. (1986) 'Suburbanisatie and Gentrification: sociaal-ruimtelijke dynamiek in de Randstad na 1970', *Geografisch Tijdschrift* 20: 64–83.

Dieleman, F.M. and Musterd, S. (ed.) (1992) *The Randstad: A Research and Policy Laboratory*, Dordrecht: Kluwer.

Eeten, M. van (1999) *Dialogues of the Deaf*, Delft: Eburon.

Faludi, A. and Valk, A.J. van der (1994) *Rule and Order: Dutch Planning Doctrine in the Twentieth Century*, Dordrecht/London: Kluwer.

Fishman, R. (1987) *Bourgeois Utopias: The Rise and Fall of Suburbia*, New York: Basic Books.

Hall, P. (1984) *The World Cities*, third edition, London: Weidenfeld and Nicholson.

Kreukels, A. and Salet, W.G.M. (eds) (1992) *Debating Institutions and Cities*, WRR V 76, The Hague: Sdu Uitgevers.

Ministry of Housing, Spatial Planning and Environment (VROM) (2001) *Ruimte Maken, Ruimte Delen: Vijfde Nota over de Ruimtelijke Ordening 2000/2020* (Fifth Report on Spatial Planning), The Hague: Ministry of Housing, Spatial Planning and Environment.

Netherlands Scientific Council for Government Policy (1992) *Institutions and Cities*, The Hague: Sdu Uitgevers.

Ostrom, E. (1990) *Governing the Commons*, Cambridge: Cambridge University Press.

Putnam, R.D., Leonardi, R. and Nannetti, R.Y. (1992) *Making Democracy Work: Civic Traditions in Modern Italy*, Princeton, NJ: Princeton University Press.

Salet, W.G.M. (1996) *De Conditie van Stedelijkheid*, The Hague: VUGA.

Salet, W.G.M. and Faludi, A. (eds) (2000) *The Revival of Strategic Spatial Planning*, Amsterdam: KNAW Edita.

Zonneveld, W. and Hajer, M. (2000) 'Spatial planning in the network society: rethinking the principles of planning in the Netherlands', *European Planning Studies*, 8 (3): 337–55.

12 Rotterdam and the south wing of the Randstad

Anton Kreukels

Introduction

Rotterdam is the second main city of the Netherlands and part of the country's western conurbation: the Randstad ('Rand' = edge; 'stad' = city). Together with The Hague it forms the urban backbone of the south wing of the Randstad (see figure 12.1 and also the map in chapter 11).

The Randstad is famous in international circles of planners and urban analysts for two reasons (Kreukels, 1992). The first is its particular urban morphology, which is expressed in its name: 'the Randstad' refers to the grouping of the four main cities in the form of a horseshoe at the edge of the western urbanised part of the Netherlands. It stretches from the city of Rotterdam and its seaport (the main one in Western Europe) in the south, to The Hague (home to both the Dutch parliament and the queen) in the west, to Amsterdam (the capital of the country and the site of its international airport) in the north, and to Utrecht (the country's railway node and central city) in the east. Between this band of cities is an open green area: the 'Greenheart' (Burke, 1966). This poly-nuclear urban morphology is famous because its functional differentiations are considered in professional circles an advantageous characteristic from the perspective of continuing growth and dynamic development, especially compared with such vast monocentric centres as London and Paris (Hall, 1977). This is even more important now that managed growth is imperative in a lot of condensed and overloaded urban regions of developed countries.

A second reason why the Randstad is attracting attention is that this particular example of an urbanised region is seen, rightly or wrongly, as the result of a powerful planning regime. Especially the well-organised, coordinated and formalised spatial planning in the Netherlands from the national level down to the subnational government layers of provinces and municipalities is seen as exceptional, even within continental Western Europe with its pronounced nation-states. This planning system got its profile especially after the Second World War and had its heyday from the late 1960s to the 1990s. It can be characterised as central control and a top-down regime. Whereas one can have doubts about its positive functions

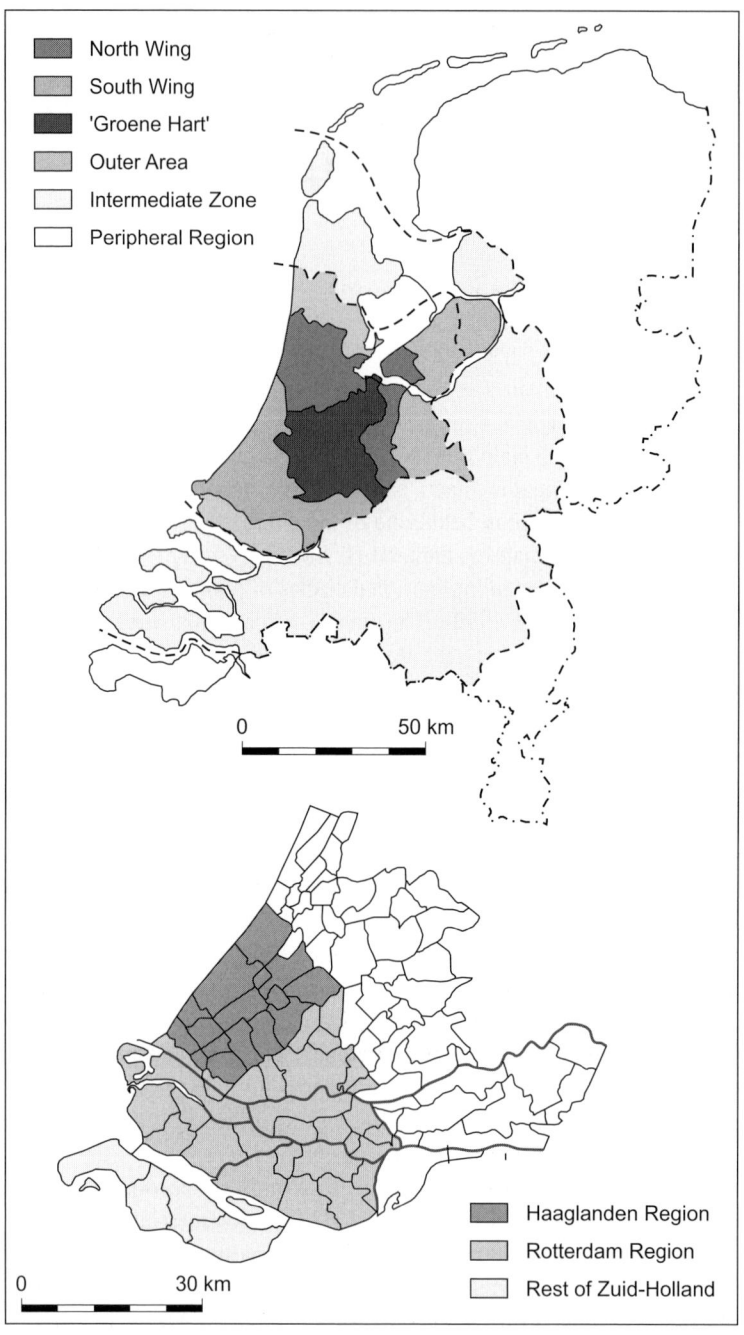

Figure 12.1 The Randstad and the south wing

in the period of the profiled welfare state (1960–80/5), this hierarchical, top-down administration is seen as a more serious obstacle now that a flexible and at the same time effective and tailor-made land-use plan is required, given the outspoken complexities and high dynamics of advanced societies (Netherlands Scientific Council for Government Policy, 1998).

In contrast to the first characteristic of a poly-nuclear structure, this second characteristic of the Randstad – the planning system, headed by the national government (Faludi and van der Valk, 1994) – is no longer seen as exemplary in our time with its high degree of required adaptation and variation. One can even ask whether the Randstad and the Netherlands have been considered rightly as an advanced planning regime in the recent past (Van Gunsteren, 1976), and even whether it is correct to interpret the particular forms of urbanisation such as those of the Randstad as the result of that regime, rather than relating them to the particular historical and cultural traits of the Netherlands since its distant past, that is, the Republic of the Netherlands of the sixteenth and seventeenth centuries as a loose federation of quite autonomous regions and sub-national units. All this results in doubts about the common connotation in planning circles of the Randstad and the Netherlands as a 'planning paradise'. Again, where these doubts apply to the past, they apply even more so to the present and the future.

Trends in urbanisation and spatial configuration

Until the late 1960s, Dutch cities – and especially the four main ones (Amsterdam, Rotterdam, Utrecht, The Hague) – offered citizens and companies a high chance of a higher income, higher employment, higher profits and better living conditions. This applied to the Netherlands as well as to north-west Europe in general: until the end of the 1960s, the best location to live was within a main city.

This privileged position of the main cities – not only those in the Netherlands but also those all over Europe – changed at the end of the 1960s when pronounced suburbanisation started to become more and more manifest. The population of the cities shrank and urban centres lost many functions to their suburban areas and to other lower ranking cities. The cities gradually became weaker in the 1970s and 1980s in terms of income, employment and as centres for profit-making, and became sites of unemployment and of people dependent on social assistance and social security. From the 1970s onwards, the best place in terms of income, employment and profits was the suburbs and medium-sized cities, which soon became robust and strong, compared with the four main cities which had become vulnerable in terms of their general functioning.

In the late 1980s, a new shift began: the four main cities gradually started to become stronger again. The profile of these cities in terms of huge unemployment and lower income changed positively. Especially Amsterdam was successful in attracting higher-income people and businesses, and thus in offering ample employment, especially higher ranking jobs. Rotterdam lagged behind in this reprofiling and restrengthening; it continued to be a city with a high degree of unemployment and an under-representation of higher income, and the economy did not regain its momentum outside the port sector. The Hague took a middle position between Amsterdam and Utrecht on the one hand and Rotterdam on the other.

However, whereas in general the main cities in the Randstad and in the Netherlands regained some of the strength they had enjoyed in the 1950s and 1960s, the situation was very different from what it was at that time. Whereas cities all over Western Europe were again strong sites in the last decades of the twentieth century, it was – in contrast to the previous periods – not as outstanding cores but as part of an extended urban region. From the 1970s onwards, the Randstad and its south wing followed, along with other Western European countries, the trend of the continuing suburbanisation of people and functions and the dispersion and diffusion of urbanisation over wider areas, a phenomenon characteristic of the USA in the 1950s and 1960s. The new urban pattern is one of a nation-state as one urban field, in which main and central cities are increasingly confronted with functionally strong, rich suburban centres. Suburban areas now have their own position and share in the urbanised reality of today. This applies to homes and businesses, as well as to institutions (Netherlands Scientific Council for Government Policy, 1992).

Changes in spatial policies, urban policies and government intervention

Central to the success of Rotterdam as the main node in the south wing of the Randstad are the concentrated and combined efforts of the main seaport and the city, being a strong coalition and experiencing the support of the national government and investing structurally over a long period in port infrastructure and port-related trade and industry. Especially investments intended to ensure Rotterdam's lasting, optimal access to the sea and to optimise the specific qualities of the Rotterdam port (e.g. oil distribution in Europe and the chemical sector related to the refineries). A strong coalition between the municipal port authority and the city administration in close connection with the 'harbour barons' (the group of the strongest entrepreneurs in the port of Rotterdam) was the motor behind the expansion of Rotterdam, first as the main port for Western Europe (Europort) and subsequently as an outstanding world port from the late 1950s onwards. During the 1960s, this symbiosis of city and main seaport was expressed and symbolised by the two-man coalition comprising the socialist mayor of Rotterdam – W. Thomassen – and the dynamic chairman of the Municipal Port Authority – F. Posthuma.

In the 1950s and 1960s, the planning mode in the Netherlands was the same as it was in the USA and other European countries: so-called blueprint planning. (It should be noted, however, that there was often a pronounced difference between countries with regard to the exact period/time of such planning.) In that period, planners, architects and urban designers made grand designs and the way of intervention was often one of clearing and bulldozing whole built-up areas, or taking over greenfield sites in favour of these blueprints. The climax of this blueprint planning in the Rotterdam area was Plan 2000+ (published in 1969). This expansion scheme for the rapidly growing seaport and city of Rotterdam within the south wing of the Randstad covered the whole south-western part of the Netherlands: the Delta region, as the wider region with the required capacity for new port-related infrastructure, new general infrastructure (e.g. an airport and new railway lines) and – last but not least – new residential areas.

The approach at the time was very top-down and professional planners were seen as being essential for the strategy. In Western Europe, this period came to an end in the late 1960s/early 1970s when a new generation of youngsters rebelled against the establishment (student revolts in Paris, Berlin, Amsterdam, Berkeley, Tokyo). Urban planning was one of the topics of the revolt. Especially the Faculty of Architecture of the Free University of Berlin promoted an alternative mode of urban design and planning. In the southern wing of the Randstad (and especially in the Rotterdam region, because of the planned development of the port of Rotterdam), this blue print planning mode came under attack in the revolt and subsequently Plan 2000+ – a symbol of the technocratic planning of the 1950s and 1960s – was rejected. Instead of an ongoing focus on technology and economy as in the Plan 2000+, the focus shifted to a more human spatial planning, considered as essential in an increasingly congested and polluted Rotterdam region, aiming at the same time at a better and more healthy living and working situation, especially for people who needed it the most.

With all this, spatial and urban planning in the early 1970s entered the second phase, one of a 'process mode of planning', meaning that planning proceeded gradually instead of being targeted at a distant time by means of a blueprint. In this way the process mode of planning can be seen as a combination of a higher professional level of planning and of more human planning (citizen-related planning by way of citizen participation). Rotterdam became one of the most pronounced testing grounds for this planning in the Netherlands, expressing itself in a remarkable urban renewal programme for residential areas in and around the inner city. The planning for the downtown area in that period even stopped the planning of central functions and offices for the inner city, setting it aside for living, culture and entertainment. This was all part of the Dutch welfare state in its heyday (1970s/early 1980s), mirrored in a strong coalition between government and social issue organisations. Here, the public sector became, as elsewhere in Western Europe, a powerful redistribution mechanism, supporting especially people and institutions which could not help themselves, especially with regard to what were considered basic human needs.

Even though the feelings, culture and mentality of the people and authorities in the city-region of Rotterdam remained focused on the port and port economy, the symbiosis between port and city that had existed from the early twentieth century to the late 1960s disappeared. The emphasis on the welfare state resulted in the neglect of the interests of the port and of the port economy. The lively formal and informal contacts between and the coalition of the economic sector, business circles, the financial sector, the port and the city administration became a thing of the past and have still not been restored (De Klerk, 1998). From the 1970s onwards the municipal administration and the municipal port authority started to function at more of a distance from each other. Also, in the 1970s Rotterdam lost – in an increasingly competitive international market for ship construction – not only its pronounced share in this market, but even ship construction at all. With this loss of ship construction (characterised by labour intensive employment) employment in Rotterdam as a whole was reduced significantly. Rotterdam has still not been able to compensate for the high degree of unemployment. Since losing its ship construction, Rotterdam has experienced the problems related to high unemployment, concentrated in inner city areas, which increasingly also became concentrations of ethnic minorities, and with this concentrations of social, economic and physical downgrading. The main urban centres of the south wing (Rotterdam and The Hague) contrasted more and more with their urban renewal and public housing regimes with the surrounding suburban areas, which became the locations of middle- and upper-class people within their own houses, besides remaining the sites of people and businesses already located there. From the second half of the 1970s onwards, businesses and facilities gradually started to leave Rotterdam (and The Hague) for the surrounding suburban areas. Besides lack of land for expansion, the absence of supporting facilities as well as traffic and parking problems played a part in this, as did the culture of indifference in that period with regard to the economy within the city politics of Rotterdam and The Hague.

Notwithstanding this contrast between Rotterdam and The Hague and their surrounding municipalities, from the 1980s onwards these urban centres became increasingly part of their wider urban region: the Rijnmond or Rotterdam region in the case of Rotterdam, and the Haaglanden region in the case of The Hague. With regard especially to housing, work and facilities, the broader region became more and more interrelated and complementary (De Klerk, 1990), even though the functional interrelations within the broader Rotterdam/Rijnmond region have remained weak and no real urban region has yet developed in the south wing of the Randstad (Jacobs, 2000).

The third, and current, phase began in the 1980s. This phase is a reaction in most European countries to the welfare state regimes that became dominant in the 1970s. It is also related to the economic recession and the oil crises of the 1970s. There was an inclination to reduce and even to withdraw from the overwhelming profile of the welfare state. This occurred everywhere in the Western world at that time. Thatcher in the UK and Reagan in the USA were the symbols of this transition, favouring the market and relating the administration more to the market. Thus in the 1980s there was a transition in spatial planning to the system of 'strategic' planning, still in a limited sense, because the continuing central rule regime of the government did not yet permit enough freedom for planning by negotiation and for planning linked to the world outside the government, especially to the profit and non-profit private sector.

The international and national economic recession of the period 1975–84 had a serious impact on the main Dutch urban centres. The statistics of transhipment in that period illustrate the decrease of the functioning of the Rotterdam port, even though it maintained its position as number one in Europe. This formed the drive behind the restoration of strategic thinking and acting in the port of Rotterdam (since 1984/6) for the first time since the boom period of the 1950s and 1960s with the expansion of the port at that time towards the sea with the port areas of Botlek, Europort and the Maasvlakte. In particular the strategic agreement in the 1980s between unions and employers with regard to the port economy, guaranteeing a calm workforce, must be mentioned here. Also the goodwill of the Rotterdam port and port economy in circles of the national government made it possible to take a number of necessary measures and to safeguard the smooth functioning of this world port. The most important factor here seems to be the continuing solid association of the harbour barons and captains of the port with each other and with the strong municipal port authority. This Rotterdam port establishment did not erode in the 1970s and kept functioning as the motor behind the new strategic investment plans for the port in the 1980s. In the second part of the 1980s the port authority and especially the city administration finally became committed to this new investment programme and strategy. The resulting Port Plan 2010 and the related Overall Spatial and Environmental Plan for the City Region of Rotterdam (ROM Rijnmond project) were settled politically in 1992–3 (Kreukels and Wever, 1998).

At the same time the city administration invested again in marketing the city centre of Rotterdam, and in relating the southern part to the centre and the northern part by means of the 'Kop van Zuid' restructuring scheme. In terms of real estate and project development, Rotterdam once again became a booming city. This was expressed in a new, modern and post-modern skyline, the first in the Netherlands (Harding *et al.*, 1994). The same applied to the cultural sector with investments in museums and art facilities. However, Rotterdam – and even the Rotterdam region – appears, unlike Amsterdam and to a certain degree also The Hague, incapable of attaining sufficient economic strength and of attracting other economic activities apart from those related to the seaport during the last 10 to 15 years. The economic vulnerability of the Rotterdam region is expressed in the ongoing outmigration of people and businesses to other regions since the 1980s (Atzema *et al.*, 1998).

Rotterdam's (and The Hague's) profiles of development and spatial and urban policies over the various periods have been embedded in the policies for urban and regional development at the national and provincial levels, especially those related to the main cities and to the Randstad.

In the 1960s, Rotterdam and The Hague were seen by the national government as main urban centres (C centres; Amsterdam was a D centre). This was expressed in a dispersal policy laid down in the First and the Second National Memorandum on Spatial Planning. It aimed at relieving the main cities and the Randstad from the pressure of growth and directing growth to other locations and parts of the Netherlands. With this early managed growth strategy for the Randstad, which was aimed at maintaining the Greenheart and the poly-nuclear structure of the Randstad, the national government targeted for the first time the specific urban patterning of the country and specified with this the sites for urban growth and of urban concentration.

In the 1970s the national government continued this dispersal strategy in the Third National Memorandum on Spatial Planning. The specific content of this strategy was the concentration of growth of population in 'growth centres' at some distance from the four main cities.

Subsequently, in the 1980s, the Fourth National Memorandum on Spatial Planning (VINEX, Vierde Nota Extra) – especially after pressure from Amsterdam and the other main cities, which had lost population and functions to the new expansion centres – meant a shift from dispersing the growth pressure from the cities and the Randstad, to a 'compact cities' strategy. Now, the main cities were seen again as centres to which growth and development should be related. The national government abandoned the strategy and policies of growth centres outside the main cities and introduced a new generation of expansion schemes on the outskirts of these cities (VINEX locations, offically selected by the Netherlands government in the VINEX report, to absorb future necessary expansion and urban growth), as well as restructuring vacant and deteriorated areas for new uses. For the open Greenheart in the Randstad, the fourth Memorandum introduced measures to restrict development. However, these measures were not very successful given the increasing pressure for expansion in the Randstad outside the main cities. While the first three national memorandums on spatial planning focused on general and social issues, the fourth concentrated on economic and ecological issues. This was expressed in a strategy of strengthening the Randstad as the main economic urban region within the nation-state. The plan was to achieve this by having central government give financial and other support to key development projects in the cities (e.g. the Kop van Zuid development in Rotterdam and the restructuring project near The Hague's central railway station). In addition, the national government expressed its intention to give financial and other support to strengthen the main seaport (Rotterdam) and the main airport (Amsterdam), both seen now as essential infrastructure related to the Randstad's economy.

Finally, the Fifth National Memorandum on Spatial Planning (2001) is a pronounced strategy of managed growth, in which the national government applies directly or indirectly strict urban growth boundaries. The emphasis is on interrelated cities in the Randstad and in the rest of the country. In favour of these 'networks of cities', the national government is inclined to invest in supporting facilities and infrastructure. However, the main aims are to maintain the quality of life and the environment, and to conserve landscapes, nature and heritage as much as possible. The economy and business are less central to the overall strategy. In this Memorandum, the Randstad has been given an impetus in the form of a new concept: the Delta Metropolis. This concept was promoted by a group of professional planners, organised around the Randstad development together with representatives of the city administrations of the four main cities, and later with people of other smaller municipalities, and finally with participants of profit and non-profit organisations.

When the national government adopted this Delta Metropololis concept, it did, however, not take over its most challenging feature: accepting urban growth and expansion also outside the urban centres and even the urbanised areas to a certain degree. However, what the national government emphasised in this new strategy was the second main characteristic of this programme: seeing the Randstad not only as the main economic area of the Netherlands, but also as a key area in north-west Europe, thanks to its position at the mouth of the Rhine and the Maas in the increased reality of the open market of the EU.

For the coming period the following evolution of the Randstad and of the south wing can be expected. The Randstad seems to be changing in two ways. First, it – like many other metropolitan areas – is becoming part of a widening regional whole which will finally embrace the whole of the Netherlands. In the southern part of the country, cities in North Brabant (Den Bosch, Breda, Tilburg, Eindhoven) are gradually becoming linked to parts of the south wing of the Randstad. The same widening of the urban configuration is occurring in the zone between Amsterdam and Utrecht. This zone continues in a corridor to the eastern part of the Netherlands, towards the cities of Arnhem and Nijmegen. In this sense, the Netherlands is gradually being transformed into one urban field of which the Randstad (the Western conurbation) is only a part, albeit a central urban core.

The second way in which the Randstad is changing is the ongoing process of differentiation within the Randstad region. The north wing of the Randstad (the Amsterdam–Utrecht zone) is currently the most powerful and robust part of the Randstad region with its own impact on surrounding areas. The south wing (the urban zone between Rotterdam and The Hague) lags behind in being manifest in its wider surroundings. In particular Rotterdam has a vulnerable economy. In this way the Randstad differentiates internally and is slowly evolving in at least two different sub-regions, each with its own profile, dynamics and potentials: the north-east wing (Amsterdam–Utrecht) and the south-west wing (Rotterdam–The Hague). Given the widening of the whole Randstad outwards, this differentiated Randstad is becoming increasingly linked to surrounding areas outside the Randstad. This will result in a new urban pattern in which the specific poly-nuclear morphology of the Randstad is only part of the country as a whole, seen as one urban complex composed of more and lesser interrelated cities, urban, semi-urban and rural areas.

A first diagnosis: agenda of development and functioning of urban regions in relation to governmental interventions

Content – agenda

Next to the fact that the planning for the Randstad is not really regionalised, there is a serious limitation in investing in the economic/technological development of the Randstad in relation to the human capital, given the continued growth of urban regions. This is especially observable in the moderate commitment to continue investing in the basic infrastructure of the Randstad (the seaport of Rotterdam and the airport of Amsterdam) and in the lack of anticipating the economic and technological geography of the Randstad in the near future. Neither seems really occupied with the social and cultural differentiation in a myriad of areas for living and working, related as these are to economic, social and cultural categories. This is also the case at the local and subregional level. However, one can note again that the north wing of the Randstad around Amsterdam and Utrecht is more proactive with regard to this than the south wing of the Randstad, the area around Rotterdam and The Hague. In general, the emphasis in both regions is more on real estate and project development than on stimulating economic and social strengths in urban areas and subsequently interrelating these economic, social and cultural policies in a regional perspective. At the national level there is the same neglect and indifference. This is particularly manifest in the latest National Memorandum on Spatial Planning. This policy document is isolated from the more central agenda (being related first of all to social and economic policies) of the Dutch government. There are exceptions to this, however. The Ministry of Economic Affairs invested over a number of years in an analysis and proposals for an agenda for the economic and technological strengths of urban regions in the Netherlands, based on its responsibility for regional economic policy. What also is not really a priority in urban and regional policies is the factual shifts and dynamics in the daily behaviour of people manifest in a spatial context, more particularly the movements and the location behaviour of people, firms and institutions, as these relate to the economic and technological development and the human capital behind it. This lack of orientation towards these shifts and emerging new patterns of behaviour results in neglecting the increasing differentiation of people, organisations and institutions, manifesting themselves in local, regional, national and international networks. None of this is at the top of the agenda in urban policies in the Randstad. This lack of orientation towards the differentiated reality is strengthened by the fragmented governmental system of municipalities and provinces, each of which focuses on its own areas and domains as closed shops. In this sense, the regional approach has been implemented only hesitantly.

When infrastructure, and land and environment policies are insufficiently related to this economic/technological development and the related human capital, the interrelations between infrastructure planning, and land and environment planning are insufficient too. Although this is particularly the case again at the national level, also at the local and regional level these policy interrelationships are weak, particularly from a regional perspective. This is related again to the institutional relationships between the three governmental layers, continuing a central rule approach, combined with strictly particular domains for each layer, even if at the same time the representatives of the layers pay lip service to negotiation and a regionally differentiated approach.

Policies – planning

As mentioned, the Randstad is undergoing a reconfiguration. The northern part and the southern part are becoming increasingly separate subsystems of policy-making, showing a proper trajectory of continued growth.

The south wing of the Randstad is hesitant to adopt a more proactive approach and to adopt institutional structures above the level of the main cities of Rotterdam and The Hague. The Hague has made more progress here. This is manifest especially in the VINEX expansion schemes around The Hague and in the rapid transport policies within the administrative setting of the urban region: Haaglanden. Rotterdam – having the exceptional facility in the Netherlands of a real regional administration for the whole Rotterdam region already in the 1970s and early 1980s – did not succeed in finding an alternative administrative arrangement for the wider Rotterdam region in the 1980s and 1990s, when an *ad hoc* law for a special administration for the Rotterdam region was voted down in a referendum by the population of Rotterdam. The Rotterdam and The Hague conurbation form together an overall diffuse and loose urban whole. Clear manifestations of this lack of organising things above the level of the separate Rotterdam conurbation and The Hague conurbation are the conflicts over the light-rail infrastructure between these two conurbations, with Rotterdam aiming at a metro infrastructure and The Hague at tram infrastructure, each approaching the overall infrastructure from the perspective of its own infrastructure.

This segmentation or fragmentation within the urban system is mirrored in the way in which regional development is handled by the municipalities concerned, but also by the attitude and behaviour of the province of South Holland – the regional authority responsible for the southern part of the Randstad. Cooperation is almost non-existent, unlike in the northern part of the Randstad. The private sector is not at all involved in a real sense in the southern part of Randstad. In the south wing there are a lot of conflicts between Rotterdam and The Hague, while within the Rotterdam area the city of Rotterdam has a lot of conflicts with the surrounding municipalities. In contrast to the northern part of the Randstad, the province of South Holland promotes no inter-municipal cooperation at all. Here the urban system that is loose in a morphological sense, is also divided and split up in terms of the institutional relations in the wider urban region (Dijkink *et al.*, 2001).

Conclusions: prospects for the south wing of the Randstad

The following is an ideal agenda for the planning of the south wing of the Randstad in the twenty-first century. First of all, one should continue investing in the economic/technological strength of the urban region. In the Randstad, this means gaining a better insight into the changing geography of this economy in a broader national and international context. This changing geography of economy and technology is closely related to the changing social geography of people. This is a core part of a proactive and future-related planning of the Randstad. This is tightly linked to the main infrastructure and the basic setting of land as related to this main infrastructure. The future planning of the seaport of Rotterdam and the airport of Amsterdam should be high on the agenda, as should the main rail infrastructure of the Randstad, as these serve this region in its changing configuration of a poly-nuclear urban system with open relations with other parts of the Netherlands and other European countries. The highway infrastructure should serve in the best way first of all the connections between the four main cities. This requires an enormous investment, because the system at the moment is used at the same time as infrastructure for local/sub-regional and for regional/national traffic. An investment strategy would lead to a much needed, more differentiated system that would strengthen the national and regional connections within the Randstad and from the Randstad to the outside world.

More in general, the basic infrastructure in the Randstad is radially organised, that is, organised around the four main urban centres. What is needed now – as in other very urbanised regions in developed countries – is an extension and restructuring of this basic system in favour of tangential connections in a regional context, with direct connections between outside centres and satellite cities, in addition to the old dominant connections to the centres of the main cities. The same applies to direct connections between outside locations, outside centres and satellite cities, and the main regional specialised distribution and traffic nodes, such as airports and main railway stations.

In this complex and dynamic urban fabric, the land and environment planning should function as a strategic intervenient. It should therefore relate first of all to the economic/social development and the infrastructure related to it. This means a land market-related planning that simultaneously makes a distinction between planning for growth and planning for maintenance, and between planning at the micro/meso level (focusing on different areas in the wider urban region) and the meso/macro level (focusing on restructuring and development in a regional context). Only a multilevel, multi-agency plan can realise this complex and interrelated agenda of urban and regional planning.

Bibliography

Atzema, O., Hooimeijer, P. and Nijstad, R. (1998) *Op Zoek in Zuid-Holland. Oorzaken en Gevolgen van Binnenlandse Migratie voor de Woning- en Arbeidsmarkt*, Utrecht: Urban Research Centre, University of Utrecht.

Burke, G.L. (1966) *Greenheart Metropolis; Planning the Western Netherlands*, London: Macmillan.

Dijkink, G., Hajer, M., de Jong, M. and Salet, W.G.M. (2001) *De Zuidvleugel van de Randstad: Instituties en Discoursen*, Amsterdam: Amsterdam study centre for the Metropolitan Environment.

Faludi, A. and van der Valk, A. (1994) *Rule and Order: Dutch Planning Doctrine in the Twentieth Century*, London, Dordrecht: Kluwer.

Gunsteren, H. van (1976) *The Quest of Control. A Critique of the Rational-Central-Rule Approach in Public Affairs*, London, New York, Sydney, Toronto: J. Wiley and Sons.

Hall, P. (1977) *The World Cities*, London: Weidenfeld and Nicholson.

Harding, A., Dawson, J., Evans, R. and Parkinson, M. (1994) *European Cities Toward 2000. Profiles, Policies and Prospects*, Manchester and New York: Manchester University Press.

Jacobs, M. (2000) *Multinodal Urban Structures. A Comparative Analysis and Strategies for Design*, Delft: Delft University Press.

Klerk, L. de (1990) 'Hoe groot is Rotterdam, Special Issue Rotterdam', *Geografisch Tijdschrift*, 24 (3): 200–10.

Klerk, L. de (1998) *Particuliere Plannen. Denkbeelden en Initiatieven van de Stedelijke Elite Inzake Woningbouw en de Stedebouw in Rotterdam, 1860–1950*, Rotterdam: Nai Uitgevers.

Kreukels, A.M.J. (1992) 'The restructuring and growth of the Randstad cities: current policy issues', in F.M. Dieleman and S. Musterd (eds) *The Randstad: A Research and Policy Laboratory*, Dordrecht: Kluwer.

Kreukels, A.M.J. (1997) *Vierde van Eesteren Lezing – Cor van Eesterenmanifestatie 1997 – Een Perspectief voor de Stad*, Amsterdam: BNSP i.o.

Kreukels, A.M.J. and Wever, E. (eds) (1998) *North Sea Ports in Transition: Changing Tides*, Assen: Van Gorcum.

Netherlands Scientific Council for Government Policy (1992) *Institutions and Cities*, The Hague: Sdu Publishers.

Netherlands Scientific Council for Government Policy (1998) *Spatial Planning Development Policies*, The Hague: Sdu Publishers.

PART IV

Prague, Vienna, Venice, Milan

13 The Prague metropolitan region

Karel Maier

Background: socio-economic frameworks from the past

1940s to 1980s: centrally planned economy and development

Nationalisation and central control were stronger in Prague than in other parts of the country owing to the high concentration of people, capital and power and, therefore, more intensive efforts by the regime to attain full control.

> Owing to … [the] totalitarian system the onset of intensive forms of development was markedly weakened and distorted. In many respects primary extensive forms of development were replaced by political decision-making, regional and local initiatives were suppressed and development activities operating 'from below' were suppressed as well. Natural tendencies, heading toward intensive forms of development, were at work in a very limited way; they appeared very late and often in hidden or indirect forms.
>
> (Hampl *et al.*, 1999, p.27)

In these circumstances, the position of Prague was much less important than it would have been in a less controlled system or a system with less egalitarian objectives of spatial development.

Changes of ownership in the 1990s: property restitution, privatisation and de-étatisme

Equal rights concerning all forms of ownership, the reintroduction of private entrepreneurship and the abolition of central economic planning were the first results in the sphere of the economy of the 1989 political changes. All property that had been nationalised since 1948 started to be returned to the original owners or their legal heirs. Also the housing stock built by the state or state-controlled cooperatives changed owners: the state transferred most of its stock to municipalities in 1991 and established basic frameworks for its privatisation at the same time. Prices were liberalised but the control of residential rents was retained. Market forces unleashed by privatisation favoured the attractive, inner-city sites where new shops and businesses mushroomed, bringing new life to many previously abandoned or misused precincts. Industrial enterprises were privatised by means of 'voucher privatisation', which converted state enterprises into joint-stock corporations. Every adult citizen was given the opportunity to acquire a certain number of shares; but in fact the immense amount of property that was privatised in this way came under the control of capital groups that were intertwined with the banking sector and with each other. This poorly transparent ownership pattern exposed many of the enterprises to mismanagement and decay.

The inherited spatial pattern of Prague

The Prague metropolitan region has preserved a hierarchical, centripetal structure more typical of a rural settlement system than a regional city. The relationship between Prague and its neighbouring region has not overcome the traditional centre-periphery pattern.

   The centre of Prague is almost identical to its historical core, which consists of several historical towns of medieval origin. The new town, which was established in the mid-fourteenth century, was transformed at the end of the nineteenth century into a modern metropolis, thanks to its original spacious layout with wide straight streets and large blocks. Some centres of the nineteenth-century historic suburbs – originally independent towns – serve as sub-centres of present-day Prague, but their role in the wider context is rather small and the relationships between the sub-centres are relatively weak. Other, less important local centres – some of them deliberately planned for new developments – seldom provide more than a basic level of services and facilities.

   Under central planning, the land market was effectively abolished by fixing land prices and imposing severe restrictions on property owners' rights. 'Location in the city became, from the point of view of the user, ... or potential investor or developer, an almost irrelevant factor' (Musil, 1993, p.901). All investments came under some form of state control. The process of urbanisation was restricted mostly to the jurisdiction of Prague. The shortage of developable land within the municipal jurisdiction after all available land had been developed led to periodic annexations of rural hinterland communities. The Prague urban fringe became a sort of no-man's land, 'a bottomless spatial reserve for aggressive road, warehousing, rubbish and recreation uses' (Blažek, 1994, p.123). Outside the immediate metropolitan region, selected industrial centres of Central Bohemia were supported in order to counterbalance the attractiveness of the metropolis.

The position of Prague and the metropolitan region

National and international context

Hampl *et al.* (1999, p.95) argue that in the post-1989 transformation only two factors have played a decisive role as regards regional differentiation in the Czech Republic: polarity between metropolitan and non-metropolitan areas, and polarity between the Prague metropolitan region and the country's other metropolitan regions. This has ranked the Prague metropolitan region greater in importance and size than the rest of the country, as it was noticed in the cases of the metropolitan areas of the national capitals all over the Visegrád countries (see Maier *et al.*, 1998). Integrating processes in the settlement systems were studied in the last decades of the twentieth century by many authors, and some considered that they transformed from hierarchies to networks (e.g. Naisbit, 1982). Hampl *et al.* (1999, p.99) argue that:

> [integrating] tendencies only have a limited and specific effect at lower levels of the scale hierarchy and partly result from the strengthened role of those forms of the hierarchisation of the settlement systems which are higher in terms of order and scale. In this sense, there is not a question of weakening the hierarchical forms of organisation, but of the scale shifts of these forms, while the frameworks of their effect are enlarged.

Prague is the only Czech centre that can compete with other major European centres. The Prague metropolitan region serves as a gateway for innovation from the most developed regions to the more backward ones. As such, the importance of Prague and its metropolitan region is vital for the rest of the country.

The Prague metropolitan region

The Prague metropolitan region was defined for the sake of planning; it has nothing to do with administration units. The region extends over a territory of about 4,000 km^2 and has 1.7 million inhabitants. The entire urban area of Prague has a total population of 1.16 million in an area covering 358 km^2, i.e. two-thirds of the inhabitants of the metropolitan area occupy less than 9 per cent of its territory. Körner (1996) commented that the extent of the metropolitan region of Prague and the share of the population outside the city are small compared with other European metropolitan regions of similar rank. The population density of the Prague metropolitan region is over 6.3 times the national average. In 1996, the 'density' of economic aggregate (expressed by the product of average wages and number of jobs) was 10.2 times higher than the national average, and wages in the Prague metropolitan region exceeded the national average by 27.6 per cent.

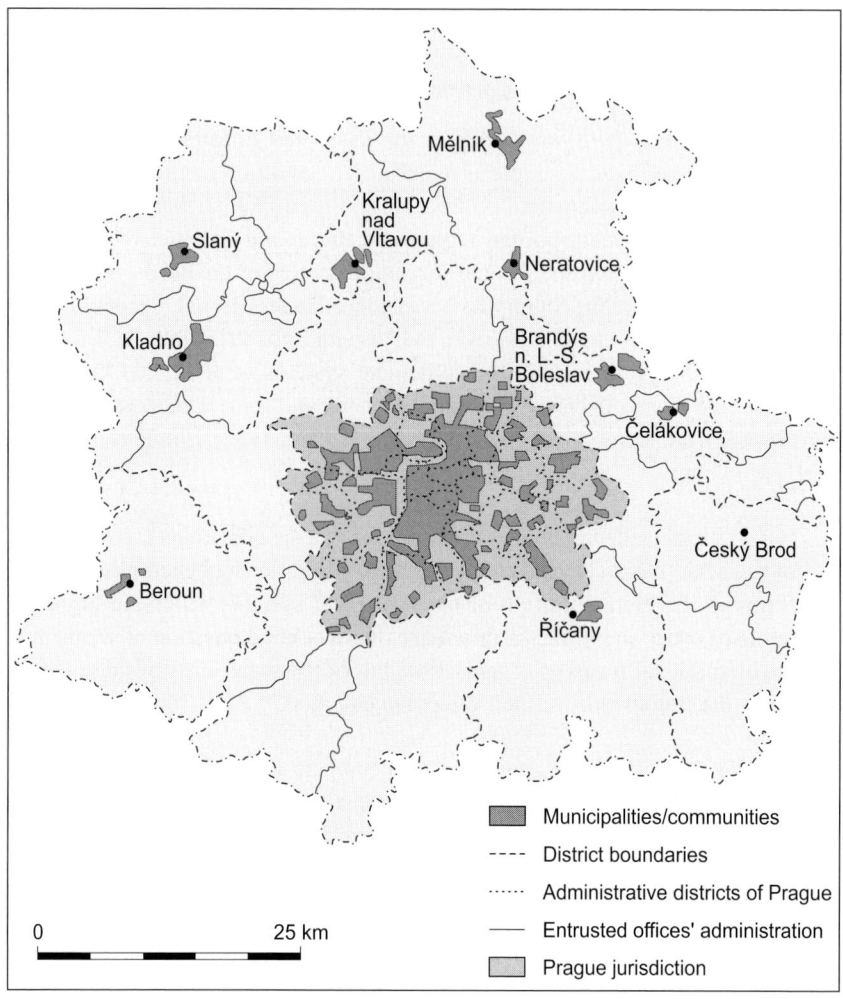

Figure 13.1 The Prague metropolitan region

The city of Prague

The population of Prague increased steadily until 1992 when it started to decline, as did the proportion of the country's total population that lived there. The net migration to Prague is not enough to compensate for the natural population decrease. Thus, the permanent population of Prague declined by 4.5 per cent between 1991 and 2000. On the other hand, the number of temporary residents from other parts of the country or from abroad is steadily increasing, and recently reached an estimated 150,000–200,000. In addition, it is estimated that about 230,000 short-term visitors (i.e. those who visit for several days at the most) come to the city each day (ÚRM, 1998, 4/2). The proportion of jobs in the national job market increased in the 1990s by 14 per cent. Prague has the lowest level of unemployment in the Czech Republic – about 3 per cent of the work force, compared with the national average of 8–9 per cent (2001). The rate of employment is also the highest in the country: 54 per cent of all inhabitants work, compared with about 50 per cent nation-wide. Recently, Prague succeeded in absorbing the work force released not only by its own factory closures but also (and mostly) by factory closures in other industrial areas in the metropolitan region.

The Prague work force has far the best average level of education in the country. Incomes in Prague were about 142 per cent of the national average in 2000. Also the price level in Prague is higher than in most other parts of the country. Manufacturing was the largest sector until 1989, when the shift towards services accelerated. Retail as well as administration, education and health services are the largest employment sectors. Tourism is currently the most dynamic branch of Prague's economy. The total income from tourism has increased by 300 per cent since 1989. Retail and tourist services are expected to continue to be growth sectors in the future.

Trends of urbanisation and spatial configuration

Spatial mobility

The diversification of destination of movement of people and goods, increased value of time and social stratification among transport users were among the immediate factors behind the tremendous change in the 1990s. The number of cars increased by 18 per cent during the 1980s, and by a further 85 per cent during the 1990s. The number of cars moving in the inner city zone increased by 44 per cent and in the outer zone by 151 per cent in the 1990s. The number of inhabitants per motor vehicle was 1:1.6 in 2000, while for private automobiles this was 1:1.9 – compared with 1:2.1 or 1:2.3 in Western metropolises (ÚDI, 2000). At the same time, public transport use dropped from 4.1 million passengers per day in 1990 to 3.3 million in 2000, i.e. by 21 per cent. Prague has succeeded in maintaining the standard of tram, metro and bus services because the decrease in the number of passengers and diminishing subsidies are compensated for by higher fares. The metro network is being continually extended. To meet the increasing demand for roads and parking places, two high-capacity ring roads are under construction. Parking and car movements should be regulated inside the inner ring and a park-and-ride system is being built adjacent to metro stations outside the city. Although investments in transportation and subsidies for public transport consume as much as 54 per cent of the municipal budget (2001), it is still not enough. The shortage of financial means and the opposition to new roads on the part of local citizens and politicians has delayed and changed some large projects.

Changes of spatial pattern and urban functions

Business and government

In the centre, the urbanisation trend has been strong since the 1990s. Newly emerging service-sector businesses prefer to be situated there: in particular the concentration of high-income and high-density workplaces increased dramatically there. At present, the central area encompasses almost half of all Prague jobs, mostly situated in the historical core, on about 1.5 per cent of the total area of Prague. Owing to the legal and urban constraints (the preservation of monuments), only a fraction of office development projects have reached completion. The projects typically combine retail and office space, and recently have started adding leisure activities and some luxurious apartments to the mix. As available sites in the centre are now almost exhausted, the pressure to demolish and replace is increasing for prestigious developments, with conflicts over monument preservation and with the local citizenry. Less central locations in the nineteenth-century suburbs seem to present an opportunity. This gives a chance to revitalise some blighted and brownfield areas adjacent to the centre, using offices as an engine for other kinds of development there.

Tourist facilities

The number of persons visiting Prague increased dramatically immediately after 1989, and has been increasing steadily ever since. Prague is now ranked seventh among European cities regarding the number of visitors. Hotels were the initial kind of private capital investment in the newly liberalised economy. Many new hotels came into being as refurbished dormitories and hostels for employees of former state enterprises. Others were refurbished rental dwellings in houses that had been returned to their owners. The accommodation market has diversified: the big-hotel boom is now over.

Housing

During the last three decades, the urban territory grew about 3.5 times faster than the population of Prague. As a result of property restitution, the housing ownership pattern changed fundamentally in the 1990s. About 15 per cent of the total number of houses in Prague were returned to the heirs of their original owners; however, in the central parts – where multi-family houses built before 1945 prevail – the figure was more than 70 per cent (Grabmüllerová, 1998). The privatisation process of non-restituted public rental housing was slower, and the final volume of the privatised stock is expected to be smaller than originally estimated. Rent control, strict legal protection against eviction, and the housing shortage have slowed down all changes in occupancy, because the law prevents the eviction of occupiers without compensation (Sýkora, 1993, p.291). In the historical core, competition from more profitable commercial uses caused the percentage of residential floor space to drop from about 32 per cent at the end of the 1980s to an estimated 26 per cent in 1994 (Grabmüllerová, 1998). Now that market rents apply to new leases, residential use is more competitive again even in the most attractive parts of the historical core. This is leading to increased gentrification of the core as well as to a spontaneous return to the original social profile in the pre-1940s higher-income residential areas. The mere share and size of housing estates inevitably makes them the issue of housing policy. However, the housing shortage has prevented housing estates from becoming socially deprived, abandoned and consequently dilapidated, despite their poor image. The number of new housing units constructed dropped to a minimum after state subsidies were abolished in 1990. Now such construction has stabilised at about 50 per cent of the average for the 1980s. Horáková (2000) shows that the housing development in the second half of the 1990s consisted of two parts: a) intensification, i.e. inner-city superstructures (e.g. attic apartments) and regenerated flats, and b) outer-city greenfields or pockets of new construction of family houses. In the metropolitan region outside the jurisdiction of Prague, housing development started from very few homes at the beginning of the 1990s, to increase 2.6 times by 1997, with a certain amount of stagnation afterwards – but this was still less than half of the amount of housing construction in Prague.

Industrial estates

The economic changes of the 1990s put industrial plants out of business. The closures were not so widespread in Prague as in other parts of the country, but the number increased towards the end of the decade when also big factories were affected. Some of the sites were converted or are being converted into retail outlets or leisure centres, but most are under-utilised or abandoned.

Changing structures of government and self-government

Nation-wide changes of governmental system

The entirely top-down bureaucratic control through the hierarchy of regional and local/municipal national committees was established after the Second World War and, despite several reforms, its nature did not change until 1989.

Municipalities

The shift from government as the absolute ruler to mechanisms that provide more socially open and responsive decision-making processes is closely linked to the establishment and position of self-government. It was quite natural that one of the

Table 13.1 Summary of major urban issues in Prague and their approach

Period	Major issues of spatial planning	Major actors to tackle the issue	Adopted/proposed solution	Side effects of the solution	Winners	Losers
1970s 1980s	Housing shortage	Central government	Subsidies for housing construction at housing estates: KBV schemes, systemic blocks	Inner-city decline; uniformity of 'new towns'	State construction monopolies; Migrants from the country	Inner-city residents (in historical core and old working class suburbs); belt of 'rural Prague'; villages along the limits of Prague jurisdiction
	Outworn and underdeveloped infrastructure	Central government	Heavy state investment in underground sewage system (not in outskirts)	High-density, mono-functional areas on urban fringe; decline outside the reach of new infrastructures		
Early 1990s	Pressure for redevelopment/ transformation of the centre/ historical core: tourist facilities and offices	Private (privatised) businesses; private investors, monument preservation authorities	Strict monument preservation and control	Lengthy and non-transparent process of development, complaints of developers	Property owners in the centre, developers who got across the red tape	
End of the 1990s	Decline of residential use in the centre	Private landlords	Tenants' rights against eviction lifting residential rent ceiling	Slum landlords	Financially strong landlords	Original city core residents (tenants)

continued...

Table 13.1 continued

Period	Major issues of spatial planning	Major actors to tackle the issue	Adopted/proposed solution	Side effects of the solution	Winners	Losers
End of the 1990s	Increase of car transportation	Municipality	Express Ring, Urban Ring, subsidies for public transport; finance by obligations	Increasing municipal debt service	Construction companies ('concrete lobby')	Other (under-nourished) services and facilities
	Inner-city gentrification	Not considered as problem yet	–	–	Property owners in the core	Original tenants
	Housing estate blight	State programmes of regeneration	Renovations; new development in estates; improvements of public spaces	Increased dependence on external support	Some estates; construction companies	Other estates; other deprived quarters
2000s	Suburbanisation (retail, housing) urban sprawl	Not on the agenda (regions?)	Coordination of major investments (inter-regional scale); preference for brown-field redevelopment and conversions?	?	Municipalities outside Prague?	Housing estates in Prague; retail inside residential areas
	Urban brownfields	Not on the agenda?	Control of residential development and large projects on regional scale?	?		

Karel Maier

first legal steps taken in all the post-totalitarian countries was to reintroduce self-governing institutions. The Act on Municipalities (1990) re-established self-government on the local level. In this law, the municipality is defined as 'the principal local government unit comprised of territorial communities of citizens with the right of self-government'. The responsibilities of local self-government are, following the pre-war tradition, pretty wide, especially if one considers that some rural municipalities in the country are very small (some have fewer than 100 permanent inhabitants). Municipalities are responsible for, *inter alia*, local infrastructure and public services. They can collaborate to develop infrastructure and provide services but they cannot collect local taxes or impose surcharges in order to finance their projects. Municipalities also prepare development programmes for their jurisdictions and are responsible for local planning. Besides the right to self-government, municipalities are an administrative district to which the law entrusts some execution of governmental administration (transferred competence). In these cases the officials have no responsibility to the local government but are controlled by the central government. The secretary of the municipal office is responsible to the mayor. For those municipalities which, mostly due to their small size, cannot assume the transferred competencies, these activities are provided by a network of 'entrusted local offices', mostly located in small towns.

Regions: abolished and renewed

When municipal self-government was established in 1990, the regional tier of government was abolished. The administration on the intermediate level (i.e. between the national and municipal levels) was entrusted to districts. The 1993 Constitution provided for self-governing units also on the regional level, but this did not come into effect until 2001. The new regions are territorial units with the right of self-government. The rights and responsibilities of regions are analogous to those of municipalities. Also regional self-governments have both representative and executive components. The districts are due to be abolished in 2003 as the final step of the current governmental reform. This will increase the importance of the entrusted local offices, which will take over some of the administration from the districts.

The governing of Prague

History: from conurbation to unicity and the two-tier model

Barlow (1994, p.125–9) distinguishes polycentric, unicentric and two-tier models for metropolitan government. For most of its history, Prague – being a conurbation of separate municipalities from medieval times till the beginning of the industrial era – applied the polycentric model. Later the ring of growing, independent

214

suburban towns encroached upon the historical centre of Prague. It was only in 1920 that Greater Prague was established as a centralised metropolitan unit. The position of Prague as predominantly a unicity started being modified to the two-tier model in 1949 (16 districts) and again in 1960 (10 districts). The annexations in 1968 and especially in 1974 made the outer districts very large and hetero-geneous, with some rural units on the fringe. The political change after 1989 opened the issue of the model of governing the capital city. Barlow's recommenda-tions, to establish a strong central administration for Prague that would be given a 'clear and substantive role: clarity is necessary in order to reduce overlap and conflict with lower-level authorities, and substance is necessary to avoid charges of irrelevance and wasteful spending', were carefully listened to and followed by the political leaders of Prague. The city has retained:

> a functional role, which relates to the provision of public services that require large-scale or area-wide organisation; a strategic role, which relates to planning and economic development; a resource-allocation role, which relates to the distribution of financial resources to lower-level governments; and a managerial role, which involves directing the various elements of the private sector in an overall system of metropolitan management.
>
> (Barlow, 1994, p.129)

Region, municipality and agency of central government at the same time

Since 2001, Prague is both a region and a municipality, and is governed by the Act on the Capital City of Prague (2000). It is completely surrounded by the Central Bohemian Region governed by the Act on Regions (2000). The Assembly of 55 Representatives is elected by means of communal elections every four years. For operative decision-making, the Assembly establishes the council consisting of mayor and 11 councillors. Municipal and regional administrative services are provided by the Municipal Office. The administration of the Municipal Office also exercises the competencies transferred from the central government. For the activities of the state administration transferred to the local level, Prague is subdivided into administrative districts. To reflect the specific position of small units in the outer parts of the jurisdiction, administrative districts were comple-mented by 57 boroughs in 1990. The boroughs do not have the legal position of municipalities: financially they are fully dependent on the city of Prague. Each borough has its own elected assembly, which selects from among themselves a council and a local mayor. Inner-city boroughs are mostly identical to the adminis-trative districts. Some out-of-town boroughs are small, formerly rural villages, which were annexed by Prague in 1974. The latest reform of the administrative division of Prague came into force in 2001. It increased the number of administra-

Karel Maier

tive districts to 22, in order to 'locate offices nearer to citizens' (Zajíček, 2001). At the same time, more activities were transferred from the Municipal Office of Prague to the administrative districts. Building Offices, which are important for the implementation of spatial policies as they issue planning permission and building permits, are now one of the typical features of the administrative districts.

Metropolitan region outside Prague

The governmental structure outside Prague follows the general nation-wide pattern. No formal representation exists for the metropolitan region. The immediate two administrative districts comprise 175 self-governed municipalities, nine of which are towns with an entrusted local office. The average population size of a municipality in these two districts is only 970.

Development of the metropolitan region: actors and strategic policies

Changing strategic objectives and policies of spatial development

Table 13.2 summarises the national objectives and regional/municipal policies connected with spatial development since the end of the 1940s.

Actors, driving forces and their interests

The arena for planning and development underwent a fundamental change in the 1990s as a result of privatisation and liberalisation. The plurality of particular group and individual interests replaced the hitherto monolithic 'societal interest' and state as the dominant investor. The controversies between local and wider (state) interests emerged soon after municipalities became subjects of planning. The political change opened the planning arena to overall control by citizens at the beginning of the 1990s, but this arena is increasingly dominated by capital groups rather than by an immature civic society and weak, small, recently-born private enterprises. The legal position of the *state* remains quite strong. The consent of state administration is needed before a master plan is submitted for approval to a local or regional assembly. Planning permission and building permits are issued by Building Offices controlled by the state, and also appeals against these decisions are addressed to the state authorities. On the other hand, the state relinquished its active role in establishing a national policy of spatial development, and the role of the state as public investor shrank to certain domains like national transportation arteries. The role of *regions* in spatial management has not been settled yet, owing to their recent re-establishment. Their effort to regulate the spatial development

216

Table 13.2 Changing strategic objectives and policies of spatial development

Period	National strategic objectives and policies	Consequent policies of	
		Capital City of Prague	*Metropolitan region outside Prague (1999–2000: municipalities in the region)*
1948–56	'Socialist industrialisation planned economy as contradiction to market: • controlled spatial development to equalise the level of development among regions	Restrictions of development Social engineering: 'working-class metropolis'	Priority for mining and heavy-industry centres
1957–89	'Scientific societal development': • 'concentrated decentralisation' of the settlement system: controlled spatial development derived from the Central Place Theory	Comprehensive Housing Development ('KBV') schemes: multi-family housing estates with basic facilities 'Showcase' projects: underground, the Congress Palace	Priority for selected industrial centres to counterbalance the attractiveness of Prague: 'KBV' schemes and industrial development Limited private housing construction
Most of the 1990s	Laissez-faire and government centralisation: • de-étatisme: transfer of property and responsibilities to municipalities • control of development compatible with market economy	Selling-off the public property, waiting for big investors	
		Get most out of the attractiveness of hisotircal Prague	Communal egoism: increasing competition among municipalities, fragmentation of local government (small municipalities)

continued…

Table 13.2 continued

Period	National strategic objectives and policies	Consequent policies of		
		Capital City of Prague	Metropolitan region outside Prague (1999–2000: municipalities in the region)	

Period	National strategic objectives and policies	Capital City of Prague	Metropolitan region outside Prague (1999–2000: municipalities in the region)
Late 1990s till present	Governmental reform: state regions, municipalities • transparency of administration • support for development • regional policy, support for less developed areas; mitigation of spatial/socio-economic disparities	Partnership with big investors Strategic planning European representation of Prague More understanding for developers: attempts for PPP Investment expansion in transportation network, obligation emissions, polycentric city?	Municipalities; • get most out of Prague • increasing competitiveness of some municipalities • microregional associations • municipal lobbying Region Central Bohemia • get most out of the state/EU? • preference of subregional centres outside the immediate influence of Prague?

would probably encounter local interests of municipalities and they would also face criticism from those who believe in the expediency of an unrestricted market. *Municipalities* now have full responsibility for planning and development programming but they do not have the power to issue planning permission or building permits. The economic weakness of most municipalities forced some of them to seek external resources for investment. Prague issues bonds to cover infrastructure investments and tries to share costs with the private sector in some projects.

In other municipalities around Prague, the dominant personalities in municipal leadership influence the local development policy; in general, the dependence on economically strong investors and developers prevails. The legitimisation of business involvement in the process of planning is fully compatible with the trend of development-oriented planning which emerged around the mid-1990s. For the rest, private capital is viewed as a 'necessary ally' in order to implement plans. The unclear or poorly pronounced mission of municipal management is behind many current issues of municipal property management and development. The attitudes of representatives and councillors sometimes oscillate between thinking like private entrepreneurs and the paternal positions of enlightened rulers. The informal power of *private investors and developers* and the influence of *real estate companies* has grown steadily since the beginning of the 1990s. The economic power challenges the role of municipalities in shaping the spatial concept of settlements. International capital prevails, transferring concepts from abroad into the local, often rather different cultural and economic environment and utilising media and advertisements to sell their products. This increases the risk of non-sustainable spatial change and conflicts with existing businesses and users of the adjacent areas.

The voice of *small and medium entrepreneurs* is less pronounced. Their lobbying is usually fragmented as they have been unable to establish their own trustworthy representation on the municipal or regional level. This makes them weak vis-à-vis the big investors (e.g. retail chains). Legally, only individual *citizens* – and not their associations – may comment on proposed plans. The general public is not invited to participate in the procedures of individual planning permission. Despite this, well-organised and informed *ad hoc* citizens' groups have proved their ability to prevent or reduce the extent of some projects. Less frequently they manage to push through their own alternatives. In the case of Prague and its metropolitan region, the attractiveness of the area created an extremely conflicting environment for development. The conflicts were not as a rule mitigated by seeking compromises between the stakeholders. The unwillingness or poor ability to communicate is typical of all the parties involved. In these circumstances, developers try to enforce their interests by force or money, while authorities seek help only in the enforcement by the power of statutory plan and other prescriptions.

Karel Maier

Institutions and instruments of spatial management

Planning

Physical plans aim at setting limits on and regulations for development, but their link to the socio-economic issues is weakly defined. From the point of view of legal requirements, the process of plan-making is an expert and governmental game with public hearings and citizens' comments at the end of each round. In Prague, the 1999 City Master Plan is currently in force. The plan identifies the sites to be developed, regulates land-use and building load and identifies areas and corridors for public projects for which sites can be expropriated, as well as zones of ecological stability within the whole jurisdiction. The plan is very detailed (map scale 1:10,000) and as such it is sometimes criticised for being too rigid. Altogether, 128 amendments of the plan were proposed at the beginning of 2001, mostly aiming at the more intensive and more profitable use of a site, but not all have been approved. The totality of these changes, and some of them in particular, can have a remarkable effect. The role of the plan as the controller of spatial development of the city is central. Numerous detailed studies were elaborated after the plan to specify the conditions for planning permissions. Most municipalities in the region outside Prague have their own local master plan. The municipalities neighbouring Prague as a rule offer all suitable land for development. The resulting surplus of supply over actual demand is often rather illusory, due to the lack of infrastructure provision, but, for the long-run, it has established the trend for urban sprawl.

Strategic planning complemented physical planning in the 1990s, aiming at setting priorities of change on the basis of wider understanding and consensus among stakeholders. The elaboration of the Strategic Plan for Prague began by

Table 13.3 Organisation and administration of (physical) planning

Tier	Statutory planning arrangement/document	Scale of main map	The 'procurer' (body responsible for planning)	Approval body
National	• Planning and building law • By-laws; guidelines • Spatial Development Policy (pending)		Ministry for Regional Development	• Parliament • Ministry for Regional Development • National Government
Regional	(Physical) plan of region – 'greater territorial unit plan'; Development principles (pending)	1:50,000 1:25,000 (1:10,000)	Region(al administration)	Regional Assembly
Local	Local (master) plan	1:10,000 1:5,000 (1:2,000)	Municipality / community	Local Municipal Assembly
	Regional (zoning) plan	1:2,000 1:1,000		

organising topical workshops assisted by the British Know-How Fund during the period 1995–7. After several stages of plan-making and discussing, the final document was approved by the Municipal Assembly in 2000. The core strategy of the plan focuses on increasing the economic role of Prague, the quality of life, the quality of the environment, transport and technical infrastructure, city management and administration. Spatial transformation is another issue of the core strategy. In order that the existing congestion and spatial conflicts in the historical core can be managed without threat to heritage, the strategic plan proposes to switch from the existing monocentric structure of urban Prague to a polycentric one. It is envisaged to expand the existing centre into a) four adjacent development areas next to the nineteenth-century suburbs; b) identified development poles next to existing inner-city sub-centres; and c) new district centres planned for the outer-city where most people live, as a rule linked to metro stations. Unlike the 'established' physical planning, strategic planning has no tools for enforcement in general legislation. Thus the implementation mechanisms have to be created mostly by further negotiations with all stakeholders in the development process. Apparently, the strategies will be easier to implement wherever they are immediately linked to concrete, clear-cut projects, and resources of funding are identified. 'Hard' infrastructure projects have been the most successful in this respect. As regards spatial transformation, private initiative seems to appreciate the development potentials of some expansion areas for the centre, while the development poles in the inner-city often attract less desirable (i.e. less urban-friendly) project proposals. In the case of new out-of-town centres, the strategy is challenged by increasing numbers of shopping developments on greenfield sites, which drain potential customers and, consequently, private investment from the planned centres.

No plan for the Prague metropolitan region has been finished and approved since 1975. In 1999 the elaboration of the Regional Structure Plan of the Prague metropolitan region was commenced. The following issues are the concern of the plan: settlement structure; development sites of regional significance; supra-regional and regional transportation systems and other technical infrastructure; corridors for public projects and environmental protection. During the process of elaboration, difficulties emerged revolving mostly around the conflicts of the proposed transportation corridors with environmental protection. The recently established regional self-government and administration of Central Bohemia will probably review the whole plan. Regional strategies were elaborated in 1998 for all (at the time, pending) regions of the country, i.e. before regional tiers of government had been established. The strategy focused on supporting investment, improving transport, providing better services in rural areas and increasing tourism. The strategy urged 'administrative support' for the projects of new roads around Prague, which are planned to be built on the territory of Central Bohemia. The regional strategy is currently under review by the new regional management.

Karel Maier

Regional policy

Governmental regional policy was formally adopted in 1998 as a response to growing unemployment and increasing disparities between regions. The agency 'Czechinvest' was established to support industrial development in the regions, especially to assist foreign investors in finding suitable sites for investment. Regional Development Agencies (RDAs) as quasi-NGOs (non-government organisations) should manage regional development in each region. The pattern of RDAs refers to the jurisdictions of the regions: thus Prague is treated separately from Central Bohemia. While the economic level of Prague is above the EU average, the economy of Central Bohemia would entitle the region to assistance from the EU. The old industrial part of the north-west of Central Bohemia is identified nationally as a problem area.

Problems of spatial coordination and institutional patterns of government

Influence of the global economy and the position within the national context

The European and national political and economic changes that occurred in the 1990s had mostly positive effects on Prague as the favoured metropolis of the country. Its westernmost geographic location among the capitals of the former Eastern Bloc countries and its cultural heritage were the most important assets in this period. International competition will increase after accession to the EU and the remaining restrictions that still preserve the national economy are abolished. The increasing exposure to global competition will obviously also affect the position of Prague on the domestic market: the hitherto unrivalled position as national centre of higher education, research, culture, banking and other financial services as well as a major industrial centre may be of decreasing importance. On the other hand, the importance of Prague as the national gateway centre will increase. The Strategic Plan envisages the future competitiveness of Prague being based on a good standard of living, attractiveness to visitors, strength and prosperity of the business sector, and resources to implement public projects. Coordination of plans and development with other central European cities (e.g. Berlin, Vienna, Budapest) are identified as vital (p.19). The Strategic Plan does not consider Prague's position towards the global market outside the European context.

Divergence of administration units and functional region

Since 2001, the administration pattern of regions of Prague and Central Bohemia has been the same as the one that was abolished in 1990. At the same time spatial problems of the growing metropolis aggravate; these were partly non-existent and partly solved by acquisition of developable areas by way of annexation in the past. As the demarcation of regions is taken for granted, the solution of the looming problems is sought in 'soft' ways of identifying common interests, bargaining and functional *ad hoc* cooperation. The ROPID (Regional Organiser of Prague Integrated Transport) agency is a good example of this. The agency was established in 1994 to coordinate urban and suburban mass transport services between several bus and rail service providers operating in the Prague metropolitan region. The size of the network coordinated by the ROPID is steadily growing, and now reaches beyond the metropolitan region. Informal *ad hoc* cooperation exists between boroughs inside Prague, but rural rather than inner-city ones. Outside Prague, a micro-regional coordination was constituted, for example, between the municipalities to the south-east of Prague but boroughs from Prague cannot formally join it.

Divergence of private profits, tax revenues and public expenditures

The existing tax system does not internalise external costs and benefits of the capital city. Tourism, which was already mentioned as a major dynamic industry in Prague, is a good example of the 'dark' side. Visitors' money is injected into the economy, but the visitors use subsidised public transport, litter the city and contribute to congestion and urban crime. As only some of the tax revenues collected by the state are returned to the municipality, Prague complains that it is not receiving enough to cover the investment in and costs of maintaining and increasing the quality of what is offered to visitors, and also for compensation for the detrimental effects of tourism. On the bright side, Prague enjoys the privileged position of being the location for the headquarters of many companies which have branches in various parts of the country. This earns the municipality a lot of extra business tax revenue. In the future, the suburbanisation of the higher-income population may become a threat to Prague's economy: the employer-income tax revenues from suburbanites will move to suburban municipalities while the burden of paying for social services for a less affluent population as well as for infrastructure will remain upon the city.

Intergovernmental relationships

In the *state-municipality relationship*, the position of the state remains dominant owing to its economic and ownership power. Therefore it is difficult for municipalities to free themselves from the 'dependence syndrome'. The state is expected to provide resources for large infrastructural investments of national importance. In the case of Prague, the state budget finances the outer ring motorway but the responsibility for financing the metro extension is that of the municipality. State institutions and state-controlled enterprises still manage large pieces of real estate, often on under-utilised or abandoned sites that are strategic from the point of view of spatial development of the city. The managers of this property do not share the objective of municipalities to recycle the property, nor are they interested in disposing of the redundant property for commercial reasons. Recent cases of the redevelopment of inner-city brownfield sites in Prague involved privately owned areas, while the state-controlled brownfield sites have remained untouched. The role of the municipality in these cases was circumscribed by its legal authority in planning.

The *inter-regional cooperation* in the Prague metropolitan region is determined by Prague's position as both a municipality and a region. Not much experience has yet been gained with the cooperation between the regions of Prague and Central Bohemia. While the Strategic Plan for Prague calls for 'greater and more effective communication between Prague and the Central Bohemian Region and the coordination of development aims and activity' (p.22), no such strategy was embedded in the Regional Development Strategy for Central Bohemia (1998). Currently, attempts are being made to establish a coordination body for development issues which would extend beyond the borders between the regions. In the inter-municipal cooperation, the gap between the city of Prague as a municipality and other surrounding municipalities with a population of several hundred (or even fewer) inhabitants makes the communication unbalanced. These boroughs, especially the small ones on the rural fringe of Prague, could be partners with the adjacent small municipalities, but the boroughs have no right to make formal agreements with municipalities on their own.

Intra-municipal relationships are of specific importance in Prague. Following Barlow's categorisation of municipal government patterns, Prague adopted an intermediate model between unicity and the two-tier system, unlike other metropolises in East-Central Europe, which now have two-tier governments. Inside Prague, overlaps and tensions repeatedly occur between boroughs and the 'big town hall'. The boroughs have no direct influence on the decisions made by the municipality, except for lobbying through their representatives in the Assembly of Prague. Also the position differs between inner-city and small semi-rural boroughs on the fringe that are struggling for improvement of basic infrastructures and services. Despite the small share of power delegated to the boroughs, some local mayors have succeeded in developing their own image, and their informal influence may reach further than their formal powers, enjoying a more immediate contact with their electorate than the remote and impersonal 'big town hall' can achieve.

Public–private partnership

The Strategic Plan for Prague identified among the weaknesses: 'uncoordinated and unclear relationships between city authorities and the business sector (potential investors)' (p.13). Among the long-term goals is mentioned: 'purposeful building of partnerships for Prague in management, the planning and financing of development measures' (p.22).

There is no legal background for it and the very concept of public-private partnership (PPP) is not quite clear. Different models of PPP can be identified:

- Some private investment is directed to the external development outside the project site, typically for technical infrastructure, roads, facilities, etc. This is made on the basis of agreements especially in the case of very attractive sites or large commercial developments. Private financial contributions to inner-city public underground car parks agreed by developers of office buildings are examples of this; in one case, the developer of an out-of-town shopping centre offered to finance a public park on the non-developable part of the site and a road bypassing the neighbouring residential area;
- a public property (land or built property) is developed or improved by a private investor. As a reward, the improved property is rented to the investor for a certain period for a symbolic fee. This method was applied for the improvement of some devastated historical palaces owned by the municipality in the centre of Prague. The rules of the partnership were set individually for each case; sometimes the municipality shares profits from the project;
- public and private partners establish a joint venture. The public partner shares the property with the private investor and the future profits or losses can be shared. The municipality can support the viability of a project by connecting it to some public investment. The project of the new exhibition complex is the most prominent example of this model. Here public financing for the extension of the nearby metro line complemented the project financed mostly by private company.

Openness of the spatial management

The Strategic Plan for Prague identified as a weakness the '… low level of coopera-tion between the city authorities, businesses and the public at large, which in turn encourages general passivity and low participation levels in decision-making processes' (p.16). One of the long-term goals of this plan is 'greater discussion between the people, public and private sectors as well as active and effective participation of the state' (p.22). Poor communication between stakeholders in development is an omnipresent problem. Developers usually try to keep their project proposals in secret for business reasons and to avoid the problems and delays caused by local opponents. This policy also suits some decision-makers who believe that only a small group of well-informed experts should be involved and the public access to project negotiation only puts sand in the wheels of bureaucratic process of planning decision-making.

The conflicts usually arise when a project is about to pass the planning permission process, or even afterwards, if the public was not informed. Here the opposing NGOs and citizens' groups are often considered as troublemakers by planners and other stakeholders. Besides *ad hoc* opponents, experts and well-known personalities offer their experience and critique especially in cases of important inner-city projects: the Club for Old Prague – which has been in existence for more than 100 years – is the most traditional of these. Some boroughs regularly organise presentations of new projects with public enquiries and discussions, to get feedback and test public opinion. Recently also the Internet has been used to inform citizens about proposed plans and to collect their comments. So far no attempt has been made by the municipality or boroughs to establish a mediator in order to prevent and/or mitigate conflicts by communicating with potentially affected people. Despite the general trend towards more openness on the part of municipalities, the level of public involvement and participation has hardly moved beyond informing and consultation (cf. Arnstein, 1969).

Evaluation of the new forms of metropolitan governance with respect to the coordination of the spatial policy

Unlike in Western Europe, municipal and especially regional self-government did not exist between the 1940s and 1990 in the Czech Republic. The experience of self-government means that both leaders and the public must undergo a learning process.

The perception of the spatial dimension of political and economic issues was very weak among political leaders at the beginning of the transitional period. The national government acknowledged the regionally disparate effects of the transformation only after 1997. The local self-governments proved to be a stabilising factor in the turbulent period of transformation. However, it was evident from the very beginning that the traditional pattern of local units based on particular villages and towns would make the viability especially of the smallest communities questionable. The need to assist them is the major argument for limited local self-governmental control of administration, and also for the large-scale redistribution of tax revenue by the state. The increasing autonomy of small municipalities gave birth to communal egoism and lessened the chance to achieve a wider coordination of development. Small municipalities are less resistant to pressures for development wherever potential investors wish. Spatially fragmented local governments may also challenge the feasibility of regionally or nationally important infrastructure projects. The gap between the size of Prague and that of other municipalities, as well as ambiguous ranking of the capital city, aggravates these problems. Facing these weaknesses of fragmented local government, the recent introduction of the regional tier of self-government with the shift of certain parts of hitherto state administration to the regional level is an important move towards a less centralised and more effective pattern of government. The spatial issues may be more negotiable on the level of regions. The territorial aspect of the introduction of regions was however not favourable for the Prague metropolitan region. The mismatch between the functional region of the capital and the spatial pattern of governance and administration was increased; this was in addition to the existing gap between the size of Prague and the small municipalities surrounding it. The position of the two involved formal regions in the spatial issues of the functional region of Prague will not be equal: while the coordination of development in the metropolitan region will be of vital interest for Prague, this will be an agenda item only for a part of the Central Bohemian region.

Thus the formal units and legal frameworks established in the governmental reforms on the local and the regional level have made spatial management in the Prague metropolitan region more difficult than before. As a result, additional efforts to coordinate spatial development will be needed and the importance of horizontal, functionally based intergovernmental coordination as well as informal cooperation outside the governmental structures will increase. These 'soft' arrangements may be quite effective in spatial management as long as the expected effects are beneficial to stakeholders in particular issues in the short- or medium-term. But they will not work if some of the key stakeholders would have to give up some gain without any compensation. Unfortunately, urban sprawl – as obviously the emerging key spatial issue in the Prague metropolitan region – belongs to the second kind. None of the key actors has enough motivation and capacity to manage this threat. The uncoordinated development in the suburban area is both a bonanza for private investment capital and promising for individual property owners. It is – at least in the short-term – compatible with the interests of the municipalities in the potentially affected suburban area. For the Central Bohemian Region it will be hardly politically feasible to enforce a more sustainable spatial policy in face of the opposing position of the affected and the disinterest of the non-affected municipalities. Prague as a potential loser has no legal word in this game as either a region or a municipality. The only actors which could prevent excessive, sprawl-like suburbanisation are the central government (in the control and restrictive line) and state organisations, such as Czech Railways (in creating the infrastructure for alternative, more sustainable patterns of suburbanisation). Political aspects and economic constraints, however, cast doubts on the active, effective and timely involvement of these actors in this issue.

The emergence of the partnership approach in governance that accepts and encompasses a larger circle of stakeholders in the management of spatial change has been delayed for historical reasons in all post-Communist countries. It can be presumed that it will increasingly contribute to compensation for the negative aspects of formal fragmentation and non-functional structuring of governmental units. More open and less formal network-like forms of governance will be crucial to manage complex issues that could be difficult to describe and tackle in simple spatial terms and control mechanisms. Indeed, even if the geography of the new governmental units is not the most important outcome of the current governmental reform, it will play an important role in the fundamental issue for the Prague metropolitan region. Due to the delayed transition from governmental control to more open governance, and owing to the expectedly high speed of the future change of spatial pattern in the Prague metropolitan region, the role of non-hierarchical, partnership- and network-based governance will be to mitigate the aftermath of the sprawl that is currently in progress.

Bibliography

Arnstein, S.R. (1969) 'A ladder of citizen participation', *Journal of the American Institute of Planners* 8, quoted from J. Stein (1995) *Classic Readings in Urban Planning*, 358–75.

Barlow, M., Dostál, P., Illner, M., Kára, J. (eds) (1993) *Changing Territorial Administration in Czechoslovakia. International Viewpoints*, Amsterdam: University of Amsterdam.

Barlow, M. (1994) 'Alternative structures of government in metropolitan areas', in M. Barlow, P. Dostál and M. Hampl (eds) *Development and Administration of Prague*, Amsterdam: University of Amsterdam.

Blažek, B. (1994) *Praha 2010. Program rozvoje hlavního města Prahy* (Development Programme for the Capital of Prague), Prague: Ecoterra.

City Development Authority of Prague (2000) *Strategic Plan for Prague*, Prague.

ČSÚ (Český statistický úřad), Data of the Czech Statistical Office.

Grabmüllerová, D. (1998) *Bytová politika* (Housing policy), Czech Technical University.

Hampl, M., Blažek, J., Čermák, Z., Drbohlav, D., Sýkora, L. and Tomeš, J. (eds) (1999) *Geography of Societal Transformation in the Czech Republic*, Prague: Charles University of Prague.

Horáková, I. (2000) 'Suburbanizace či urbanizace? Nová bytová výstavba v Praze a v jejím zázemí' (Suburbanisation or urbanisation? New housing development in Prague and its background), unpublished thesis led by L. Sýkora, Charles University, Prague.

Körner, M. (1996) *Prognosis of development for the Prague Metropolitan Region*.

Lacina, K. and Vajdová, Z. (2000) 'Local Government in the Czech Republic', in T.M. Horváth (ed.) *Decentralisation: Experiments and Reforms*, Budapest: LGI Books.

Maier, J., Dittmeier, V., Chen, Y.-L. and Grasselli, N. (1998) *Regionale Disparitäten in Ostmitteleuropa: Die Notwendigkeit von Raumtypisierungen dargestelt am Beispiel der Tschechischen Republik und Ungarns*, Universität Bayreuth.

Ministry of Regional Development (2001) *Proposal for the new Planning and Building Law*.

Musil, J. (1993) 'Changing urban systems in post-communist societies in Central Europe: analysis and prediction', *Urban Studies*, 30.

Naisbit, J. (1982) *Megatrends. The New Directions Transforming Our Lives*, New York: Warner Books.

Nedović-Budić, Z. (2001) 'Adjustment of planning practice to the new Eastern and Central European Context', *APA Journal*, 1 (67).

Pešek, J. (1999) *Od aglomerace k velkoměstu* (From Agglomeration to Metropolis), Prague: Scriptorium Praha.

Regional Development Strategy for Central Bohemia (1998).

Sýkora, L. (1993) 'City in transition: the role of rent gaps in Prague's revitalization', *Tijdschrift voor Economie en Sociale Geografie* 4.

ÚDI (Ústav dopravního inženýrství, Transport Engineering Institute) (2000) *Ročenka dopravy* (Transport Yearbook), Prague: ÚDI.

Zajíček, Z. (2001) 'Radnice jdou blíže k občanům' (Town halls move nearer to citizens), *Metro* (6/6/2001).

Act on Municipalities 2000 (Zákon 128/2000 Sb., o obcích (obecní zřízení)).

Act on Regions 2000 (Zákon 129/2000 Sb., o krajích (krajské zřízení)).

Act on the Capital City of Prague 2000 (Zákon 131/2000 Sb., o hlavním městě Praze).

Act on Support for Regional Development 2000 (Zákon 248/2000 Sb., o podpoře regionálního rozvoje).

Planning and Building Law 1976, last amendment 2000 (Zákon 50/1976 Sb., o územním plánování a stavebním řádu, ve znění zákona 132/2000 Sb.).

14 Metropolitan governance and regional planning in Vienna

Michaela Paal

Introduction: changing planning conditions since the fall of the Iron Curtain

After decades of stagnation in relation to population and economic development, Austria's capital is now on the way to integrating itself into the new system of leading European metropolises. New geopolitical conditions and the internationalisation of economics and migration have brought new prosperity to urban development. At the same time, urban planning partly rejects the traditional paradigm of municipal socialism and seeks to find a new balance between planning prescription and planning strategy.

Compared to other great European urban centres, until 1990 Vienna was a relatively conservative city, largely spared the effects of many short-lived fads in urban development. This oversized capital of a country on the fringe of Europe was characterised by stagnation in an economic and demographic context. Decades of shrinking populations led the Urban Development Plan to project a population of 1.4 million residents for the year 2001 – a remarkable decline considering that in 1900 Vienna had 2 million inhabitants.

At the beginning of the 1990s this prognosis had to be completely revised. Between 1987 and 1994 the number of residents increased by 120,000, and in 1999 reached a stable plateau of 1.61 million. This subsequent growth was one of the results of the fall of the Iron Curtain in 1989 and of Austria's accession to the EU in 1995, which changed Vienna's geopolitical situation dramatically. The city was no longer the easternmost European outpost of the Western economic system, but had acquired a new centrality within the European Community.

Within the external pressures of internationalisation, the patterns of urban planning also changed dramatically. Fossilised spatial structures of urban settlement and socio-economic configurations were suddenly influenced by international demands and new liberalism. At the same time the political conditions of urban planning also changed. The Social Democrats lost their majority on the city council, and the era of municipal socialism seemed to have been modified or even brought to an end. To understand the consequences of this break, a brief retrospective of Vienna's urban development and urban planning strategies since the era of industrialisation is in order.

Vienna's urban development since the middle of the nineteenth century

The development of Vienna did not take place in a more or less continuous fashion but in what were sometimes major bursts (see table 14.1). In 1857 the imperial capital of the Hapsburg monarchy was an almost quaint urban relict. While the town walls of other great European cities had been demolished during the seventeenth century, Vienna remained a medieval city constrained by massive bastions, ramparts and walls that had long since lost any military significance. Beyond the walls, the suburbs crept towards the city, but were kept away by an open expanse of land several hundred metres wide, called the Glacis.

At this time, a decision taken by the Emperor, Franz Joseph I, changed everything. His autocratic decree to demolish the town walls marked the first great upheaval in modern Viennese history. An international competition was launched to bridge the gap between the medieval town and its suburbs by means of a *via triumphalis* of the emerging Austrian haute bourgeoisie: the *Ringstraße*.

At the same time, rapid industrialisation and mass immigration brought about an explosive growth in terms of area and population. A broad fringe of industrial production and tenement blocks characterised the western quarters outside the old fortifications (*Linienwall*) and established the urban social structure up to the present day. The Danube control scheme provided new building land close to the city centre, which was developed in kilometre-long street grids. Towards the end of this *Gründerzeit* (Founders' period, 1857–1914; the Viennese equivalent of the Victorian era) the city was equipped with an extraordinarily efficient infrastructure, planned for 4 million inhabitants.

One of the most important planning tools used to develop the main structure of the expanding city was the *Bauzonenplan*. One of the main goals of this plan was to limit the floor space related to the different building zones from the city centre to the old villages situated on the mountainside of the Viennese Forest. The Bauzonenplan was in force up until 1990 and helped to preserve the urban structure of a dense and compact built-up area.

The explosive development ceased abruptly after the First World War, the disintegration of the dual monarchy and the founding of the Republic of Austria in 1918. After their election victory in 1918, the Viennese Social Democrats launched a programme to ameliorate aspects that had been neglected by the Christian Socialists, especially the extreme shortage of housing and the charging of exorbitant rents. The new policy was directed towards providing social services, a balanced

231

Table 14.1 The main planning periods since 1857

Founder's period 1857–1914	Intermediate war period 1918–34	Post-war period 1945–70	Consolidation 1971–89	internationalisation 1990–?
• demolition of the town walls	• communal housing	• reconstruction of demolished buildings	• rediscovery of the inner city	• relief for the traditional economic centre
• Danube regulation	• amelioration of the technical infrastructure	• satisfaction of housing demand	• new traffic infrastructure	• high-rise buildings
• traffic infrastructure				• public–private partnership
urban extension	increasing urban development	urban extension	urban renewal	urban transformation
regulation plan; 'Bauzonenplan'	land development plan; expropriation established in law	concept for urban development	municipal plan for urban development (STEP84)	STEP94 and strategy plan

strategy of land-use and the construction of municipal housing units. Supported by the existing infrastructure, around 64,000 apartments were built between 1918 and 1934, which were contained in large, municipal housing complexes known as 'people's palaces' or – to urban planners – 'super-blocks'. Mainly they were integrated into the suburban green belt of the western districts in order to infiltrate their upper-class population structure.

The construction of municipal housing units was halted after the establishment of an authoritarian state in 1934. With the aid of the *Assanierungsfonds* (revitalisation fund) the construction activities of the community were replaced and boosted by private-sector building programmes. The main objective was to demolish older buildings that were a hindrance to automobile traffic and create a dense, compact, modern city.

Shortly after the *Anschluß* the National Socialists began to develop fantasies about the city's future as the second capital of Greater Germany. A new Vienna was to evolve on both banks of the Danube with marching routes and administrative complexes that would have relegated the historical centre to being a mere architectural attraction for tourists. The idea of creating a Greater Vienna by extending the city's borders to include satellite communities was not prompted by the practicalities of progressive and far-sighted urban and regional planning, but only served as an extension of the territorial administrative mandate of the governor of Vienna.

Unfortunately, the ideology of a large conurbation survived the Nazi era and the policy of dispersion was introduced. The years of reconstruction between 1945 and 1960 were partly characterised by the concepts of National Socialism and partly by modern architecture. This can be explained by the fact that most of the architects involved in this reconstruction period had worked or studied during the Nazi era. The well-established model of residential blocks was hardly ever used. New buildings were constructed in the periphery of the city, but it is remarkable that this wave also penetrated the inner districts where vacant lots in the densely built-up nineteenth-century area were also subject to ribbon development.

The general trend towards the periphery was encouraged – as in other European metropolises – by the improved access for cars. The use of precast concrete elements was introduced in Vienna in 1960, at the beginning of a decade of urban extension towards the outer districts on the northern bank of the Danube. Most of these very large housing estates were not erected in the vicinity of the local suburban railway because they were intended to be reached by car. But all in all, compared to other European cities, the measures to turn Vienna into an automobile-friendly city were of marginal significance.

Vienna was around ten years behind the rest of Western Europe as regards the economic and cultural development of the 1960s. The stagnation in population development helped to maintain the infrastructure at the 1914 level without the need for modernisation and modification.

From the middle of the 1970s onwards a change in planning strategy took place. In context with the national minority government of the Socialist Party and the opening up to international trends, two great planning projects altered the city's fabric in the same way as the Ringstraße or the Danube's control had done: construction of UNO City (City of the United Nations) on the northern bank of the Danube, linked to the inner city by the first metro line, and the creation of the Donauinsel (Danube's Isle) in the course of the excavation of an overflow channel to control river flooding. The huge building complex of UNO City – the third UN headquarters after New York and Geneva – was located on the historic north–south axis and represented the first step towards bringing Viennese development to the river.

At the same time – and within the context of the first metro line – the inner city attracted attention again. The establishment of pedestrian zones and the high density of cultural attractions helped this trend, and the planners began to develop a new concept of urban renewal. The city's older fabric was in poor condition. Because of the law protecting tenants (a result of the city's social housing policy during the 1920s) and low rents, landlords could not afford to renovate. Vienna had never applied the practice of demolishing old houses, but the burden of 150,000 inadequately equipped (by international standards) flats caused the Social Democratic city government to create *Sanfte Stadterneuerung* (the 'preservative urban renewal'). The concept entailed not only improving housing and renovating residential buildings but comprehensively renewing densely built-up areas and improving the urban environment in general. Its major goals were in the fields of social and housing politics, that is, to prevent segregation, to deal with houses as well as with individual flats or sections of streets, and to protect the Founders' period fabric as well as the functional mixture of apartments, offices, workshops and shops.

'Preservative urban renewal' acted – and still acts – on different legal levels and with different instruments. First of all, a 'protective zone model' (1972) included 10,000 buildings, where designation and construction plans declared areas to be worthy of preservation because of their local visual context as an integral whole. At the same time a reassessment of the building stock took place together with the critical evaluation of the sustainability of the older fabric. The social needs of the residents had to be respected during the whole construction work for the revitalisation process. Tenant participation involved residents and contributed substantially to the success of the block rehabilitation.

Planning conditions in Austria

It is important to know that Austrian regional planning is in the hands of the nine Austrian provinces. Only decisions of national importance – such as those affecting railways, mining, forests and water resources – are within the government's competence. The conception and the performance of the land development plans depend on the communities (see table 14.2).

Vienna is both a province and a community. Regional planning and land-development planning are drafted by the Department of Urban Planning as a part of municipal administration. All decisions about future urban development – for the whole city and for certain districts – have to be approved by the city council. Before approval is granted, new land-development plans are open to public discussion.

In reality the land development plans and the limitation of construction height (which was already approved during the Founders' period) are the only binding framework of Viennese urban planning. The municipal plan for urban development as well as its Strategy Plan (see the section 'Spatial effects of new urban planning') may only propose future development.

Vienna is one of few European metropolises without a working collaboration between the core city and the suburban communities. One reason for this is the growing competition in business location decisions, especially in services (some of the richest Austrian communities are situated to the south of Vienna, participating in agglomeration advantages).

Urban planning conditions and planning tools in the 1980s

In the early 1980s, Vienna's urban planners were confronted with the stagnation of the Viennese population and slower economic development. The real estate market for both living and office space was predominately oriented towards demand and was not at all dynamic. Nevertheless, the urban planners agreed on the need for a superordinated concept for sustainable urban development. In 1984 the

Table 14.2 Financial and planning responsibilities in Austria

Level	Political	Financial	Planning responsibilities
Nation	Election	Raises taxes (except trade tax and tax on alcoholic drinks)	Planning of national infrastructure
Province	Election	National grants, equalization of revenue between government and provinces	Regional planning
Community	Election	Trade tax, tax on alcoholic drinks, equalization of revenue between government and communities	Land development planning

municipal government drew up *Stadtentwicklungsplan STEP84* (municipal plan for urban development), a long-term instrument to establish a spatial concept to enhance the quality of life, social justice, solidarity with the poor, urban diversity and urban culture.

The planning-oriented integration of inhabitants was intended as collaboration with all communities in the urban agglomeration (see figure 14.1). The main goals of STEP84 were:

* *Special emphasis on urban renewal and the gradual reduction of densely populated urban areas*
  With the implementation of the Urban Renewal Fund (1984) the first legislation of measures took place and was designed to facilitate the material implementation. In the following 16 years, over 3,100 buildings throughout the administrative territory received financial support.
* *Moderate density in the new settlement axes at the city's edges*
  Necessary urban growth was planned to take place along a few development axes along efficient public transport lines and between green belts. Ten of these development axes were instituted within municipal territory. The advantages of this concept were described by the planners as follows: '… this axis model has significant advantages for urban growth, because by concentrating construction in areas within easy reach of public transport, optimal access can be ensured and the dependency on private cars can be ruled out. Over and beyond this, the model allows relatively flexible settlement development while at the same time facilitating quicker or slower urban growth characteristic of different periods of urban development' (Kotzya, 2001).
* *Planning cooperation with Vienna's hinterland*
  STEP84 called for closer cooperation with the Province of Lower Austria, but also with the surrounding communities in the Lower Austria hinterland. The spatial model proposed concentrating settlement activities along the main axes of the public transport network.
* *Changing patterns in international and local politics: from STEP94 to the Vienna Strategy Plan*
  At the beginning of the 1990s – following the collapse of the Eastern Bloc and the changing geopolitical situation – Vienna's urban development had a new dynamism. The burst of development was reflected in an increasing demand for both accommodation and workspace, caused by increasing immigration and the lack of well-equipped offices. For the first time since the end of the Second World War, the Viennese real estate market changed from a demand to a supply market because international large-scale enterprises chose Vienna as their principal headquarters to open up the Eastern European markets.

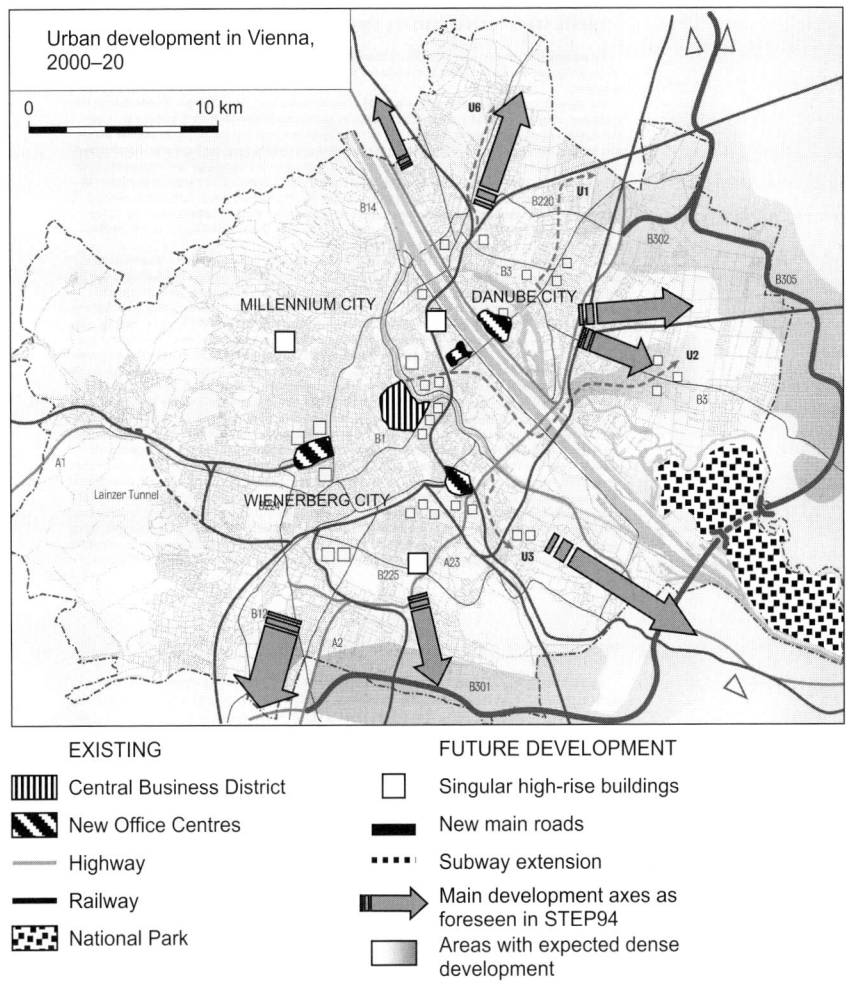

Figure 14.1 Urban development in Vienna, 2000–20. *Source:* Based on MA18 (2000)

A new Founders' period was stimulated by the decision to organise a world exhibition in close cooperation with Budapest. The intended location was the vacant site between UNO City and the Danube. This district had been enormously enhanced through metro access and the Donauinsel, and clamoured for development as a new urban centre.

After the EXPO was rejected by plebiscite, the discussion of urban development was implemented swiftly and with (by Viennese standards) unusual intensity. The height of the UN buildings meant that a long-held planning dogma proscribing high-rise buildings in Vienna was scrapped. A group of prominent architects, closely connected to the municipal government, insisted that it would have been pointless to develop the extremely valuable site with small-scale buildings. At the same time, underused, partially vacant, unattractive but more or less centrally situated areas which had hitherto resisted refurbishment for various reasons became more and more attractive for investors. However, attempts to thin out densely built-up areas, as had been made in the past, were now out of the question.

In the context of the new accommodation, STEP84 was no longer applicable and fell victim to euphoric growth. Its successor was STEP94, which attempted to reconcile the need for the continuity of a model that had been recognised as being valid in a long-term perspective, and the necessity of providing for extra areas for inevitable urban growth.

Although the increasing immigration brought about by the fall of the Iron Curtain and the war in the Balkans foreshadowed a massive increase in urban growth, STEP94 maintained the priority of gentle urban renewal. The great development axes were extended, supplementary axes were introduced and the building density in all of them was increased, but the basic political principles of STEP84 remained untouched. In questions of traffic development STEP94 was more in favour of environment-friendly transport (pedestrians, cyclists, public transport); it wanted to influence the choice of means of transport through improving the public transport system and by means of a comprehensive parking management system to avoid superfluous automobile traffic.

Like its predecessor, STEP94 remained on the level of recommendations without having any force in law. The main planning goals – such as closer cooperation between Vienna and the surrounding communities – were not attained because of

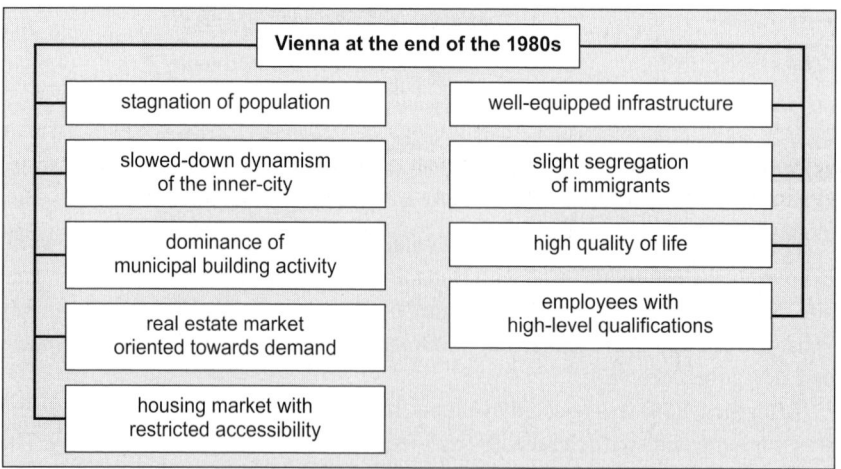

Figure 14.2 Vienna at the end of the 1980s

Austria's eastern region's administrative structures (the communities close to the administrative territory of Vienna are part of the province of Lower Austria, whereas Austria's capital is both a community and a province). Financial and economic competition between Vienna and the suburban communities had also been an important reason to delay making an agreement concerning future urban development (in the previous two decades, the neighbourhood communities to the south of Vienna in particular had been extremely successful in enticing small- and medium-sized enterprises from the inner city).

In 1998 the Municipality of Vienna decided to draw up a strategy plan for the city – 'Quality sets standards: innovation for Vienna' (Klotz, 2001). In it, five main strategy areas were defined: increasing regional cooperation; creating new perspectives in economics and employment; investment in knowledge, education, leisure and culture; increasing the quality of natural and urban spaces; and ensuring the high quality of life and the environment. The central objective was to establish Vienna as a cultural city with a high quality of life and with new fields of competence, while preserving and utilising existing resources. This was intended to ensure that Vienna gained a higher profile as an international commercial centre. A recognisable orientation towards action and realisation was to be ensured by the consequent implementation of strategic projects.

These projects were to have a stimulating effect, as their implementation illustrated good practice, such as the economic, scientific, life and environmental qualities that can be strengthened in Vienna. For instance, the strategy plan concerning trade and employment featured such projects as the Vienna Technology Park and the Main Railway Station. Special attention was paid to the strategic field in context with metropolitan competition on an international level and the specialisation in knowledge, education and culture. This strategic area embraced projects such as the Technology and Provision Fund and the Viennese Education Network; the latter connects the majority of Viennese educational facilities via a high-performance data network (Klotz, 2001).

One prerequisite for an effective implementation of the strategic projects was to adapt the administrative structures within the municipality to their future assignments. For this reason, a strategic project of modernising Vienna's municipality was initiated concurrently with Vienna's Strategic Plan. The activities of the municipality and its employees should be evaluated on the basis of their output for the people and businesses according to the concepts of a 'new public management', that is: '... organisational measures in the sense of contract management, controlling and reporting will allow the administration to self-confidently fulfil the demands posed by increasing partnership of the public and private sector' (Klotz, 2001).

In comparison with the strategy plans of other European metropolises – especially with the measures presented for the urban development in Berlin – the Vienna Strategy Plan is not exactly defined. The Plan – like STEP84 and STEP94

– is not legally binding; even the financing of the strategy projects is not safeguarded. An evaluation of the progress of the strategic projects is not foreseen.

The Strategy Plan may be interpreted as a result of the increasing liberalisation of the Vienna municipal government. In 1993 the Social Democrats lost their absolute majority and formed a coalition with the Christian Democrats, and – after 80 years of municipal socialist planning tradition – the chair of the city councillor for urban planning was transferred to the Christian Democrats. The new policy of liberalism in urban planning forced the demise of the dictum proscribing high-rise buildings in Vienna. The consequences for spatial urban development are far-reaching. Vienna's skyscraper boom is the result of increasing financial commitment of private investors as well as international investment groups. Reality is overtaking urban planning measures.

Spatial effects of new urban planning

The physical appearance of the city has changed more profoundly in the last two decades than in the previous 80 years. The demise of the dictum to proscribe high-rise buildings remodelled the densely built-up area of the Founders' period in an impressive manner.

From the middle of the 1990s onwards the extremes in demand for housing were covered, so that the programmes to build new apartments could be reduced. This process took place against the background of increasingly scarce financial resources on the part of the public sector because the investments needed for the social and technical infrastructure drew excessively on the budget of the municipality. In context with the demand for offices in the densely built-up area, more attention was paid to the economic development of the city. Already in STEP94 and also in the following designation and construction plans, locations for industrial and commercial urbanisation and for the service sector had been foreseen.

Already during these first years it seemed to be clear that it was impossible to satisfy the increasing demand for floor space in the form of technically state-of-the-art offices only in the inner districts. Despite concerted attempts to mobilise enough reserves of building land within the inner city areas, the dynamics of the first period of urban development after the fall of the Iron Curtain had been concentrated in the north-east of Vienna, especially in the Danube-orientated part of the twenty-second district (which is not too far from the historical centre) which had been chosen as the new economic pole to relieve the pressure from the inner-city real estate market.

At present, urban development is concentrated on three sites: Danube City, Millennium City and Wienerberg City. Danube City can be seen as the inspiration for the significant development of *Transdanubia*. The area is the only Viennese metropolitan project that can compare with other international projects such as the Docklands in London, La Défense in Paris or Potsdamer Platz in Berlin. The development includes offices, laboratories with a high quality technical infrastructure (such as TECH GATE, Vienna's first step towards a service specialisation in research and knowledge) as well as apartments, schools, services and recreational facilities.

In contrast to the PPP investments in Danube City, the other development projects – Millennium City and Wienerberg City – were inspired and are being financed by private investor groups. Millennium City, which is located on Handelskai near the river and a metro station, has the characteristics of a super-block that encompasses everything, even public space. With its shopping mall and layer of residential accommodation, the Millennium Tower is an eye-catching landmark in the waterfront development zone (and at 202 metres, the fourth highest tower in Europe).

Wienerberg, which is situated in an extraordinary topological and natural environment on the southern border of the Vienna administrative area, represents the new peripheral expansion. One of the new constructions here is the 137-metre-high Vienna Twin Tower, but the development also includes residential buildings and a cineplex centre. Wienerberg City is not integrated into the public transport system, a location decision pointing the way forwards for urban planning. An analysis of future high-rise building projects in Vienna reveals a remarkable distribution of skyscrapers all over the densely built-up area without any spatial or functional concentration. This means that the public transport system has lost its function of modelling urban development.

But also the strategy of urban renewal seems to have changed. With Austria's accession to the EU, the creation of benefits for urban development projects opens up new financial prospects for the municipality. One of the most impressive examples of the new paradigm to enhance urban renewal with help from Brussels within the framework of the EU initiative URBAN PLUS, is the Gürtel area.

The history of planning in the Gürtel area was characterised by a wide range of concepts and projects. The projects of the *Gürtelkommission* between 1984 and 1988 included the transfer of the vehicle carriageway as well as excavating a tunnel under the thoroughfare; but financial constraints together with a certain amount of scepticism about the project's feasibility led to the adoption of a new planning philosophy, which intends the gradual adaptation and improvement of the treatment and utilisation of the region of the overhead railway arches along the Gürtel, which would represent an initial catalyst for the urban structure of the region. In attracting EU funding for the project within the framework of the communal initiative URBAN PLUS, the programme should form the decisive impetus for the implementation of measures in the Gürtel area. In the last five years, musical venues, fashionable bars and restaurants, galleries and shops especially for young people have been built in 30 of the arches of the overhead railway. This is commercial gentrification at the interface between the inner-city middle-class districts and the outer quarters, which are dominated by immigrants.

The extensive policy of gentle urban renewal is heading for replacement by a strategy of pilot projects in relation to private initiatives of rehabilitation. In the long term, this will mean the dropping of equal distribution of finance resources all over the densely built-up area which has been one of the most efficient tools to prevent the segregation of minorities.

In the meantime, spatial patterns of internationalisation of migration and the development of ethnic segregation can be observed. While highly qualified managers prefer to live in the suburban belt of western districts near the Viennese Forest, immigrants from the Balkans and the Far East are concentrated in the fringe of low-rise tenement blocks dating back to the Founders' period near the Gürtel.

Vienna's new location: the consequences for urban development

Vienna itself was not responsible for the change of location in context with the new fault-line of a politically and economically reunited Europe; in fact, it was basically caught unawares. What does it mean for Vienna to be located at what can be called a new European front behind the leaky Schengen border? And what does it mean for Vienna's location policy and its inner-city development?

In a globalised, interlinked world, different location qualities are very carefully assessed and exploited by enterprises, leading to increased direct and indirect competition between metropolises. This competition takes place on two levels. Superficially it is a matter of attracting international enterprises and high-level management. However, this competition only forms a small fraction of urban economic output. These enterprises do not produce merely to cover local needs, but offer their goods and services to the domestic or international market. A rapidly changing and innovative milieu is of decisive importance to this critical part of the urban economy, as is the cooperation between public and private research facilities, technological transfer of cultural variety and quality of life.

Extension of the transport infrastructure and the increasing significance of the modern service sector will have considerable effects on the spatial development of Vienna. The following tendencies can be inferred:

- The projected traffic access in the direction of the north-east and south-east will bring considerable residential development to prime locations over a large area, initiate a wave of suburbanisation and lead in the long-run to the formation of a second ring around the city.
- Highly accessible locations for modern service utilisation remain attractive and offer themselves as starting points for the formation of further centres across the rest of the urban area.

Residential building will adhere only to a certain extent to this economically determined spatial pattern. It is to be hoped that the redevelopment potential of the municipality will direct the focus on highly accessible areas and the extension of the metro and railway system. A central challenge for urban planning is to hinder the construction of high-rise buildings all over the densely built-up area with no development focus. There is the option on the one hand of constructing office spaces for modern service enterprises, and on the other hand of constructing sprawling, automobile-oriented suburbs in peripheral areas, as can be seen at the Wienerberg City.

With the completion of the south-eastern bypass and its extension over the Danube, a central challenge to urban planning and property policy will emerge. Whether it will be possible to prevent the development of a new ring of residential and economic suburbanisation is – although in context with the new social democratic majority since May 2001 – still an open question.

Bibliography

Bobek, H. and Lichtenberger, E. (1966) *Wien – bauliche Gestalt und Entwicklung seit der Mitte des 19. Jhdts*, Wien: Böhlau.

Bökemann, D., Giffinger, R., Knötig, G. and Riedl, R. (1990) 'Sanstrat Wien – Strukturanalyse zur Stadterneuerungspolitik', *Beiträge zur Stadtforschung, Stadtentwicklung und Stadtgestaltung,* 23.

Kohlbacher, J. and Reeger, U. (1999) 'Ethnische Segregation und Fremdenfeindlichkeit in Wien', *Mitteilungen der Österreichischen Geographischen Gesellschaft*, 141: 19–52.

Kotyza, G. (2001) 'Übergeordnete Stadtplanungskonzepte', *Wien Städtebau. Der Stand der Dinge*, 18: 27–33.

Klotz, A. (2001) 'Stadtentwicklung und Städtebau in Wien', *Wien Städtebau. Der Stand der Dinge,* 18: 8–15.

Lichtenberger, E. (1990) 'Stadtverfall und Stadterneuerung', *Beiträge zur Stadt- und Regionalforschung,* 10.

Magistratsabteilung 18 (1994) 'Stadtentwicklungsplan für Wien', *Beiträge zur Stadtforschung, Stadtentwicklung und Stadtgestaltung,* 53.

Magistratsabteilung 18 (2000) 'Stadtregion Wien', *Werkstattberichte*, 33.

Magistratsabteilung 18 (2000) 'Stadtentwicklungsbericht 2000. Beiträge zur Fortschreibung des Wiener Stadtentwicklungsplanes', *Werkstattberichte*, 38.

Magistratsabteilung 18 (2000) 'Strategieplan für Wien. Qualität verpflichtet – Innovationen für Wien', *Werkstattberichte*, 32.

Purtscher, V. and Tabor, J. (2001) 'Städtebauliche Entwicklung Wiens seit der Mitte des 19. Jhdts', *Wien Städtebau. Der Stand der Dinge*, 18: 21–6.

Schremmer, C. (2001) 'Standort Wien – eine regionale Metropole im Osten des neuen Europa?', *Wien Städtebau. Der Stand der Dinge*, 18: 43–51.

15 Venice

Mariolina Toniolo and
Turiddo Pugliese

Metropolitan development in Venice: ordinary trends in an extraordinary city

Phenomena associated with suburbanisation appeared in Venice earlier than in similar Italian cities due to the peculiar nature and shape of the city, clearly divided as it is into (at least) two parts, namely: the ancient, water-based one – consisting of the city core with a smaller lagoon island – and more recent developments on the mainland.[1] The relationship between the old and the new parts of the city – or between the archipelago and the mainland – have always been uneasy (see figure 15.1).

During most of its existence, Venice was a maritime republic having closer relationships with the eastern shores of the Mediterranean than with the nearby regions on the mainland. Since Venice ceased to be an independent state two centuries ago, the task of preserving the peculiar character of this unique city was often associated with isolating it from the rest of the world.

Shortly before the First World War, industrial and residential overspill from the old city caused the development of a new city around the villages of Marghera and Mestre. New developments were, and still are, neither just peripheral to the old core nor do they constitute a totally independent city. Therefore, in Venice the typical dilemma, integration-oriented movements opposing those supporting the self-sufficiency of different parts, common to every metropolitan area, does not occur only among municipalities but is deeply felt even within the city itself.

This is why in Venice special attention was always devoted to suburbanisation processes, and statistics were provided to distinguish the different parts of the city earlier than for similar Italian cities. As early as in the 1960s the outflow of population and economic activities was detected from the old core to what was then the periphery on the mainland, but was explained in light of the peculiar nature of the city rather than being seen as part of a trend common to most European and northern Italian cities. For people who cared for the city's preservation – and many people all over the world do care – this was a clear symptom of urban decline (see UNESCO, 1969, for probably the most relevant example).[2] As a consequence, solutions stressed the need for special policies for this very special city rather

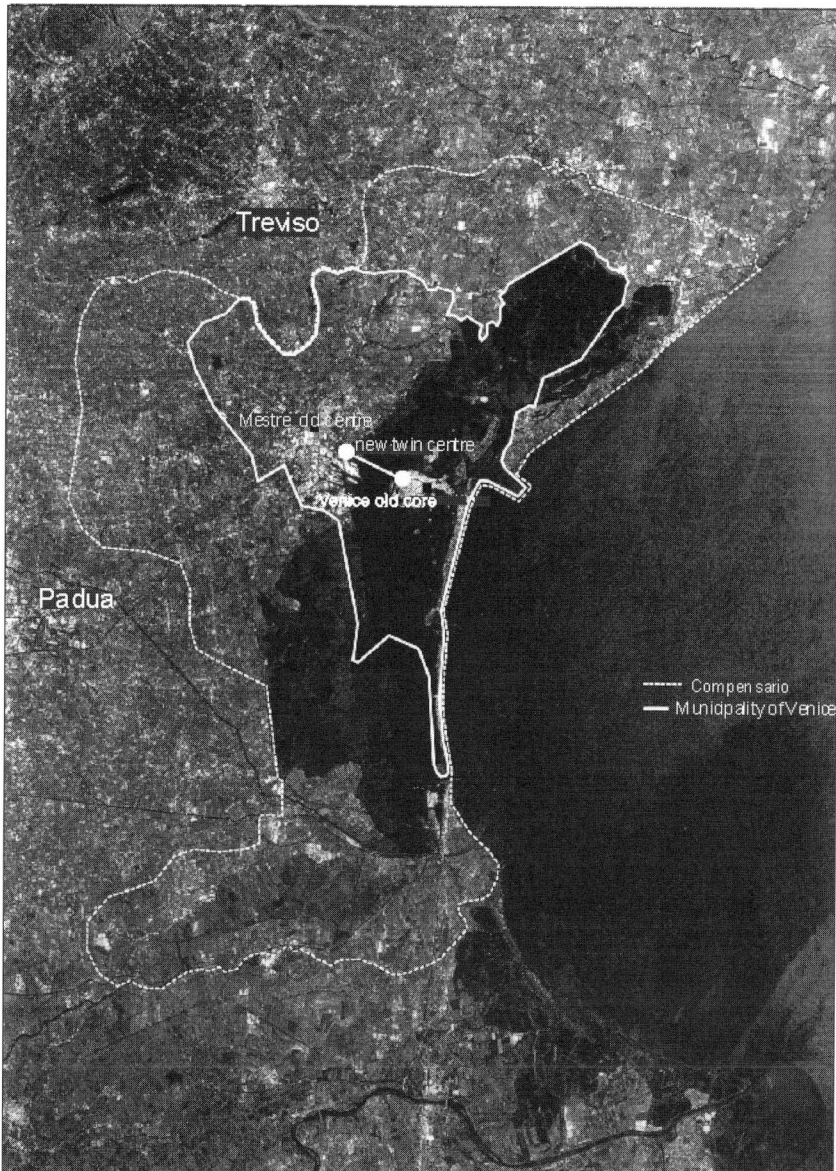

Figure 15.1 Venice and its metropolitan region

than envisaging a metropolitan government, as was being suggested for 'ordinary' cities even in Italy (Aquarone, 1961). In fact, a special law for the rescue of Venice was passed by the Italian parliament in 1971. This law, which was subsequently passed in different versions several times, devotes a considerable amount of money to the city's salvation, and also concerns the physical planning issue, asking for a comprehensive plan involving a region larger than the municipal boundaries. Since then, suburbanisation phenomena have become both more apparent and better understood, but policy solutions for Venice still oscillate between creating a larger reference area – for whose boundaries several proposals have been put forward – or splitting the existing city into smaller, self-governing parts. Currently, both options are still open, although a decision may be taken in the near future.

Redistribution of population and activities

According to the 1951 census, the number of people living in the old part of Venice in that year had reached the unprecedented peak of over 180,000. This was probably a higher than desirable figure and involved the overcrowding of dwellings. In time, population overspill affected Venice, just as it had in other cities in the rich part of the world. Table 15.1 shows the population change between the last two censuses (data from the 2001 census are not yet available) and – from a different and not perfectly comparable source – more recently.

But since in 1960 the population living in the new part of the municipality became larger than that in the old core (see figure 15.2), the fact was perceived by the public opinion as proof of the mainland's economic success and of the decadence of the ancient part of the city. Additional proof of this decline was found in the ageing population in the city centre (see figure 15.3).

Nowadays, most European cities exhibit the same pattern; however, gross population figures are very poor indicators of a city's success, especially in the case of Venice, where the needs of historical preservation drastically limit the provision of additional floor space. In fact, if the 'city lifecycle' paradigm is assumed, Venice seems to be undergoing the 'absolute decentralisation' phase characteristic of any other Western metropolitan area.

If one ignores the commonplaces about the decline of Venice and looks at the evidence, one sees that the old part of the city still works as the business core of

Table 15.1 Population change in the Venice metropolitan area, 1981–91 and 1992–9

Origin/ destination	Population 1991	% change 1981–91	% change 1992–99	Population 1999
Venice	309,422	−10.61	−10.20	277,305
inner ring	127,264	7.54	5.80	206,211
outer ring	98,958	7.47	3.20	130,625
total metrop. area	535,644	−3.76	−3.36	614,141
Province of Venice	819,530	−2.23	−0.60	814,581

Source: Municipality of Venice.

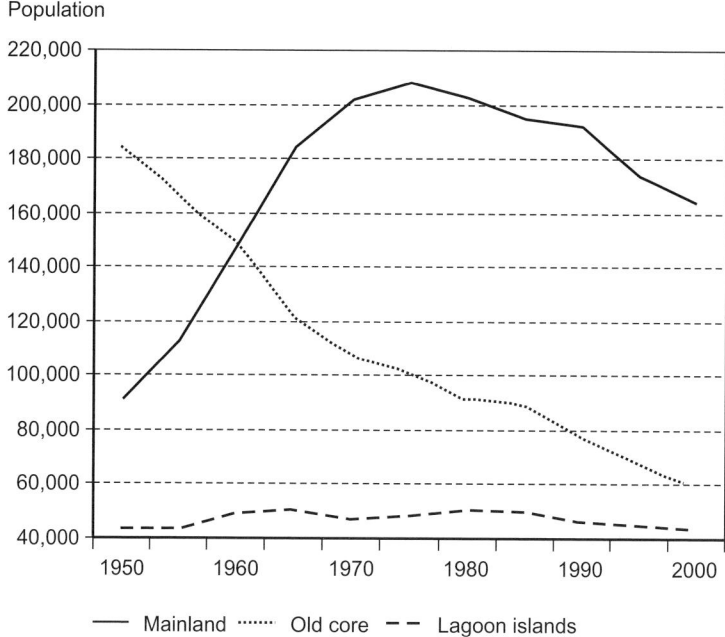

Figure 15.2 Population in different sections of Venice, 1950–2000. *Source:* Municipality of Venice

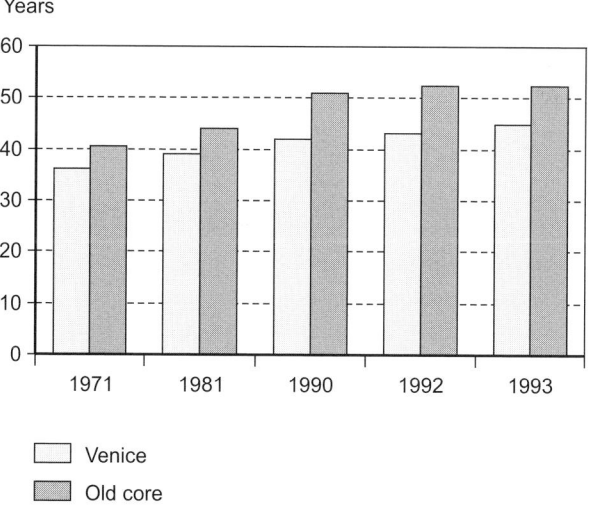

Figure 15.3 Average population age in Venice and in the old core, 1971–93

the metropolitan area, the decrease in gross population is the result of important redistribution flows within different parts of the metropolitan area (see figure 15.4) and daily commuter flows are prevailingly centripetal (see table 15.2). Gross employment data may also give the impression of an economic decline, because of recently shrinking work opportunities in the Marghera industrial area.[3] In fact, if quality is considered instead of quantity, recent data would show a post-industrial centralisation process (see table 15.5).

The same is true if we consider social change in the city's various sections, according to the employment position of the population (see table 15.3). We then see that while the total population sharply declined in every part of the city between the last two censuses, higher income positions (namely entrepreneurs, executives and professionals) have been increasing in absolute terms, and more so in the old core, where of course real estate prices are high and continuing to grow (see table 15.6).

This provides evidence of a clear gentrification process, which can hardly support any picture of Venice as an economically declining city. It is nevertheless true that the two parts of the city are often at odds. There are differences in the economic base – the city centre being oriented towards the government, cultural institutions and tourist-related activities. The two parts are also different from the social and cultural point of view. And, last but not least, in the old part no car circulation is allowed, which makes it hard to access by car-dependent people living on the mainland. All these reasons contribute to making the cultural conflict

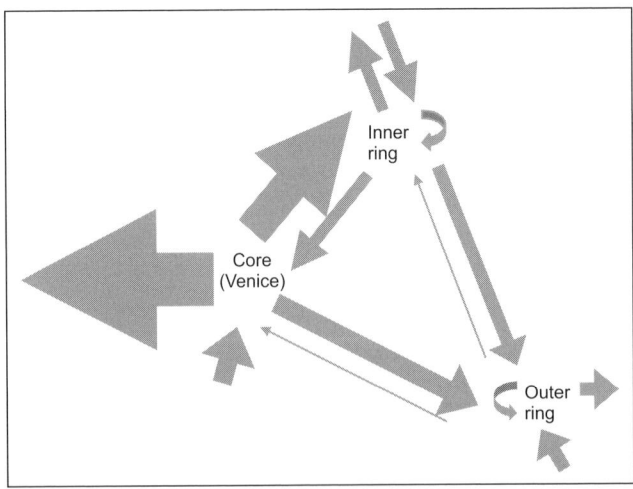

Figure 15.4 Population flows among parts of the Venice metropolitan area, 1986–87. *Source:* Municipality of Venice

Table 15.2 Commuters' flows within the Venice metropolitan area, 1991

Origin/destination	Venice, old core	Venice, mainland	Inner ring	Outer ring	Total metrop. area	Other destinations
Venice, old core	–	2.958	230	122	352	1,712
Venice, mainland	14,934	–	4,180	1,403	5,583	6,971
inner ring	4,408	16,280	–	–		
outer ring	1,692	5,626				
total metrop. area	6,100	21,906			–	–
other origins	2,900	4,420				
Total	30,034	51,190				

Source: Municipality of Venice.

Table 15.3 Employment in the Venice area by position, 1981–91

1981: absolute values

	Old core	Lagoon islands	Main land	Venice
Executives	777	242	822	1,841
Clericals	13,375	4,590	28,968	46,939
Manuals	10,361	7,562	31,743	46,684
Entrepreneurs	691	263	1,080	2,034
Professionals	1,160	330	1,626	3,116
Self-employed	5,288	3,697	9,132	18,133
Total*	32,384	17,006	74,765	124,195

1991: absolute values

	Old core	Lagoon islands	Main land	Venice
Executives	1,051	308	1,254	2,613
Clericals	10,577	4,561	30,845	45,990
Manuals	7,791	7,286	28,769	43,881
Entrepreneurs	1,402	663	2,051	4,117
Professionals	1,507	427	2,506	4,440
Self-employed	5,021	4,081	10,745	19,855
Total*	27,349	17,326	76,170	120,896

*Totals 1981 include 'Others'

1981: % over total

	Old core	Lagoon islands	Main land	Venice
Executives	3.84	1.78	1.65	2.16
Clericals	38.67	26.32	40.49	38.04
Manuals	28.49	42.05	37.77	36.30
Entrepreneurs	5.13	3.83	2.69	3.41
Professionals	5.51	2.46	3.29	3.67
Self-employed	18.36	23.55	14.11	16.42
Total	100.00	100.00	100.00	100.00

1991: % change over 1981

	Old core	Lagoon islands	Main land	Venice
Executives	35.26	27.27	52.55	41.93
Clericals	-20.92	-0.63	6.48	-2.02
Manuals	-24.80	-3.65	-9.37	-11.68
Entrepreneurs	102.89	152.09	89.91	102.41
Professionals	29.91	29.39	54.12	42.49
Self-employed	-5.05	10.39	17.66	9.50
Total	-13.59	3.85	3.81	-0.70

Source: Census.

between the central city and the metropolitan ring, which is common to every metropolitan area in the world, a bigger problem here.

To make things more complicated, the same conflict exists between Venice and the rest of Veneto, the region of 4 million inhabitants to which Venice belongs. Venice is its administrative capital as well as the region's most famous city but not its most important business centre nor its indisputably accepted reference point.[4]

State and local authorities in Italy

According to the Republican Constitution, Italy is divided into 20 *regioni*, 90 provinces and over 8,000 *comuni*.[5] Table 15.4 shows how local authorities are organised with special reference to the Venice case. Some large comuni, including

Table 15.4 State and local authorities in Italy (with reference to Venice)

Level	Population	Finance	Responsibilities
Nation Italy	56 million	Raises income taxes and redistributes to lower levels	Sets legislative framework. Makes decisions on major infrastructure.
Regione Veneto	4 million	Raises taxes on fuel and a few minor items	Issues laws on physical planning, agriculture, housing, healthcare, transportation, within the national framework.
Provincia Venezia	800,000	Almost entirely dependent on national transfer	Flood prevention, local roads, school buildings. Physical planning for the province and control on planning by municipalities.
Comune (municipality) Venezia	300,000	Property taxes + national transfers + own resources including casino, parking, museums, lease of public spaces	Planning, public works, welfare, housing, environment, childcare and kindergartens. Owns (or holds stock in) agencies for water resources and refuse collection, local transport, real estate, and other activities.
10 Quartieri (boroughs)	5,000 – 50,000	Transfers from municipality	Citizen participation. Advise on locally relevant planning issues.

Source: Municipality of Venice.

251

Mariolina Toniolo and Turiddo Pugliese

Table 15.5 Distribution of employed per productive type, 1996

	1	2	3	4	5	6	7	8	9	Total
Padua	16.74	1.02	5.75	27.12	4.79	9.73	7.19	24.01	3.65	100.00
Treviso	20.83	0.89	6.65	23.57	4.09	11.41	6.87	22.13	3.56	100.00
Venice	21.11	3.69	7.08	19.72	10.49	18.41	3.89	13.24	2.38	100.00
Veneto	44.53	0.80	9.15	19.19	5.23	6.13	3.12	9.24	2.61	100.00

Source: Coses.

1: goods production
2: energy, gas and water production and distribution
3: building
4: commerce
5: hotels and restaurants
6: transport, warehousing and communications
7: financial intermediation
8: property management, rentals, research, professionals and entrepreuneurs
9: school, health and social services, civil service, social and personal services

Venice, have also chosen to promote *Consigli di Quartiere* (boroughs) in order to foster citizen participation. Such bodies are elected together with the city council.

Italy is not a federal state. Much power is still held by the central government. In recent years, though, demand for decentralisation has grown. The decentralisation issue is a high priority on the agenda of almost all political parties, but is specially supported by those political groups (the prominent one being Lega Nord) which feel the wealthy north to be unduly disadvantaged by central state compensation in favour of the south. While *province* and *comuni* have existed since the birth of the Italian state in the nineteenth century, the *regioni* were only introduced by the 1949 Constitution, which entrusted them with legislative power over a well-defined bundle of issues, and were actually not implemented until 1970. Their implementation resulted in a subtraction of power from the state and, to a lesser extent, from the *province*, whose responsibilities were already not very significant. In fact, some think that the only reason the provinces still exist is that they are written into the Constitution. This is why, when metropolitan area authorities were introduced by law, they were identified with a new sort of province. Italian *comuni* can be very different in size, ranging from 3 million inhabitants to less than a thousand, but in theory they have the same power. The *commune* remains by far the public authority which is perceived as closest to citizens in their daily life; nevertheless, in large cities the need is felt for more decentralisation.

The Veneto region is a wealthy manufacturing area, whose fortune has been skyrocketing in the last three decades. Within the region, Venice is not the most successful city, economically speaking. Two other cities, Padua and Verona, are of more or less equal size and are no less endowed than Venice with institutions (cultural, economic and otherwise) typical of the urban environment and with

252

Table 15.6 Medium prices for dwelling in different types of urban areas, 2001 (€/m²)

	Padova			Treviso			Venezia		
	new	non-refurbished	old	new	non-refurbished	old	new	non-refurbished	old
Old core	2,840	2,324	1,704	2,686	2,169	1,601	5,681	4,906	3,202
Intermediate areas	2,066	1,549	1,291	2,066	1,601	1,110	2,944	2,298	1,730
Outskirts	1,549	1,214	1,033	1,498	1,136	852	2,169	1,653	1,136

Source: Scenari Immobiliari, September 2001.

urban infrastructures; they are also much better integrated into the rest of the region. Also, while the city and province of Venice tend to be politically oriented towards the left of centre parties, the opposite is true for the rest of the Veneto. The *provincia* encompasses an area some parts of which, though well integrated into Venice in the past from a cultural point of view, are so far away in terms of actual physical distance that their populations increasingly look towards other urban centres. The splitting of the *provincia* of Venice into two different provinces is being actively promoted by relevant local groups. This is why the integration versus competition dilemma for Venice has twofold dimensions: with respect to its immediate surrounding area as well as in relation to the larger regional context.

Governing metropolitan change

Responses to the above outlined change, and to emerging problems, were similarly ambiguous, corresponding to the different ways such changes were perceived. The 1973 special law intended to save Venice acknowledged the need to coordinate spatial policy within a wider than municipal area. A physical plan was required for a metropolitan region (*Piano Comprensoriale*) whose boundaries were identified as those of the Daily Urban System plus the whole Lagoon (whose salvation is strictly connected with that of the ancient city). A special council (*Consiglio di Comprensorio*), made up of councillors named by the councils of the participating municipalities, was responsible for approving it. In fact, this plan was issued as a technical document in 1978 but never approved by the council because of political change that had occurred during the 1975 local elections. Later on, the regional government issued a plan – the PALAV (Piano di Area per la Laguna di Venezia), a plan issued by the regional government affecting the area of Venice, including the lagoon and the Daily Urban System, with a prevailing environmental scope – for the designated area in order to meet the national law requirement for comprehensive physical planning to encompass the whole area. But of course, while this document provided for technical requirements, the failure of the *Comprensorio* to issue its own plan proved, again and not for the last time, the inability of local authorities to reach agreement over common problems concerning the metropolitan area.

Meanwhile, a number of Venetian citizens in both city sections were fighting to split the municipali into two parts. A referendum on the issue was held three times (in 1979, 1989 and 1993), and always failed. By the end of the 1980s the need for special metropolitan government bodies was felt at the national level. In 1990 an opportunity was provided by a new Local Authorities Act. According to this new law, the provinces – including the nine largest cities in Italy, of which Venice was one – could become metropolitan authorities, with new boundaries and new powers. At the same time, the central city would be split into smaller parts. Regional governments (Regioni) were asked to define the boundaries and powers of metropolitan area authorities.

Again, after much debate (Costa and Toniolo, 1992), this reform failed in Venice and in other Italian metropolitan areas. Most probably the reason lay in the law itself, which entrusted the regional government to promote the birth of a new local authority that would have very likely become more powerful than the regional government itself. Still, an important debate was initiated by the law during the three years in which efforts to implement it were made. The debate about the boundaries and powers of the metropolitan area shed light on important concepts concerning the future of Venice and the kind of relationships it ought to have with its regional environment. Those who supported boundaries like those of Piano Comprensoriale, basically defined in terms of the Daily Urban System, wanted to strengthen the links between the city and its immediate hinterland; these kinds of boundaries were consistent with a metropolitan government endowed with strong powers – a brand-new local authority that would take the place of the existing province. Problems to be confronted (besides the protection of the lagoon eco-system) were the coordination of transportation, land use and population-oriented facilities – problems that are common to all other metropolitan areas. To others, such problems did not appear as important as those posed by emerging competition between cities at the global (or at least, European) level. Their point was that, if a middle-sized city like Venice were to be competitive, it would have to merge its assets with those of other cities on a wider regional level. Thus, a three-cities metropolitan area, made up of Venice, Padua and Treviso – two cities that are less than half an hour apart with existing transportation facilities – was envisaged (see map). Of course, such a wide area could not have the same powers. It was conceived to be more an alliance of three independent cities seeking stricter interaction without really merging; moreover, more attention would be paid to the problems of the three central cities rather than those of the metropolitan ring.

But focus on global competition could also suggest an opposite solution. All over the world the current trend is towards the increasing importance of inner cities relative to their periphery. If this is to continue, then probably the best chance for Venice would be to stress its special character by explicitly ignoring the link with its surrounding area: that is, by envisioning the city's future as part of a network having closer connections with other European cities, no matter how far away, than with the closest area on the mainland. After all, modern forms of trans-portation – particularly air-based ones – and communication technologies are redefining distances in terms of time. And Venice has the third largest airport in Italy. Of course, it is the ancient part of the city that has the best chance to compete in a global network. The recurrent proposal to split the municipality was supported not only by people living on the mainland – bitter as they are about the presumed privileges the central city enjoys – but also by old-fashioned supporters of the

Venice tradition, as well as by some who saw the special character of the city as an asset to be used in global competition.

In 1994 almost all the municipalities involved reached agreement concerning the creation of a metropolitan area authority based on the Daily Urban System concept – but the regional government failed to approve it (Zanon, 1996). This failure was perceived to be a betrayal of the popular will. Some attributed the failure to the fact that the regional government was ruled by a coalition politically antagonistic to the city of Venice and the province. In fact, similar opposition to the birth of metropolitan authorities occurred everywhere in Italy, so that a conflict between institutions, and not so much between politically opposed coalitions, could better explain what happened.

The contribution of physical planning to metropolitan development

The election of the strongly determined philosopher Massimo Cacciari as mayor in 1993 was a turning point in urban policy. His ability to give the city a new drive was fostered by innovations that were introduced in the same year by the Local Elections Act, which grant the mayor more freedom in choosing his team and therefore provide more stability to local government. Mayor Cacciari held office for seven years. His successor – Paolo Costa, who was elected mayor in April 2000 – explicitly wishes to continue Cacciari's policy. Therefore the 1993 turn has not been reversed so far. Stricter and better relationships with the surrounding region were a primary concern for the new administration. In the beginning, as we have seen, it tried hard to have the metropolitan authority approved by the regional government, but without success. When this reform was frustrated, an alternative policy was put forth. Informal agreements were sought with the mayor of Padua[6] in order to coordinate policy issues, such as major transport facilities including commuter trains and freight management. But such agreements were based only on the partners' goodwill and did not prove very effective when it came to serious conflicts of interest. An important effort was devoted to physical planning by the new administration. It conceived a new Master Plan for Venice and linked it to the mayor's urban strategy (Benevolo, 1995). An important goal of the Master Plan, which was completed in 1999, was to foster closer relationships between Venice, the metropolitan ring and the whole Veneto region.

At the same time, the provincial administration was designing its physical plan. The municipality and the province agreed to coordinate the two plans by means of informal, flexible agreements. One of the most important projects the two administrations developed together was the one for a new turnpike in Mestre. This was badly needed because, after the opening of Eastern Europe to trade with the West, the quantity of traffic had been skyrocketing on the existing highway, which was and still is the only highway linking Eastern Europe to Milan and Rome and is now one of the most congested sections of the whole Italian highway network. To make things worse, the highway passes very close to the centre of Mestre.

A number of relevant issues were addressed by the city's Master Plan, but these cannot be mentioned here. Concerning metropolitan relationships, however, two topics were crucial: transportation and land use. In terms of transportation, Venice faces problems common to every metropolitan area – the need for efficient local and long-distance connections while minimising congestion – and problems related to the unusual character of its ancient core, from land-based transport modes to its peculiar pedestrian and boat transit system. Addressing the transportation problem within the framework of the new Master Plan was a very important contribution to metropolitan development, even though it failed to create the metropolitan authority. Solutions provided by the Master Plan include: conversion of local trains into a metropolitan network[7] that will double its capacity in ten years; three points of interchange from car and buses to boats along the lagoon shores (which will supplement the only interchange point that now exists, one which creates unnecessary congestion in the old city by taking cars right into the island); a tramway linking Mestre to the ancient part of the city; and a belt of interchange car parking places around Mestre for daily commuters. City design also contributes to better cultural integration among the different parts of the city and within the metropolitan area by enhancing the lagoon waterfront, which, besides protecting a valuable environment, will ideally help the people living on the mainland to feel part of a water-based city.

Crucial for the Master Plan's strategy to open up Venice to the metropolitan and regional horizon is the project for a new city centre. The centre would have two linked sections on either side of the existing bridge, which links the two parts of the city across the lagoon. At present, each of the two main parts of the city has its own centre: the old city predominantly around Rialto and St Mark's Square – which is not so different from what it was a thousand years ago – and Mestre around its old main square, which is not so different from what it was a hundred years ago, when it was a farmers' marketplace. The two centres have different roles: the old city is more oriented towards cultural and tourist facilities and to the public sector. A number of finance- and business-oriented services are inefficiently located in both places, thus failing to profit from scale economies while the two centres are more than an hour apart via the existing transportation network, and both are poorly linked to regional and long-distance transport. This prevents the two parts of the city from working as a whole and thus as a real capital city of the region. The result is that the city's facility supply is not the one required by a city of 300,000 inhabitants. The new twin centre envisaged by the Master Plan will be in a better position to serve the metropolitan area and the rest of the region; it will also be well served by the railway, which is the most appropriate access mode to a congested pedestrian city like ancient Venice. By rail, Padua – the most important business city in the region and a major university – will be only 20 minutes away from the new centre; currently it is more than an hour away from the old city centre near St Mark's Square, and 45 minutes from what is now the centre of Mestre. Consistent with the city's Master Plan, the plan for the province encouraged new residential developments to grow around the railway stations in order to promote the use of trains for metropolitan transportation and to foster integration within the metropolitan area. It is thus not an exaggeration to say that the new city centre could probably do more in order to integrate Venice into the rest of the region than any government reform. For the same reason, it has both supporters and opponents.

From planning to implementation

In 1999, elections were held for the government of the province of Venice. The new administration was part of the same coalition (centre and left) as the city of Venice. Nevertheless minor political shifts to come were sufficient to break a still fragile equilibrium. The new administration of the province, probably fearing disagreement from many small-size municipalities, discontinued the previous policy of planning agreements with the city of Venice. The new provincial plan dropped the attempt to control residential development by encouraging sites near railway stations, again fearing disagreement by small municipalities who wanted to be free to set their own development strategies. Even worse, it failed to promote a badly needed agreement between small municipalities concerning the Mestre highway, despite the province offices having designed the preliminary project together with those of the municipality. In Padua, local elections changed the make-up of the old political coalition. This shift was sufficient to reverse the policy of flexible agreements that had been established with the city of Venice. In addition, as we write, a new referendum is being promoted, once again concerning splitting Venice into two different municipalities (no matter how many times the question is rejected, the law allows for it to be proposed again). In 1999 a similar referendum succeeded in separating a small part of the peninsula (Cavallino) from the rest of Venice. Cavallino is not essential in terms of the integrity of the metropolitan area, but is still important both because it is part of the lagoon environment and because such a separation was perceived to be auspicious for the more important splitting up of the rest of the city into different parts.[8]

The Master Plan was completed in 1999. Regarding many relevant issues that are not strictly connected with this chapter's scope (e.g. historical and natural resources preservation, the conversion of distressed industrial areas and the cleaning up of polluted sites, and the supply of new moderately-priced housing), the plan is proving very effective. But the part of it whose implementation is proving most difficult is the one concerning the twin city centres across the lagoon. This is surprising considering that little support for the suggested project came from land-owners whose property values would have been positively affected. In fact, this was also the most controversial issue of the new Master Plan, clearly reflecting the support that the goal of splitting the city into parts still enjoys in public opinion.

At the same time, a major project, also envisaged by the Master Plan, was promoted by the administration, involving the rescue of the ancient shipyard (*Arsenale*). The Arsenale is the oldest and largest industrial site still existing in Europe, having been established in the thirteenth century and still preserving its sixteenth-century setting. It is also a crucial site for the city's memory, if we consider that it is from here that Venice drew its power as a maritime trading centre. At the moment it is of little use to the city because its current use as a military centre renders it inaccessible to ordinary people except during special events like international art exhibitions. The municipal offices are presently promoting its acquisition by a group of public and private investors in order to turn it into a part of the city open to daily use. The project seems to be appealing even to private investors. Still, the most important disadvantage of the site is that it is located at the very eastern end of the old city. With existing transit facilities it now takes 45 minutes to reach the Arsenale from the railway station. It was therefore seen as a preliminary condition for the whole project to improve its connections with the mainland. The most effective and cheapest solution was found to be a lightweight train using a subway under the lagoon and reaching the airport. Such a solution was innovative relative to the Master Plan, and is supported by possible investors in the Arsenale project. No final decision has been made so far on the project as a whole and on the transport facility issue in particular; the latter may be a major problem because it implies challenging long-established opposition by a large fraction of public opinion against the introduction of any modern technology, and underground transportation in particular, in Venice. Regarding the integration of Venice and its metropolitan area, it has to be pointed out here that, if approved, the connection of the Arsenale with the rest of the city will probably work as an additional hurdle to metropolitan integration because the fastest link between the water city and the mainland (8 minutes, instead of 20) will be provided via the airport, which is located outside the physical boundaries of the city, rather than via Mestre. The effect of the new underground, then, could possibly be to reverse recent efforts to more effectively link Venice to its metropolitan ring. With the new underground (and by plane, of course) Venice would be easier to reach from some faraway places than from its own surroundings. Again, physical planning appears to be extremely relevant to the effective constitution of an integrated metropolitan area.

Recent developments

In August 2000 a new Local Authorities Act was passed by the national parliament, revising the 1990 law specifically in reference to metropolitan authorities, for which even a change in the republic's constitution was introduced. According to the new law, metropolitan authorities will be acknowledged as local authorities of the Italian republic, just like provinces and municipalities.

In order to make their birth easier, the role of regional governments was downscaled, the metropolitan municipality is now entitled to take the initiative in promoting the new authority, and the procedure for approval was made easier. The new law is the final act of a process aimed at four main actions: modifying the region's role in the process of territorial delimitation of the metropolitan area, so far limited to the ratification of the proposal put forth by the local authorities involved; acknowledging the capital city's role in promoting the establishment of the metropolitan authority; acknowledging that the municipalities involved in the establishment of the metropolitan city can ask that the delimitation of the metropolitan city be an ambit of coordinated exertion of functions; and defining the electoral procedures of the metropolitan city's organs of government.

The amendments to the constitution led to the acknowledgement of the metropolitan city as an ordinary local authority, with autonomy, powers and duties comparable to those of the municipalities, provinces and regions. The referendum to approve these amendments was held in October according to law and passed with over 60 per cent of the votes. In the Venetian area the percentage was even higher. Not unexpectedly, the regional government of Veneto did not respond promptly to such innovations. In April 2001 a cautious regional law was passed on the subject. In contrast, the municipality of Venice was more active in two areas that were selected to continue the experiment on decentralisation. The municipality thus created sufficiently autonomous communities in two peripheral parts of the city: Marghera – part of recent developments on the mainland – and Lido-Pellestrina, two islands located between the lagoon and the sea. Already in February 2001, the municipal council approved the amendments to the regulations that permitted municipalities to experiment. These experiments have so far been limited to Marghera and Lido-Pellestrina, but in the near future are likely to include all the local communities of which Venice is made. Once agreements are signed permitting the transfer of responsibilities from the city to smaller communities in the name of a 'principle of mutual subsidy', this long-lasting devolution process will finally be accomplished.

This initiative is aimed at establishing the Venice Urban Community, which will be a first step towards creating the Metropolitan City of Venice. It is a response not only to a problem of efficiency, but also to the necessity of meeting the need for enhancing local identity expressed by the homogeneous communities that form Greater Venice. This change is a tactical anticipation in view of possible future new referenda on the city splitting issue, but it is also the answer to real problems considering how scattered the parts of the city are.[9] The new communities – called *municipalità*, which does not mean, of course, municipalities – will have the role of promoting active participation by citizens within a project common to the whole city. Other Italian cities are pursuing the same goal along different paths.

Along with institutional change, the city of Venice is actively pursuing flexible agreements with the cities of Padua and Treviso together with the other small municipalities in the adjoining area, in order to create a large metropolitan system encompassing the whole central part of the Veneto region. In September 2000 a special agreement to promote a free association among local and other public authorities of the area, public agencies and even single persons or private companies, was signed by the mayors of Padua and Venice. Mayors of other cities signed later.

The Association of Municipalities approved by the municipal council of Venice, which had long before been proposed to the municipalities of the PATREVE (Padova–TREviso–VEnezia) area in order to spur them to translate the enthusiasm shown in the agreement protocol into an effective adherence, is one of the means that can be used to promote the establishment of the Metropolitan City of Venice.

The idea is thus beginning to gain substance. Many of the municipalities that signed the protocol have now confirmed their adherence to the initiative, even though the region does not play an active role and the provinces can hardly hide their aversion to the project, which they fear could limit their role and their physical reference ambit. The Association will make decisions concerning its own boundaries and negotiate with the state concerning the transfer of appropriate powers. Here, of course, 'metropolitan area' has a totally different meaning from that of the Local Authorities Act mentioned above. The two streams of the initiative are meant to be synergetic. While the smaller metropolitan area will according to bylaw provisions become a real local authority, the large one will be more grass-roots, oriented towards the making of an effective community, fostering economic development and creating a common living environment for the population involved.

The new provisions will allow the city of Venice to move faster towards the creation of a metropolitan city, through a process tailored to the city's features (in terms of forms of organisation, functions and schedule). The specific initiatives that have been undertaken include a plan for the development of the local system (Strategic Plan), the improvement of the centre/periphery relationship (for both the devolution process and the establishment of the metropolitan city), the drafting of a statute of the metropolitan city, and the study of interests and large-scale services that local communities of the Venetian system can share in view of the opportunities offered by the aggregation process.

Technical support for the initiative is being provided by CoSES, a public agency whose ownership is shared by the city and the province of Venice. So far, the following proposals have been put forth: provisional boundaries for the area, a project for a single metropolitan bureau of information providing information and all required permits for business enterprises in or wishing to operate in the area, a database concerning settlement opportunities for business enterprises in the area, an agreement for railway development, a single centre for the booking of healthcare facilities, and a single ticket system for public transport. Rapid though limited results from the initiative are expected to help people believe in the possibility and opportunity of pursuing the creation of a metropolitan community, after the deception involved in the failure of the 1994 initiative.

Conclusions

Venice, just like any other city of similar size and economic development, feels the need to integrate its metropolitan area in terms of both effective living conditions and institutional change. As in similar cities, the issue appears to be controversial among the public, where locally-oriented views are strongly represented. What makes public opinion influential is the fact that it includes not only conservative people, who are unaware of emerging problems, but also opinion leaders – usually long-established citizens whose daily routine is either locally very limited (because they are rich enough to live close to the city centre) and/or based on long-distance connections, ignoring the relationship with the immediately surrounding area. Also, opposition to any solution to metropolitan problems involving institutional change comes from existing authorities who fear having to share part of their power with new local authorities. In contrast to what happens in other cities, movements in Venice supporting extreme local pride not only oppose metropolitan integration, but also wish to promote the splitting of the existing city into parts.

Repeated attempts to achieve better integration and to resist it were made during the last two decades, and are still ongoing. Such efforts involve the whole range of available tools: institutional reform, flexible institutional agreements concerning more or less crucial issues, and actions aimed at promoting effective integration in terms of both comprehensive planning and incremental policy steps. No important change has been successfully introduced so far in either direction. This fact is making the public increasingly sceptical about any suggested change. Despite all that, the city of Venice is again trying to create both a real Venice metropolitan area authority and, along with other municipalities, a more grass-roots community encompassing a vast region including two other cities of comparable size. The two initiatives are assumed to be mutually supportive. While we wish success to the ongoing initiatives, past experience may suggest some considerations.

In the past, institutional change failed because of conflicts between existing authorities over power-sharing. In spite of legal innovations, the making of a new metropolitan authority remains a distant goal. Flexible agreements may provide a faster response to the needs of people living in the metropolitan area, while also helping to reverse a generalised sense that politics has little impact on the quality of life. Flexible agreements, however, can also be easily reversed by any change in the administrations involved. What should not be forgotten is the contribution physical planning can give to the birth of an integrated metropolitan environment. The shape of a city – its internal and external accessibility, the location of its facilities – is not neutral in making it a self-contained or an open community. And it usually lasts longer than the will of contingent governments. This is also why, if the planning process involves adequate democratic participation, decisions concerning the physical setting of an area may play an important role in fostering people's involvement in metropolitan integration.

Notes

1 What most people call Venice – namely the ancient city – is now the core of a municipality with approximately 300,000 inhabitants. Two-thirds of the inhabitants now live on the mainland, in city sections that were built in the twentieth century, mostly after the Second World War. The old core houses no more than 70,000 inhabitants – but a larger daily population and typical central city activities. About 30,000 inhabitants live on lagoon islands.
2 In fact, metropolitan decentralisation had been already detected around major Italian cities but the fact was only known to a limited number of scholars.
3 The Marghera industrial area, whose construction was begun during the First World War, covers 2,000 hectares. Created to be the most important petrochemical pole in Italy, it is now widely dismissed and in need of reclamation and redevelopment.
4 In fact, when regions were created as local authorities in 1970 (see next section), Venice's status as capital city for the Veneto was contested.
5 Reformed at the end of 2001, this article of the Constitution now states that Italy is 'constituted by', instead of 'divided into', comuni, province, metropolitan cities and regioni. Metropolitan cities are thus legimimated at the highest level of the Italian law and their existence does not substitute that of province.
6 It was impossible to reach similar agreements with the mayor of Treviso, whose views were strictly bound to local issues.
7 The project is being carried on by the regional government and half of its cost is covered by national funds.
8 In fact, the referendum according to which Cavallino seceded from Venice was recently declared illegal, so the integrity of the city's boundaries will probably be established again for an indeterminate time.
9 The organising committee of the referendum for the splitting of Venice from Mestre has already sent the 6,000 signatures collected to support the initiative to the Region of Veneto. The Region has been slow to express its views about the legitimacy of the proposal, because in the absence of a law governing referenda procedures, it is always possible that the referendum could be invalidated by appeal to the Constitutional Court.

Bibliography

Aquarone, A. (1961) *Grandi città e aree metropolitane*, Bologna: Zanichelli.
Benevolo, L. (ed.) (1995) *Venezia, il nuovo piano urbanistico*, Roma-Bari: Laterza.
Costa, P. and Toniolo, M. (1992) *Città metropolitane e sviluppo regionale*, Milano: F. Angeli.
Dorigo, W. (1973) *Una legge contro Venezia*, Roma: Officina.
Toniolo Trivellato, M. (1995) 'Venice: population decline, change in economic base and housing', in L. Padovani (ed.) *Urban change and housing policies*, Venezia: DAEST.
UNESCO (1969) *Rapport sur Venise*, Paris.
Zanon, G. (1996) 'Metropoli Veneta, un parto difficile', in CoSES *Alfabeto Veneziano*, Bologna: il Mulino.

16 The region of Milan

Enrico Gualini

Trends in urbanisation and spatial structure: the last twenty years

According to a consolidated geo-historical pattern, Milan represents the core of a highly integrated metropolitan agglomeration situated at the centre of the polycentric urban system of 'Padania'. In the course of the centuries – and especially since the industrial age, as this pattern turned into the foundation for Milan's role as 'Italy's economic capital' (Dalmasso, 1972) – the area has developed strong complementary relations between the central city, with its superior 'metropolitan' functions, and its peripheral territorial systems, featuring relatively autonomous paths of socio-economic development.

While traditionally the origin of Milan's fortunes as a complete, internally balanced and functionally differentiated economic region, such a pattern of socio-economic and spatial integration has given rise in recent decades to new emerging phenomena, which have challenged traditional views of monocentric metro-politanisation processes. Geographic research has drawn attention to the variety of specific socio-economic and territorial production systems that lie behind the aggregate levels of performance of the Milan economic region as a whole. Reinter-preting the metropolitan region as a 'territory of differences' (e.g. Lanzani, 1991; Boeri *et al.*, 1993; Palermo, 1997) has led in particular to an appreciation of the intense dynamics of intra-peripheral relations of a non-centripetal kind that have developed in the area. This kind of relationships involves a plurality of 'territorial systems' that feature recognisable individual patterns of spatial and economic development, establishing increasingly complex patterns of autonomy and inter-dependence with the metropolitan core. Accordingly, the increasing attention to 'local' dimensions of development has highlighted the need for more differentiated, area-based approaches to spatial policy, contributing to a critical revision of compre-hensive approaches to metropolitan government and planning.

In light of recent geographical analyses of its features of internal socio-economic differentiation, the traditional inadequacy of references to administrative regions for addressing issues of governance in the Milan area becomes even more apparent. The provincial territory, in particular, has been traditionally inadequate in account-ing for the complexity of its internal functional relations. Even if recent detachment

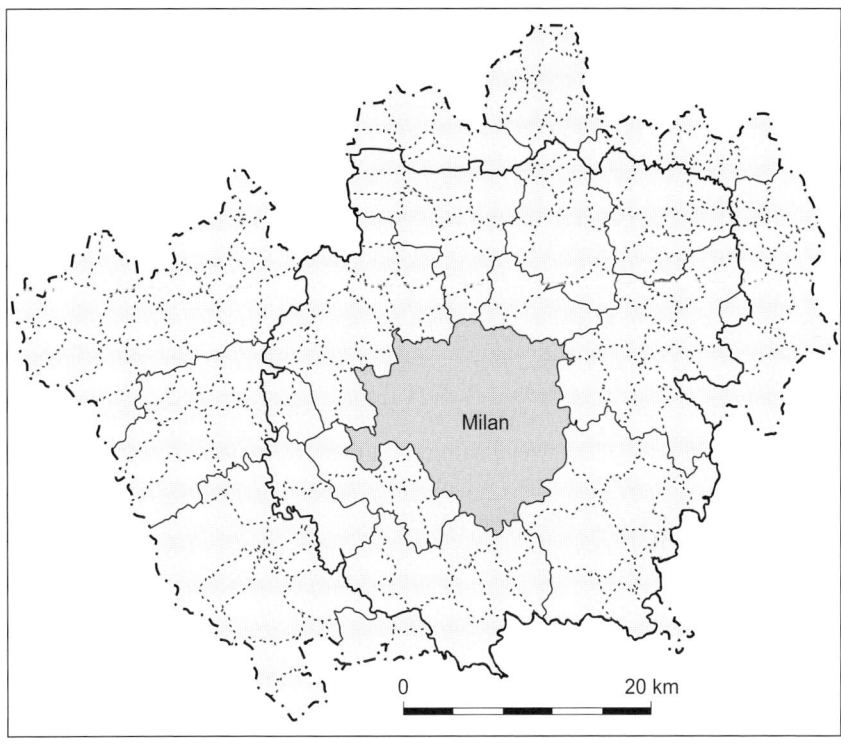

Figure 16.1 The metropolitan region of Milan. The city of Milan (dark grey area) is at the core of the Province of Milan (light grey area) with its municipalities (dotted lines) and subprovincial subdivisions (thin black line); the black line comprises the municipalities joining the consortium of the *Piano Intercomunale Milanese* (PIM), established in the 1960s

of the prevailingly rural territory of the new province of Lodi has rendered it spatially more homogeneous, the territory of the Milan province remains hardly representative of the features of Milan's metropolitan region. With its 4 million inhabitants, the Province of Milan – one of eleven in the Region of Lombardy – lies in fact at the core of a much broader metropolitan region, counting about 10 million inhabitants and extending along the north Italian urban system beyond the jurisdiction of Lombardy itself, a region of 9 million inhabitants characterised by a strong north–south urban–rural divide.

The population of the metropolitan region has witnessed in recent decades a significant shift in core-periphery balance: Milan (558,575 inhabitants in 1901, and 1,274,245 in 1951) reached its peak in 1973 with 1.7 million inhabitants, followed by a long-lasting trend in decline (1,655,000 in 1980, and 1,370,000 in 1991) despite the stability of the province (4,059,000 in 1980, and 4,091,000 in 1991). During this period, population mobility was extremely high within both core and periphery areas, with a distinctive population growth in minor outer centres of the agglomeration (87 per cent of the total growth in municipalities under 20,000 inhabitants, 30 per cent in municipalities under 5,000), according to more 'suburban' land-use patterns.

The Milan agglomeration – as shown by 1991 figures referring to the new provincial delimitation (3,707,134 inhabitants, 185 municipalities) – features a population density of 1,901 inhabitants/km^2, distributed over a territory 34 per cent of which is urbanised, 57 per cent is mainly agricultural, and 39 per cent is subject to measures of regional or local landscape or open-space protection. Such average figures, however, overshadow high internal disparities in land-use intensity. Urbanisation rates range from figures typical of the urban districts and towns of the northern old-industrial sector (50–88 per cent urbanised land) to much lower figures in the south-east sector (between 2–29 per cent). Similar differences are found also in the recent relative dynamics of urbanisation. During the 1980s, this was particularly high in the less urbanised southern, south-eastern, eastern and western sectors of the agglomeration, with average rates in the increase of urbanised land of 20 per cent, and with peaks of up to 90 per cent in some individual municipalities, which testifies to a progressive erosion of rural land at the urban fringe. Differentials in distribution of industrial land-use – representing 21 per cent of urbanised land on average – are also significant, with particularly high concentrations in the traditional locations of the northern old-industrial sector, but also in the more recent growth areas of the north-east and north-west (Centro Studi PIM, 1990).

The trends in urbanisation emerging in the 1980s in connection with a persistent economic dynamic also express the territorial patterns taken by processes of industrial restructuring and sectoral specialisation. The most notable phenomenon has been the persistence of high levels of industrial employment in small-medium size enterprises, located according to diffuse and fragmented spatial patterns, along with its rapid growth in emerging high-tech sectors, prevailingly concentrated in new growth areas featuring high accessibility, amenities and more flexible locational conditions. The overall results have been a high turnover in land-use, but also increased rates of urbanisation. Reuse of industrial land – amounting in the late 1980s to 5 million m^2 in Milan (i.e. to 2.5 per cent of the municipal surface) and to about 4.8 million m^2 in the province – has been constrained by the high territorial fragmentation of processes of industrial restructuring, resulting in a large number of small, derelict or under-utilised sites spread throughout the agglomeration, next to large-scale sites in areas witnessing structural processes of industrial decline (e.g. Sesto S. Giovanni and Arese).

High employment rates in both manufacturing and service industries are the expression of an economy traditionally characterised by high levels of intersectoral balance, and of core-periphery and intra-regional integration. Since the 1970s, these features have been strengthened by a rationalisation in supply, quality and territorial distribution of business and production services, which has favoured a stricter adherence to local patterns of specialisation within the agglomeration. This is well expressed by the dynamic taken by the service industry in the province in the 1980s, resulting from diffuse processes of modernisation of production, which has contributed to a significant functional re-equilibrium relative to the core. This has been on the other hand backed by a further centralisation of superior services and of 'gateway' functions in the metropolitan core. Overall, the impressive regional growth of the service industry during that decade (+25.6 per cent in employment in Lombardy, of which 50.2 per cent was in the Province of Milan) has strengthened the centrality of Milan at both the regional level (expressed by the concentration in the city of 90 per cent of the regional labour force employed in financial activities, 83 per cent of that in advertising and marketing, 78 per cent of that in consultancy and 57 per cent of that in informatics and telecommunication services) and the national level (with by far the highest levels of specialisation in financial markets, fairs and international trade).

Precisely such patterns of intra-regional relations however, have progressively highlighted the burdens on Milan as a functional system. Consequences of the extremely intense conditions of urbanisation – such as the lack of locational flexibility, the intense rates of intra-urban mobility, and the decrease of environmental quality – have been perceived since the late 1980s, particularly in connection with European market integration, as a major source of diseconomies and of inefficiency of the metropolitan system as a whole. Several studies of the 'comparative advantages' of cities have pointed accordingly to the increasing threat represented for Milan in international competition by sub-optimal conditions in the supply of key metropolitan functions and by losses in locational attractiveness. Whereas earlier studies highlighted Milan's unchallenged position at the 'second level' of urban functional ranking and its primacy in the central-southern European space in terms of productive performance, business services, executive functions, technological assets, and labour market qualification, more recent surveys underlined a worrying downward trend. Along with a perceived as well as 'objective' lack in living standards – the most striking indicators being the levels of inner-city congestion, automotive mobility, watershed exploitation and pollution, and the quantitative and qualitative standard of green/recreational areas (less than 8 m^2 per inhabitant in Milan) – research has pointed to other important shortcomings in urban modernisation (e.g. CCIAA Milano, 1992; Ciciotti *et al.*, 1994; Morandi, 1994): a relative backwardness in superior business services, a lack in supply of attractive high-level office space, and a low level of efficiency of the public administration. A particular issue is the deadlock in improvements of metropolitan and regional scale infrastructure: the completion of the regional public transport network (the *Sistema Ferroviario Regionale*), the establishment of an effective metropolitan logistic system, the realisation of measures for improving intra-regional mobility (such as the highly contested Pedemontana and Milan-Brescia highway connections), the upgrade of exhibition and congress facilities, and the modernisation of Milan's airport infrastructure (which resulted in the opening of Malpensa in the late 1990s, after over 20 years of controversies).

Approaches to metropolitan government, 1959–90

The struggle for metropolitan government in Milan may be seen partly as an aspect inherent to the complexity of its agglomeration and of its recent evolution; it is however also the result of a more general 'unsolved institutional question' at the national level (Rotelli, 1996) and of its repercussions on local politics. Milan, the capital of the Region of Lombardy, is embedded in a three-tier system of territorial jurisdictions (region, provinces, municipalities), with the province – the level most approximate to metropolitan areas – traditionally being its weakest element. The ambiguity in their relations is a path-dependent result of the failure in addressing a reform of sub-national governments in post-war years: while the principle of 'local autonomies' contained in the republican constitution granted municipal and provincial governments significant degrees of autonomous competence, their relations with central powers remained defined in practice – at least until reforms of the 1990s – by a nested-hierarchical conception, as inherited from the Franco–Napoleonic administrative system, defining them as subordinate secondary units of the state. A further crucial aspect is the late implementation and the unfulfilment of the regionalist project delineated by the constitution, which added to such ambiguities.

Consequences of this situation are apparent in the field of urban and regional planning. In line with the principle of 'local autonomies', framework legislation (Law 1150/1942) entrusted municipalities with planning tasks such as the adoption of master plans and building regulations, within the scope defined by the legislative power granted by the constitution to the regions. A further provision of the law was the entitlement to establish supra-local plans, an authority that – according to the constitution – should have been taken over by the regions. However, while provinces were substantially bypassed as intermediate planning jurisdictions, ordinary regions were established as autonomous entities only in the 1970s, leaving supra-municipal planning tasks in an institutional vacuum.

Under such conditions, the need for an intermediate level of planning emerged early as a major issue of debate and institutional experimentation, but was also bound to depend on extensive conflicts of competencies and contrasting political claims. Milan's first application to adopt a supra-local plan for 79 metropolitan municipalities – the *Piano Intercomunale Milanese* (PIM) – was approved in 1959 by the Ministry of Public Works in a restricted version for 35 municipalities, seven of which – including large centres like Busto and Gallarate – were external to the Milan province. Lack of collaboration by municipal governments, however, undermined the required unanimous approval of the plan: almost a third of the involved municipalities formally opposed the dominant role assumed by the City of Milan, alleging threats to their autonomy in adopting local master plans. A way out of the conflict was pursued through a voluntary 'associational' model, leading in 1961 to the constitution of a consortium of municipalities committed to establishing the PIM, acting through an indirect representative body – the assembly of mayors – and an executive committee.

The consortium – soon extended to include 94 municipalities – envisioned an ambitious strategy of metropolitan decentralisation. The outcome was in 1967 the adoption of a plan, which was, however, soon delegitimised by a crossfire of vetoes: the complexity of the decision-making environment and the weight of party politics, emphasised by contrasting local governments' affiliations along centre-periphery lines, determined a substantial watering-down of the strategy and, finally, its formal abandonment.

The constitution of 'ordinary' regions that occurred between 1970 (with the establishment of regional councils) and 1977 (with the transfer of central legislative and administrative functions) introduced a decisive shift in attention towards the new governmental entity and its competencies as an intermediary actor of spatial planning. This also resulted in a significant shift in debates on metropolitan government. Attention increasingly focused on the contrasting claims expressed on the one hand by regional governments (endowed with significant but yet limited powers) and on the other hand by local autonomies (provinces, municipalities, and possibly new metropolitan entities). This contrast of claims between territorial government institutions was exacerbated by the fact that the new regional level had been established without contextually addressing a long-overdue reform of local governments. The result – even in a region like Lombardy, in which awareness of the metropolitan issue was most developed – was paradoxical: the constitution of the new regional government did not contribute at all to a quick solution to the issue of a metropolitan government, but rather made it even more wicked (Rotelli, 1996).

In the late 1970s, regional governments developed a first attempt to counter the tendency towards a territorial fragmentation of sectoral policies: the establishment of supra-municipal entities (the *comprensori*) that were meant primarily to take over programming tasks from the provinces, thus underlining the latter's mere administrative function. *Comprensori*, however, not only lacked a coherent territorial identity, being defined in highly diverse ways across different regions, but were also devoid of the political backing and powers necessary to become an institutional alternative to provinces.

In Lombardy, *comprensori* faced strong municipal opposition. The *Comprensorio Milanese* established in the early 1980s – including 106 municipalities and entrusted with tasks of spatial and socio-economic planning – suffered similar difficulties in reaching consensus over policy options as the PIM had: municipal opposition resulted in a referendum which expedited recognition of its failure and its final abolition. As an outcome, the original consortium was turned into an agency for planning research and consultancy – the *Centro Studi PIM* – which was to become a major informal actor of metropolitan policy through its role in assisting local administrations and framing public debate.

Failures in establishing an intermediate tier of government nurtured dissatis-factions with comprehensive territorial-institutional approaches to metropolitan government among regional political elites. In the late 1980s, hence, a new phase of the controversy began, defined by two contrasting positions. On the one hand, a 'structuralist' position – represented by the city and Province of Milan, mainly through contributions elaborated within their think-tank, the *Istituto per la Scienza dell'Amministrazione Pubblica* (ISAP) – envisioned a two-tier system based on reframing the size and competencies of existing territorial entities: in particular, on the substitution of the province with a new 'metropolitan province', and on the establishment of a 'metropolitan area' formed by merging and subdividing existing local bodies into homogeneous units. This position was grounded on an appraisal of internal and external core-periphery disequilibria in the metropolitan region, pointing to the need for a re-articulation of territorial scales questioning the unitary character of the central city and introducing more adequate local administrative units. On the other hand, a 'functionalist' position – represented by experts and officials of the Region of Lombardy – pleaded for innovative ways of coalition-building, such as negotiating arenas and intermediary institutional settings, as means for achieving effective decision-making and coordination; this envisioned the pursuit of 'political' rather than 'structural' solutions, supported by an inter-mediate metropolitan body with a council of municipal representatives and a directly elected presidency endowed with autonomous and flexible strategic tasks and with powers for resource mobilisation.

The rejection of a 'structural' solution by regional actors originated in their alleged incompatibility with their constitutionally legitimate political claims: an institutionalised Milan metropolitan entity would have necessarily extended over territories of the provinces of Varese and Brescia, potentially conflicting with the Region's new and yet too weakly defined territorial competencies. The issue, however, was also tied to the delay in rationalisation of existing territorial juris-dictions, most notably the provinces. The emerging fortunes of political localism – which found a significant terrain in new claims for provincial autonomy – were in fact partly a result of their persisting territorial imbalances (particularly between the rural south and the northern industrial districts of the Province of Milan). Local political ambitions, however, were also dealt with outside a general design of territorial rationalisation, leading in the 1990s to the establishment of the new provinces of Lecco and Lodi (the latter by detachment from the Province of Milan) – as well as to further claims for autonomy – without a parallel definition of solutions for the metropolitan region.

Strategies and policies for the metropolitan regions, 1975–95

Before addressing recent reforms and experiences in metropolitan governance, we turn to the main stages of urban strategies and policies since the 1980s, interpreted as an expression of Milan's struggle in defining its competitive position in the face of institutional failures in metropolitan coordination and in conditions of political instability and administrative fragmentation.

The early 1980s: the new ideology of centrality

A significant turn in Milan's development strategies emerges in the early 1980s, in connection with the failure of 'associational' approaches to metropolitan government like the PIM and with the crisis of the ideology of urban management pursued by the city's master plan. The *Variante Generale al PRG* (Piano Regolatore Generale, General Master Plan) (1976–80) – a major effort of the left-wing Communist-Socialist party coalition governing the city since 1975 – expressed a basic conservationist attitude towards contrasting counter-urbanisation trends through urban containment, inner-city re-equilibrium and functional decentralisation. In pursuing a distinctive proceduralist approach to urban development processes, the *Variante Generale* introduced significant innovations in planning instruments (particularly by providing tools for the timing and sequencing of development initiatives), but also expressed a rather technocratic attitude which soon proved to be both instrumentally and cognitively inadequate in keeping up with the nature and scope of the forces which were shaping development in the metropolitan region.

A crucial step towards the dismissal of the plan's regulatory approach was introduced in the early 1980s by the rise of a new discourse on Milan's role in a competitive European environment. In connection with the leadership taken by the Socialist party, the city's second left-wing coalition introduced a 'managerial style' of policy-making in approaching local planning and development issues, with unprecedented openings to the private sector, frequent use of negotiations with corporate actors and in general a new 'managerial', corporate-inspired rethorics in urban policy focusing on the valorisation of Milan's centrality and on the constitution of a composite coalition of interests around a strategy of metropolitan centralisation. Planning tools and procedures were coherently subdued to such a strategy, turning Milan – until the corruption scandals of the early 1990s – into the symbolic centre of a new urban ideology. The nature of Milan's urban policy in the 1980s may be best understood by observing its 'dual' nature, i.e. the complementarity between its strategic and its tactical, 'everyday' dimension.

On the one hand, the urban development discourse grounded its political support on matching the entrepreneurial ambitions of a highly heterogeneous and fragmented range of development actors. Key in this direction was what may be called the 'tactical' dimension of the new planning approach, represented by the deregulation of incremental urban change. The strict regulatory measures for containing urban tertiarisation and industrial decentralisation introduced by the *Variante Generale* were loosened from the early stage of implementation through the adoption of more permissive rules and through the flexible and largely discretionary introduction of *ad hoc* variants of the general plan, with the aim of overcoming the deadlock of small and medium-size development and redevelopment initiatives that was allegedly affecting the building and real estate market, and of revitalising the urban economy. This turn towards a sort of 'deregulatory proceduralism' resulted in a remarkable development dynamic, which disproved in fact the existence of an alleged crisis in the urban development industry. The booming of real estate initiatives – with about 4.0 million m^2 built between 1980 and 1985, about 2.1 million m^2 of which were realised on derelict industrial land, against the 1.8 million m^2 foreseen by the plan – also bore the seeds of new problems, however, like the oversupply-crisis in office space that became apparent at the end of the decade. Moreover, systematic resort to plan variants favoured the structural embedding of speculative development interests into public policy-making. The most striking case is represented by *Progetto Casa* (1982–4), an extraordinary public housing programme of the municipality, which provided for 3.0 million m^2 on 19 mainly privately-owned greenfield sites in the southern urban fringe.

On the other hand, deregulation was accompanied by a shift from the ideology of urban containment and re-equilibrium to a strategic reconceptualisation of Milan's centrality in the 'wider' urban region. The reappraisal of urban centrality in the framework of inter-regional and supra-national competition favoured a project-oriented approach to metropolitan governance, standing in sharp contrast with previous attempts to establish 'meta-decisional' settings of metropolitan government, and rather strictly tied to the valorisation of the interests and assets of a series of public and private actors. Plan-making hence became part of what may be called the strategic dimension of the new approach: the constitution of a new discourse around Milan's centrality as a framework for the constitution of a new development coalition.

The new urban strategy entailed the invention of a new 'extraordinary' format for policy-making – formally distinct from statutory planning tools – and a new approach to knowledge as a framing and legitimising resource. The former aspect was represented by the adoption of a non-binding document, the *Documento Direttore*, which defined a framework of actions related to the effects of a major infrastructure project, the *Progetto Passante*; the latter by *Progetto Milano*, an initiative involving the main territorial institutions and knowledge centres of the Milan region under the coordination of IReR (Istituto Regionale di Reicerca della Lombardia, the research institute of the Region of Lombardy) in surveying and conceptualising the socio-economic and territorial prospects of the metropolitan region in the increasing internationalisation of urban competition.

The *Documento Direttore* (Comune di Milano, 1984) represented an absolute novelty, putting Milan in an exceptional, 'unorthodox' position in the Italian planning landscape. Polarising the distinction between plan-led and project-led urban change that dominated scholarly debate during the decade, the *Documento Direttore* explicitly aimed at representing an alternative to comprehensive planning tools, introducing a proactive and flexible approach to urban modernisation, based on development projects (*progetti d'area*) defining the physical and contractual requirements for *ad hoc* variants to the master plan.

Key to the strategy of the *Documento Direttore* was the combination of public assets and private capital around a big infrastructural project – the new underground railway track (called *Passante Ferroviario*) – connecting the existing system of railway stations and a series of new stations throughout the inner-city along an axis running from the north-west to the south-east. The *Passante* was conceived as the backbone of the new integrated regional railway system as well as a unique occasion for the valorisation of urban locations located at its intersection. The concept relied on the integration of public–private resources around a series of urban nodes – most notably located on key derelict industrial sites – defined by the *Passante*, ensuring the mobilisation of private capital for the valorisation of a sequence of new central places. The urban section of the tunnel was to be financed according to a 1983 intergovernmental agreement by an equal share of one-third of capital investments each between the City of Milan, the Region of Lombardy and the state railway company FFSS, with the addition of further state funding for external connections.

The *Passante Ferroviario* represented the rebirth of a concept advanced by PIM in 1965, aimed at strengthening functional decentralisation in the polycentric urban system around Milan by means of enhanced intra-regional accessibility. In its revised version, however, less than a 'solution' to perceived problems, the *Passante* became the catalyst for new ambitions: the upgrading and specialisation of Milan's central functions in the European urban hierarchy.

The late 1980s: the fragmentation of urban development coalitions

With the shift from a left-wing to a five-party Socialist-led coalition in 1985, Milan witnessed a progressive ineffectiveness in making decisions and in implementing strategic projects. The implementation of *progetti d'area* proved to be highly constrained by difficulties in building credible commitments among actors with divergent interests. On the one hand,

> the public or para-public actors whom the city administration intended to involve to ensure [...] the success of initiatives proved to be scarcely interested in taking co-leadership in implementing the strategy [...], rather attaching to

the projects in which they were involved corporate rationales often conflicting with the aims of the planning document.

(Balducci, 1988, p.58–9)

Such divergences often forced highly controversial redefinitions of the initial concepts, leading to breakdowns in the development coalition supporting the *Progetto Passante*. This evolution is well represented by some of Milan's major urban projects. In the case of both the Garibaldi-Repubblica financial district and the Portello fair district, the complex integrated features of the projects as well as the ambiguities of the nature of public aims contributed to the inability to reach binding agreements among the main final users (the Region of Lombardy and the Milan Stock Exchange in the former, the broadcasting company RAI in the latter), leading to their radical redefinition or to their abandonment.

On the other hand, uneven relationships between public and market actors resulted either in the stagnation of projects (Bovisa, Porta Vittoria) or in priority shifts towards more market-led initiatives (Bicocca, Montecity), relocating leadership from public to private promoters and undermining the overall coherence of the strategy. A similar evolution marked one of Milan's few 'success stories', the realisation of the Bicocca technology pole: delays and difficulties in fulfilling mutual commitments among the actors progressively changed the nature of the initiative, turning it from an ambitious public–private joint project – targeted at the establishment of a cluster of superior metropolitan activities according to a strategic pattern of functional decentralisation – into a rather traditional, private marketing initiative, rising to the status of a new urban location in a somewhat incremental rather than a 'planned' way.

Even more crucially, the ill-structured approach featured by many projects – in terms of the definition of the problem as well as of the conditions for implementation – contributed to consistent delays in responding to the need to upgrade key metropolitan functions, as in the case of the fair district. This led in most cases to lengthy and ineffective decision-making processes characterised by ambiguous intertwinings of public and private interests, which came to light in their full dimensions in the 1990s. The end of the decade is hence marked by a remarkable combination of continuity and change in urban policy. While planning strategies defined by the *Progetto Passante* continued to shape development initiatives along a pattern of incremental adjustments, the need for new 'structural' measures was increasingly perceived.

A paradigmatic expression of this climate is the *Documento Direttore delle Aree Dismesse*, the city's first comprehensive strategy for the reuse of derelict industrial sites (Comune di Milano, 1988). While a previous version realised in support of the *Progetto Passante* had focused exclusively on the strategic potential represented by big areas included in the *progetti d'area*, the new approach addressed the issue of the fragmentation of derelict land in the urban fabric in a more differentiated way, pointing both to the need for contrasting speculative pressures on this urban resource and to its potential for diffuse improvements of urban quality. The document accordingly proposed a dual strategy, pursuing on the one hand objectives of functional decentralisation at locations contributing to a strategic framework of higher-level metropolitan specialisation, in line with the *Progetto Passante*, and on the other hand objectives of urban regeneration on smaller-scale sites earmarked for neighbourhood-based projects. The new strategy, however, proved to be undermined by shortcomings similar to those experienced by previous initiatives: the difficulty in establishing stable commitments among development actors by binding their actions to a shared and consistent strategy. Significantly, in the end, its failure was marked by the inability to find a compatibility between the prevailing regulatory rationale of planning tools and the need for a more proactive public approach to the management of urban change.

The early 1990s: 'competition without strategies'?

At the beginning of the 1990s, Milan's score in the pursuit of its strategic goals appeared to be dramatically low. Besides difficulties and failures in implementing strategic projects as well as other initiatives in urban modernisation, decision-making deadlocks and mismanagement – and soon the outburst of corruption scandals – hindered the implementation of infrastructural projects crucial for an efficient level of metropolitan functions (the system of logistic centres, the new water-purification site, the new fair district, the layout of high-speed railways, and Malpensa airport). The completion of the *Passante* itself had been subject to huge delays. In summary, Milan – despite its unquestionable factors of excellence – appeared contradictorily split between a diffuse capacity in promoting and an acute incapacity in implementing urban development initiatives (Fareri, 1991).

In light of recent failures, the 1990s brought new policy-analytical elements for the critical scrutiny of project-led approaches, highlighting crucial constraints to their effectiveness, like the lack of political stability and accountability, the weakness of technical bureaucracies, the persistence of vested interests and conflicting objectives. Certain contributory factors have been increasingly identified regarding the difficulty of Milan's polity in establishing a stable and accountable coalition of metropolitan interests: the poor level of communication and of creative policy interchange among urban actors (Fareri, 1991, 1995); the inability of the political and institutional sphere to enhance networking relationships (Ciciotti *et al.*, 1994); the reliance on 'meta-decisional' institutional settings; and also – as experience has shown – the naivety entailed in the assumption of project-oriented policies as a solution to the complexity of conjoint action implied by initiatives in urban transformation (Balducci and Dente, 1992; Bobbio *et al.*, 1994).

The pursuit of new sources for policy innovation through social dialogue and concerted action thus became high on the agenda during the decade, particularly

Enrico Gualini

in response to the dramatic loss of legitimacy of the Italian polity in the early 1990s. Paradoxically, the increasing activism of civil society and stakeholders during the decade – as witnessed by the emergence of such associations as *Associazione per gli Interessi Metropolitani* (AIM) and *MeglioMilano*, and by the role taken by foundations like the *Fondazione Cariplo* and functional autonomies like the chamber of commerce in promoting research and public debate – has been often characterised by a distinctive unrelatedness, if not overt competition among initiatives. As a consequence, the aim of creating new recognised arenas for debate and cooperation among stakeholders and civil society has been hindered by the very constraints to cooperation that it aimed to overcome (e.g. Fareri, 1995). Remarkably, a distinctive feature of this phase has been the difficult integration of innovative policy aims with statutory planning tools like the master plan. The reasons for this lie in an overall crisis in legitimacy of regulatory means, as well as in the perceived inadequacy of traditional comprehensive approaches in addressing the needs of an advanced, highly dynamic metropolitan society.

As a result, the 1990s have by and large witnessed the coexistence of projects and small-scale initiatives developed in continuity with previous rationales and of the tentative pursuit of a 'new pragmatism' in planning. *Nove Parchi per Milano* (Comune di Milano, 1995) – the only significant initiative taken by the city administration taken over by Lega Nord after the 1993 elections – is paradigmatic of this attitude. The valorisation of a key urban resource – the embeddedness in the urban fabric of medium- and large-scale derelict areas – is turned into an inter-subjectively appealing urban design vision: a new crown of nine urban parks, meant to upgrade living standards through the supply of green recreational areas. The operational foundation for this design, significantly, is identified in a strategically selective orientation to market actors and rationales, allegedly capable of realising patterns of credible commitment; and its medium is identified in the least common denominator for public-private cooperation in the market domain, the exchange of values, realised through the granting of exceptional building densities and of public locational betterments.

New forms of governance and spatial policy: developments in the 1990s

Recent governance approaches in the Milan region are the result of a combination between developments in the Italian institutional landscape and original responses to typically metropolitan issues. In this, the dialectics of continuity and change that characterised the 1990s appears particularly complex. In this final section, after having delineated the trajectory of Milan's urban and metropolitan policies, we highlight developments in the Italian public administration – in particular the rise of contractual forms of relationships among policy actors – which define some crucial administrative conditions and political 'opportunity structures' for

276

experimenting with flexible and innovative forms of metropolitan governance. Their features may be summarised in a highly pragmatic approach to the spatial aims and scales of strategic planning, addressed according to a new concerted-collaborative attitude developing in the framework of inclusionary, weakly institutionalised policy arenas.

From metropolitan governments to 'flexible' modes of governance?

In 1990, Law 142 – as part of a broader reform of local governments and of the public sector – introduced the first statutory approach to metropolitan government in the Italian legislation. The comprehensive model of metropolitan government represented by this initiative, however, far from bringing this long-lasting controversy to an end, was the expression of a compromise soon doomed to fail for two sets of reasons. On the one hand, it pursued a conception that for a long time had been the subject of open controversies on both the scholarly and the political level (e.g. Dematteis, 1989; Dente, 1989); on the other hand, it did not adequately address but rather harshened conflicts over the distribution of functions among sub-national jurisdictions (between the state and the regions, and between regions and provinces) by the addition of a new level of territorial government.

The reform was grounded on a double-tier system of metropolitan government, based on existing municipalities and on the establishment of a new authority, the *città metropolitana*, endowed with powers by partial assumption of previous powers of municipalities and provinces. Two assumptions supported this approach: first, the need for correspondence between a territory, a community, and its government, typical of classical principles of territorial jurisdiction, and for an unequivocal identification of metropolitan areas and their boundaries; second, the possibility to establish a criterion for identifying areas (on the part of the state) and boundaries (on the part of the regions) from the top down in an effective and viable way.

The contradictions and ambiguities of this model – which soon made it appear as an 'old-born reform' (Dente, 1995) – were related to the failure to address a thorough reform of intergovernmental relations and to the intergovernmental conflicts thus originated:

- between the regions and the state (the former objecting to strong metropolitan authorities and to state intervention in defining their boundaries, in fear of their ability to enter into direct negotiations with the state);
- between the provinces and the new metropolitan authorities (as a result of the former's allegations about their prospective loss of power in favour of the new entity);
- between smaller municipalities and the new metropolitan authorities (due to the former's fear of a centralisation of powers).

Enrico Gualini

Significantly, the result has been a substantial disregard of the law's requirements (as of today, no *città metropolitane* has been established according to the procedures of Law 142/1990) and its reframing within the recent reform of local governments (Dlgs. 267/2000) in line with a concerted approach similar to that adopted by the city and province of Bologna: *città metropolitane* are expected to be formed upon the proposal of local autonomies (and subject to local referenda) according to varying models of constitutional order, to be consensually defined by participant authorities.

Nevertheless, the path of reform introduced in 1990 has set important conditions for turning intergovernmental relationships towards a concerted approach to coordination. A first step in this direction was the introduction of tools for negotiated coordination in public-public and public-private relationships – the so-called *accordi di programma* (Law 142/1990) and *conferenze di servizi* (Law 241/1990) – focusing on the need for anticipatory agreements in order to ensure coherence between different agendas, programmes and regulatory frameworks in realising complex coordination tasks. (An important example of the role played by such arenas in overcoming decision-making deadlocks in the Milan area is given by the agreements for the relocation of the fair district on the derelict industrial site of the former petrolchemical pole of Rho-Pero.) A second step is represented by the rationalisation and institutionalisation of concerted policy-making approaches as a tool for regional policy, introduced in the mid-1990s under the label of 'negotiated programming' (Law 662/1996), which has extended the range of negotiated policy agreements from public-public intergovernmental contracts to public–private initiatives for the promotion of integrated local development initiatives (like *patti territoriali* and *contratti d'area*). A third step is represented by the 'Bassanini reform' (Dlgs. 143/1997, 469/1997, and 112/1998), a complex in-progress programme for the 'devolution' of competencies to local governments in key areas of public regulation and intervention. Besides the aim of a generalisation of principles of subsidiarity and negotiated intergovernmental coordination, the reform has introduced new corporate forms of public action – like local development agencies – which represents a further step towards a 'territorialisation' of development policies and contributes to the diffusion of more proactive entrepreneurial attitudes in local administration. A final aspect is the rise of a 'new municipalism' as a result of reforming the system of local governments (Law 142/1990) and elections (Law 81/1993) – which introduced the direct election of mayors, a shift towards more executive powers and autonomy, and perspectives of modernisation and greater effectiveness of municipal action through the introduction of partnerships and *ad hoc* agencies – and of the progressive devolution of taxing powers to regions and localities.

Together, such innovations have fostered a change in attitude in the Italian public administration in the direction of a broader effectiveness and accountability as well as of a better responsiveness to the requirements and rationales of EU funding programmes and community initiatives: they have contributed to introducing opportunities for local administrative modernisation, favouring collaborative intergovernmental relationships, and embedding partnership in the policy process. Furthermore, they have jointly contributed to a substantial renewal of the sources and forms of legitimisation for local governmental actors, contributing to the rise of new and more proactive local polities and leaderships (Bobbio, 2000; Gelli, 2001; Gualini, 2001).

Planning in the shadow of hierarchy: innovative experiences in concerted territorial governance

Since the early 1990s, as a response to institutional deadlocks and political crises, a series of loosely institutionalised experiments in the Milan metropolitan region have been exploring new approaches to planning. Moving from pioneering approaches to open landscape preservation involving voluntary cooperation between neighbouring municipalities (such as the consortium for the *Parco Agricolo Sud Milano*), more recent initiatives have addressed the opportunities for multidimensional approaches to territorial restructuring in areas undergoing structural change and in conditions of socio-economic emergency. Their common feature is an attempt to redefine the appropriate level of policy-making within a broader social and economic environment through the promotion of concrete courses of action, supported by flexible institutional arrangements among the involved actors, in order to match supra-local, 'structural' conditions for development with the resources and potentials that can be activated through 'local' mobilisation (Pasqui and Bolocan Goldstein, 1998; Pasqui, 2001).

A significant anticipation of this trend in local development strategies is the approach promoted by the Region of Lombardy and elaborated by IReR – but never implemented – as an alternative to traditional end-of-pipe approaches to the issue of environmental pollution pursued by state legislation for the critical area of the rivers Lambro, Seveso and Olona in the northern Milan agglomeration (IReR, 1995). Inspired by innovative experiences like that of the IBA-Emscher Park, the alternative strategy proposed for the area pursued a combination of measures for environmental recovery and measures for the valorisation of territorial specificities, as a condition for promoting self-centred patterns of local development. Accordingly, an important focus was placed on the promotion of alternative organisational patterns – relying on the decentralised involvement of local communities, agencies, and civic initiatives – that openly challenged comprehensive views on metropolitan coordination, and rather put the emphasis on the need to adopt flexible, 'experimental' institutional scales and settings for territorial governance.

The role of territorial partnerships and of development agencies as their intermediaries became a policy focus of the Province of Milan in the mid-1990s

Enrico Gualini

(Provincia di Milano, 1998), in partial convergence with perspectives of 'negotiated programming' introduced by national legislation. The pursuit of a local dimension of competitiveness emphasises organisational innovation as a key factor, promoting cooperation among different societal sectors by integrating the flexibleness and the streamlining of procedures in the public administration, the adoption of active labour training and job creating policies, and the development and involvement of the 'third-sector' economy and initiatives in policy-making and service provision. In this respect, the new development agencies promoted by the province in crisis areas like Sesto S. Giovanni, Legnano and Arese soon moved beyond the initial single-dimensional definition of their mission of industrial conversion, addressing the more general aim of matching the needs of local economic structures – based on highly specialised SMEs (small and medium enterprises) clusters facing severe innovation challenges – through integrated development concepts and by directing funding sources to demand-driven initiatives.

Among these, the *Agenzia di Sviluppo Nord-Milano* (ASNM) has become the most advanced experiment in local development in the Milan area. Originated by three-party agreements of 1993 and 1996 between the state, the unions and private companies about the closing and redevelopment of the steel and machinery industries of Sesto S. Giovanni, ASNM was founded in 1996 as a corporate public agency involving four municipalities, the Province of Milan and the main shareholders of the area. Its mission was soon extended beyond the original task of redeveloping portions of the industrial sites into a science park for environmental technologies, towards a more general assumption of issues of local development, addressing the radical transformation of the social and economic environment and the need to promote active processes of local re-identification around new development strategies in order to address a viable perspective of economic transition. ASNM has been entrusted with such tasks as channelling and administering sources, promoting economic activities and joint programmes, and developing projects for land reclamation, urban regeneration and environmental decontamination and recovery. The role of the agency has been particularly strengthened in this respect by measures for the ecological conversion of the environmental crisis area Lambro–Seveso–Olona provided by laws for the steel districts of Bagnoli and Sesto S. Giovanni. Through its integrated approach to economic and environmental development and the promotion of local environmental initiatives, ASNM may in fact become a pilot project of the integrated and self-sustained development strategy for the Lambro–Seveso–Olona region developed by IReR. The scope of its formal responsibilities has constituted the background for an ambitious development strategy directed at valorising the endogenous resources present in the area – like a highly developed industrial and entrepreneurial culture and a diffuse social capital – by linking policies for innovation, employment and sustainable development.

A 'new pragmatism'? Strategic spatial planning as a framework for new governance approaches in the Milan region

The experiences described express a renewal of strategic approaches to metropolitan governance currently in search of a difficult balance between experimentation and institutionalisation. A crucial arena for this search will be defined by the process of 'federalist' reform of state-local relationships constitutionally sanctioned in 2001. Meanwhile, nevertheless, some common features distinguish actual experiences. On the one hand, a 'new pragmatism' has emerged in dealing with issues of public-private coordination. The aim of establishing credible commitments among policy actors is increasingly connected to the definition of strategic frames of reference in support of concrete courses of action. On the other hand, a need is perceived for stable, legitimate and accountable policy frameworks and for new institutional arenas of interaction and mutual adjustment.

Caught in this dualism of claims, approaches to strategic planning are gradually changing in meaning. An understanding of strategic rationality is emerging that conceives of planning as a means for consensus-building, for constituting stable patterns of mutual commitment among policy actors. Strategic planning becomes a way of defining legitimate and effective urban policy agendas and coalitions. From such a perspective, plan-making, rather than as a technical tool, tends to be assumed mainly as an arena for deliberative processes, in which the constitution of reliable coalitions in support of a public policy is at stake. In the wake of failures of institutional attempts to regain political effectiveness and legitimacy, practices of strategic planning have come to be viewed as flexible and experimental ways for reconstructing the polity, for redefining the public sphere (Mazza, 2000; Balducci, 2001).

An outstanding example is the strategic development process for the northern Milan area promoted by ASNM in 1997. The approach builds on the experience gained from the first incremental redevelopment initiatives conducted in the area – in particular, the competition for a plan for a new 'central park' on the core derelict industrial site – in which use was made of methodologies of participation and strategic visioning (such as holding 'awareness scenario workshops'). Acknowledging the importance of public involvement in the process of the 'social construction' of shared symbolic-cognitive frames of reference is at the basis of the agency's approach to defining a comprehensive strategy for local processes of social, economic and environmental transformation, intended as a focus for ongoing collaboration within informal stakeholder arenas – like the 'Forum for Northern Milan' – and as a foundation for establishing effective commitments among the involved actors.

A similar attitude characterises the approach recently adopted by the *Progetto Pianificazione Strategica* of the City of Milan. Spatial planning is redefined, again,

Enrico Gualini

as part of a broader strategy of the city's new political elite in order to regain legitimisation through a new working method and the establishment of an ongoing dialogue with social forces. The periodic convocation of the city's States General promoted since 1998 is conceived as an occasion – in Major Albertini's words (1998 opening address) – for 'gathering all public and private actors in order to listen to needs, evaluations and suggestions, and to commit ourselves to achieving defined results within defined timeframes, valorising the free initiative of private actors and associations'. Similarly, the new strategic document – defined, in apparently modest fashion, as a 'framework of coordination for the city's urban policies' (Comune di Milano, 2000) – explicitly aims at making sense of and at valorising ongoing initiatives, projects and plans within an easily communicable framework of spatial development: a strategic vision is intimately targeted at enhancing collective commitments, at reconstructing a stable urban development coalition.

Bibliography

ASNM (ed.) (1999) *Verso il Piano Strategico. Manifesto del Nord Milano. Un patto locale per lo sviluppo*, ASNM, Sesto S. Giovanni.

Balducci, A. (1988) 'Le vicende del Piano: una periodizzazione', *Urbanistica*, 90: 50–9.

Balducci, A. (2001) 'New tasks and new forms for comprehensive planning in Italy', in L. Albrechts, J. Alden and A. Da Rosa Pires (eds) *The Changing Institutional Landscape of Planning*, Aldershot: Ashgate.

Balducci, A. and Dente, B. (1992) 'L'operatività delle scelte di piano', in IReR *Per un piano territoriale strategico della Lombardia anni 2000*, Milano: IReR.

Bobbio, L. (2000) 'Produzione di politiche a mezzo di contratti nella pubblica amminis-trazione italiana', *Stato e Mercato*, 58: 111–41.

Bobbio, L., Fareri, P. Morisi, M. and Dente, B. (1994) *Metropoli per progetti*, Bologna: Il Mulino.

Boeri, S., Lanzani, A. and Marini, E. (1993) *Il territorio che cambia*, Milano: Abitare Segesta Cataloghi.

CCIAA Milano (ed.) (1992) *Monitorare Milano*, Milano: CCIAA.

Centro Studi PIM (1990) *Uso e consumo di suolo e dinamiche insediative nell'area metropolitana milanese*, Milano: Centro Studi PIM.

Ciciotti, E., Florio, R. and Perulli, P. (1994) *Milano: competizione senza strategie?*, Milano: AIM.

Comune di Milano (1984) *Progetto Passante. Documento direttore*, Milano: Comune di Milano.

Comune di Milano (1988) *Linee programmatiche per il Documento Direttore sulle aree dismesse o sottoutilizzate*, Milano: Comune di Milano.

Comune di Milano (1995) *Nove Parchi per Milano*, Milano: Triennale di Milano.

Comune di Milano (2000) *Ricostruire la Grande Milano. Documento di inquadramento delle politiche urbanistiche comunali*, Milano: Comune di Milano.

Dalmasso, E. (1972) *Milano capitale economica d'Italia*, Milano: Franco Angeli.

Dematteis, G. (1989) 'Regioni geografiche, articolazione territoriale degli interessi e regioni istituzionali', *Stato e mercato*, 27: 115–37.

Dente, B. (1989) 'Del governare le metropoli: obiettivi sostanziali e strumenti istituzionali', *Stato e Mercato*, 26: 279–303.

Dente, B. (1995) *In un diverso stato. Come rifare la pubblica amministrazione italiana*, Bologna: Il Mulino.

Fareri, P. (1988) 'Se il Passante è la soluzione quale è il problema?', *Urbanistica*, 90: 84–90.

Fareri, P. (1991) 'Milano: progettualità diffusa e difficoltà realizzativa', in CRESME *La costruzione della città europea negli anni '80*, Vol. 2, Roma: Credito Fondiario.

Fareri, P. (1995) *Urban Center: l'esperienza statunitense*, Milano: CCIAA.

Gelli, F. (2001) 'Planning systems in Italy within the context of new processes of region-alization', *International Planning Studies*, 6 (2): 183–97.

Gualini, E. (2001) 'New programming and the influence of transnational discourses in the reform of regional policy in Italy', *European Planning Studies*, 9 (6): 755–71.

IReR (1995) *Bonifica, riconversione e valorizzazione ambientale del bacino dei fiumi Lambro, Seveso e Olona*, Roma: Urbanistica Edizioni.

Lanzani, A. (1991) *Il territorio al plurale*, Milano: Franco Angeli.

Mazza, L. (2000) 'Strategie e strategie spaziali', *Territorio*, 13: 26–32.

Morandi, C. (ed.) (1994) *I vantaggi competitivi delle città: un confronto in ambito europeo*, Milano: Franco Angeli.

Palermo, P.C. (ed.) (1997) *Linee di assetto e scenari evolutivi della regione urbana milanese. Atlante delle trasformazioni urbane*, Milano: Franco Angeli.

Pasqui, G. (2001) *Confini milanesi. Processi territoriali e pratiche di governo*, Milano: Franco Angeli.

Pasqui, G. and Bolocan Goldstein, M. (eds) (1998) *Sviluppo locale in contesti metro-politani. Trasformazioni economiche e territoriali nel Milanese*, Milano: Franco Angeli.

Provincia di Milano (1998) *Le azioni della Provincia di Milano per lo sviluppo locale e l'innovazione tecnologica delle PMI*, Milano: Provincia di Milano.

Rotelli, E. (1996) 'Le aree metropolitane in Italia: una questione istituzionale insoluta (1956–1996)', *Amministrare*, 26 (2): 273–302.

PART V

Paris, Brussels, Marseilles-Aix, Barcelona, Madrid

17 Paris – Île-de-France region

Christian Lefèvre

The Paris–Île-de-France area dominates France, not only because Paris is the capital and as such contains the symbols and resources of political power, but also because it contains the economic and cultural power. No other European metropolis has the same importance vis-à-vis its nation-state, as is shown in table 17.1. The Paris area is considered by many (Kantor *et al.*, 1997) as the model of the *dirigist* planner regime. If once there was some truth to this description, the ongoing changes which have been taking place for the last five years indicate that the Île-de-France can no longer be presented as the model of a state-controlled territory. Today, new actors are emerging at the local level who potentially challenge the state as the *deus ex machina* of the French capital. After a synthetic presentation of the socio-economic and political evolution of the Paris area, this chapter will focus on the changes taking place there, using the planning sector in a broad sense as an illustration of such changes.

Table 17.1 Some data regarding the weight of the Île-de-France region versus France in 2000

	Numbers Île-de-France	Relative to France (%)
Population	10,952,000	18.6
Labour force	5,400,000	21.4
Foreign (non-French) population		39.0
Employment	5,000,000	21.9
GDP		29.0
Part of the national income tax		33.0
Number of students	550,000	25.0
Number of researchers		45.0

Source: IAURIF, 40 ans en Île-de-France, Etudes et Développement, 2001.

Christian Lefèvre

The evolution of the Île-de-France over the last decades

The economic and social evolution of the Île-de-France

In 1965, the Region of Paris Master Plan (*Schéma Directeur d'Aménagement et d'Urbanisme de la Région Parisienne*, SDAURP) projected a 65 per cent increase in the population of the area by 2000, bringing the total to 14 million. In order to accommodate such considerable growth, the state decided to establish several new towns on the outskirts of Paris. However, the demographic forecast turned out to be wrong and was adjusted in the Master Plan of 1976 (*Schéma Directeur d'Aménagement et d'Urbanisme de la Région Île-de-France*, SDAURIF) which projected that there would be 12 million inhabitants by 2000, representing only a slight increase. Five new towns were established in the 1960s and 1970s, and a large part of the population increase took place in these towns between 1975 and 2000 (these towns account for 43 per cent of the regional population increase during that period, that is, 475,000 people). Most of the remainder of the increase occurred in the outer ring (*grande couronne*), which accommodated 2.1 million people in 1960 as compared to 3.6 million in 1975 and 4.1 million in 2000. In the 1960s and early 1970s, demographic growth was housed in high density areas called ZUPs (*Zones à Urbaniser en Priorité*), that is, in social and collective housing. This situation started to change in the 1970s when more and more single housing units were built, resulting in the tremendous urban sprawl in the Île-de-France region. Indeed, the last decades have seen a significant increase in the urbanised land in the outer ring, that is, 600 km² in the 1960s against 1,000 km² in 1980 and about 1,300 km² today.

Consequently, the population of Paris has declined over the last three decades. Between 1960 and 1975, the city lost 500,000 inhabitants, or approximately 18 per cent of its population. The decrease was less sharp in the 1975–90 period, that is, there was a decline of 'only' 160,000 people. Between 1990 and 2000, the rate of decrease slowed to about 3,000 per year. Today the city's population is 2.1 million compared to 2.8 million in 1960.

These urbanisation trends have presented the public authorities with quite a problem. In 1990, the governmental White Paper on the Île-de-France (DREIF *et al.*, 1990) permitted the release, between then and 2015, of approximately 50,000 hectares for urban use, but required the balancing of the land supply against environmental protection, notably to preserve the city's green belt. This was established in the 1994 Master Plan (*Schéma Directeur de la Région Île-de-France*, SDRIF).

Economically and socially, the Île-de-France has undergone tremendous changes over the last two decades. Like most other European metropolitan areas, the Paris region underwent a major shift in its production system in the late 1970s and 1980s. Industrial decline was severe, with a loss of 650,000 industrial jobs between

1975 and 1994, and was not completely offset by the tertiary sector growth until the mid-1990s. Today, 82 per cent of jobs are in the tertiary sector, and 18 per cent in construction and manufacturing. In addition, in the tertiary sector, the Paris area contains the most qualified and executive functions in research and development, finance, logistics, etc. In the industrial sector, half of the jobs involve medium and high technology activities.

Economic growth has obviously influenced the evolution of the social composition of the population of the Île-de-France, and there has been a significant increase in social disparities, which have taken a specific spatial configuration. In 1998, about 70 per cent of the total regional employment was in Paris and the first ring (*petite couronne*). Jobs requiring high qualifications have continued to be concentrated in the central city and the first ring, notably on the west side of the region (mainly the Hauts-de-Seine department, in which La Défense is located). Today, Paris and the Hauts-de-Seine account for 67 per cent of these jobs. In addition, economic urban decentralisation in the outer ring has not been homogeneously distributed. On the contrary, so-called *pôles d'excellence* have been established around the Roissy-Charles de Gaulle airport in the north, the Plateau de Saclay in the south, and in the new towns of Marne la Vallée in the east and Cergy Pontoise in the north-west (see figure 17.1).

Briefly, the Île-de-France suffers from two major problems: social exclusion and bad transport. Industrial and urban decline has mainly affected specific territories, such as the Seine-Saint-Denis department to the north of Paris (the former 'red belt'). This is where social problems are the most acute, even though the local economy is showing some signs of recovery. Massive public investments in the eastern part have not offset the traditional west–east divide (the major executive functions and most of the wealthy social groups are to be found in the west, while less qualified and poorer households are concentrated in the east). These economic and social changes have had serious consequences for the transport system. Although the Paris area has one of the best transport systems in the world, traffic congestion (and as a result, air pollution) and the downgrading of the public transport system are becoming serious problems. Urban sprawl and the west–east divide have strongly contributed to the increasing mobility of Parisians and to the significant increase in car use. Suburb to suburb trips are becoming more and more important while the road and public transport systems are still focused on the core of the metropolitan area. The massive investments in the highway system (new highways in the 1970s and 1980s, construction of two ring roads in the 1980s and 1990s) and in public transport (building of the suburban railway network (*Réseau Express Régional*, RER) in the 1970s, extension of the metro and RER systems in the 1980s and 1990s, construction of peripheral tramway links in the late 1990s) have not been able to alleviate the problems of increasing traffic and the spatial evolution of trip patterns.

Christian Lefèvre

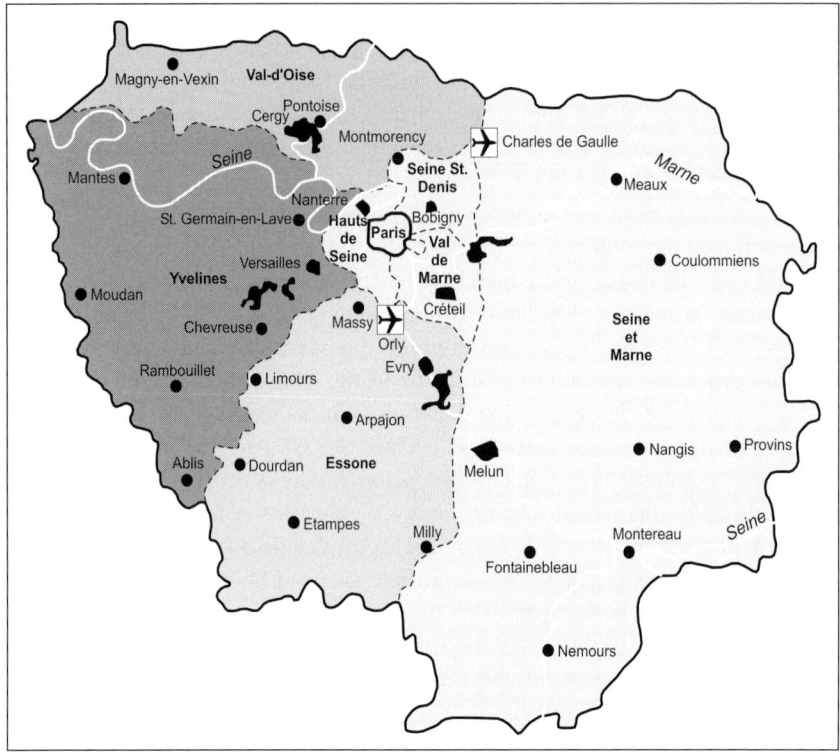

Figure 17.1 The eight départements 'Franciliens'

Changing patterns of governmental structure over the last two decades

These significant economic and social changes with their considerable spatial impacts have occurred while France and the Paris area in particular were in a period of strong political and institutional evolution. Since the early 1980s, France has been undergoing a process of decentralisation. Long known as the epitome of a centralist state, France has been gradually moving towards a more balanced system. In 1982 and 1983, the first decentralisation acts came into effect, transferring some state powers – notably in the fields of public transport, urban planning and social affairs – to local governments, that is, to municipalities and departments. In addition, the 1982 Act created a new local governmental tier, namely the regions. Although the regional level of government pre-existed as a state-controlled unit, the 1982 Act established regions as local governments in their own right, and in 1986 regional institutions were established with the first regional elections. Thus, since 1986 the Île-de-France area has had a democratically elected regional council.

However, for political as well as economic and social reasons, the Île-de-France region has been treated differently from other regional tiers. Because Paris is the capital of France, the state was reluctant to transfer as many powers to the Île-de-France as to other standard regions. Consequently, decentralisation has not been implemented in Paris in the same way it has in the other parts of France. Several significant policy sectors such as transport and regional planning (i.e. basically the elaboration and implementation of the Île-de-France master plan, since the Île-de-France area covers more or less the functional region) have remained under the tight control of the central government. For instance, in public transport, the state chairs the Public Transport Regional Board (*Syndicat des Transports Parisiens*) and as such holds 50 per cent of the seats and has a casting vote. In addition, the state controls the two major public transport operators, the *Régie Autonome des Transports Parisiens* (RATP) – which operates the subway, major bus and tramway lines and part of the RER network – and the *Société Nationale des Chemins de fer Français* (SNCF), the French national railway, which operates all suburban trains and the other part of the RER network.

In the field of urban planning, the central government's control has been as strong as it is in the public transport sector. In other regions and metropolitan areas, master plans are elaborated and implemented by local governments by means of complex intergovernmental joint authorities. In the Île-de-France, however, master plans were under the state umbrella until this year (2002). Although local governments have been associated with the elaboration of the various master plans, final approval remained in the hands of the state, as demonstrated by the 1994 SDRIF, which was imposed by the state on all local governments who had all voted against it. Consequently, although decentralisation has brought about significant changes in France, notably in the policy-making process, this is less the case in the Île-de-France – a situation which is less and less accepted by all partners.

The state's attitude as the *deus ex machina* of the Île-de-France has some rationale, beyond the classical motives suggested above. With about 37,000 municipalities, the French territory is very fragmented. The Île-de-France area – with eight departments and over 1,200 municipalities – is no exception to this, although two elements have contributed to a state of fragmentation which would be more damaging should the state decide to withdraw. First, although French municipalities have joined more and more integrated joint authorities – such as *communautés urbaines* (urban communities) and *communautés de communes* (communities of towns) – in order to compensate for territorial fragmentation and to be able to carry out various policies (economic development, strategic planning, public transport, social cohesion, etc.) in 'relevant' territories, until very recently the Île-de-France municipalities showed no real interest in such ventures. The reasons for this are rather complex, but as a result territorial fragmentation has been more acute in the Paris metropolitan area than in any other metropolitan area. Second, Paris itself is the largest municipality in France. It is, as we say, a state within a state. Just as the Île-de-France dominates France, the municipality of Paris dominates the Île-de-France. With slightly over 2 million inhabitants, a consolidated budget of over EUR 5 billion, a staff of over 40,000 and extensive powers (Paris is a municipality as well as a department), Paris is a giant whose support is necessary in order to govern the Île-de-France. However, the city of Paris has always refused to enter into any cooperative structure with either other municipalities or departments, and this attitude plays a strong role in the fragmentation of the Île-de-France territory, although some changes seem to be on the way with the establishment of an office for 'territorial cooperation' by the newly elected left majority in March 2001. Already some contacts have been made to start joint projects involving Paris and municipalities or joint authorities in the first ring (e.g. Seine-Saint-Denis, in the north).

Paris and the Île-de-France: between national balance and territorial competition

While these changes have been taking place, there has been a paradigmic shift in the way the French state regards the Île-de-France area. Following a much publicised book, *Paris and the French desert* in 1947 (Gravier, 1947), the state considered Paris responsible for the growing imbalance in France. The book's thesis – which until recently was predominant in the central government ministries – was that Paris was a monster, which grew at the cost of other French metropolitan areas. It was thus considered essential to limit its growth by implementing restrictive policies. This was the job of DATAR (*Délégation à l'Aménagement du Territoire et à l'Action Régionale*), which was created in 1963. Five years later, DATAR introduced the policy of counterbalancing metropolises (*métropoles d'équilibre*), the aim of which was to slow the growth of the Île-de-France to the advantage of the provincial areas. In order to achieve this, various policies were set up, such as the authorisation procedure (*procédure de l'agrément*) – which required firms wanting to settle in the Paris area to seek permission from the state, which in many cases was refused – and the transfer policy (*politique de délocalisation*), by means of which central government transferred ministerial agencies or national public bodies located in Paris to other metropolitan areas in order to better balance the location of national organisations.

However, these policies have turned out to be rather inefficient, since they have been unable to combat the 'natural' economic growth of the Île-de-France. Today they are seriously criticised to the extent that in recent years, central government policy regarding the Paris area seems to have changed. It is increasingly being acknowledged that Paris and its development are to be considered less from a national perspective than from a European and world one. Clearly this means that the state is acknowledging the specific needs of the Paris area as a world-class city in competition with London, Tokyo and New York. There are clear signs of this conceptual shift. The authorisation procedure was abandoned in 2000 and new, 'world-class' infrastructure has been built in the Île-de-France, for example, the Soleil project (the construction of a nuclear particle accelerator) in the *pôle d'excellence* of Orsay-Saclay (the Île-de-France won this infrastructure in competition with the Lille area, a state decision which would have been unthinkable just a few years earlier). In 2000, the Île-de-France was authorised for the first time to receive European Objective 2 funding, the state thus considering that the Île-de-France region, although being the richest part of France, had pockets of poverty and economic decline which deserved to be assisted in order for the area to improve its position in the international context.

The changing scales of power

Until the end of the 1980s, the Île-de-France area was not a place of conflicts between the state and local governments, nor was it a place of cooperation. State dominance was so strong that most relationships between local actors and power took place with the various ministries, not to say the heads of central government. This, however, is changing – as is the territorial location of the locus of power. The regional level is becoming a new place for the regulation of power relations, not only between the regional government and the state, but also between all local governments and private actors.

The Île-de-France as a new territory of collective action

State dominance was strong regarding land-use plans and strategic planning. It was the state that imposed the existing master plan (SDRIF) on all local governments, the regional council included. As such, the state undertook a revision of the SDAURIF in the early 1990s because the problems of the Paris area were becoming so large that a new master plan had to be drawn up to accommodate the need both for more land to be urbanised and for natural areas to be protected. For the first time, the 1976 Master plan had introduced some environmental elements with the creation of balanced natural areas (*zones naturelles d'équilibre*). In 1994 the SDRIF called for more land to be urbanised within an accepted context of environmental protection. Urban sprawl had become a problem and its reduction was now a target of the state planning policy, notably because it entailed transport problems that were already considered dramatic.

But the state could use other instruments to impose its policies on local governments. The decentralisation acts had created a new instrument of cooperation between the state and newly established regional councils, the State-Region Planning Agreements (*Contrats de Plan Etat-Region*; CPERs). CPERs are documents signed by the state and a region, specifying the priorities of both actors in all policy sectors. By signing these documents, both institutions agreed to

293

Christian Lefèvre

participate in the financing of specific actions over a five-year period. Indeed, CPERs have become the most significant tool of cooperation between the state and local governments. However, the first CPERs (1984–99) were strongly controlled by the state and were considered a mere reflection of state policies. This was all the more true in the Île-de-France, where the regional council (*Conseil Régional d'Île-de-France*, CRIF) had no definite policies in many sectors, notably because it had no political majority and was not able to set up a clear list of priorities. In addition and as a consequence, the CRIF could not play a mediating role between the state and other local governments, such as the eight departments. The state could run the Île-de-France all the better because the local government system was fragmented.

This has begun to change in recent years and can be illustrated by the new CPER and the debate around the urban travel plan, both planning and programming documents having presented a more open and more balanced decision-making process. The new CPER (2000–06) was approved in March 2000. For the first time since its establishment in 1986, the CRIF came to the table with a regional plan, that is, a document listing the priorities of the regional council in various policy sectors and specific actions it wanted implemented through the CPER. For that reason, since the elaboration of the regional plan had been the locus of discussions between the region and other local governments, the CRIF was able to act as the spokesman of the eight departments vis-à-vis the state. Its political and bargaining position was thus all the stronger. The state accepted that because it realised it could no longer play the role of the master of the game, notably because it had no specific territorial policy regarding the Île-de-France area, which was a requirement of the central government for all new CPERs. So, although the discussion process remained largely in the hands of public authorities, the decision-making process was more balanced and more open than previously.

The same can be said regarding a policy sector dominated by the state, that of transport. In the 1980s and 1990s, several acts introduced significant changes in the way transport planning and transport policies were elaborated and implemented. Urban travel plans (*Plans de Déplacements Urbains*; PDU) are now the common instruments through which transport policies are elaborated, and they concern not only public transport but also road transport, safety, parking, the environment, etc. The Île-de-France PDU was launched in 1998 and approved in December 2000. For the first time the regional territory was considered in terms of a comprehensive travel policy. Its elaboration became a process where the private sector (chambers of commerce, employers' unions, private operators, the auto industry) as well as the public sector and civil society were able to discuss setting up policies on a regional scale. The state was very important in that process, with an essential role played by the Regional Directorate of the Ministry of Public Works and the Regional Prefect, but the regional council, departments and municipalities were also much involved, notably through the establishment of local (inter-municipal) travel plans. Thus, these changes have gradually put public policies into a regional context. The Île-de-France has become a stake between public actors as a relevant territory. However, many (e.g. DATAR) consider the Île-de-France too small and not matching the functional area of Paris. DATAR speaks of the *Grand Bassin Parisien* (a larger area including part of the adjacent regions) and in 2001 the Regional Planning Institute (*Institut d'Aménagement et d'Urbanisme de la Région Île-de-France*, IAURIF) drew a map of the Paris functional urban region (FUR) which extends largely beyond the Île-de-France perimeter.

From government to governance?

In 2002, the SDRIF will be revised and for the first time its revision will not be conducted by the state. According to the last 2000 Act on 'Solidarity and Urban Regeneration', known as the *Solidarité et Renouvellement Urbain* (SRU) Act, the elaboration of the new SDRIF will be directed by the Regional Council. The state, however, will not be left out of the process – in fact, far from it. First and foremost, it will be in charge of assessing the previous SDRIF; this assessment will be made in 2003. Second, it will work on the new regional Master Plan through its own regional services located in the prefecture. The SRU will also change the governance of some policy sectors, notably that of transport. Indeed, the SRU has finally established a significant change in the decision-making process of transport. As mentioned previously, it is the state which enacts transport policies in the Île-de-France by chairing the transport board (STP). The strange thing was that the regional council was never part of the STP, although the CRIF participated heavily in the financing of infrastructure, transport being in fact the most important item in the investment budget of the CRIF. To correct this 'strangeness', and after almost two decades of debate and proposals of reform, the SRU created a new body, the *Syndicat des Transports de l'Île-de-France* (STIF). The most important change is the entry of the regional body in the STIF board, this being a mere acknowledgement of the increasing role of the CRIF in the transport domain. However, the state remains in charge, by chairing the STIF board and having as many votes as the rest of the members put together, CRIF included.

The decision-making process at the regional level is thus becoming more open and more a matter of partnership, as the case of the new CPER has shown. However, the state is still in charge in various significant domains. True, the role of the state is changing, becoming less dictatorial, but it nevertheless remains the strongest actor. The question is of the nature of this new state role. In France – and here the Paris area is no exception – the state is becoming more regional with the regional prefect assuming a real function of directing the various state administrations at the local (deconcentrated) level. In the Île-de-France, it is helped by several regional directorates, notably the Public Works and Planning Directorate (DREIF) which

Christian Lefèvre

possesses important competent staff and resources which exceed by far those of the regional council. In addition, the regional state wants to play a mediating role between local governments and is more legitimate to do so because it is in charge of significant policy domains like transport, health, housing and economic development that will not be transferred to the region in the near future.

New actors are also entering the governance system. Decentralisation has brought the departments back on stage and, after a decade or so, some have been able to establish themselves as significant players. More recently, this has been the turn of associations of municipalities using the 1999 Inter-communality Act as a tool to create joint bodies which are now gaining importance. These changes are significant since they bring to the political and economic fore new actors at the infra-regional level which in the near future may well be the most important partners of both the state and the regional council. The eight Île-de-France departments are young (they were created in 1964) and some of them are trying to create their identity on the grounds that neither the state nor the regional council can act in their interest. The behaviour of the department of Val d'Oise in this context is particularly significant. The Val d'Oise, which is located to the north-west of Paris, has over 1.2 million inhabitants spread over 185 municipalities. It has a very active economic strategy conducted by a specific development agency, the *Comité d'Expansion Economique du Val d'Oise* (CEEVO). Since 1998, the Val d'Oise has approved a strategic development plan, based on high-tech small and medium-sized enterprises (SMEs) and on the department's favourable location, notably being near the international airport, Roissy-Charles de Gaulle. The department is particularly active in the international marketing of its economy and of its quality of life with good accessibility to the whole Île-de-France region and at the same time a good environmental quality with a lot of parks and forests, small villages, etc. It has 'embassies' in several countries, notably Japan (over 50 Japanese firms are located in its territory). Other departments are following the same proactive logic, such as Hauts-de-Seine (the richest department after Paris), which includes the area of La Défense, one of the most economically dynamic areas in the Île-de-France with many international firms having their headquarters there.

The same applies to the infra-departmental level, with the recent establishment of very active joint authorities. The 1999 Inter-municipal Cooperation (*Inter-communalité*) Act has created new joint bodies, the communities of agglomeration (*communautés d'agglomération*) which are in charge of economic development, strategic planning and environment policies in their area. These *communautés* must bring together more than 50,000 people and several municipalities. By law, they are given fiscal powers and receive the business tax of member municipalities, which is all the more important since the business tax is the largest source of revenue for the French municipalities. While, as mentioned, the Île-de-France municipalities have always been reluctant to embark on cooperation, the 1999 Act

296

has so far been a success with the establishment of about ten *communautés d'agglomération* in the last two years. It is now the policy of the state and of the regional council to support these joint authorities as long as they are able to approve a strategic plan and to elaborate sectoral policies in their domain of competence according to this strategic plan. On that ground, the *communautés d'agglomération* receive significant amounts of extra money from the state and their priorities are taken into consideration in the new CPER. Today, the most active *communauté d'agglomération* in the Île-de-France is the Plaine Commune, which is located to the north of Paris in the department of Seine-Saint-Denis, one of the most distressed areas of France. The Plaine Commune encompasses five municipalities with 230,000 inhabitants between them. It is currently drawing up its strategic plan and has become a major partner of public authorities, the local chamber of commerce and the employers' union in the north of Paris.

Many elements mentioned above indicate that the regional council is emerging as a more and more significant actor whose legitimacy is being reinforced by the relevance of the regional territory to address such important issues as strategic planning, economic development and environmental protection. Regional governments are, however, weak governments because they have only limited powers, lack expertise and staff in several domains (e.g. economic development and professional training for the Île-de-France), and have limited legitimacy and sometimes limited capacity to act because of a lack of a stable political majority. Indeed, regional councillors are elected on a proportional system on a departmental ballot. Departments are the constituencies for the regional elections, which reduces the capacity of the regional council to speak as a true regional voice. This is all the more true when, as in the Île-de-France, the regional council has never been able to achieve a stable majority, preventing it from agreeing on specific policies. The president of the region must indeed be very diplomatic and strive for a delicate consensus between the Greens and the Communists which, for instance, disagree on transport and environment policies – which is why the 1999 Regional Plan has not been formally approved.

However, the period looks favourable for the regional councils to gain more autonomy and be more active. In 2001, the government agreed to enhance decentralisation and to transfer more powers to local governments (notably the regions), especially in the fields of professional training and education. In addition, regions seem to be an increasingly relevant partner for the state, as confirmed by the new CPER. The CRIF and especially its socialist president (elected in 1998) seem to be increasingly keen to embark on actions aimed at positioning the regional body as a key actor in the governance of the Île-de-France. The recent creation of the Regional Development Agency (*Agence Régionale de Développement*, ARD) is a good illustration of such an evolution as well as a good test of the CRIF's capacity to act on its own.

Until 2001, the region Île-de-France had no structure for creating a development strategy. The only actor capable of elaborating and carrying out a strategy in that territory was the state, but the strategy it elaborated and partially implemented in the CPERs was at best piecemeal, depending as it did on the policy sector. In 2001, the ARD was established as a partnership body between the CRIF and the chambers of commerce; soon after, the departments were asked to participate. Seven of the eight have accepted the invitation. However, the ARD is largely a creation of the CRIF, which provides 95 per cent of its budget. The CRIF wants the ARD to be a strategic body, in charge of economic and social development. It is too soon to tell whether the CRIF will achieve that objective, but conflicts are already emerging with some departments and the chambers of commerce which were and still are the major actors in that field and which do not want the ARD to become a powerful agency.

The SDRIF revision may also soon become another source of conflict between the players. According to the SRU Act, the new regional Master Plan will be a Territorial Cohesion plan (*Schéma de Cohérence Territoriale*, SCOT). The SRU Act will indeed profoundly transform the French system of spatial planning, replacing municipal land-use plans and Master Plans (*Schémas directeurs*) as well as other sectoral planning documents. The future SCOT will bring together in a single document a strategic plan, transport plan, environmental plan, landscape plan, etc. Elaborated by the CRIF and approved by the region, it will be the legal framework for all local (municipal and inter-municipal) new land-use plans, the Urban Local Plans (*Plans Locaux d'Urbanisme*, PLU). Its elaboration process will be a good test of the capacity of the CRIF to establish itself as a true regional authority.

All these changes can be considered timid for the time being, although they do have the potential to bring about a significant evolution. However, the governance of the Île-de-France remains largely a public-public affair. It is not going too far to stress the fact that, generally speaking, the private sector is not very welcome in the decision-making process. The last CESR[1] report on the governance of the Île-de-France (CESR, 2001) is a good illustration of such a situation, as it calls the public transport sector the best example of an efficient and democratic policy-making process, whereas public transport policy in the Île-de-France is totally in the hands of public authorities (state, local governments and national public operators). Although chambers of commerce are *de jure* members of a lot of committees and working groups in charge of elaborating planning documents and policy reports, their representativeness of the business community is being increasingly contested by employers' unions and large firms.[2]

However, some slight changes in the involvement of the private sector (and indeed of the voluntary sector and citizens' participation) in the policy-making process can be seen. The last PDU, for instance, showed a significant involvement of the *Mouvement des Enterprises de France* (MEDEF), one of the major employers' unions. Considering the interests of their members were not taken into account by the chambers of commerce, the MEDEF asked to participate in the various working groups of the PDU, a request which was formally accepted. On a more positive side, in 1999 the CRIF launched a one-year debate (the *Assises pour l'Emploi*) on the regional strategies and priorities in the field of economic development and employment, calling for a strong involvement of the private sector. Chambers of commerce, all employers' unions and trade unions showed up and some were active participants. The changes are real – but they are timid. Indeed, there is a fear that the CRIF and the state will consider the CESR involvement sufficient, because this regional body is supposed to represent the civil society, including the business community. This position is severely contested by employers' unions which have not been involved in the elaboration of the new CPER, which largely remains a public-public document although it establishes the state and regional strategies and priorities – which also concern the business community – for the coming six years.

Conclusion

The polycentric system of policy-making that exists in most metropolitan areas of Europe has some value for the Île-de-France. Planning policy – be it in its spatial or strategic dimension – will be a good domain for observing and assessing the evolution of relationships within the political sphere as well as between public authorities, the business community and civil society. However, it is too soon to say that the reign of the state is over and that policy-making is definitely moving towards becoming more a matter of partnerships and balanced relationships between the major protagonists, at least at the regional-metropolitan level. The direction that the Île-de-France will take as far as its government is concerned is clearly a matter of territorial political leadership (Jouve and Lefèvre, 2002) and several scenarios are likely. The first will maintain state control, albeit in new forms, over the area; the second will see the establishment of the Regional Council as the new centre; the third will show a territorial division at inter-municipal and départmental scales with the state and/or the region playing a mediating role. The fourth will present a fragmented regional area with no institution or arrangement of institutions able to act as a pilot. This may be not the less likely one.

Notes

1 CESR: Conseil Economique et Social Régional. It is the second regional assembly. Established by the decentralisation Acts, the CESR gathers the representatives of the economic sector (CCI, employers unions, trade unions) and civil society (NGO, citizens associations, etc.). It is a consultative body.

2 It is important to know that in France (as in such other countries as Italy and Germany), chambers of commerce are public organisations, essentially funded by taxes. As such they have been criticised on the grounds that they tend to represent their own interest rather than that of their members.

Christian Lefèvre

Bibliography

CESR (2001) *De l'efficacité en démocratie: rapport sur la gouvernance de l'Île-de-France*, Paris: CESR.

DREIF (Direction Régionale de l'Equipement d'Île-de-France) *et al.* (1990) *Le livre blanc de l'Ile-de-France*, Paris: DREIF.

Gravier, J.F. (1947) *Paris et le désert français*, Le Portulan.

IAURIF (Institut d'Aménagement et d'Urbanisme de la Région Île-de-France) (2001) *40 ans en Île-de-France, Etudes et Développement*, Paris: IAURIF.

IAURIF (2001) *Les métropoles d'Europe du Nord-Ouest: limites géographique et structures économiques*, INTERREG Programme 'GEMACA II', Paris: IAURIF.

Jouve, B. and Lefèvre, C. (2002) *Local power, territory and institutions in European Metropolitan Regions,* London: Frank Cass.

Kantor, P., Savitch, H. and Vicari, S. (1997) 'The political economy of urban regimes: a comparative perspective', *Urban Affairs Review*, 32 (3).

Lefèvre, C. and Roméra, A.M. (2001) *La gouvernance en Île-de-France dans le domaine économique: contexte et évolution*, report for the IAURIF, INTERREG Programme 'GEMACA II', Paris: IAURIF.

18 Brussels

A superimposition of social, cultural and spatial layers

Evert Lagrou

Most significant trends in urbanisation and spatial configuration

Brussels is the capital of Belgium, of the Flemish region, of the French Community, of the Brussels capital region and of the European Union – which means it has to deal with a complex system of competencies. Urban planning is also characterised by the superimposition of so many different layers.

Brussels within the socio-ecological evolution of European city-centres

The general trend in the spatial configuration in the Brussels capital region is similar to that in other European capitals of the same size. Increased welfare has led to a growing need for space and thus to suburbanisation and social and spatial segregation within the metropolitan area. The Brussels capital region has a higher degree of social and functional mix (in age, income classes, spatial distribution of activities) than most European cities. The reason is the relatively low proportion of social housing units in the total housing stock: in Belgium (and Brussels) the percentage is 8 per cent, whereas in neighbouring countries (and their capitals) the figure is at least 35 per cent. Large-scale housing estates concentrating lower-income classes (*Großsiedlungen*, *grand ensembles*, *new towns*) are almost non-existent in Brussels. These population groups stay in the city centre and the nineteenth-century ring around it in old, poorly renovated, low-comfort buildings and thus pay cheap rents. But they are mixed with higher-income groups because of the recent spectacular growth of couples without children preferring to live in the city: Their preference for the city has resulted in a recent increase of the inner-city population and a spontaneous revival of inner-city quarters. The low degree of publicly owned housing indirectly causes strong suburbanisation. Seventy per cent of Belgians own the house they live in.

Table 18.1 The Brussels capital region within the federal state Belgium

Region (*)	Community (**)	Surface (km²)	Inhabitants (2000)
Brussels capital region	Dutch and French communities	162	960,000
Flanders region	Dutch community	13,522	5,860,000
Walloon region	French and German communities	16,844	3,305,000
Kingdom Belgium		30,528	10,125,000

Notes:
(*) regions are responsible for urban planning, environment, nature, housing, water resources, economic development, energy, custody on lower political bodies, employment, public works, scientific research on regional level.
(**) communities are responsible for culture, education, social welfare and matters directly linked to persons.

Table 18.2 Some key figures on the Brussels capital region, 1991 and 2000

Density Region (inhabitants/km²)	5,926	daily incoming commuters	350,000
Density Pentagon (inner-city 4.45 km²)	8,988	commuters car trips (in and out)	160,000
Loss of inhabitants per year (% 1991–2000)	–0.1	number of dwellings	454,000
Office spaces (m²)	9,600,000	vacant houses	25,000
Jobs	670,000	houses occupied by owner	125,000

To compensate for the shortage of publicly owned rental housing, the state facilitates the access of lower-income classes to residential ownership. One of the means used is a flexible building permit policy. The offer of residential land in the official land-use plans largely exceeds the demand. The result is low land prices and thus easy access to residential property. Negative effects are excessive urban sprawl, difficulties in organising a reliable public transportation system and the generalised suburbanisation of urban functions. This trend is opposite to the recent spontaneous residential return to the city. There is a social differentiation between the east and the west in the Brussels capital region mostly due to a different environmental quality. The eastern municipalities within the Brussels capital region and in the Flemish and Walloon periphery attract higher-income dwellings, families with children and strong economic functions (e.g. the headquarters of international companies). The western part of Brussels, historically identified with the downtown area, attracts low-income classes, refugees, singles and – more recently – more affluent young couples.

Permanently changing urban planning concepts

Modernism in Brussels (up to 1968)

Following the concepts of the CIAM (Congrès Internationaux d'Architecture Moderne), in 1965 the government proposed a regional land-use plan for the Brussels region providing urban motorways and radical urban renewal projects in old quarters following the well-known examples (e.g. La Défense, Barbican, Hötorget). The Manhattan project at Brussels North Station was the most exemplary project of the concept: 50 ha of low-standard dwellings were demolished and replaced by high-standard offices. The project was implemented during the economic boom of the 1960s. The economic crisis that started in 1970 played an important role in the shift from large-scale, centrally-managed urban reconstruction to the protection and reinforcement of the existing urban fabric with an active involvement of the local population.

Offices, motorways and new buildings became symbols of capitalism and provoked a strong political movement fed by the French neo-Marxist school of H. Lefebvre-M. Castells. A high level of unemployment, low pressure on land values and the far-reaching proposals of the 1965 regional land-use plan strongly incentivised the establishment of 150 local action committees. The government rejected the plan in 1970.

Economic decline and step-by-step urban planning (1970–85)

The final regional land-use plan officially approved in 1979 took the existing land-use as the absolute standard for the new planning. Exceptions (e.g. offices in residential zones) could only be allowed following an inquiry organised by the municipality. The building activities (mainly of office space) were welcomed as a rare sign of economic recovery and their developers easily obtained building permits after mostly unproblematic public participation procedures. Urban planning became a step-by-step policy. During this period the strict protection of historical monuments and sites was elaborated and applied. The demolition of many important monuments (mainly nineteenth-century *Jugendstil* buildings) when modernism was rampant in Brussels explains the strong impact of heritage protection on urban planning both by the official authorities and private *ad hoc* organisations. The academic world took the opportunity provided by so many local action groups to elaborate further on an 'anti-capitalistic' urban planning theory mainly supported by Leon Krier and Maurice Culot. The sociology of poverty and anti-CIAM ideas became (and in fact still are) favourite thesis and PhD themes (mainly in sociology and social-geography). The final study projects for architects and urban planners dealt only with urban renewal and insertion, and 'alternative' architecture. The movement invented the term 'Bruxellisation' – the capitalistic destruction of a city with a compromising collaboration of the public sector. Meant as a means of putting political pressure on the authorities, the final result was that Brussels was branded with a negative, simplified and persistent image on the international platform. The protagonists have now disappeared, but the negative image has not.

Economic recovery (1985–2001)

After the economy recovered in the 1980s, deviations from the official land-use plan became the rule. The building permits given to office developments in residential zones led to an increase in land prices and to residential expulsion. This provoked demands for the strict protection of homogeneous residential zones. The 1995 Regional Development Plan met this requirement by introducing the 'enhanced protection of housing' zone, covering a third of the territory of the Brussels capital region – mainly in areas surrounding the CBD (Central Business District in Brussels, the European Quarter) under high land price pressure. Current urban planning is trying to concentrate the office development following the ABC location method. The Regional Land-Use Plan approved in 2001 is based on a comprehensive mobility concept. Only the class-A locations (i.e. those with excellent accessibility via public transport) are allowed to obtain considerable quantities of additional office space: Etterbeek and the North and South Railway Stations in the short term, and the West Railway Station in the long term. The translation of these objectives into planning regulations differs depending on the political party in power: strict limitation of offices in the indicated areas and high levels of protection for surrounding residential areas (the Left, Greens); or a more flexible permit policy allowing office development also in residential areas (Liberals). Current planning mainly has to cope with four problems:

- The legal obligation to realise the HST (high speed train) route through Belgium and Brussels necessitated important public works for a new HST terminal North and new metro connections. Should this purely technical intervention be linked to an important new urban development – or not? The project has been related to the extension of the European Union to 27 states in the long run and the location of its spatial needs (mostly additional office space).
- The authorities are trying to influence the modal split of commuters. Seventy per cent of commuters living within a radius of 25 km commute by private car. In order to promote the use of public transport, the Brussels government proposes to use the rails of the National Belgian Railway Company as a metropolitan network (*Réseau Express Régional, Gewestelijk Express Net*). Several authorities will finance this operation: the federal state (which owns the railway company), the Brussels region (which is eager to relieve the clogged entrance roads) and the Flemish and Walloon regions (which want the relief of traffic jams in the Brussels periphery).

- The EU bureaucracy currently occupies approximately 1,800,000 m² of office space. The accession of a further eight states to the EU, which will entail an additional 1,000,000 m², raises the question of the most appropriate urban model: a new, mixed campus at the HST terminal site (Brussels North) with an important public participation, or a dispersed addition to the existing stock by free market mechanisms. As for the 21,000 'international' employees, the housing of the newcomers will be spontaneously absorbed within the existing residential areas without explicit planning interventions. The political dimension of this question is obvious.
- The discussion about the economic feasibility of the theoretically so praised mix of functions as a planning standard is ongoing. The Left and the Greens are promoting the priority of the residential functions. The employers' organisations are more flexible regarding the situation. The combination of living and working in the same space in a compact city-model seems easier in concept than in reality.

Political changes in planning competencies

Since the 1989 revision of the Constitution, the political competencies have been divided between the federal government, the three regions (Brussels, Flanders, Wallonia) and the three communities (Dutch-, French- and German-speaking communities). The federal state is responsible for the finances (taxation, the mint), justice and interior security, external affairs (competence shared with the three regions), national defence, social security and retirement funds, national economy and international trade, and some 'national' aspects of the regional matters. The regions are responsible for urban planning, environment, nature protection, housing, water policy, regional economy, supervision of municipalities, public works and transportation policy, and the 'regional' aspects of some federal matters. The communities are responsible for matters related to persons (language, culture, training). The communities are thus less involved in urban planning. Since the regionalisation of the 1989 Constitution, political power has been divided into regional matters (Brussels, Flanders, Wallonia) and community matters (Dutch, French, German).

Each region and community elects its own parliament. Soon after regionalisation, the three regions voted their urban planning laws. The Brussels urban planning law dates from 1991. All contacts between the regions have a purely bilateral character without any federal arbitral authority. The borders of the Brussels capital region are delimited on a purely cultural criterion (bilingual Brussels versus Dutch-speaking Flanders). The natural economic metropolitan region being much larger, urban planning has to cope with a multitude of common problems: road planning (the ring-road of Brussels is located in Flanders), the Brussels National Airport (in Flanders), metropolitan public transportation, harbour policy, environment

Table 18.3 The three regions in Belgium after the regionalisation of 1989

Kingdom of Belgium (federal state)		
Flanders Region (Dutch)	Brussels Capital Region (Dutch and French)	Walloon Region (French and German)
6 provinces	–	5 provinces
308 municipalities	19 municipalities	262 municipalities

policy, waste disposal, all zoning matters, and environmental standards. Common sense and pragmatism prevent most conflicts, but the political and the administrative procedures are time- and energy-consuming.

The federalisation of Belgium, a process which started in 1963, hampers the coordination of planning in the three regions encompassing the Brussels metropolitan area. The delimitation of the Brussels region does not correspond to the economic and social reality. Matters of urban planning in a broad sense are the sole competence of the regions without any coordinating instance at federal level – unlike in other federal states such as Austria or Germany. All common points have to be discussed on a bilateral basis.

Changes in the structure of government

From a strong, central power to decentralised decisions?

After a 150-year period of a strong, 'unitary' Napoleonic system within which Brussels decided on everything, in 1989 Belgium became a decentralised state with decisive competencies given to the three regions: Brussels, Flanders and Wallonia.

Since its foundation in 1830, Belgium has had three hierarchical levels in the public management: kingdom, province and municipality. It is notable that in 1962 – when Belgium was still a highly centralised country – the urban planning law did not provide a national plan, as in France or the Netherlands. The province had no planning competence. The municipalities had to elaborate plans but under the strict control of the central government. The central government's reasons for not approving plans could relate to any aspect, either legal (e.g. 'non-conformity with hierarchically higher plans') or due to precise individual interpretations ('not in accordance with the rules of good planning'). This centralism was even more evident in the building permit procedure. The municipality was only allowed to grant a building permit based on binding advice from the central administration. Municipalities could only decide themselves without the advice of the central government if the plot for which the building permit was requested was located in an area covered by central government-approved land-use plans or detailed urban planning regulations. In any case the final decision was for the central government to make. Since regionalisation in 1989, this situation has not changed funda-

Table 18.4 The urban planning law of 1962 – valid until the three regions made their own legislations (1991)

Planning type	Legally stated content	Authority	Application in reality
Regional Plan[a]	General measures for urban planning	Kingdom	Not implemented
District Plan[b]	Measures for urban planning	Kingdom	All 47 drawn up but as 'general land-use'
Master Zoning Plan[c]	General land-use plan	Municipality	Further implementation stopped
Special Zoning Plan[d]	Detailed land-use plan	Municipality	Only executed as framework for realisation

Notes:
a Streekplan/Plan Régional;
b Gewestplan/Plan de Secteur;
c Algemeen Plan van Aanleg/Plan Général d'Aménagement;
d Bijzonder Plan van Aanleg/Plan Particulier d'Aménagement.

mentally: the centralised Belgian 'kingdom' has been replaced by the three regions. Real competencies in urban planning for the municipality are very restricted.

The governance culture

More important than legislative regulations is the governance culture in the relationship between the various authorities. First, the lack of power of the municipalities led to a systematic low degree of activity in the elaboration of municipal plans ('The national authorities decide all important cases, so why should we elaborate local urban planning with all the locally political troubles land-use planning entails?'). Second, the Latin tradition of the accumulation of political mandates (France, Italy, etc.) is also applied in Belgium. Most members of the regional parliament or government combine this 'central' function with a post within their municipality as mayor or alderman. This accumulation seems to be a much more efficient way to obtain building permits than the official land-use plans. The legal incompatibility between the mayoralty of larger towns (greater than 20,000 inhabitants) and national mandates does not decrease the real impact of the member of parliament – 'mayor temporarily off duty'. This generalised system in all political parties is undermining the logic of the legal separation of the different political levels. Third, the decisions on difficult 'transborder' topics with a high economic impact on the Brussels capital region are mostly postponed; these topics include the development of the airport area, new industrial estates and shopping units, coordination of the public transportation systems, and environmental standards. The result is not a fight between the regions, but worse: indifference and non-planning. Only the economic law of the free market is taken into account.

More political power for the municipalities?

The urban planning policy in the three Belgian regions tends to give more urban planning competencies to the municipalities. The prerequisite for this decentral- isation is that they elaborate master zoning plans for their whole territory as well as municipal urban planning regulations. Both documents have to be approved by the regional government. There are several reasons for this policy. The complexity of sectoral evolutions (industries, housing, road system, etc.) is increasing to such a degree that a central authority can no longer master this. It is up to the local level to make a synthesis of sectoral spatial needs. Central authorities (region or province) have difficulties assessing local, often complicated situations related to building permits. The position of municipalities in planning is also linked to a political vision. The Left/the Greens tend towards a more central decision-making power, while the Liberals prefer a more decentralised model.

The two other regions have a similar planning system (Flemish region 1996; Walloon region 1998), though its implementation has not gone as far as it has in the Brussels region. This leads to some coordination problems at the border of the Brussels region. Most municipalities in the Brussels periphery lack an overall plan ('Structure plan') which leads to decisions being postponed in the Brussels region. Because of this lack of global planning, important building permit demands around the airport and the ring motorway are decided by step-by-step decisions.

The official regional and municipal development plans have no real impact on planning: they are too careful in their statements, avoiding clear options in key problems in urban planning. Even the Regional Land-Use Plan – although detailed and strict concerning the enforced land-use of all blocks – does not formulate proposals for today's major spatial challenges, that is, the HST terminal North, the expansion of the European institutions, the future of the 10 ha former shunting yard at the West Station, the planning of the surroundings of the Regional Express Net stations, the expansion of the public transportation system (metro or an express tramway on its own site), park & ride areas, and the fate of the 50 ha former customs transportation area Thurn & Taxis in the city centre. Too many political parties are sharing power for there to be an efficient policy. The eight members of the Brussels Government belong to six different political parties: there are five French (two Liberals, two Socialists, one Nationalist) and three Dutch (one Catholic, one Liberal, one Socialist) ministers. Obtaining a political consensus requires clear urban planning statements. Because of its heterogeneous

Table 18.5 Legal levels in urban planning for the Brussels capital region (law 29 August 1991)

Planning typology	Validity term	Planning authority and legal impact	Number and period
Regional Development Plan[a] 1: 25,000	5 years (legislature)	Regional government 'planning objectives' not binding for citizens	2 (1995 and 2002)
Regional Land-Use Plan[b] 1: 10,000	No term	Regional Government land-use binding for authorities and citizens	2 (1998 and 2001)
Municipal Development Plan[c] 1: 5,000	6 years (legislature)	Municipal Councils (19) 'planning objectives' not binding for citizens, contract planning Region-Municipality	19 (1998–2001)
Special Zoning Plan[d] 1: 500 to 1: 2,500	No term	Municipality detailed binding land use at the scale of cadastral parcel	+/– 350 (1962–present)

Notes:
a Gewestelijk Ontwikkelingsplan/Plan Régional de Développement;
b Gewestelijk Bestemmingsplan/Plan Régional d'Affectation du Sol;
c Gemeentelijk Ontwikkelingsplan/Plan Communal de Développement;
d Bijzonder Bestemmingsplan/Plan Particulier d'Affectation du Sol.

composition, the government is too sensitive to action groups, most of which do not want any urban development at all (NIABY – 'Not in any backyard').

Strategic policies for the metropolitan region

The Brussels capital region, a cultural – not a metropolitan – entity

As a political entity Brussels has a population of 950,000 and covers 162 km²; as a morphologic region, it has 1,400,000 inhabitants and covers 413 km². The delimitation of the Brussels capital region based on the language difference is a result of the historical social evolution in Belgium.

The Belgian State was born in 1830 when it seceded from the Netherlands. Simultaneously, Dutch was banned as the official language. In 1920, Cardinal Mercier commented that: 'La Belgique sera Latine ou elle ne sera pas' ('Belgium will be Latin or will not be'). Only in 1932 was Dutch recognised as a language for university education. Although Dutch was recognised as an official language in 1950, the language difference still represented a social barrier: French was the upper-class and Dutch the lower-class language. Bilingualism was only practised by the Flemings. The language frontier moved permanently northwards to the detriment of the Dutch-speaking community. Although the French dominance has since changed into a positive acceptance of Dutch, the suspicious Flemish politicians refused to make any changes to the frontiers of the Brussels region (bilingual with a Dutch-speaking minority) which is limited to the 19 municipalities.

Changing strategic policies

Urban planning strategies are closely linked to a country's economic dynamism. The economic boom of the 1960s created the opportunity to make drastic public interventions in the urban fabric. The 1970s and 1980s, which were characterised by economic crisis, reoriented the public finances and political involvement to welfare and employment within a static, preservationist urban planning. The high demand for new developments during the new economic boom of the 1990s was met by means of the public-private partnership (PPP) formula.

Successive political strategies

Populism – or 'the People's Voice' (1968–85)

Between 1960 and 1970 the impact of the planners' model was decisive for many transformations in the city ('his Master's Voice'). The negative consequences of this model both socially and spatially became apparent soon after the economic decline of the 1970s. The action research of the academic world and the professionally organised action groups largely supported by the media created a political threat to the politicians in power, who elaborated new urban planning regulations which fitted in with populism. The balance between organising public participation and keeping real political power became an important political issue. At the same time the government had to cope with the negative image of Brussels caused by the Bruxellisation action of the academic world and the Flemish and Walloon media, by means of a professional city marketing strategy. To cope with 'people's power', several strategies were developed.

- A new version of the 1979 Land-Use Plan scrupulously protected the existing land-use ('small is beautiful', 're-use instead of new', 'pedestrians and public transportation have priority over private car use'). If a building project deviated from the existing situation it had to be submitted to the advice of a local participation committee. As long as the building activities were very low under the influence of the economic crisis, the procedure functioned rather well.
- The politicians tried to co-opt institutions coordinating local actions and action groups with a considerable influence on the public opinion: *Inter-environnement Bruxelles* and BRAL (*Brussels Raad voor Leefmilieu*), and

Table 18.6 Strategies in urban planning and impact of the main parties involved (1970–2001) with typical Brussels examples (the strongest parties are highlighted in the table)

	PUBLIC INTERESTS (comprehensive planning)			PRIVATE INTERESTS (sectorial planning)	
	power	technics		local	sectorial
	elected politicians	design urban planners	management public servants	NIMBY local action-groups	land developers, railway company, monuments conservation ...
Until 1968 Modernism 'His Masters Voice'	*'Manhattan' North Station area:* high-rise, offices, urban motorways, building for the future				hidden partners
1968–85 Populism 'People's Voice'				*1979 Regional Land Use Plan:* existing land-use strictly confirmed, strong impact local committees, small scale, 'old is beautiful'	low economic activity
1985–99 P.P.P. 'The Region invites'	*1995 Regional Development Plan*: economic viability of the Region: housing policy, concentration of offices				European Quarter, Manhattan project, HST-terminal South
1999–now P.P.P. 'Developers invite'					Economic globalisation, HST terminal North, Music Centre T&T

some other action groups (e.g. *Ateliers de Recherche et d'Action Urbaines* and *Sint-Lukasarchief*). The region partly paid for their personnel and publications, commissioned them to perform with several urban planning studies and even appointed some of their leaders to the minister's personal staff.

- The enlargement of the European functions in the European quarter provoked a conflict with the local community. The local action committees supported by the Green-Left political parties insisted on stronger protection for the existing social and spatial urban fabric. The federal government on the other hand had to ensure the international role of Brussels and hence flexibility in granting building permits. The strategy of the Brussels government was to organise the participation of the action groups in a steering committee which had to give advice on all projects in the European quarter. The main conflicts were over scale, degree of functional mix, transparency, etc. When the federal government was obliged to start the building of the European parliament, consultations stopped and the building permit was granted (1987).

The left's version of PPP: 'The authorities invite the private sector' (1985–98)

The residential and commercial exodus to the periphery of the Flemish and Walloon regions resumed after the economic crisis and threatened the financial, social and spatial viability of the Brussels region. Stopping the exodus of the economically most interesting activities was the main concern of the Brussels regional government, as concretised by two main planning strategies.

- The 1995 Regional Development Plan strictly protected the existing residential zones in order to stop the residential exodus and attract new middle-class dwellers. The care for the housing of the lowest income classes of the 1970s was broadened to the middle-classes by granting special subsidies for buying and restoring existing houses and by sponsoring the Brussels Regional Development Society as a public real estate agency for the construction of dwellings for the middle-class. The formally stated political bodies, which lacked any managerial flexibility (because of institutional complexity), established many 'semi-official' bodies like the Brussels Development Society. They showed better performance in operating within the real estate private market but enhanced the lack of transparency in the already complicated Brussels institutions. The region also imposed 'urban planning charges' on developers: they had to build/have built 1 m² of residential space for every 5 m² of office space. The Brussels Development Society constructed within this structure many new dwellings.

- The Brussels region itself managed several important office developments under the PPP formula: the European Parliament and about 250,000 m² of office space in its environs, the HST terminal at the South Station with a functionally mixed project (offices, shops, conference centre, parking garage) and many new office buildings for public use (mostly for the Flemish region ministries) at the North Station. All office developments out of the office zoning around the main railway stations (North, Luxembourg, South) are severely restricted. This should stimulate the use of public transportation rather than cars.

The Right's version of PPP: 'The private sector invites the authorities' (since 1998)

The Liberal's success in the 1998 elections reoriented the planning objectives by stimulating economic development and reinforcing Brussels as the European capital on the international forum. The restrictions on office development in residential areas have been reduced. The compensations for new offices spaces ('urban planning charges') can now be realised by a new layout of public spaces, and no longer by dwellings. The private sector has an increasing influence in the PPP. During the post-1995 economic boom many new office buildings, ICT enterprises and shopping units have been built in the Flemish periphery bordering the Brussels region. Coordination with the Flemish region is becoming a high priority. Strong public interventions are not to be expected as the Liberals increased their influence also in the Flemish government – the prime minister and the minister of urban planning being members of the Liberal Party.

Problems of institutional and spatial coordination

Basic problem: considerable divergence between morphological and legal delimitation

In 1962, the area of the Brussels Capital region was 'definitively' restricted to 19 municipalities. Since then, the delimitation of the Brussels metropolitan area has been a delicate political issue. Many scientific studies are trying to define the Brussels region: French research centres are mostly in favour of a maximum and Dutch centres of a minimum delimitation. The underlying fear of the latter is the political linking of the notion 'socio-economic metropolitan region' to the extension of the bilingual region.

A global planning approach to the metropolitan region of Brussels seems to be an institutional impossibility. No planning competencies are left to the federal government. The relations between the Dutch- and French-speaking communities and the three regions have been normalised since the 1989 regionalisation: most problems are solved during informal, pragmatic consultations. However, this cannot be the proper method to deal with a scientifically founded and binding metropolitan planning with all the conflicts this entails.

The 1989 Spatial Structure Plan for Flanders contains an ambiguity: 43 municipalities with a total surface of 2,250 km² located in the 'Flemish Lozenge' and encompassing the entire Brussels region obtained the status of 'economic node', allowing them to attract new 'industries and commercial developments of a high, international added value'. This creates strong competition between Brussels and Flanders. The urban development in the 1998 Structure Plan for the Walloon Region is more oriented towards the west–east axis Lille–Liège–Cologne. The orientation towards Brussels regarding commuting, higher education, etc. is not retained as an important objective in the regional development plan but offers enough space for the suburbanisation from Brussels in the district land-use plans (*plans de secteur*). Meanwhile the five Flemish provinces have started to elaborate provincial structure plans. The draft Provincial Structure Plan for Flemish Brabant (2001), which completely surrounds the Brussels capital region, does not take into account

Table 18.7 Several delimitations of the Brussels metropolitan region

Denomination	Inhabitants (1999)	Area (km²)	Inh./km²
Political Brussels: 19 municipalities	960,000	162	5,944
Morphological agglomeration: 33 municipalities	1,293,000	529	2,443
Agglomeration and periphery: 59 municipalities	1,863,000	1,401	1,330

the options of the Brussels planning regarding the recuperation of a part of the residential exodus, the insertion in the housing market of the roughly 25,000 empty houses, and the concentration of the new industrial estates at nodes of rapid public transportation systems. The reason is not a conflict between cultures but between economic interests.

Dynamics of responses to coordination

The process of regionalisation started in 1971 is still going on – even since the federalisation of 1989. There is a paradox between the struggle for more decentralised competencies in the 'Europe of regions', and the need for more comprehensive and coordinated planning for the transborder problems. The Flemish and Walloon aversion to centralised Belgium has some similarity to the aversion of the former communist states to central planning structures. Problems of coordination are nevertheless resolved mainly by bilateral agreements, and a high degree of pragmatism and problem-solving by personal network contacts. It is not the optimal 'plan-o-logical' solution but it works for problems with a highly political and economic impact.

Functional solutions

Some planning developments are linked to a strict time schedule imposed by international agreements, such as the realisation of the HST lines and stations and the additional office space for the EU. In these matters the federal ministers intervene informally to force the regional authorities to improve the proposed projects to be realised within the schedule.

Collaborative solutions

The planning of technical infrastructure and environmental matters is mostly organised in bilateral agreements: the realisation of the Regional Express Net (federal state and the three regions), common inter-regional refuse- and wastewater-treatment, etc.

Delayed planning objectives

The coordination of important projects between the regions is often difficult: industrial or commercial developments, residential zoning, park & ride facilities in the Flemish and Walloon towns 25 km from Brussels, and the harbour and canal infrastructure.

The already mentioned reason is the lack of a federal coordinating authority. A second reason is the different position in the planning competence of the intermediate planning level between the region and the municipality: the province. The provincial level is non-existent in the Brussels capital region. The five Flemish provinces received an important planning competence in the 1998 Flemish planning law but lack any planning tradition. The Walloon provinces received no planning competencies. Also the position of the municipalities in the planning process differs according to the region. In 1977, the Flemish and Walloon municipalities increased their territory, population and management capacity after 2,500 municipalities were merged into 650. The 19 Brussels municipalities not included in the 1977 merger are no longer the logical subdivision they were a hundred years ago. They no longer represent any social-economic entity. This hampers logical urban planning. The municipalities are too small for urban planning management but compensate for their incompetence by accumulating mandates of their burgomasters and aldermen with regional mandates. The recent urban planning regulations give them some planning competencies but most of them are not eager to actually implement them.

Major planning issues in the Brussels metropolitan region

1   Project areas
   • Brussels has hosted European institutions since 1958. The debate about where to locate these institutions was and still is an interesting one from both an institutional and an urban planning viewpoint. Unlike in Luxembourg and Strasbourg, the European institutions in Brussels are located on the edge of the inner city and within residential quarters. This location has the advantage of the high degree of mix of the European activities with the local urban fabric, and accessibility by public transportation. Disadvantages are the effect on land prices, leading to social expulsion and the involvement of different authorities in the decision process: the federal government is directly responsible to the European authorities, the Brussels government is more sensitive to the attitudes of the local population, and the municipalities want residential functions to be fully protected from the European Moloch. Local action groups oppose any further extension. The result is an open discussion about the alternatives – an example of the democratic decision-making process.
   • The planning of highway infrastructure has been a regional competence since 1989: there are no longer any national motorways or waterways. The ring-road around the Brussels capital region is 72 km long but only 12 km of it is inside Brussels' territory. It has a key function in the mastery of the modal split and the distribution of the car traffic on the regional road network. The ring has 30 access points mostly in Flemish and Walloon territory, each of them offering attractive poles for commercial and industrial development. The demands are seldom refused by the three regions because of the tax advantages for the municipalities and the regions. The

negative impacts on the modal split are not taken into account, because most of the areas are not served by public transport. A federal arbitral instance could intervene but is non-existent. The effect on the increase of car traffic in Brussels and its periphery typifies the lack of planning. Between 1990 and 1998, the evolution of car traffic was as follows: on the outer ring: +3.30 per cent; on the roads between the outer and the middle ring: +0.82 per cent; between the middle ring and the inner ring: –0.44 per cent and on the inner ring: –0.37 per cent. Most new industrial estates cannot be reached by public transport.

- The Brussels National Airport is a strongly growing pole located within the Flemish region. The National Railway Company is planning an HST terminal North (on the territory of the Brussels capital region) with a shuttle connection to the airport (Flemish region). Comprehensive planning is needed to elaborate a global scope on the planning of traffic centres (HST, national rail, metropolitan and urban transportation), new industrial estates, commercial development, congress and hotel facilities, and housing. The solutions realised in reality are too pragmatic, are not based on a global concept and neglect the impact on car traffic.
- The former Brussels Sea Canal linking Charleroi (Wallonia) to Antwerp (Flanders) is gaining goods traffic as an alternative to the congested roads. After regionalisation, the administration of the canal was split into three separate companies, one per region. Even though the relations between the three companies are good, it is difficult to elaborate a comprehensive global plan for water transportation – not only on this route but nation-wide.
- The planned Regional Express Network involves the insertion of the national railroads into the Brussels public transportation system (similar to the Berlin S-Bahn and the Paris RER). Only 27 per cent of Flemish and Walloon commuters use public transport. To increase this percentage is the main objective of the RER network but it has to be approved by the three regions and the federal government. The desirability and positive impact on the Brussels capital region is a political issue. The RER/GEN (Réseau Express Régional/Gewestelijk Express Net) is expected to encourage commuters to use public transport. The opening of about 20 new stations within the Brussels region will improve inner-city mobility and foster economic development around the stations. A negative element is that a considerable improvement of the relation between city and suburbs could enhance suburbanisation. Implementation has finally been forced by the federal minister responsible for public transportation (a member of Green Party, Ecolo) threatening to withdraw her party from the government coalition if the system is not realised.

2   The environmental policy encounters many coordination problems due not to unwillingness to realise a better environment but to differences in political priorities: river-water purification, sewage treatment, location of incinerators, different standards for noise nuisance (the national airport is located just 15 km from Brussels' city centre), etc.
3   Competition between the three regions in the field of land-use planning and management.

   The estimate of the necessary surfaces for residential, commercial and industrial areas in the more affluent Flemish and Walloon periphery did not take into account the planning objectives of the Brussels Regional Development Plan. Both the

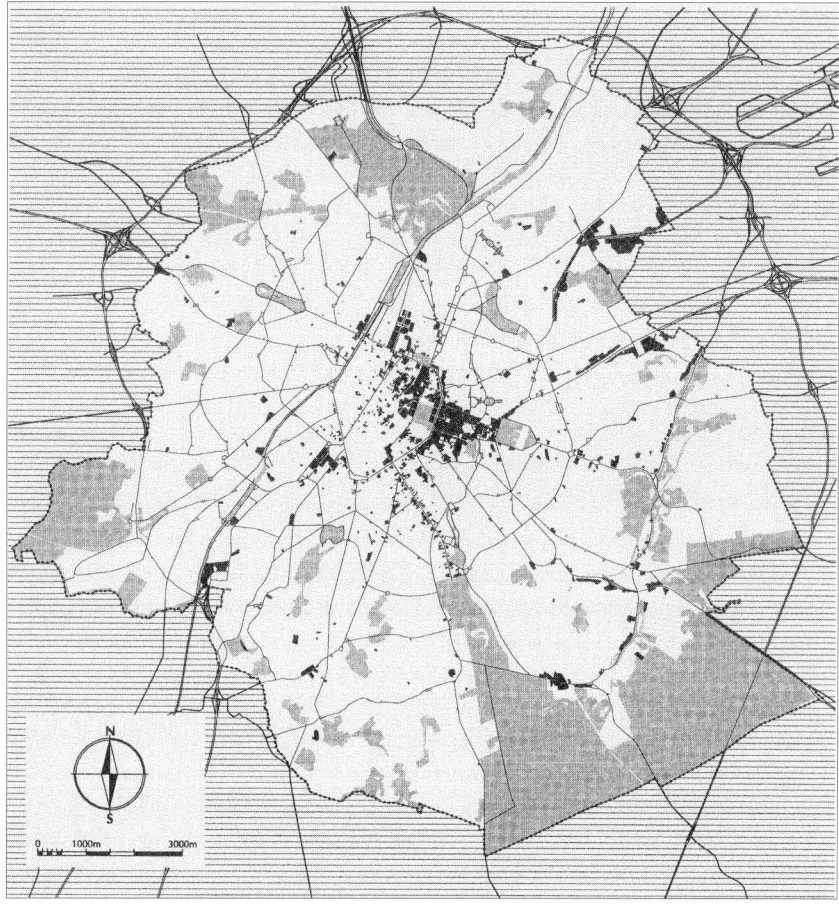

Figure 18.1 Map of Brussels with the location of the main office concentrations

Flemish and the Brussels region appeal to the same active population in order to justify additional urban space.

The Central Administration for Public Properties – which managed 6.5 million m² of office space before regionalisation – has been split into three regional administrations. The Brussels one is responsible for 2.6 million m². This subdivision has caused a loss of technical and financial skill and has increased overheads. This is an example of the high costs of the splitting up of so many public bodies in Belgium as a result of regionalisation: social housing, land reclamation, water and green policy. The public finances of the Brussels capital region are a mirror of the complexity of Belgian regionalisation. Public finances play an important role in the political fight for more competencies for the regions. They have to enable the realisation of the competencies given to the region, the two communities in it (Dutch and French), the 19 municipalities and the capital and international functions. The public finances of Brussels take a central place in the planned further regionalisation. The (mainly Flemish) 'regionalists' dispute the amount of the federal budget for the Brussels capital region: too high federal subsidies for the capital functions, too high subsidies from the Brussels capital region and the 19 municipalities on French education with a structural deficit, and high income for the region and municipalities from real estate and corporation taxes. The Brussels viewpoint accentuates high costs for both private and public transport caused by the 300,000 commuters, the significant loss of taxes from the tax-free statute for publicly used buildings, extra costs for security and culture due to the capital functions, and the care for marginal groups for which the European Capital seems to have a special attraction.

New forms of metropolitan governance and coordination of spatial planning

- The far-reaching constitutional reforms in Belgium hamper good metropolitan governance rather than improve it. The Belgian regionalisation – which is ideologically supported by the 'Europe of regions' movement – is in fact mainly a fight for more regional competencies. How to coordinate spatial planning among the regions and to tune the fragmented competencies to each other, is not (yet) a political issue.
- There is no 'Brussels metropolitan region' – Brussels being restricted to 19 municipalities based solely on language differences between Brussels and the periphery. The advantages taken of the suburbanisation by the Flemish and Walloon periphery are not compensated for or even discussed. There is no common planning for important planning fields: the environs of the national airport, regional mobility, environmental planning, road system, etc.
- Politicians in the Brussels capital region are hesitating over the necessary merger between the 19 too small and too illogically bordered municipalities.

The political effect of the greater distance between citizen and elected politicians in spatial planning matters is unclear, although most researchers conclude that the actual situation ('the municipal baronies') is hampering good governance.

- Many planning topics are decided between the regions in a pragmatic way based on personal networks not incorporated into a global planning concept. The federal government has withdrawn from all competences in planning matters and no arbitral instance is left over for planning conflicts between the three regions (Brussels, Flanders and Wallonia).

- The elaboration of comprehensive planning is an urgent matter, given the increase of transborder problems mainly in the field of environment and mobility. Transborder refers not only to the relations between the three Belgian regions, but also to the planning within north-west European metropolises – Belgium being part of one urban continuity extending from the Dutch Randstad to the French Département du Nord-Pas de Calais and even to the German Ruhrgebiet.

Bibliography

Abeels, G., Sint-Lukasarchief *et al.* (1983) *Straten en Stenen. Brussel Stadsgroei 1780–1980, Pierres et Rues. Bruxelles: Croissance urbaine 1780–1980* (two separate editions), Brussels: Generale Bank Maatschappij/Société Générale de Banque.

Archives d'Architecture Moderne (1982) *La Reconstruction de Bruxelles*, Brussels: Archives d'Architecture Moderne.

Brussel-Bruxelles (Government of the Brussels Capital Region) (2001) 'Projet d'Affecation du Sol/Ontwerp van Gewestelijk Bestemmingsplan', *Moniteur Belge-Belgisch Staatsblad*, p.528.

Billen, C. (2000) *Brussel – Steden in Europa*, Antwerp: Mercatorfonds.

Lagrou, E. (1979) 'Ruimtelijke ordening in Brussel. Analyse en diagnose', PhD thesis, Antwerp.

Lagrou, E. (2000) 'Brussels: five capitals in search of a place. The citizens, the planners and the functions', *GeoJournal*, 51: 99–112.

Michiels, M. (1996) *Bruxelles est Malade ... mais son coeur bat*, Brussels: Edition Le Livre.

Ranieri, L. (1973) *Leopold II Urbaniste*, Brussels: Edition Hayez.

Sint Lukaswerkgemeenschap (1985) *Grootstadsplan voor Brussel. Un Plan metropolitain pour Bruxelles. A Metropolitan Plan for Brussels* (map with text), Brussels: Brussels Capital Region.

19 Marseilles-Aix metropolitan region (1981–2000)

Alain Motte

The case

The Marseilles-Aix metropolitan region developed in a geographic location which conditioned its urban organisation. This Mediterranean littoral territory is structured by coastal mountains (massif Cassis la Ciotat, Calanques, Côte Bleue), fragile humid spaces (Etang de Berre, Camargue) and a river (the Rhône and its tributary, La Durance). The littoral land itself has constraints: the mountain amphitheatre of Marseilles commune, Alpilles and Lubéron. All these elements have imposed the circulation corridors and influenced the urbanisation processes.

A Marseilles metropolitan planning scheme was elaborated in the late 1960s and early 1970s by local representatives of the central state in consultation with the communes. This scheme was used by the central state to coordinate its major investments in the urban region. It has also had a major influence on the urbanisation processes in this urban area since the 1970s, mainly through the highway system. No metropolitan strategy has been elaborated since the 1970s. The decentralisation process during the 1980s and 1990s developed competition between communes. The local institutional culture is historically one of autonomy and non-cooperation[1] between communes. Since 1990 the central state, using the institutional national reforms (1992 and 1999–2000), and by specific policies, has worked on the emergence of metropolitan policies in the Marseilles-Aix urban region. What should be acknowledged first is the fundamental role of the central state and its representatives in the urban region. This role is not a role of imposition of policies. Since the beginning of the decentralisation reforms of the 1980s the central state has been encouraging local public institutions (*Commune, Département, Région*) to volunteer (Duran and Thoenig, 1996) for new policies.

How has it been possible for the territorial public institutions to cooperate more and more during the 1990s? What has been the precise role of the central state and its representatives? Has it be done specifically by national reforms? Have any metropolitan policies developed? A further aim of this case study is to provide an understanding of the rapid changes in the economic, social and environ-mental dimensions of the metropolitan space during the 1980s and 1990s. Is it possible to characterise the metropolitanisation processes? What have been the consequences of the non-institutional guidance of the metropolitan dynamics?

Before answering these questions it is necessary to define the Marseilles-Aix metropolitan region. There is a plurality of spaces which could be taken into consideration, and we will have to deal with them simultaneously. The first category of spaces is the territories of the main communes of the metropolitan region. First Marseilles[2] (797,491 inhabitants in 1999) and second Aix-en-Provence (134,324 inhabitants in 1999) which are the poles of the metropolitan region. They had very different dynamics during the 1980–90s period. Marseilles started a severe decline process and Aix showed economic growth.[3] The second category of space to take into consideration is the agglomerated space[4] around the two main communes. The Statistical Office (Institut National de la Statistique et des Etudes Economiques, INSEE) gives two classic definitions: first 'agglomeration' (1,349,772 inhabitants in 1999) in which the main delimitation criterion is the continuity of the built environment, and second 'urban area' (1,398,146 inhabitants in 1999), for which the criterion is the intensity of work–home daily travel. We will use mainly the urban area definition. The third category of space is what could be called the metropolitan region of Marseilles-Aix. Most of the actors[5] or academics have positioned themselves in relation to the Bouches du Rhône départe-ment territory: either infra (study limits of the AMM[6] in 1967–70) or supra (study limits of the DDE[7] in 1996). The Bouches du Rhône département limits are very interesting from an analytical point of view, and many statistics are available. A precise definition[8] of the metropolitan region will include the Marseilles-Aix urban area and the urban areas around Berre l'Etang (west: Fos, Istres; north: Miramas, Salon). The fourth space is the Mediterranean Grand Delta urban space[9] (approx. 3,500,000 inhabitants in 1999) which includes Toulon to the east, Montpellier-Sète to the west and Avignon to the north. This space has strong demographic and economic dynamics.

Trends of urbanisation and spatial configuration

The Marseilles-Aix metropolitan region changed rapidly during the 1980–90s period due to many factors, the most important of which were:

- changes in productive systems linked to globalisation developments;
- residential restructuring (peripheral developments, village growth);
- social and spatial segregation developments.

In the absence of a metropolitan strategy during the 1980s and 1990s, the metro-politan region structured itself as a multi-polarised space, mainly on the basis of the 1970 Planning Scheme and the highway system which was built during the 1960s and 1970s.

The Marseilles commune has the largest population of the metropolitan region but does not dominate it: the central city and peripheral cities not only function independently but the development dynamics are very different. Growth during the 1980s and 1990s took place outside Marseilles. Marseilles was declining demographically and economically. Metropolitanisation was happening outside the Marseilles territory.

Residential changes appear very clearly when one reads the demographic statistics for the period 1982–99.[10] The Bouches du Rhône département grew from 1.7 million inhabitants in 1982 to 1.8 million inhabitants in 1999,[11] but the area of the département outside Marseilles grew by 8.2 per cent (+188,911 inhabitants) whereas Marseilles lost 6.7 per cent of its population (–73,360 inhabitants).

Metropolitan housing growth outside Marseilles is segregative. The urbanised space is structured by fragmented residential spaces: individual/collective; subsidised/non-subsidised housing; in a liberal mode and with competition between the communes to attract the most affluent population. Residential redistribution is directly linked to the employment poles: families are reducing their daily work–home movements (67 per cent of individuals work in their residence commune compared to a national average of 30 per cent).[12] The residential peri-urban growth is based on individual housing. The residential urban growth is based on collective housing. From an economic point of view the Marseilles-Aix metropolitan region is organised in three main production areas, each of which has it own development dynamics.

- A Marseilles area, which collapsed during the 1960-70s period. It dragged the city into a severe decline during the 1980–90s period;
- A Fos-Martigues area (west of Marseilles) dominated by large, traditional industrial plants (chemicals, fuel, gas), which developed mainly during the 1960s and 1970s. They were under severe economic threat during the 1970s and 1980s;
- An Aix area (Les Milles, Rousset, Saint Paul les Durance) with high-tech development, on the basis of central state investments during the 1960s and 1970s (CETE[13] in 1968; CEA[14] in Saint Paul in 1969). This area was at the heart of the urban development processes during the 1990s.

Two other areas have to be taken into account. Their dynamics have been very important for the metropolitan region.

- Vitrolles and Plan de Campagne, near the airport and the TGV (high-speed train line), with big industrial and commercial zones developing since the 1960s;
- Aubagne and Gémenos (east of Marseilles), which received the relocation of Marseilles industries during the 1980s.

Two other areas with traditional industries are under threat:

- Gardanne, a mining city between Aix and Marseilles (closing date 2002);
- La Ciotat (east of Marseilles), whose shipyards were closed at the beginning of the 1980s.

The structuring/destructuring of productive poles are fundamental: they explain most of the residential changes. The metropolitan region has a concentration of national and international road, rail and air infrastructures. It is at the crossroads of a north–south axis which ends at the Mediterranean coast and of a west–east axis linking Spain to Italy. The central state was strong during the 1960s and organised the Fos development. It built the highway system which focused on road transport between the Rhône Valley and Spain/Italy. This highway system has also contributed greatly to the urbanisation processes of the metropolitan region since the 1970s in facilitating residential developments around the main cities.[15] The metropolitan railway infrastructures have been largely abandoned, due to the priority given to the car between the 1960s and the end of the 1990s. Only the national dimension has been taken into account with the construction of a TGV line at the end of the 1990s. The consequences of these policies are shown by the commuting surveys in 1997: 91 per cent of trips are made by private car. The motorway system is saturated during peak hours every day, particularly the Marseilles-Aix motorway, which is the spinal column of the network. In 2000, the

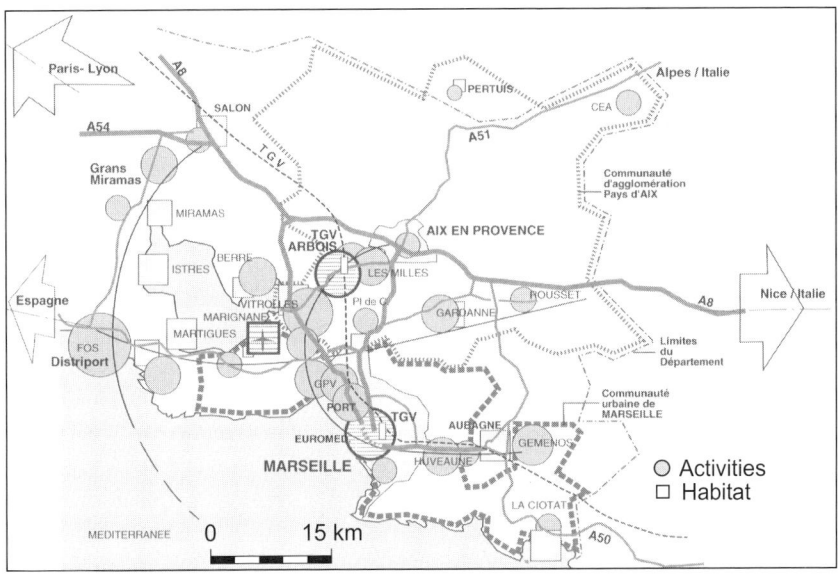

Figure 19.1 Planning issues and governance in the Marseilles-Aix metropolitan area. *Source*: Michel Chaippero, urbaniste architecte, 2001

Marseilles-Provence airport was the third busiest in France[16] (6.4 million passengers). Its development was very fast during the 1980s and 1990s.

The Marseilles-Aix metropolitan region has also many high quality environmental and landscape spaces: Camargue, Alpilles, Sainte-Victoire mountain, Côte Bleue, Frioul isles, Calanques and Cap Canaille, to name just a few. The most prestigious spaces are legally protected but the general environmental quality of the metropolitan region declined during the 1980s and 1990s due to the urbanisation processes.

Changes in the structures of government

France is a unitary state, which built its local institutional system (communes and départements) during the Revolution (1789–99) and the Consulat and Empire (1799–1814), on a highly centralised working. Local powers were in the hands of the *Préfet*, the local representative of the government. Local representatives were progressively introduced and given powers during the nineteenth century, culminating in départements in 1871 and communes in 1884, the préfet still having a crucial role. Local powers were structured between the end of the nineteenth century and 1982 along two networks: the administrative network dominated by the préfet, and the political network based on decentralised local institutions (communes, *Conseil général*[17]); the two networks working on centralisation processes.

The dramatic evolution of post-Second World War French society, and its very quick urbanisation and industrialisation, increased the political and administrative importance of mayors, particularly those of large cities (Bordeaux, Lille, Lyon, Marseilles). The 1980–2000 period was one of sea change in the development of the powers of local elected representatives, and the role of the préfet. The first main reform of 1982/3 moved the centre of gravity of French institutions from central spheres to local and regional spheres, and from the administrative network to the political network. This decentralisation process, though it maintained the same institutions, changed the role of each of them.

The generalist territorial local and regional authorities (communes, départements, régions) have largely developed their own responsibilities and now have the competence to define their own agendas. The commune has been reinforced in its role as manager of the local territory (planning permission, *Plan d'occupation des sols*, *Schéma directeur*). The département is no longer directly dependent on the préfet: it has its own elected president (by département representatives). It has developed its importance in education (investments in secondary schools), roads and transportation, social and sanitary policies. The région was transformed into a full public territorial authority with a president elected by a regional council.[18] The région has a crucial role in coordinating investments of the local authorities (regional planning and *aménagement du territoire*), education (investments in secondary schools), professional training and transport. All these authorities can also promote economic development.

With reduced power over the local and regional authorities, the préfet – the local and regional representative of the government – has become an intermediary, encouraging local authorities to adopt national policies. He or she is also in charge of controlling the legality of the public authorities' actions. His or her main role is to coordinate the actions of the administrative network at regional and departmental levels. The central ministries are still working on a vertical basis and the horizontal functioning at région and département level is difficult to put into practice. This is weakening the position of the préfet because territorial problems have to be managed on a horizontal basis by the local authorities, and only the communes, départements and régions have the capacity to coordinate and establish hierarchies in their policies.

In this new system the main difficulty is coordinating public policies within the central administrative network, within the political network, and between the two networks. An institutional mechanism was set up in 1982 to link the networks: the five year state–region contract. This contract is dedicated to national and regional investments and policies. It is a multipurpose contract. It is necessary for each institution to define, rank and negotiate its priorities for a five-year period. The state–region contract was directly linked at the beginning of the 1980s to planning at national and regional levels. This system worked fairly well during the first (1984–8) contract, but national planning collapsed progressively and the central state was not able to plan the ranking of its sectoral priorities, as it was the case during the 1960s. Nevertheless, the contract survives and the région has been reinforced in its role of coordinating local authorities and policies of the central state, particularly by the 1999 reform of *Aménagement du territoire*.

Another mechanism to coordinate public policies in the metropolitan regions has been the development of cooperation between communes. The first big attempt to develop that cooperation was in 1966: urban communities were created in some large cities (Lille, Lyon).[19] The next important attempts occurred in 1992 and 1999: new institutions (*Communautés de Communes, Communautés d'Aggloméra-tion, Communautés Urbaines*) were set up, successfully, particularly in the Bouches du Rhône département.

In the Marseilles-Aix metropolitan region, political powers were structured between 1953 and 1986 by the mayor of Marseilles, Gaston Defferre (Socialist Party).[20] 'He dominated the political sphere from the 1960s until the beginning of the 1980s in the Bouches-du-Rhône département, the Provence-Alpes-Côte-d'Azur région and even the administrative networks'. He died in 1986 and the increasing importance of the right-wing parties in the région completely changed the coordination modes of local authorities, which were acting separately. New institutions appeared in 1992–3, particularly around Marseilles and Aix. They developed progressively and the 1999 national reform gave birth to an urban community (18 communes) around Marseilles, and an agglomeration community around Aix-en-Provence (33 communes). Spatial planning is one of the main tasks

Alain Motte

Table 19.1 The levels of governance in France (2001)

Level	Political	Financial	Planning responsibilities
Nation	Election	Income tax and VAT Redistribution to lower levels	9 National Planning Schemes[a]
Région	Election at Département level (1984–2004)	Local taxes and grants from nation on neutral indicators	Schéma régional d'aménagement[b] Nation/Region (2000–06) Contract
Département	Election	Local taxes and grants from nation on neutral indicators	
Communautés	Representatives of Communes	Local taxes and grants from nation on neutral indicators	Région/ Communautés contract (1982–2002) Schéma directeur or Schéma de cohérence territoriale[c] (2002–...)
Communes	Election	Local taxes and grants from nation on neutral indicators	Plan d'occupation des Sols (1982–2002) or Plan Local d'Urbanisme[d] (2002–...)

Notes:
a Loi 'Voynet' : Loi n° 99–533 of 25 June 1999 (J.O. 29 June 1999, pp. 9515–27) and Loi 'Pasqua': Loi n° 95–115 of 4 February 1995 (J.O. 5 February 1995, pp. 1973ff.)
b Ibid.
c Loi 'Gayssot-Besson': Loi n° 2000–1208 of 13 December 2000 (J.O. 14 December 2000, pp. 19777ff.)
d Ibid.

of those new institutions, and the new 2000 Planning Law has made spatial planning an important issue at the local level.

The central state played a crucial role during the 1980–2000 period in structuring and modernising the institutions of this metropolitan region, first by national reforms and second by the restructuring of its administrative practices. At the end of the 1990s the central state's position was explicit: 'If we succeed in structuring this département with three or four [intercommunal] institutions for big issues of the agglomeration, we can easily find the appropriate structures'.[21] However, there was no metropolitan power in place during the 1980–2000 period. Nevertheless, there is now a strong possibility of public policy coordination between the two communities, reinforced in 2001 by the election of mayors from the same political sphere (the Right).

Strategic policies for the Marseilles-Aix metropolitan region

A metropolitan strategic policy was defined by local representatives of the central state in 1969–71 with the *Schéma d'Aménagement de l'Aire Métropolitaine Marseillaise* (1970).[22] This planning document is based on a projected population of 3.2 million inhabitants in 2000 (the real figure in 2000 was approx. 1.7 million). Its main focus is to articulate the development of high level services in Marseilles and the industrial development of Fos-Martigues.[23] The Aix-en-Provence area is dedicated to high-tech sites in order to complement its service vocation[24]. Furthermore the areas of outstanding natural interest must be developed but with a conservational attitude.[25] Recreation sites are planned between Aix and Marseilles in order to maintain green areas. To end this short summary the document supports the idea of promoting railway public transport. Many of these policies were received reluctantly by local authorities. Nevertheless this planning scheme structured the national public investments in the urban region, particularly the Marseilles, Fos and Aix developments. The motorway infrastructure has also evolved according to the scheme since the end of the 1960s.

During the first period of the decentralisation process (i.e. 1981–90), no metropolitan initiatives were taken by the regional or local authorities or the central state. A second period started in 1990. The central state had a very important incentive role for the emergence of a metropolitan policy, a role which was developed both at national level (new laws and policies) and in the Marseilles-Aix metropolitan region. All the initiatives came from central government, with some directness at times. One can list all the initiatives taken by central state government during the 1990–2000, and it developed them regularly, through all the political evolutions of governments at national level.

- At the beginning of the 1990s, the DATAR launched a specific local mission to make metropolitan strategic policy proposals (de Gaudemar, 1990; de Roo, 1992): the *Aire Métroplitaine Marseillaise* was again considered top priority for the *Aménagement du Territoire* policies. The critical focus was to promote the role of Marseilles as a trade and service centre.
- From 1990 till 1999: the Exchange Club of the Metropolitan Area was set up by the Préfecture de Région. It was an informal network of the metropolitan area planning practitioners, who met roughly every two months to argue their points of view on the main metropolitan issues, without referring formally to their institutional or political membership. They published numerous reports

and two books in 1994[26] and 2000.[27] They analysed and debated the metropolitan economic, social and spatial issues and challenged local authorities
about their incapacity to develop adequate policies to cope with those issues.
- From 1991 till 1996, the Capital Works Ministry (DDE) proceeded more
  formally, as in other metropolitan areas, to a 'strategic planning exercise'
  which was concluded by a book.[28] The role of the central state, and particularly
  that of the DDE, was to enhance the reflections on the urban issues and to
  develop a shared point of view among public planning officers. Many meetings
  were organised with all the 'partners' of the Capital Works Ministry (région
  préfecture, urban agencies of Aix-en-Provence, Marseilles, DATAR,
  Agricultural Ministry, etc.).[29] This 'partnership' was very large and developed
  independently of the elected representatives. It is a good illustration of the
  way the central state is proceeding, developing a common representation of
  the public necessity to act to face the new challenges. This 'planning exercise'
  was concluded in 1996 by a book published locally by the Director of the
  Direction Départementale de l'Equipement des Bouches du Rhône. His attitude
  was very critical for local authorities. He said, for example: 'The metropolitan
  area remains a virgin of any long-term planning'. Why is this so? Because
  there is 'an historic hostility of this territory to any form of planning, risks of
  incoherent development and perverse effects of *laissez-faire*'.[30]
- In 1996, the implementation of the Pasqua Planning law of 1995 led to a
  Directive Territoriale d'Aménagement (DTA) procedure. In this new procedure, the central state could unilaterally define spatial policies on a territory.
  The only condition was that it had to be defined in consultation with the
  elected representatives. Since 1996, the préfecture and the DDE have elaborated this DTA at the metropolitan level, with many political and administrative
  difficulties. It was nevertheless a possible way of defining a metropolitan
  strategic policy. Jean-Paul Proust, regional préfet, said in 1999: 'This document
  will give us a coherent organisation of the whole metropolitan area'.[31]

All those initiatives are emerging from the central state sphere: DATAR,
ministries and their local representatives. Local initiatives outside this central state
sphere are rare, particularly the initiatives coming from the employers' community.
The employers community is in fact fragmented,[32] as is the metropolitan region
itself. That heterogeneity is the consequence of destructuring the traditional
economic activities since the 1960s, and the arrival of large national and international enterprises during the same period. These large enterprises do not structure
the local employers' community, but coexist with the traditional employers'
communities. The heterogeneity is also linked to the fact that they benefit from
the communes' competition to attract enterprises at any cost. Therefore economic
interests are the main priority for the communes.

The end of the 1990s was again a new phase. The convergence of national
reforms both in institutional terms and strategic planning terms led to a completely

new situation. The implementation of the 1999 Sustainable Development Law makes quite compulsory the elaboration of a strategic spatial policy (*Projet d'agglo-mération*) for the urban area. The DATAR set up an agglomeration working group[33] between Marseilles and Aix communities to start the definition of an agglomeration strategic policy. This attempt was not successful but did structure the emergence of a political debate on this issue.

At the same time the region had a new role during the 1998–2001 period as a result of the elaboration of the 2000–6 Regional-National Contract and the Regional Planning Scheme (*schéma d'aménagement régional*). The contract has some elements of a new metropolitan policy. It is also linked to national service schemes and European programmes for the same period. It shows the link which is emerging between four levels of policies: Europe, France, region and local communities.

The attitude of the central state was defined by Jean-Paul Proust, prefect in 1999. It shows clearly the new role of the central state: 'My ambition, as a representative of the state, is certainly not to say what has to be done, but to try to federate all the energies to create a large project, an ambitious project for the metropolitan area'. The central state effort has been on the institutional side, which could support the emergence of a metropolitan strategic policy.

Problems of institutional and spatial coordination

Institutional and spatial coordination at the metropolitan level has been linked in France to the national decentralisation reforms. It took its local configurations according to the characteristics of the institutional local cultures and coordination is very different from one metropolis to another.[34] Decentralisation during the 1980s was organised with no hierarchy between the main levels of local and regional governments. Communes, départements and régions could act separately and were formally independent. The central state gave up many elements of its hierarchical power over local authorities. The existence of horizontal relations and the coordination of agendas depended on the willingness of the local governments (Duran and Thoenig, 1996). During the 1980s, in some urban areas this new situation led to the development of cooperation (e.g. Lille, Lyon, Rennes). In other urban areas, limited cooperation or non-cooperation was dominant (e.g. Bordeaux, Grenoble, Toulouse, Nantes). In the Marseilles-Aix metropolitan area non-cooperation was the main characteristic of the institutional relations, and competition developed between communes.

The 1990s period was different. The 1990 census revealed the new growth of the Paris region, leading the government to launch national incentive policies to expand regional metropolises in the context of European cities competition. In the Bouches du Rhône département the central state developed actions to promote the building of new supra-communal institutions. The objective was to coordinate the production of public goods and services at the metropolitan level in order to scale up the competitiveness of the Marseilles-Aix metropolitan region.

The regional, departmental and communal political scene was dominated during the 1970s and the beginning of the 1980s by a very strong leader, Gaston Defferre. He was a member of the Socialist Party and became the Interior Minister responsible for the decentralisation laws of 1982–3. He played an integrative role between the three levels of local and regional government. Since his death in 1986 the local political sphere has evolved very rapidly.

In Marseilles, another Socialist leader, Robert Vigouroux, was mayor (1986–95) but a shift to the Right occurred. Jean-Claude Gaudin (Liberal Democrats – the Right) was elected in 1995 (and re-elected in 2001). The Département des Bouches du Rhône kept its Socialist leadership (1986–2001), but not a strong link with the Marseilles commune during the 1986–95 period. The Provence-Alpes-Côte-d'Azur Région became dominated by the Right between 1986 and 1998 (with Jean-Claude Gaudin as president of the regional council). In 1998 a Socialist president was elected after the regional elections. His power is weak as he does not have a majority on the regional council.

Robert Vigouroux (mayor 1986–95) had an affirmative policy for Marseilles, aimed at dominating – without much success – other communes of the département. He nevertheless started to cooperate in 1993[35] with other communes around Marseilles, creating a Community of Communes: the Marseilles-Provence Métropole (MPM), which in 1993 consisted of 13 communes. Jean-Claude Gaudin developed a strategic spatial scheme for Marseilles, and expanded, on a consensus basis, the MPM (20 communes in 1999). In 2000[36] he transformed it into a new urban community (18 communes) which has strong powers in planning, economic development, housing, the environment and infrastructure provisions (water, sewage, transportation). In this process Jean-Claude Gaudin proposed to the Aix-en-Provence mayor to integrate this urban community, without success. One should note that the MPM did not develop much during the 1993–9 period. Policies were developed with an informal veto principle from the small communes, which prevented any large project from emerging. Aix-en-Provence used the 1992 and 1999[37] laws to strongly develop cooperation between communes. The Pays d'Aix Community of Communes was created in 1993 (six communes in 1993 and 19 in 1999). The agglomeration community was created in 2001 (33 communes). It has strong powers in planning, economic development, housing and the environment. Other agglomeration communities are developing (2001): Aubagne-Garlaban, Nord de l'Etang de Berre, Ouest de l'Etang de Berre, Nord-Ouest de l'Etang de Berre, Arles.

Competition between the main public institutions (communes, Département des Bouches-du-Rhône, Région Provence-Alpes-Côte-d'Azur) was nevertheless the main characteristic of the 1980s and most of the 1990s. This can be seen from the main metropolitan projects:

- *Arbois* projects (TGV station, road infrastructure development, activity zone development): with conflicts between Aix, Marseilles and the Département;

- *Euroméditerranée* project (311 ha of urban redevelopment of Marseilles harbour area) which was not welcomed at first by the Département;
- Logistics: three projects developed separately, without much cooperation;
- Commercial zones: Grand Littoral development in Marseilles was set up autonomously by the Marseilles (Vigouroux) municipality.

A clear illustration of this lack of cooperation is the case of the large music halls built in the mid-1990s by Marseilles (Le Dôme – EUR 15 million) and Vitrolles (Le Stadium – EUR 10 million). In 2001 the Dôme was working well and the Stadium was collapsing.

What was new at the end of the 1990s/beginning of the 2000s was that communes had started to experiment with some new cooperative relationships. Why is there such an emergence of cooperation between communes after such a long period of competition? Is it due to government policy in place since the beginning of the 1990s and to the considerable financial incentives in the 1999 law[38] which grouped together the communes? This factor is certainly important but alone it does not suffice, as cooperation is much more limited in some neighbouring départements (e.g. Var, Hérault). Is this linked to the fact that the councillors in communes on the outskirts of cities have become aware of the need to offer their citizens a greater standard of amenities and services than is possible according to the actual means of these communes? This factor must certainly play a role, for many outlying communes are not able alone to take on, for example, the cost of public transport or the collection and processing of household waste. Since the 1960s these services have been organised by resorting to forms of syndicate cooperation, but the boundaries of the syndicates vary from service to service. By the end of the 1990s the network of syndicate boundaries had become inextricable. In this respect the 1999 Chevènement Law provides an opportunity to reduce the overly complex workings of the management of local public services and the provision of amenities.

Is this linked to the chance hereby offered to mayors to be less isolated when dealing with the great complexity of the regulations that apply to the communes? Many municipalities are no longer capable of taking these regulations into account (e.g. the application of European standards as regards environmental issues), which periodically leads to legal action against mayors. The communauté is an institution which allows management to be simplified but the process involves the unification of power which leads to mayors being very dependent on one another. Why have the mayors agreed to enter into this new reasoning that completely breaks with the isolationist traditions built up[39] since the end of the nineteenth century? In the setting up of communities, there are very important domains which are of the community competence (planning, economy, housing, social quarters). The communes are at risk of losing large powers in these domains. The mayors agreed to join because two new rules of the game appeared both in the communauté urbaine de Marseilles and in the communauté d'agglomération d'Aix: subsidiarity and consensus. This means first that each commune has potentially a large possibility to choose the policies which are really granted to the level of the communauté. In order to transfer a policy to the communauté it must be declared to be of benefit to the communauté. This question of benefit has started to be framed by regulations but it is interpreted by the *conseil de communauté*. If this council works by consensus then the mayors obey the unwritten rule, namely they respect the choices of the other municipalities. The mayor thereby has considerable room to manoeuvre when it comes to policies that are to be transferred to the level of the communauté. To this level, conversely, he is able to transfer policies that he finds difficult to manage, those which pose awkward questions or those which he thinks are too costly, such as the provision of public transport and the collection and processing of waste.

Did the financial aspects motivate the grouping together? There are two financial incentives. The first consists of an additional substantial grant, granted to the communautés, which may benefit, at one time or another the communes. The second concerns local business tax. Historically this tax has exacerbated competition between communes wishing to attract businesses into their area. This led to great inequalities in the collection of revenue between communes with many businesses and those with none. The Chevènement Law introduced a single local business tax for communautés d'agglomération and for communautés urbaines. We can see why the poorest communes accepted joining a system that would potentially bring them greater resources, by redistribution of services or infrastructures. But what of the rich communes? The regulation was constructed in such a way that the rich communes keep the total sum collected upon entry to the communauté. The increases alone are redistributed. We can see therefore that the system as a whole allows every commune to gain financially when it enters a communauté.

Did business leaders play a role in the incitement to group the communes together? We can consider their role to have been important. For several decades business leaders have been calling for a standard rate of local business tax. The sum payable by businesses in the same sector can vary greatly from one commune to another depending on the number of businesses in the commune in which they are situated. This inequality between the rates distorts competition between businesses. The reform will allow the rates of local business taxation to be standardised across the communauté area and will then in all likelihood allow the highest rates to be reduced.

One of the consequences of the homogenisation of the rates of local business taxation will be far less fierce competition between communes wishing to attract businesses. After the transitional period the redistribution of revenue from the local business tax will actually be submerged into the rest of the resources of the communauté. The allocation of funds will be carried out according to criteria concerning communauté policies and no longer according to the direct revenue collected by each municipality.

The question we can now ask is why certain communes are not taking part in this reform. First, there can be reasons concerning increased isolationism. In some cases there are reasons pertaining to political allegiance (e.g. Communist municipalities do not wish to be linked with right-wing municipalities, as is the case for Aubagne with Marseilles, or even with left-wing municipalities, such as Martigues and Istres) or to historical conflict that cannot be resolved (Aix, for example, has been opposed to Marseille for several centuries, this relation was historically created by central power). Finally, the mayors may be concerned about communautés gaining power. National debates lead to a recommendation for présidents de communautés to be elected by direct universal suffrage (in 2007) which could subsequently lead to a greatly strengthened manner of cooperation (around 2015).

These institutional developments could contribute to the emergence of a metropolitan spatial strategy elaborated by the local authorities. The intense local activity of the central state during the 1990s identified the main problems which have to be solved. Consequently new appropriate metropolitan policies have been identified. The communes working together in new intercommunal institutions provide a strong possibility of coordinating these new metropolitan policies.

Evaluation of metropolitan governance and coordination of spatial policies

Why is coordination so difficult? Despite the fact that it is a common tendency in many metropolitan areas, the Mediterranean hypothesis is strongly supported. Marseilles-Aix 'belongs to a Latin, Mediterranean space and historically in this space cities and elite social groups struggle for complete autonomy. This generates very strong economic and social inequalities' (Braudel, 1966, p.94). In this respect, the central state policies in France are much more redistributive and egalitarian.

What are the consequences of this historical absence of coordination at metropolitan level? Public resources are spoilt by competition between communes, for example in terms of activity zones created at too high a level. The absence of public resources for metropolitan infrastructures is a handicap in the European and international cities competition. The Marseilles-Aix metropolitan region, for example, is unable to organise large international conferences (which go to Nice instead). The absence of a public transport system in the metropolitan area increases the social spatial segregation and intensifies the traffic jams. There is also a strong differentiation of land and property markets, of the fiscal bases, and of the site qualities from one commune to another. What is influencing this tendency to non-coordination? Who is benefiting from it?

For example, the most innovative high-tech industries are located in Rousset, a small commune near Sainte-Victoire mountain, a few kilometres from Aix (which has a good national and international reputation), and outside the declining main city (Marseilles). Rousset is also very well located on the motorway system and very close (when there are no traffic jams) to the international airport and now the TGV. This activity zone was built with European funds and benefited from low local taxes. This development is linked to the globalisation processes: innovating enterprises are reducing their installation costs and recruiting high-flying engineers who benefit from a pleasant environment and good residential costs, and enjoy access to a high level of services.

Those developments are quite close to the development of many American metropolitan areas, in which the social and economic inequalities of social groups can be read in the institutional spaces differentiations. The metropolitan area is a market of territories.

Can the development of communauté institutions improve this situation? All will depend on the local application of central government laws and therefore on the way in which local councillors adapt them to suit the local context. The dynamics in place are very strong and constitute a well-suited response to the development of globalisation. Nevertheless there is great potential for structuring between communauté policy (the agglomeration project, the Territorial Coherence Scheme; SCOT[40]), regional policy (the Regional Territory Planning and Development Scheme; SRADT[41]) and national policy (Collective Service Schemes; SSC). In this respect the national level holds important influential power.

National policy in 2001 is clearly directed towards housing densification (in order to contain urban sprawl), the development of rail networks for public transport (in order to overcome the clogging-up of the road networks), the protection of endangered natural environments, and the social mix (the just allocation of council housing in all communes). Can these four policies be adopted and implemented by the Communauté urbaine de Marseilles and by the Communauté d'agglomération d'Aix-en-Provence? If so, they will break with the reasoning that has been prevalent in this metropolitan region for the last 50 years.

Notes

1 During the 1960s 'urban communities' including a large number of municipalities were legally imposed by the government in many big cities, including Lille and Lyon. Marseilles rejected the project of the urban community. Gaston Defferre (socialist) who had the political leadership in the Marseilles commune and the département of Bouches du Rhône, resisted strongly – partly for political reasons (he was in the opposition and there was a strong Communist Party in the nearby communes) – the new intercommunal structure.
2 Marseilles is the most important commune in the Marseilles-Aix urban area with 57 per cent of the total population and covering 43 per cent of the département.
3 Those communes have very large territories, which is specific to that part of France.
4 Marseilles-Aix ranks as the second or third agglomeration, depending on the chosen definitions.
5 Varies according to periods and political issues.
6 Aire Métropolitaine Marseillaise: limits defined by central government in 1967.
7 Direction Départementale de l'Equipement (département level institution of the Capital Works Ministry).

8 1999 delimitations.
9 Grand Delta Méditerranéen.
10 Statistical census.
11 Statistics of the Bouches du Rhône Département. In the 37 years between 1962 and 1999, there was growth of 46.9 per cent.
12 This is partly due to the fact that these communes have large territories, which is an exception in France.
13 *Centre d'Études Techniques du ministère de l'Équipement* – Research Centre of the Capital Works Ministry.
14 *Centre d'Études Atomiques* – Nuclear research centre
15 Residential development has also been reinforced by the massive investments in water supply by central government during the 1960s and 1970s.
16 Paris airports (73.6 million passengers in 2000), Nice (9.3 million), Lyon (6.0 million).
17 Département elected body.
18 Elected body.
19 Not in Marseilles.
20 He was the 'father' of the decentralisation laws of 1982 and 1983.
21 Préfet de Région declaration in Langevin and Chouraqui, 2000, p.182.
22 Planning Scheme of the Marseilles Metropolitan Area.
23 Ministère de l'Equipement – OREAM (Organisation d'Etudes d'Aménagement de l'aire Métropolitaine), 1970, p.119.
24 Ibid., p.129.
25 Ibid., p.121.
26 Club de l'AMM (1994): 'la métropole inachevée'.
27 Langevin, Chouraqui, 2000: 'encore un effort'.
28 Brassart, 1996.
29 DIREN (Direction Régionale de l'Environnement), DRE (Direction Régionale du Ministère de l'Equipement), CETE (Centre d'Etudes Techniques du Ministère de l'Equipement), EPAREB (Etablissement Public d'Aménagement des Rives de l'Etang de Berre), Euromed (Etablissement Public d'Aménagement Euroméditerannée).
30 Brassart, 1996, p.10.
31 30 April 1999.
32 Zalio, in Donzel, pp.19–35.
33 The same experience started in 15 other French agglomerations.
34 See Motte (1997).
35 Using the 1992 law.
36 Using the 1999 Chevènement law.
37 Loi 'Chevènement': Loi n° 99–586 du 12 juillet 1999 (J.O. du 13 July 1999, pp.10361–96).
38 'Chevènement' Law: Law N°. 99–586, 12 juillet 1999 (J.O. 13th July 1999, pp.10361–96).
39 See Crozier, Friedberg, 1977 for a detailed description of the characteristics of the '*système politico-administratif départemental français*', pp.218–34.
40 Schéma de Cohérence Territoriale – SCOT.
41 Schéma Régional d'Aménagement et de Développement du Territoire – SRADT.

Bibliography

Becquart, D. (1994) *Marseille: 25 ans de planification urbaine*, La Tour d'Aigues: Ed. de l'Aube.

Brassart, E. (ed.) (1996) *La région urbaine marseillaise*, La Tour d'Aigues: Ed. de l'Aube.

Braudel, F. (1966, 6th edn 1985) *La méditerranée et le monde méditerranéen à l'époque de Philippe II*, Paris: Armand Colin.

Alain Motte

Club d'échanges et de réflexions sur l'aire métropolitaine marseillaise (1994) *La métropole inachevée Les ferments d'une démarche de prospective partagée*, La Tour d'Aigues: Ed. de l'Aube.

Crozier, M. and Friedberg, E. (1977) *L'acteur et le système*, Paris: Seuil.

De Gaudemar, J.P. (1990) *SAM 3 ou l'esquisse d'une métropole euroméditerranéenne?,* Marseilles: Mission AMM de la DATAR.

De Roo, P. (1992) *Livre Blanc: l'aire métropolitaine marseillaise ou la métropole éclatée*, Marseille: Mission AMM de la DATAR.

Donzel, A. (2001) *Métropolisation, gouvernance et citoyenneté dans la région urbaine marseillaise*, Paris: Ed. Maisonneuve et Laroche.

Duran, P. and Thoenig, J.-C. (1996) 'L'État et la gestion publique territoriale', *Revue Française de Science Politique*, 580–623.

Fellmann, T. and Morel, B. (1989) *Métropolisation et aires métropolitaines. Les effets de la polarisation sur la métropole marseillaise mobilité économique, concurrence, complémentarité* (Rapport de recherche pour le Plan Urbain), Marseilles.

Julien, Ph. (1999) *Au delà de l'urbanisation, l'étalement urbain caractérise la région*, Marseilles: INSEE.

Langevin, Ph. and Chouraqui, E. (2000) *Aire métropolitaine mareillaise encore un effort...*, La Tour d'Aigues: Ed. de l'Aube.

Ministère de l'Equipement, OREAM (1970) *Schéma d'aménagement de l'aire métropolitaine marseillaise*, Marseilles: Ministère de l'Equipement.

Ministère de l'Equipement, Plan urbain, (1997) *Qui fait la ville aujourd'hui?*, Paris: Ministère de l'Equipement.

Morel, B. (1999) *Marseille, naissance d'une métropole*, Paris: L'Harmattan.

Motte, A. (1987) 'La restructuration du pouvoir régional en Provence-Alpes-Côte d'Azur', in P. Perrineau (ed.) *Région: le baptême des urnes*, Paris: Ed. Pédone.

Motte, A. (1987) 'Continuités et ruptures dans les politiques d'urbanisme et d'aménagement du Conseil Régional de Provence-Alpes-Côte d'Azur', *Urbanisme*, October, pp.106–9.

Motte, A. (ed.) (1995) *Schéma directeur et Projet d'agglomération: Un renouvellement du mode de gestion des espaces urbanisés français (1981–1993)*, Paris: Juris Service éditions.

Motte, A. (1997) 'The production of spaces in France (1981–1995): a comparison of Rennes, Nantes and Toulouse', Paper for the Association of European Schools of Planning (AESOP) Conference, Nijmegen.

336

20 The case of Barcelona

Marisol García

Introduction[1]

Barcelona – the capital of Catalonia and the second largest city in Spain – was the most industrialised urban metropolis in the country until Madrid took the lead relatively recently. The city of Barcelona has a population of about 1.5 million. The population of metropolitan Barcelona – which is constituted by the city along with another 26 municipalities – is about 2.8 million. Finally, the metropolitan region of Barcelona – which comprises 162 municipalities – has a population of about 4.2 million. Given the fact that Catalonia has 6 million inhabitants, the social and economic relevance of the three 'Barcelonas' is considerable. However, the internationally well-known Barcelona is the city itself, especially since the 1992 Olympic Games. The international profile acquired by the city as a result of this event increased international tourism during the 1990s. Urban tourism is one important sector of the development of the service sector in the city, while industry has moved out to the rest of the Barcelona region. As it has expanded, Barcelona has met up with other long established cities generating an urban continuum which plays a strong social and economic role in Catalonia, but has no government or central management institution.

In fact the Barcelona region has seven layers of administration intervening in the territory with various levels of discretion. Barcelona is not an exception in the Spanish context. Politically, the decentralisation of Spain into autonomous communities has involved considerable devolution of resources and functions at the regional level since 1980; however, further decentralisation to metropolises and localities has been very limited. Thus, Barcelona as a metropolitan and regional city lacks a government and governance is fragmentary. Why is this the case? There is no single answer, and yet the explanation falls more in the sphere of politics than in that of socio-economic interests, as this chapter shows.

Local debates about the promotion of the metropolitan region are polarised around two strong leaders: the previous city mayor and current opposition leader in the Catalan government, Pascual Maragall, along with his political party and partisan professionals, and the long-lasting Catalan president, Jordi Pujol.[1] The former has been arguing that the real Barcelona is the region, with central Barcelona as the leading and articulating city and that the institutionalisation of the urban

337

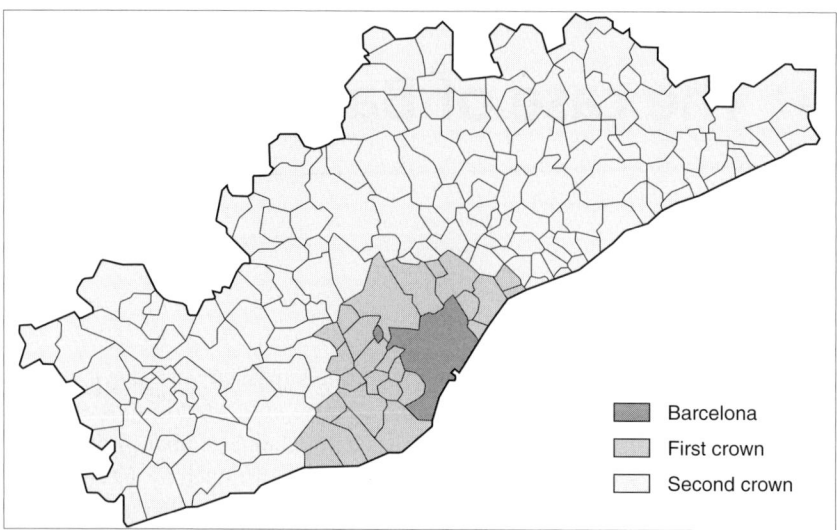

Figure 20.1 The metropolitan region of Barcelona. *Source:* Servei d'Estudis Territorials de la Mancomunitat de Municipis. Dinamiques Metropolitanes a l'Area i la regio de Barcelona, 1995

region – formed by a network of modern, relatively large cities that have considerable economic and social interaction – should be organised around the leadership of Barcelona. On the other hand, the Catalonian president argues that the socioeconomic dynamics of the relatively large, medium and small cities needs to be promoted in order to balance the overpowering presence of Barcelona. He abolished the Metropolitan Corporation in 1987 and since then has prevented the establishment of any formal government institution that could reinforce the already unequal balance between Barcelona and the other cities. His argument favours a decentralised system of governance coordinated and supervised by the Catalan government.

The previous political disagreements have had consequences on the regulation of the territory. Whereas the metropolitan region has had an urban plan since 1976 (before the restoration of democracy), the Catalan Region Plan was only passed by the Catalan parliament in 1995. However, the Barcelona region is still awaiting a comprehensive plan.[2] General plans at the county level have been formulated and in many instances implemented to a considerable extent. The fact that the region is a social and economic reality with increasing job and residence mobility between towns, poses the question of the price the population is paying as a result of political dissent, in terms of efficiency and justice in the location of infrastructures and services. Thus the Barcelona case is an interesting one in terms of institutional and territorial regulation conflict and power relations between levels of governance.

Changes in the structure of government

In the last 20 years, Spain's governance structure has undergone important changes. The 1978 Constitution opened the way for the formation of 17 autonomous communities. In the following years, negotiation between political parties established the decentralisation model to be followed in Spain. There was a strong political will to increase autonomy in the historical 'national' communities (e.g. Catalonia) and considerable debate about the formula that would be accepted by these communities and others that emerged artificially.[3] However, the decentralisation process was also seen by the municipalities as an opportunity for further autonomy in decision-making. In fact, the devolution of power to the regions (and nationalities) has not been paralleled by a similar devolution to municipal governments.

To provide a general picture, Spain has 17 autonomous communities (some of them referred to as nationalities given their historical tradition). The country is divided into 52 provinces and 8,022 municipalities. The state structure has several levels: central, autonomous, provincial and municipal. In the case of Catalonia the provincial level is seen by local political parties as an external imposition. The provinces (which correspond to the French *départements*) have served since 1833 as a territorial basis for the central state organisation. In order to maintain central state control over the provinces, executive powers were concentrated in the figure of the civil governor. The role of the governor was reinforced during the dictatorship and then increasingly minimised after the establishment of democratic governance. An added level of administration in Catalonia comprises the county councils, which, although established in 1988 by the Catalan government, have not been given financial support and therefore are practically ineffective.

One of the main difficulties for municipal autonomy has been the lack of resources. City government participation in public spending has been lower than elsewhere in Europe, increasing slowly from 9.95 per cent in 1970 to around 12 per cent in 1990 and 15 per cent in 2001. In contrast, regional administrations have rapidly increased their share of public spending since their creation from just 0.2 per cent in 1980 to over 23 per cent in 1991 and 35 per cent in 2001. Moreover, the salient role of autonomous communities has been reinforced by the EU regional policy, that is, by the active part regional governments played in the negotiation over Structural Funds. As a result of these negotiations it was agreed that while regional administrations should manage 33.8 per cent of the structural funds, local governments should manage only 7 per cent, with 59.2 per cent to be managed by the central government.

As other autonomous governments have done, the Catalan government has not redistributed to the local level proportionally the increasing financial transfers it receives from the central state. Whereas 67.3 per cent of the current income of the Catalan government comprises transfers from the central state, the city council's income is to a large extent comprised of local taxes. In 1999 the transfers from other state levels to the city council amounted to 34 per cent of total income. The central state provided 91 per cent of this amount. Welfare services, education infrastructure and social services, although managed by municipalities, are directly financed and to a large extent supervised by the Catalan government departments. In fact, local welfare systems are increasingly requiring the involvement of municipalities in the management and coordination of services (social assistance is a good example). This requires considerable coordination between municipal and Catalan governments as well as with the private and – in some spheres – voluntary sectors. Thus a clear constraint on municipal autonomy is the cooperation between levels of governance. The flexibility established by the 1985 Local Government law concerning the role of provincial and city councils has increased the importance of city-regional government relations. These relations have effectively favoured autonomous communities' governments, which have acquired supervisory functions over areas of city council competence.[4] Thus, the expanding role of local councils in managing planning, education, culture, health and social services requires more coordination with the regional administrations. This can create problems when negotiations become over-politicised. The relations between Barcelona city council and the Catalan government are a case in point.

Trends of urbanisation in Barcelona

The process of decentralising population and economic activity took shape in Barcelona from the 1970s onwards. What is particularly significant is the quality of this process. While central Barcelona, like most other large cities in Europe, has increasingly specialised in the service sector, the Barcelona region exhibits a productive diversification, with a high degree of specialisation of production and services in the territory. However, industrial production is not located in the metropolitan region but around the more distant industrial cities. Thus the immediate cities that form the metropolitan region – or 'first crown' – are also losing position in favour of the 'second crown' (see figure 20.1). Since the early days of industrial expansion, companies have been basically small and medium-sized, which has encouraged territorial fragmentation. This was especially the case prior to the democratic control of land regulation, which officially began with the 1979 local elections. Since then, and taking as a point of reference the 1976 Metropolitan Plan, each municipality has had an important role within the region in the regulation and provision of services. However, the Plan only affected the metropolitan area and not the rest of the region. Sectional plans were developed subsequently at a county level, as it will be shown in the following section.

Since the industrialisation of the city in the nineteenth century, the urbanisation of Barcelona has been based to a large extent on being a major centre of labour immigration. This pioneering industrial region attracted internal migration from the rest of Catalonia and Spain up until the 1970s. However, whereas in the early 1960s the central city was still attracting immigrants from the rest of Spain, by the 1970s the metropolitan area was becoming the main focus of immigration. From the mid-1970s the population of Barcelona city started to stabilise, internal immigration from other regions of Spain came to a halt, and migrants now come either from nearby areas or the rest of Catalonia or in various proportions from other countries. What was more salient during the last decades of the twentieth century was a process of dispersion towards the metropolitan area, followed by an increasing relevance of the rest of the Barcelona region as a recipient of population and economic activity: during the 1990s, the region beyond the metropolitan area (the city's 'second crown') has been gaining in population, whereas the 'first crown' is losing population. Population dynamics have been closely related to the dynamics of the production and housing sectors, which have the same dispersion patterns of expansion.

The dispersion of people and economic activity has caused increasing inter-regional mobility. In 1998, 31.5 per cent of the total working population in the Barcelona central city lived in towns located mainly within the metropolitan areas, but also in further away towns within the Barcelona region. On the other hand, 21.2 per cent of the residents of the central city worked outside the city, mainly in the rest of the Barcelona region (Mur, 2001). Moreover, there is increasing forced commuting within the region not only from the periphery to the centre and vice versa, but also between medium and small towns as a result of the expansion of job opportunities in these towns. In fact the distance from the place of residence of those who continue to work in the Barcelona municipality is increasing each year. Whereas in the years of rapid urbanisation of the metropolitan area, the place of destination was the nearest large town in the first crown, in recent years those leaving Barcelona are settling down in towns located more than 30 km from the central city and with a population of 10,000–50,000 (Serra, 1997). The majority of those who leave the central city for these towns are young couples and families with children.

The territorial expansion of Barcelona is characterised by the fact that each new urban extension meets an existing town which has a strong historical person-

Table 20.1 Population by extension of territory, 1970–96

Territory	1970	1981	1991	1996
Barcelona-city	1,741,979	1,752,627	1,643,542	1,508,805
Metropolitan Area	2,724,603	3,145,103	3,037,763	2,904,941
Barcelona-Region	3,565,962	4,238,876	4,264,422	4,228,048
Catalonia	5,107,606	5,956,414	6,059,494	6,090,040

Source: Dinàmiques metropolitaness a lÀreas I la Regió de Barcelona, 1995.

ality. Local identities are strong and exhibit a rich cultural heritage reinforced by the reawakened nationalism of the 1980s encouraged by the Catalan government. Only the new towns built in the 1970s to house internal immigrants constitute an exception. These towns were defectively constructed and lacked infrastructure and cultural amenities for the immigrant population housed in them, and have been more sensitive to the problems of unemployment and stigmatising labour of social exclusion patterns. In contrast, the traditional localities with an historical identity are seen as the locus of a more successful social integration, especially since the newly elected democratic local governments put considerable efforts into generating services and attracting investments. Thus, some cities have flourished and others have languished.

The core-periphery population mobility trend is partly explained by the fact that the municipality of Barcelona has undergone deindustrialisation. Industry either closed down or moved to other municipalities within the region, mainly from the 1980s onwards. Reorganisation of the industrial sector (types and volume of companies, productivity, externalisation of services, relocation of companies and participation of foreign capital) has been remarkable. The process is by no means simple, thus part of the decrease in industrial employment is related to the externalisation of jobs from industry to services that operate as subcontractors of what before was industrial employment. When taking into consideration productivity instead of industrial occupation, it appears that the industrial sector continues to play a crucial role in the economy of Barcelona. However, during the period 1970–86 there was 'negative' deindustrialisation causing considerable losses in industrial jobs: 249,861 industrial jobs were lost in Barcelona city, and 225,006 industrial jobs were lost in the metropolitan area in the same period, mainly in the textiles and metal industries, but also in related sectors. The city's process of 'regionalisation' meant that by the 1980s Barcelona's metropolitan area had concentrated almost 60 per cent of the total investments in Catalonia. In this period there was a tendency towards spatial specialisation, in which industry was located increasingly in the most distant parts of the metropolitan territory and the service sector was concentrated in the city (Busquets, 1992).

Since 1986 (the year Spain joined the EC) and especially since 1992, Barcelona has undergone an important internationalisation of industrial capital, improving technological developments and increasing the size of companies. This new injection of capital did not, however, affect industrial production within the central city, which lost a further 81,090 jobs between 1986 and 1995. What has been considered 'positive' deindustrialisation during this period translated into the loss of jobs in traditional industrial sectors in favour of the creation of jobs in new industries and the related service sector, which involved an increase of 154,294 new jobs in services within the central city (Gómez, 2002). However, what is clear is that in recent years, industrial production has increasingly taken place in the second crown beyond the metropolitan area.

Table 20.2 Active population by economic sectors in Barcelona's municipality, 1975–96

	1975	1981	1991	1996
Services	52.2	61.4	65.7	71.8
Industry	41.7	35.3	29.7	24.4
Construction	5.6	3.0	4.4	3.3

Source: Martinez, 2001, p.75.

In the central city, services have continued to increase mainly in the commerce and catering sectors, financial services, and communications and transport sectors. The growth of the tourist sector since 1992 has given a further impetus to the expansion of services in Barcelona. Barcelona city council's urbanism department planned several 'areas of new centrality' where offices and large commercial centres were to be built, thus generating job opportunities. These new job opportunities are taken not only by residents of the central city, but increasingly so by residents of the rest of the Barcelona region.

The expansion of the housing market and the development of public transport infrastructure and road systems complement the picture of how and why Barcelona has experienced decentralisation of population and activity. The housing market has been relatively stable in the central city. Major residential developments took place in preparation for the 1992 Olympic Games (e.g. the Olympic Village), which involved the gentrification of one of the traditional industrial neighbourhoods of the city. In recent years another large development has been underway in the nearby area of the sea front, where the Olympic Village is located and a new festival will be held in 2004 (*Diagonal-Mar*). However, these developments have proved to be incapable of fulfilling the real demand. Between 1987 and 2000, only 69,456 new housing units were completed within the central city. During the same period, the numbers for the first and second crowns of the Barcelona region (excluding Barcelona) were 113,112 and 207,582, respectively. This trend in the housing market explains the exodus towards the regional territory. Moreover, some families have sought alternatives to buying a new house by using their second residence as their first residence. In 1991, approximately 30 per cent of all housing in the second crown was used as a second residence.[5] According to senior officials of the Catalan government, an increasing number of second residences are being converted into first residences.

Table 20.3 shows that the total number of housing units constructed in the second crown increased considerably in the period 1992–2000 compared to the number built in the period 1981–91. This increase applies not only to Barcelona city, but also to the metropolitan area (first crown). The housing supply has been not only greater in the rest of the Barcelona region (i.e. the region minus the metropolitan area) but also cheaper. As table 20.4 shows, prices in Barcelona have

Table 20.3 Finished housing units by territorial areas, 1981–2000

	1981–91		1992–2000				
	Total	Mitjana (11 years)	Total	Mitjana (9 years)	Population 1996	Housing units per 1000 inhabitants/year	
Barcelona	37,919	3,447	31,537	3,504	1,508,805	2.32
Rest AMB (1ª Crown)	43,104	3,919	69,908	7,768	1,410,805	5.51
AMB	81,023	7,366	101,445	11,272	2,919,610	3.86
Rest RMB (2ª Crown)	87,533	7,958	120,049	13,339	1,308,438	10.19
RMB	168,556	15,324	221,494	24,611	4,228,048	5.82

Source: García, E., Area Metropolitana de Barcelona, 2002. (Table compiled for this chapter.)

increased so much that young couples with a middle or low income cannot afford to buy there, and thus have to look elsewhere. In fact, these new households are formed in the larger towns of the rest of the Barcelona region, where there is economic activity growth or good road connections with industrial and service economy locations. Housing prices increased proportionally more in the first and second crown between 1987 and 2000; however, the difference between prices inside the central city and in the two crowns remains substantial. In the central city, the price per m^2 continues to be almost double that in the second crown (EUR 2,170 and 1,277, respectively), with prices in the first crown falling in between (EUR 1,657). The larger supply combined with the more affordable prices explains the population dispersion throughout the larger area of the second crown.

Increasing housing supply and relatively lower prices in the second crown have been supported by the modernisation of urban infrastructure and the improvement of communications. These transformations in the location of population and economic activity have reinforced a pattern of daily commuting not only between Barcelona central city and the periphery (and vice versa), but also between towns throughout the territory. In the region, currently 45 per cent of the working population works in a locality other than the one in which they live. The speed of the increase in commuting is growing rapidly (in 1986 the figure was only 33 per cent) (Nello, 2001, 153–4). This poses an important question concerning transport and communication infrastructures. Some of the contentious issues between the Catalan government and the opposition concern extending the metro from Barcelona to some of the metropolitan towns, and constructing new railway lines and ring roads to connect towns in an octagon around Barcelona. Major infrastructural work will require the financial participation of the central government, and this needs to be negotiated at a high level by the Catalan government. Thus two matters are problematic: overall planning, and decision-making.

The development of the city planning

Since 1976, Barcelona's metropolitan planning has been guided by the General Metropolitan Plan of Barcelona (Plan General Metropolitano de Barcelona, PGMB).[6] This plan has been fully implemented following the re-establishment of democratic local governance in 1979. The PGMB meant a new territorial ordering creating a clear regulation of public spaces, especially of transport and communications road systems. It also defined a considerable space reserved for green areas and collective consumption services. Moreover, between 1976 and 1987 metropolitan territorial planning was approved and managed by the metropolitan government (*Corporación Metropolitana de Barcelona*; CMB). The fact that the mayor of Barcelona was the president of the metropolitan government facilitated the implementation of the PGMB after initial reluctance on the part of

Table 20.4 Average price of new housing in Catalonia (Euros/m^2)

Municipalities	1987	1990	1987/ 1990	1992	1997	2000	1996/ 2000	1999/ 2000
Barcelona	618	1,224	25.6%	1,376	1,461	2,170	10.9%	13.2%
First Crown	400	1,038	37.3%	1,131	1,065	1,657	12.5%	18.4%
Second Crown	353	689	24.9%	791	826	1,277	12.5%	20.0%
Rest of Catalonia	340	598	20.9%	934	966	1,346	9.2%	8.1%

Source: García, E., Area Metropolitana de Barcelona, 2002. (Table compiled for this chapter.)

some of the mayors was overcome.[7] Later on in this chapter we will return to the issue of metropolitan governance.

The PGMB has undergone numerous modifications over the years and there are voices that express a need for a new plan. An alternative interpretation, however, is that the plan has consistently demonstrated its good quality by allowing considerable changes without changing its essence. Some of the discussions concerning the plan's modification have been of a political nature (and could have been avoided) and took place between the Catalan government and the municipal governments. These discussions did not prevent negotiations being held, resulting in concrete implementations (Esteban, 1999). Depending on the scope of the project, implementation has three forms: a) small operations to regenerate the urban fabric; b) intermediate scale projects affecting entire neighbourhoods (these two types of planning correspond to 'the reconstruction of the city' stage that took place between 1979 and 1986); and c) large projects for the whole city, such as the Olympic project (1986–92). This stage has been denominated the 'Olympic stage'. A fourth one started with the 'post-Olympic stage' (Font, 2001).

Numerous small operations were carried out in the period 1980–2. During this period, the city council aimed at demonstrating its good will by making the city more habitable and human; however, the projects also revealed the imbalance between good will and public investment in the urban sphere. It could be argued that city councils lacked resources to implement relevant changes. These were testing years for the new, democratic local councils in the cities and towns in the Barcelona region, especially because many of the councils were now comprised of left-wing politicians, professionals and managers. The special plans of interior reform (Planes de Reforms Interior PERIS)[8] had been more significantly implemented in the period 1980–6. These plans have allowed in most instances the participation of neighbourhood associations in the redesigning of the areas affected. The guidelines in these projects were to correct the original imbalance in favour of private housing and against public spaces and collective services. This type of planning has also favoured the strengthening of the neighbourhoods' identities.

The Olympic project was the key project in the transformation of the city in the 1990s. This project also demonstrated the metropolitan vocation of the city government. Not only were infrastructures connecting the city with its metropolitan hinterland improved, but also sports facilities were constructed in order to house sporting events during the Games in some of the surrounding municipalities. Moreover, this project created a dynamic of seeing the city as a whole and giving an impetus to urban projects, such as opening up the city to the sea and developing the sea front,[9] improving communications infrastructures, and distributing and improving sports facilities. Finally it also stimulated other projects that followed the Olympic project within Barcelona city, such as the creation of areas of new

347

centrality, i.e. ten new central zones with improved infrastructure or collective services, most with new, large commercial sites.[10]

It has been pointed out that Barcelona's city planning has a double aim. One is to monumentalise the periphery, the other to revive the city centre through urban planning on different scales, from the small city-quarter that needs improvement to large topological projects (Esteban, 1999, p.62). The PGMB continues to be the main framework. This plan is aimed at controlling growth and limiting density, while increasing the provision of open spaces in order to address both existing and emerging deficiencies, particularly within the urban continuum. Large-scale growth has been limited to one zone.[11] Physical structuring by means of road infrastructure has been carried out in order to cover the metropolitan area with a network of motorways, urban trunk roads, ring roads and tunnels. This new system has given the metropolitan area a global structure linking the major arterial networks of each municipality into a single network, conserving large natural areas while controlling processes of settlement, which damage the landscape and the environment.[12]

So far it has been stressed that Barcelona central city is very prominent within the Barcelona region and within Catalonia. The ambition not only to institutionalise the metropolitan government but also to confer it with political power provided the Catalan government with ammunition for presenting an alternative project of territorial management, which was going to affect the implementation of territorial planning. What was the Catalan government doing during this time in terms of planning and urban expansion? To what extent have institutions guided territorial development, or vice versa? The Catalan Statute for Autonomy, approved in December 1979, established the exclusive responsibility of the Catalan government for the ordering of the Catalan territory; a year later, the Catalan Land Institute (*Institut Català del Sol*) was created. This Institute has been steering the main territorial transformation by purchasing urbanised land to be used for residential and industrial purposes.[13] Through this institute, the Catalan government has been managing urban development for the last 20 years.[14] Opposing the Spanish government's policy of building new towns, the Catalan Land Institute has implemented a policy of strengthening already existent, relatively large and medium sized towns throughout the Catalan territory, especially those located in the rest of the Barcelona region beyond the metropolitan area. This policy is aimed at creating what the Catalan government representatives and managers call the 'Catalonia city' model – that is, a system of large and medium size cities well connected around the whole Catalan territory – which will strengthen the territorial balance. In order to do so successfully, Barcelona and the metropolitan area must be decentralised. Thus, this polycentric city model was presented as an alternative to the defused city around the large metropolis acting as leader of subordinated metropolitan towns. The implementation of this polycentric model has been based on a strong concentration of power and decision-making in Catalan government officials, combined with negotiations with large and medium sized municipal government according to specific planning interventions. From the planning perspective, the Catalan officials favoured the development of general plans of the counties that belong to the second crown, rather than institutionalising a wide general plan for the region.

The Territorial Plan for Catalonia (PGTC)[15] was finally approved by the Catalan parliament in 1995 – 15 years after the territorial policies were implemented. The PGTC considers the metropolitan ambit and the seven counties bordering it as Region I. This means that although there is not an institutionalisation of this area, the Catalan government has finally accepted its socio-economic and territorial reality. The implementation of this plan is envisaged in partial territorial plans according to the existing territorial divisions, such as the counties (one should remember that the Barcelona region is composed of seven counties). The Plan also envisages the implementation of large-scale infrastructures – such as road networks – and the definition of land uses.

More specifically, the strategy the Catalan government has followed for the last 20 years has been one of regenerating part of the early twentieth-century *Ensanches* as well as facilitating the links between neighbouring cities and towns. This strategy basically involves the allocation of the purchase of land to either private developers, cooperatives or other associations, or alternatively the construction of housing on it by the Catalan institution to be mostly sold (but also rented) at a relatively cheap price to lower-income groups.[16] On the other hand, industrial land has been promoted in the periphery of towns in order to house large industries as well as medium and small sized industrial and service companies within the second crown, achieving the aim of deconcentrating economic activity in the metropolitan area of Barcelona. The Institute has facilitated infrastructure services in order to attract economic activity to the areas designated for those purposes. Urban management of land for residential and industrial purposes[17] has needed the collaboration of municipal governments and land owners. Negotiations have been complex and difficult at times, especially as other urban agents (e.g. developers) have also been involved. Undoubtedly, some conflicts arising from the diversity of views and interests have led to delays in the final implementation of some of the original projects.

This chapter started with the hypothesis that politics matters dearly in the transformation of the territory, and that a major element to be taken into account is the fact that in Barcelona party politics revolves around two charismatic leaders. These leaders have said in their own words what their party members have been implementing:[18]

> Catalonia has to be vigilant in not unbalancing itself in many aspects: culturally, economically, socially … The possibility of the metropolitan region of Barcelona marginalising the rest of the country (Catalonia) is a constant danger

... The question of the territorial disequilibria continues to be a pending issue even though there has been unquestionable progress in this area in the last 20 years.

(Jordi Pujol)

In Barcelona converge a series of flows that go beyond the city itself and that draw a map of an urban system that goes beyond the frontier of the municipality ... Often the argument is framed with the idea of re-equilibrium in a way of compensation as if half the country – the more urban – is in debt to the other half – rural, marginalised by the other part.

(Pascual Maragall)

The two previous visions of the socio-economic development of Catalonia by the two key political actors, who have determined the urban and regional policies in Catalonia and Barcelona, have led to the governance tensions concerning territorial planning. The fact that the New Metropolitan Plan was initiated in 1990 but has never seen the light of day (only a draft has been presented to professional forums) shows the impasse created by the two positions.

Strategic planning

The process of strategic urban planning began in Barcelona in 1988. Its orientation had more of a citizens' (including all sectors of civil society) perspective than a purely business perspective. The point of departure was the following. Until the nomination of Barcelona as the site for the 1992 Olympic Games, the relationship between Barcelona's city council and the city's business sector was hardly existent. The public and the private sector had little knowledge about and virtually distrusted each other (Santacana, 2000).

Since then, three strategic plans have been ratified. These plans have been socio-economic and indicative. They have integrated major works that were already underway as well as promoted new ones. Their major role was to coordinate key sectors of the city's economy and policy-making, creating a debate on the model Barcelona should take in the European arena. The first Strategic Plan was ratified in 1990, the second in 1994 and the third in 1999 (covering the period 1999–2005). The first Plan aimed at consolidating Barcelona as a European metropolis; the second aimed at strengthening business companies in international markets; and the third aims at linking the city 'through its specific characteristics and identity' to the new globalising reality. Of the three, the first plan was more inclusive in the sense of wanting to modernise the city as well as providing guidance for improving social redistribution. In this sense it was more oriented towards citizens than the other two.

The territorial scope of the first plan (which guided the subsequent plans) was not to limit the objective and measures to the municipal reality (the city of Barcelona) but to consider a wider area, which could be extended according to the matter in question. Thus in some of the measures, the municipal city takes precedence, while in others the metropolitan city, Catalonia and finally the European macro-region, respectively, are taken as the frame of reference. Barcelona is therefore seen as the centre of a macro-region made up of Toulouse, Montpellier, Zaragoza, Valencia and Palma de Mallorca.

From an organisation point of view, the first plan established a general council, a coordinating office and several special committees. The general council is presided over by the mayor of Barcelona. About 200 organisations have been integrated into different forms of participation. The executive committee comprises delegates representing the city's key economic and social institutions, such as the chamber of commerce, industry and shipping, the Economy Debating Society, employers' organisations, trade unions, etc. The achievement of the first Plan was to create consensus in order to have a coherent design for Barcelona in terms of its economic expansion and identity, its transportation and communication networks and its quality of environment.

The contents of the three plans varied according to the city's contextual characteristics. When the first plan was designed, Barcelona was emerging from an industrial crisis, and one of the strategic lines put emphasis on giving impetus to industry as well as to advancing service to industry. Another line (there were three) was to improve the population's quality of life. In fact this line was a result of the trade unions' participation in the plan, with objectives such as increasing the life chances of people. However, the first plan had as a whole a stronger emphasis on the articulation of the territory through the development of infrastructures and the improvement of human capital through training as well as by recommending the development of R+D.

The local political context of the first plan was not neutral. The Metropolitan Corporation had been abolished a year before, and the technical team that initiated the design of the first plan was very close to the mayor of Barcelona city. Thus the metropolitan reality was emphasised. For example, the impact of the metropolitan region was made explicit in publications closely related to the first plan. The economic relevance to Catalonia of the metropolitan region was explicitly pointed out: the region's population constituted 70.6 per cent of the total Catalan population, jobs 68.3 per cent, investments in industry 68.8 per cent, and advance services to companies 77.4 per cent (de Forn and Pascual, 1991). The implicit argument was that the Barcelona region was the main engine driving the competitive position of Catalonia in Europe. Politically, the elaboration of the first Strategic Plan involved the gathering of support from key institutions for the arguments put forward by the city council against the policy of the Catalan government. However, no open debate emerged along these confrontational lines; on the contrary, the strategy was to find as much consensus as possible.

By 1992, 41 per cent of the measures were in an advanced stage of implementation, 31 per cent were in a stage of intermediary implementation and 28 per cent were far behind their target. Moreover, several of the largest cities in the metropolitan area had established their local strategic plans in order to develop a clear idea of the problems and opportunities they faced and may have to face in the future (Santacana, 2000).

The second Strategic Plan (1994) was more explicit concerning the territoriality of the objective by emphasising the metropolitan dimension. However, most of the objectives included in this plan could be considered a further development of the objectives of the first plan. In the third Strategic Plan (1999), the primary aim is to achieve an active, cohesive and sustainable metropolitan region. However, a stronger emphasis is put on making Barcelona a city of knowledge encouraging the development of technological and scientific parks related to universities. As in the previous plans, emphasis is also put on improving infrastructures and providing support for small and medium sized companies. Despite the allusions to the metropolitan regional reality of Barcelona, the three plans have had only Barcelona city as the ambit of focus analysis and implementation. Nonetheless, a fourth Plan has started in March 2002, in which the ambit of analysis will be the metropolitan region, acknowledging in this way its socio-economic reality and providing yet another argument for a future metropolitan region government. The fact that the Barcelona Strategic Plan was considered a success, in terms of creating a culture of consensus and providing fuel for specific projects, has been a model for the other counties comprising the Barcelona region. In fact, all seven counties have drawn up a strategic plan. Their design and management has been in the hands of the largest city of each county and the issues have been mainly socio-economic. Some of them have not gone much further than establishing a diagnosis. However, the basis for a coordinated regional strategic plan is there, as the practice has become familiar to city councils. The county councils have not been particularly active in these plans; all have been promoted by the municipalities.[19]

Public–private partnerships

The entrepreneurial role of local governments through the 1980s and 1990s is well documented in the urban literature (Preteceille, 1994, Logan and Molotch, 1987). Competition between cities to attract national and foreign investment became fierce at the end of the 1970s. Two major motors have guided the increasing role of public and private partnership. One was the need felt by local leaders to counteract the increasing numbers of unemployed in the cities they represent. This was the case in Barcelona, where between 1975 and 1985 there was a considerable fall (25 per cent) in industrial employment. The other motor was the perceived need to make the administrative machinery of the local government more efficient by downsizing the number of employees. This was also the case in Barcelona. Thus one of the roads taken by the mayor was to rationalise the functioning of the city council and to promote private companies in order to externalise some of the local administration services. The number of direct personnel and personnel working in municipal companies and institutions was downsized from 24,000 to 12,560 between 1985 and 1997 (Raventos, 2000).

The introduction of a culture of public-private partnerships (PPPs) in Barcelona has also been associated with the organisation – which started in 1986 – of the 1992 Olympic Games. Several factors have been stressed as relevant, such as the strong leadership of Barcelona's municipality, which took a large number of initiatives in which the private sector became engaged. Moreover, there has been, on the one hand, a gradual recognition by the municipal government of the important role that private companies could play in the economic regeneration of the city, acknowledging the positive elements of market regulation. On the other hand, the private sector has come to recognise the importance of municipal government in the economic sphere. When the city council created the first municipal company (with the objective of developing economic activity) the major business organisation took legal action to prevent it from developing.[20] Since then, mutual trust between the business community and the city council has developed. It has been argued that the PPP was also facilitated by two other elements related to the international event: strategic planning and citizens' empathy with the city. First, the global project of the Games encouraged overall planning for the city to develop a 'model' around which wide support could be gathered. This model was delineated by the lines defined by the Strategic Plan, Barcelona 2000. It consisted of promoting Barcelona as a city of production and consumption with a high quality of life based on certain levels of redistribution. Second, the international event acted as a catalyst to involve the citizens of Barcelona in a common project in which the identity of the city became symbolically merged with the identity of the citizens. A consensus was reached among the major social and economic actors (e.g. chamber of commerce, business and trade union organisations, etc.) to give an impulse to major transport, redevelopment and infrastructure projects.

In fact the positive outcome of this model has been the improvement of the transport system in the city and between the city and other metropolitan cities and towns, and the creation of public spaces and improvement of the existing ones. PPPs have developed in the last 15 years in several forms according to whether they are relevant to the public or the private sector. These are: a) public leadership with a strong contribution from the private sector (Olympic Games, strategic planning); b) mixed public–private (Barcelona Fair, tourism, *Zona Franca* Consortium, *Port Vell*); c) public interventions with a certain private participation (urban regeneration of the old town, *Procivesa*, technological park of *Valles*); and d) limited public participation (port, airport, savings banks).

Marisol García

Problems of institutional and spatial coordination

The metropolitan government: a brief experience

Currently there are 162 local entities governing the Barcelona region, as well as seven different levels of administration, as pointed out at the beginning of this chapter. Three of the seven levels of public intervention are elected bodies (local, regional and state governments). The provincial councils are administrative bodies with very limited competence to redistribute resources for public investment, and the county councils are symbolic institutions, which were established by the Catalan government but are still waiting for executive powers. Only the Association of Municipalities and two metropolitan entities managing services are effective bodies implementing territorial policy and active in decision-making. In order to clarify their significance, it is better to provide a short historical account of their origin and development.

In 1974, the year in which the revision of the 1953 Comarcal Plan was started, the Metropolitan Corporation of Barcelona (CMB) was created. This corporation had two basic areas of jurisdiction: 1) the approval of urban planning and 2) provision of services of particular interest to the metropolitan area. With the introduction of the Law of Local Regime (*Ley de Bases del Régimen Local*) in 1985, the scope of the metropolitan reality was recognised by the central state; this meant that the Corporation was also responsible for the coordination of the actions exercised by the different central state ministries intervening in the metropolitan territory. From a decision-making point of view, this involved the incorporation of the municipalities in the metropolitan area into the commission responsible for the metropolitan government. The metropolitan government had two democratically elected Socialist leaders, since the mayor of Barcelona automatically became the CMB president. Both were in power thanks to the support of two small left-wing parties. The second and last president was Pascual Maragall.[21] The functioning of the CMB had two major periods.[22] During the first (1979–85), considerable impetus was given to planning projects, as well as to the management of metropolitan public transport and other inter-municipal services. During this period investments were increased by a factor of four. However, it was in the second period (1985–88) that the CMB became financially more significant as it received a considerable budget, partly due to the incorporation of the National Municipal Cooperation Funds. In this way the central state recognised the right of Barcelona's municipal corporations to participate financially in the Corporation (Artal, 1997). In this period more ambitious projects were developed with the aim of creating a redistributive mechanism in order to balance the living conditions of the population of the metropolitan areas by such means as the major redevelopment and creation of public spaces, and better communications systems. While investments grew by the year the international profile of the Corporation gained weight, but the ambition to become a political institution (a flag and an anthem were created to celebrate 'The Day of the Metropolitan Area of Barcelona' during the city's fair) provoked considerable concern within the Catalan government by 1986. Thus, the Metropolitan Corporation of Barcelona acquired considerable power, especially because at the time the metropolitan area included more than 50 per cent of the population of Catalonia.[23]

In 1987 the Catalan government introduced a law that repealed the Decree Law that had created the metropolitan body in 1974. The abolition of the Metropolitan Corporation generated considerable political tension between the two leading Catalan parties – *Convergencia i Unio* (CiU) and the Catalan Socialists (PSC) – and particularly between their leaders. The Socialists (and observers) interpreted this decision as political without technical justification. Since then, attempts by the Socialist leadership backed by professional proposals to restructure territorial governance have always encountered considerable resistance from the Catalan government.[24]

The solution adopted to manage the existing coordination of services within the metropolitan area was the creation of two corporations or entities, one to manage transport (*Entidad Metropolitana de Transportes*) comprising 18 municipalities, and another to manage hydraulic services and waste treatment (*Entidad Metropolitana de Servicios Hidraulicos y Tratamiento de Residuos*) comprising 33 municipalities. Moreover, the Metropolitan Corporation before its dissolution constituted the Association of Municipalities of the Metropolitan Area (*Mancomunidad de Municipios*) (27 municipalities) for the provision of services not covered by the other two entities. These institutions and the county council of Barcelona constitute the resulting metropolitan institutional structure. Although they act independently, some of the leading managers have been present in more than one entity or worked closely with each other. Since then, the Catalan government has had discretion and responsibility for planning, which has weakened the negotiating capacity of the metropolitan entities with the private sectors involved in redevelopment within each municipality, especially concerning public works and the redefinition of land uses (Artal, 1997, p.241). Despite the emerging difficulties in coordinating the works of the metropolitan entities with those of the Catalan government concerning investment and expansion of service and infrastructure, the metropolitan entities have continued to be active agents in the territory. Thus, for example, outside Barcelona municipality the Metropolitan Land Institute manages housing development (mainly publicly subsidised housing) in a similar way as the Catalan Land Institute does within the metropolitan area. However, their actions are not coordinated at all. Moreover, the Association of Municipalities has become more prominent over the years. This association – which is voluntary, and therefore municipal governments may join and leave it freely – receives funds from its members, particularly from Barcelona's municipality which contributes 71 per cent of the total budget. The Association operates effectively on the basis that it can eventually become the managing government for the Barcelona region, although the proportion of municipal members is still relatively small if the whole region is taken into account, as members are basically located in the metropolitan area (or first crown).

Since the abolition of the Metropolitan Corporation, new attempts have been made to create a system of governance that will correspond to the real city, that is, the metropolitan region. The most salient political attempt has been the configuration of the Municipal Charter of Barcelona. One of the main goals of the Charter is to surmount the limitations that the common local regime puts on the government of the city. One of the most ambitious challenges of the Charter is to expand the local domain according to the subsidiarity principle. The Charter claims different autonomous and state government domains in order to guarantee a larger municipal presence in urbanism, infrastructure, education, social services and culture. Moreover, the Charter proposes a consortium as a formula to achieve the joint management of domains between the Catalan government and the city government. The Charter is awaiting approval from the Spanish parliament and is currently under discussion as the Spanish government does not favour its institutionalisation on the grounds that all large Spanish cities should have a similar charter, rather than Barcelona having a special one. Even if the Charter does not provide the Barcelona region with a government, at least it can act as a stepping stone in the process of the institutionalisation of regional governance and local autonomy.

Notes

1 I thank Francesc Artal, Joan Ignasi Coll, Emili García and Joan Anton Solans for providing very rich accounts and information as well as Lidia Garcia for assisting with the research. I also thank the editors of this book for their comments on a previous draft.
2 A leading urban planner was given the assignment of drawing up the Territorial Plan of the Metropolitan Region in 1990. There is a draft of the plan, but this has not been institutionally integrated or discussed.
3 On the peninsula, only Catalonia, the Basque Country and Galicia have distinctive cultural traditions other than Spanish. These communities claimed a distinctive treatment in the constitution of the emerging autonomous communities. They were only partly placated by being denominated 'nationalities'.
4 Regional governments opted to provide local councils with *subsidios finalistas* – financial subsidies allocated by higher state institutions for specific purposes.
5 For a detailed database taking into account each municipality, see Otero and Serra, 1998.
6 The origin of the metropolitan concept was established in the *Plan Comarcal* in 1953. This plan included Barcelona and 26 surrounding municipalities.
7 Reservations about the predominance of Barcelona's interests were discussed politically without a formal revision of the Plan.
8 Legal instrument to regulate specific urban areas equivalent to partial plans, usually affecting complete neighbourhoods.
9 Project Barcelona 2004 (urban renewal via festival organisation) and Poble Nou 22@ (new technological activities park) are two major development projects located near the sea front Olympic Village.

10 This project was published in 1986.
11 Sant Cugat-Cerdanyola, where new urban centres were envisaged and have developed since the design of the Plan.
12 The most significant areas are: Garraf massif, the Ordal, Collserola and Serra de Marina, and agricultural land in the Llobregat Delta.
13 In terms of numbers, between 1981 and 2000, a total of 48,893 ha were urbanised, 17,221 for residential use and 31,672 for industrial use in the whole Catalan territory.
14 From the start and until 2000, the head office was led by the same General Director of Urbanism, who has imprinted a highly personalistic approach on territorial development.
15 *Plan General Territorial de Catalunya.*
16 The Institute has followed the policy of promoting the construction of officially protected housing to cover part of the demand from families not able to afford the market prices as well as creating a stock of public housing units to be rented to the most vulnerable social groups. An added line of action has been the improvement of the existing housing stock in the inner cities and some peripheries where housing was built cheaply in previous decades.
17 Involving the expropriation of land, the management of planning and the reconfiguration of land ownership.
18 The two fragments are from the book by Tobaruela and Tort, 2002, pp.115 and 69.
19 This information is based on the revision of the existing strategic plans drawn up by the cities located in the metropolitan region of Barcelona.
20 This was the case of Iniciativas SA, a company created by the city council.
21 The first elected president, Narcis Serra, became Minister of Defence in 1982.
22 For a detailed summary of the CMB functioning, see Artal, 1997.
23 The proportion has increased in the last 15 years as production sector and population have moved towards as well as being created in the second crown of the metropolitan area.
24 Whereas there is considerable literature on the proposals that support the Socialists' position, there is comparatively very little written against those proposals.

Bibliography

Artal, F. (1997) 'Política I adminstració del territori: el drama de l'Area Metropolitana de Barcelona', in J. Roca i Albert *El municipi de Barcelona i els combats per govern de la ciutat*, Barcelona: Institut Municipal d'Historia de Barcelona.
Busquets, J. (1992) *Barcelona: evolución urbanística de una capital compacta*, Barcelona: Mafre.
Esteban, J. (1999) *El projecte urbanístic. Valorar la periferia i recuperar el centre*, Barcelona: Aula de Barcelona.
Font, A. (2001) 'La experiencia reciente de Catalunya. Planeamiento urbanístico para el s.XXI', *Revista Urban* 5, Barcelona: Federació de Municipis de Catalunya, pp 60–82.
Font, A., Llop, A. and Vilanova, J.M. (1999) *La construcció del territori metropolita*, Barcelona: Area Metropolitana. Mancomunitat de municipis.
De Forn, M. and Pascual, J.M. (1991) 'Aproximació a l'impacte de l'Acta Única Europea en el sistema productiu. El paper de Barcelona i la competitivitat de Catalunya', *Regió Metropolitana de Barcelona*, 3.
Gómez, A. (2002) 'Cooperativas, sociedades laborales y autoempleo. La capitalización del desempleo como política activa de inclusión laboral', PhD thesis (unfinished), Universidad de Barcelona.
Institut Català del Sol (1995) *Anuari*. Generalitat de Catalunya, Departament de Politica Territorial i Obres Publiques.

Marisol García

Institut Cátala del Sol (2002) *Anuari* (unpublished draft paper). Generalitat de Catalunya, Departament de Politica Territorial i Obres Publiques.

Logan, J. and Molotch, H. (1987) *Urban Fortunes. The Political Economy of Place*, Berkeley: University of California Press.

Martinez, S. (2001) 'El retorn al centre de la ciutat. La reestructuració del Raval, entre la renovaciió i la gentrificació', PhD thesis, Universidad de Barcelona.

Mur, R. (2001) 'Pobresa i rendes Mínimes a Barcelona Ciutat', PhD thesis, Universidad de Barcelona.

Nello, O. (2001) *Ciutat de Ciutats*, Barcelona: Editorial Empuries.

Otero, M. and Serra, J. (1998) 'Regió metropolitana de Barcelona. Indicadors estadistics municipals', *Regió Metropolitana de Barcelona*, 30, 7–191.

Preteceille, E. (1994) 'Paradojas políticas de las reestructuraciones urbanas, globalización de la economía y localización de la política', in A. Alabart, S. García and A. Giner (eds) *Clase, poder y ciudadanía*, Madrid: SigloXXI.

Raventos, F. (2000) *La collaboració publicoprivada*, Barcelona: Aula de Barcelona.

Santacana, F. (2000) *El planejament estratègic*, Barcelona: Aula Barcelona.

Serra (1997) 'L'emigració neta a Barcelona com a factor de desconcentració demográfica a Catalunya i a la Regió Metropolitana 1988–1994', in *VV.AA. Expansió urbana i planejament a Barcelon*, Barcelona: Institut Municipal d'Historia de Barcelona, Proa.

Serratosa, A. (1997) 'La revisió del Pla Comarcam de 1953: alternatives a lórigen i organizació del treballs', *Regió Metropolitana de Barcelona*, 28, 9–14.

Solans, J.A. (1997) 'Els canvis que el Pla General Metropolita va introduir a la pràctica Urbanística. Un balanç', *Regió Metropolitana de Barcelona*, 28, 85–105.

Tobaruela, P. and Tort, J. (2002) *Darrere l'horitzó. Quinze converses per descobrir Catalunya*, Barcelona: LA Magrana.

Trullén, J. (1998) *Noves estratègies econòmiques i territorials per a Barcelona*, Barcelona: Ayuntament de Barcelona.

Various authors (1993) 'La Regió Metropolitana el el planejament territorial de Catalunya', *Regió Metropolitana de Barcelona*, 14, 7–107.

Various authors (1995) *Dinàmiques Metropolitanes a L'Àrea i la Regió de Barcelona*, Barcelona: Area Metropolitana. Mancomunitat de municipis.

21 Metropolitan government and development strategies in Madrid

Jesús Leal Maldonado

High rate of urban growth

Like many other metropolitan areas, that of Madrid is widespread and delimited by towns of various densities. The old delimitations have remained and, if we wish to determine the area's size and expansion, we can distinguish three concentric rings around the old city centre. The centre is formed by the seven central city districts, with a population of 910,000.[1] It is composed mainly of the old city centre and the extension planned in the middle of the nineteenth century: the 'ensanche', sourrounded by a highway ring (M-30).

The peripheral fifteen districts of the city constitute the first ring area, with approximately 1,947,000 people living inside it. Most of the ring area had been initially composed of separate municipalities, but in the mid-twentieth century they were all integrated into the Madrid municipality. This was a way to coordinate the city, and as a result Madrid is now a big central city within which are concentrated more than half of the population of its Functional Urban Region.

The second ring is formed by 26 towns which, together with the municipality of Madrid, compose the Metropolitan Area, which was legally constituted at the end of the 1960s. This ring area, which radiates 20 km from the centre of Madrid, adds a residential population of 1,711,000 inhabitants to the urban region, and accommodates most of the population growth of the last 20 years. The institution of the Metropolitan Area, together with the COPLACO (Comité de PLAneamiento y COordinación del Area Metropolitana de Madrid, Committee for Planning and Coordination of the Madrid Metropolitan Area), which coordinated the municipalities planning, was scrapped at the end of 1970s when the Madrid Autonomous Community was established.

The third ring area of the urban region is constituted by a series of towns located outside the legal metropolitan area. This ring is currently undergoing rapid sub-urbanisation, and has a population of over 300,000.

Outside the urban region, but belonging to the Madrid Autonomous Community, is a series of rural towns, most of which have a high proportion of second homes,[2] with a population of slightly over 100,000. Thus one can say that the Functional Urban Region of Madrid fits the space defined by the Autonomous Community (Regional Government). This fact is important because the city-community of Madrid it is a strong institution with many resources and competencies to govern its urban region. It facilitates the coordination between the municipalities and contributes to the definition of a singular urban policy for all the municipalities that come under this unitary political power.

At the beginning of 1996 the population of the Community of Madrid exceeded 5 million with a slight demographic growth due to positive immigration. The dynamics of the spatial distribution of the population is characterised by a decrease in central areas and an increase in the periphery, with the spreading of its area of influence. In the period between 1991–6, the municipality of Madrid lost 158,000 inhabitants, representing 5.5 per cent of its population, whilst the third ring (area of influence) grew by 27 per cent in a strong process of suburbanisation. This suburban expansion process does not match the traditional forms of Spanish urban development in terms of a compact city.

The Madrid Urban Region is the third largest such region in the EU, but is substantially smaller than its precedents, London and Paris. This great, densely populated city, located at an altitude of 650 metres above sea level in the centre of the Iberian Plateau, is surrounded by scarcely populated territory. Once outside the city limits, one has to travel more than 200 km to find a city with more than 100,000 inhabitants, and 350 km to reach the nearest seaport. However, the city's location in the centre of the Iberian Peninsula is also one of its main strategic advantages, as the majority of the larger cities of the Peninsula are located on its periphery. This privileged position contrasts with its marginal character with respect to the main European urban population concentrations which also implies a continued risk of isolation from the rest of Europe.

Table 21.1 Population distribution by zones in Madrid, 1991–6

Zones	%1991	%1996
Madrid core	20.2	18.0
First municipal ring	38.9	37.3
Metropolitan area ring	33.8	35.3
Area of influence	5.0	7.0
Rest of the region	2.1	2.4
Total	100	100

Source: Census 1991 and 1996

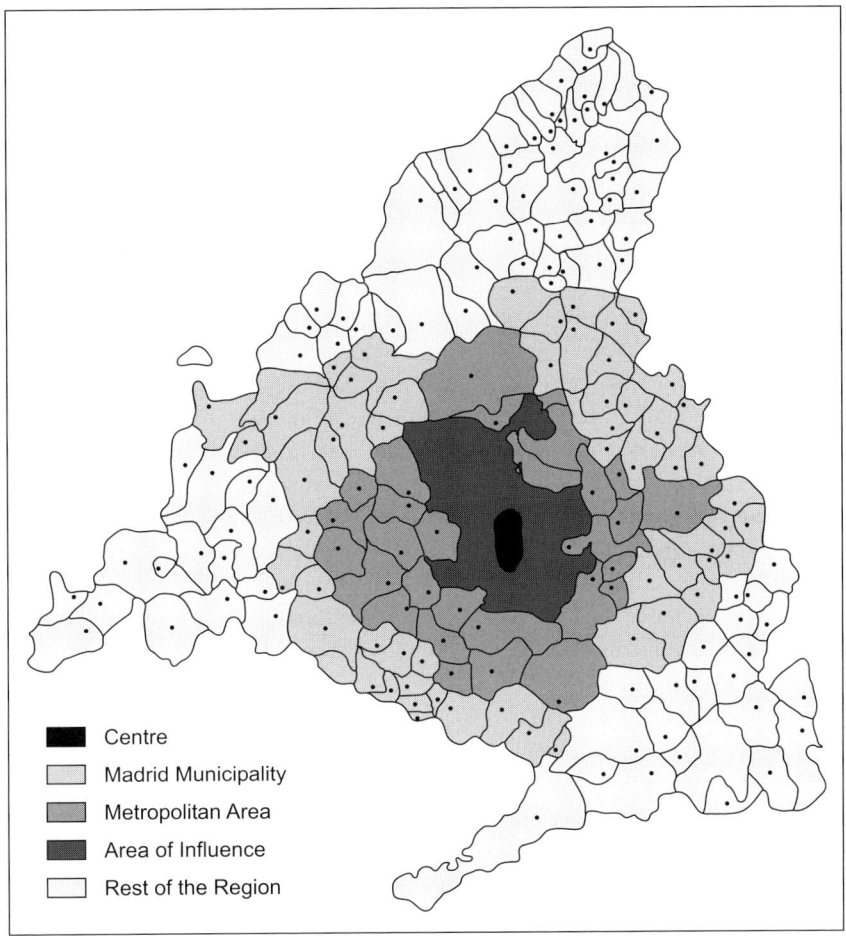

Figure 21.1 The Madrid metropolitan region

Historically, being the seat of the National Government, the condition of the Capital has required reinforcement with regard to communications with the rest of the country. As the central point of the radially structured rail and road network, most of the main routes between the largest Spanish cities pass through Madrid, and Madrid's Airport is an important hub for the Spanish airports. This demand for radial communication has had a major influence on the structuring of the city growth, based on a supportive structure composed of eight main routes linking Madrid to the rest of the Peninsula (Estébanez, 1990).

In spite of the almost desert land in the surroundings, urban density continues to be very high, although the recent impact of the suburbanisation process contributes to reduce the density. In 1991, only 13.5 per cent of the total housing stock comprised one family houses. More than 50 per cent of all housing units were in buildings more than five storeys high, and 15 per cent were in buildings more than ten storeys high.

The forecast for Madrid for the period 1996–2016 is for a population growth of 5 per cent and for a housing stock growth of over 30 per cent (Leal, 1999a). Madrid is a city experiencing at the beginning of the twenty-first century a high urban growth rate with all the usually determining factors (gross investment in urbanisation, new infrastructures and reshaping of the urban area). This type of growth, with a high increase in housing stock and a mostly stable population, is mainly a result of the changes in household size, with an increase in one-person households (mainly in the central areas), and a decline in the average family size from 3.5 household members in 1981 to 2.9 in 2001. This household size – one of the highest among European cities – contrasts with the low fertility rate amongst women in Madrid (in the year 2000 the rate was 1.14), a figure similar to the Spanish average. This contrast, between low fertility rate and large household size, can be explained by two residential practices: a delay in leaving the parental home on the part of young people, and the return of widowed elderly people to their children's homes after the age of 80. The average age of leaving the parental home is 29, an increase of 3.5 years between 1981 and 2001. This delay is due to cultural reasons and also to a high unemployment rate. The proportion of older people living with their children is decreasing but is still high (40 per cent of people over 80), and it is related to weak welfare provision of special housing for the elderly, and low pensions for widows (Fernández Cordón and Blane, 1999).

During the 1990s, housing conditions have noticeably improved with an increase in the available usable space to 24.3 m² per person in 1991 and an average home size of 79.1 m², which continues to grow despite the progressive decline in household size and the stabilisation of new housing size at around 110 m². This improvement has been brought about by considerable investments in the condition of public spaces and by a bettering of housing conditions, especially in the periphery of the city. The process of urban growth and the recent suburbanisation has been made possible by a strong development in transport infrastructure. These changes have various aspects, but the three most important ones are:

- A considerable expansion of the metro network.
- The improvement of suburban trains.
- The improvement of roads around and leading into the central city by transforming the eight main radial access roads into highways and building three principal ring roads (M-30, M-40 and M-45) around the central city, thus allowing improvements to the slip roads to be carried out in a more organised manner.

However, these interventions do not prevent the occurrence of traffic jams in peak hours. Traffic is one of the biggest problems in managing the city, and is the consequence of a high density in residential urban space and also of the high concentration of offices and business activities taking place in the city centre. The substantial investments in infrastructure, made at the end of the 1980s and early 1990s, were parallel to a noticeable increase in the use of cars in the daily commuting of the Madrilenians. Today the standard of motorisation is high (more than one car per each household) and is approaching that of other large European cities. The strong growth of car stock means constant saturation of a large part of the new infrastructure network.

Changing the government of the urban region

Since 1975, Spain's political and administrative structure has undergone profound changes, and this process is now almost complete. In the 1970s there were two levels of authority – the central and the municipal – but today there are three, the new one being the autonomous (regional) authority. This new authority, the autonomous government, has taken responsibility over duties from the central government but kept the municipal government with limited resources and limited capacity of investment (one of the lowest in Europe). The 17 new autonomous communities yield more political power than the regions in any other industrialised country. Madrid is one of them, third by population size after Andalusia and Catalonia.

The historical division of the country into autonomous regions poses the question of what is to be done with Madrid, which has traditionally been included in the region of Castilla La Mancha. However, the fear of being tied up with the problems of the capital caused this region to consider itself apart and reject its inclusion with the capital city. The result is that the province of Madrid became an independent autonomous community, which includes those outskirts that did not have their own entity as a region. From a political perspective it had to confront the birth of a new administrative entity, which had to deal with a problem of housing the central government and settling in a region, in which more than half the population was concentrated in a single municipality.

The Autonomous Community of Madrid is a politically independent entity, formed by an assembly whose members are elected. The community assembly has fairly extensive legislative powers regarding its competencies. The community has drafted its own land law and a regional development law, and makes a strategic regional plan to coordinate all the local master plans. A government whose president is elected by the assembly of the community manages these laws and plans. The urban and regional policy of the region depends mainly on this government, which controls the majority of health, education and housing competencies, as well as an important number of infrastructural and regional activities. It also includes some powers that are subtracted from those of the local councils (e.g. in the case of urban planning, whose approbation requires the consent of the regional governments). In this sense, Madrid's regional government determines or controls the essence of urban policies. Coordinating urban planning, transportation systems and basic services is now easier than before. In terms of transportation, a regional consortium has been created to integrate public transport (e.g. the metro, railway and public buses of the municipality of Madrid) with the mainly private, regional buses. There is a single ticket that applies for all regional transportation (*abono*) with different tariffs according to the zones covered. Water supply is run by a public company, whereas the supply of energy (electricity and gas) is a private enterprise affair. Currently, a second cable telephone company is being developed in order to encourage competition and to give citizens a choice.

This political structure has the advantage that apart from three sparsely populated areas situated in its three corners, the rest coincides with the Functional Urban Region boundaries. This facilitates to solving coordination problems between municipalities. It should be taken into account that Spanish local councils have insufficient economic resources to manage their local needs, even though their legal capacity to act is high (Castells, 1990). The existence of this autonomous community with a strong regional authority means that there is a powerful force that governs the urban region and is able to solve most of the problems. The consequence is that the autonomous community government defines the urban policy, even though the councils can specify their urban plans and interventions.

The inter-municipal coordination does not pose a big problem because the community solves most of the conflicts. The average population of the 26 municipalities in the second ring of the old legal metropolitan area is 66,000, enough to define their own urban policy by means of an urban master plan and to manage some of their own local services. This administrative structure has faced a problem from its early beginning, namely, how to the enable participation of the city dwellers in the drawing up of urban policies, the construction and renewal of their city. Theoretically, this structure could be very efficient because of the strong urban regional powers, though it usually implies having weak municipalities. A weak municipal capacity implies difficulty in access of the citizens to the decision-making authorities. This is amplified when civil society is poorly structured and the local associations, which play an important role in organising this participation, must survive on public financing.

Even if the coordination does not present a great problem in managing services, there are problems in controlling urban growth. The regional government develops a Strategic Regional Plan according to which the growth is controlled and directed, giving a quota which corresponds to every municipality, enabling possible developments in some areas with relation to the capacity to bring to the forefront the necessary infrastructure. However, the reality is that this distribution of urban growth depends substantially on the potential of the existing transportation systems and the capacity of each local council to apply political pressure. The difficulty is that each municipality is supreme in defining its urban growth, and most of them try to develop into their maximum possible size, because this is a way to solve local urban problems and to get more economic resources, and consequently is a source of money and power. The result is that in practical terms the trends in urban growth are derived from the existing investments in infrastructure, transport systems and also in the location of the new jobs, especially new offices.

Urban master plans are clearly defined by laws, and their best tool – zoning – has a long tradition in controlling urban development and illegal building was not so frequent as in other Southern European cities. However, territorial plans are hindered by weak legal conditions (because they are first defined by the regional law as director plans and only later as strategic territorial plans) and do not have the instrumental power, as master plans, to impose a trend on the urban development of municipalities. Territorial plans have played an important role in orientation, information, and above all in the comprehension of the territorial process (Ezquiaga, 1995). Some of these regional plans have become valuable documents because they synthesise quite well the territorial processes that are developing in the region, and serve to inform and ameliorate public administration and private management, but they are not accomplished in the same way that local urban plans are. The reason for this difference lies in their different legal basis. These regional plans define quite well what is not to be developed as urban space: the regional green parks and the principle parts of the principal transport infrastructure, such as high roads, new railways (for fast trains), new metro lines, new airports and so on, which are the real conditioning for urban development in the functional urban region.

The community has another series of non-spatial instruments for improving economic development, from the public investment in innovative businesses and public performance in the creation of urban spaces for productive activities, to the initiation of agreements with private partners (consortiums) for the development of urban operations with private entities. In the case of Madrid, the physical presence of the central government, together with certain elements that compete with it, implies a greater demand for coordination between the three administrations in other Spanish urban regions, although in general the involvement of the central state in relation to metropolitan policies is related mainly to the building of large transport infrastructures (national roads, stations, new railway lines and airports) and intervening in some coordinated projects in which the three administrations collaborate, such as some operations in city-centre renewal (*contrato-programa*). This is customarily carried out after the the proposal of the programmes by the central government, in accordance with a series of specific policies.

Strategic policies for the growing urban region

The first democratic municipal elections after almost 40 years of the Franco regime were held in Spain at the end of the 1970s. As a result of those 40 years, the country's municipalities suffered from four deficiencies:

- Shortage of urban services such as schools, health centres, recreation and sports areas, as well as cultural centres.
- Huge deficit in urban infrastructure and urbanisation, ranging from a lack of pavements and streets to a lack of recreational areas, car parking and roads.
- A large proportion of the housing stock was in bad condition because the units were self-built (shanty towns) or, those publicly owned, were built with little capital and were of extremely poor quality.
- Lack of basic elementary democratic communication channels between the citizens and the decision-making powers. In the pre-democratic period, urban interventions were often attained as a result of powerful demonstrations sustained by a strong social urban movement, which acted as a substitute for prohibited political parties.

This lack of correlation between social demands and urban projects during the last years of the Franco regime led to an urban policy characterised by stressing the rhetorical image of the projects rather than the actual satisfaction of needs. This urban policy was implemented with singular projects which were used as the image of a very limited action: for example, one large hospital instead of a network of smaller hospitals and health centres, or a large sports arena instead of a series of small playing-grounds distributed throughout the city. The lack of services and urbanisation in many parts of the city engendered a wave of social urban movements fighting to ameliorate urban conditions.

The many urban movements which sprung up during the last decade of Franco's regime were transformed during the transition to democracy. Some of their leaders became local politicians, holding high positions in the local administration of the municipalities of Madrid. The principal uneasiness of the new local government, composed of people with no previous experience, was how to efficiently organise municipal management. As a consequence, these new local governments have considerably increased efficiency and improved the local investment to ameliorate urban conditions. They balanced most of the principal deficits in urban services, built schools and health centres, and little by little developed a wide programme for improving urban conditions in the more deprived areas. Hwever, on the other hand, citizens' participation decreased, with few exceptions. This occurred because it was not a priority on the local agenda: political leaders originating from grass-roots social movements did not find it necessary to gain better knowledge of the local problems.

The social demands to improve working and living conditions led to a national agreement between the government, the political parties, the trade unions and the economic powers (the Moncloa Agreements). Trade unions and all political parties agreed to reduce the conflictivity and improve the economic conditions of the country, and the central government promised to make a large investment in equipment and services, and also in the development of a welfare state that primarily had to increase pensions and unemployment benefits. A little later, at the end of the 1970s, urban social movements in Madrid obtained a promise from the government to renovate the shanty towns and public housing units that were in bad condition. This programme – *Remodelación de Barrios* (Neighbourhood Remodelling) – was a large operation involving 47,000 new dwellings, and brought about a major change in the residential conditions in the periphery of the municipality of Madrid. This great success of the urban grass-root movements also brought about their decay, because after their demands had been honoured and their leaders were elected to local councils, they lost their reason to fight.

The strong increase in the welfare budget in relative terms in the 1980s made Madrid an exceptional city in the European context in the period of 1981–96, because the process of globalisation had not brought with it an increase in income inequalities, nor an increase in social segregation, though social and economic differences were very large at the beginning of this period. The reason for this change was the increase of the social budget: at the beginning of the period, the budget was as small as the inequality rates were large. Pensions and unemployment benefits had played an important role in preventing income inequalities, and the growth of services played the same role in reducing social differences in terms of social structure and segregation. Ruiz Huerta *et al*. (1993) concluded that income differences in Spain decreased in the period 1981–91, although the more affluent experienced a large increase in income. Social inequality changes in Madrid Region are described by Leal (1994) in the same way. Nevertheless, inequalities in property and education increased in this period at least in spatial terms.

Urban policy in the 1980s – when the Socialist party was in the majority in most municipalities, in the autonomous community and in the central government – focussed on the renewal or amelioration of the urban quality of the areas in the first and second ring areas built under Franco in the 1950s and 1960s, in which the working class lives. This was a consequence of several programmes, most of them stressing investment in social services, parks and urban conditions. The result was not as spectacular as the urban centre renewal in Italian cities, but it did change the image of the near periphery of the city, and brought about a noticeable change in the living conditions of the majority of inhabitants of the first urban ring.

Planning urban and regional development

The amelioration of conditions in the urban peripheries was also possible because of a series of urban plans whose objective was to 'change and complete Madrid' (this was the slogan of the master plan approved in 1985). The first wave of plans were PAIs[3] (Immediate Action Plans) made at the end of the 1970s. There was a series of urban district plans whose primary function was to recognise the principal demands of the citizens and transform them into town-planning proposals, in one of the largest citizen participation programmes in urban planning in Spain. But the results of these PAIs were contradictory. The results too hastily multiplied proposals of services, and the large number of these new services exceeded the capacity of public investment. The need to coordinate all proposals led to the revision of Madrid's General Urban Plan (*Plan General de Urbanismo*) which, based on these PAIs, proposed changes in the urban structure of the municipality of Madrid. At the same time, most of the new democratic councils in the second ring revised their plans, adapting them to the new urban policies.

In 1985, the principal objective of Madrid's General Plan was to end the indefinite growth and regain the organised form, as well as to meet the demands of a remarkably strong urban movement. In this sense, it was a plan to improve infrastructures and social services of the first ring, but, unlike Barcelona's plans, the city centre was left alone and the image of the city did not change remarkably. This General Master Plan was completed during a period of economic crisis and uncertainty, and was partly inspired by the ideas of the Italian planner Campos Venuti (1981) about the need to be austere in urban proposals. This orientation affected the proposals for the new urban developments, which resulted in a lack of new land for urban use. This approach contributed to the huge increase of housing prices in the second half of the 1980s.

The second half of the 1980s had such an impact on the growth of Madrid that it can almost be described as spectacular. The economic growth which Europe experienced had significant repercussions in a country such as Spain, in which the entrance to the European Community provoked a considerable increase in foreign investments, especially in real estate. Employment grew considerably, as did income. However, this growth encountered a series of problems: the severe philosophy of the plan of 1985 did not adapt to the enormous pressure of expansion. The result was a strong increase in real estate prices; offices, factories and housing prices more than doubled in just six years. This dynamic together with the change in the political composition of the council led to a new Urban Master Plan for Madrid, which was completed in 1997 and – in contrast with the previous Plan – proposed a huge increase of urban space. The new proposal included the urbanisation of the empty space between the first and the second rings, with a proposal for 350,000 new dwellings (Martínez Vidal, 1999).

Coordinating the management of the metropolitan region

Getting new employment

The first challenge to the regional policies of Madrid in recent years has been the promotion of new jobs in order to reduce the high level of unemployment in the urban region (22 per cent in 1985). The arrival of numerous generations in the work market and the increase in the number of women seeking employment contrasted with the small number of workers reaching the age of retirement.

Unemployment affected primarily those looking for their first job. In 1997, the unemployment rate among young people (15–24 years old) was 36 per cent; 12 years earlier, this figure had been 50 per cent. The considerable growth of the job market, which had increased by 28 per cent in those 12 years (Izquierdo and Jimeno, 1999), was not enough to solve the problem. The case was clearer for female employment: between 1986 and 1991 the number of working women increased by 48 per cent, but despite this growth female unemployment increased from 17.5 per cent to 18.4 per cent in the region. That gives an impression of the impact of two simultaneous processes: more young people searching for their first job, and – a more structural process – the increase in the number of working women. Total employment grew by 15.3 per cent in the period 1977–97, but not enough to significantly reduce unemployment rates. The composition of employment in relation to gender changed dramatically: male unemployment dropped from 20 per cent to 15.4 per cent in the period 1985–97, and that of women dropped from 25 per cent to 22.5 per cent (Izquierdo and Jimeno, 1999). But the direct means used by local and regional powers to counteract unemployment were limited. They were concentrated in improving activities, especially industrial activities, by offering land for new factories below the market price, and facilities to allow easier access to labour contracts for people searching for their first job. But in fact these industrial activities brought to a decrease in employment though sustained the level of production.

Developing transport infrastructures

The second challenge was to build new urban transportation infrastructures that at the same time will facilitate the development of activities and the mobility of workers. The coordination problems are fairly complex in this respect, public transportation in Madrid, as in most big cities, is not profitable and the losses are shared by various authorities. In the Metropolitan Transport Council of Madrid, each administration has a different weighting in paying the deficit. The Municipality of Madrid maintains the public buses network, the metro is managed by the autonomous community and the rail network is managed by the State. The size of the loss incurred is different for each administration – Madrid council being the one worst affected.

This difference in deficit for each mode of transport and for each administration made it difficult to turn the Metropolitan Transport Council into an institution to coordinate the whole transport system and unify the tickets for the whole urban region. Private companies operating suburban buses are also involved in this council, because they manage the most profitable mode of transport: buses linking the distant periphery with the centre. As a consequence of these agreements the investment in transport infrastructure has been considerable and more than 40 new metro stations opened within four years (the metro is the mode of transportation most used by Madrilenians, with 534 million passengers annually, closely followed by public buses, with 423 million passengers in 1997). The increased frequency of trains in the second and the third rings has significantly increased the number of passengers over the past ten years (Iranzo and Llanes, 1999).

The enlargement of Madrid Airport has become one of the priorities of regional policy. The airport has experienced a continuous growth in traffic. In 2000, more than 30 million passengers passed through it, pushing its capacity to the limit. Spanish airports depend on the central government, and the lack of agreement with respect to required alternatives with other administrations led to a paralysis at the end of the 1990s. We should also take into account that Madrid Airport is the principal hub for the other national airports and its problems have important consequences for all Spanish air traffic. The enlargement of the airport required an investment in a new terminal made by the national public enterprise (AENA), a considerable enlargement of land area (obtained from the municipality), and a new ground transport system built by the autonomous community. The result is not totally satisfactory, because the proximity to the city and the constraints of the new development block any further expansion and mean that a new airport will have to be built within 15 years.

Nevertheless, the need for building new infrastructures implied the use of new policies, allowing the incorporation of private partners. Some parts of the fourth ring road network (M-40) have been financed by commercial entities that built shopping malls in privileged positions in the junctions and flyovers between motorways, and the latest ring (M-45) is being financed by private companies by means of 'shadow tolls': for 20 years, these companies will be paid a certain amount per vehicle using it by the autonomous community. Apaprt from that, Madrid City Council has appealed to the larger construction companies to develop their plans for tunnels under the main roads entering the city. Sometimes the payment was a permission to build car parks under the main streets.

Privatising urbanisation

The third challenge is to obtain the Required urbanised land to restructure the activities, industry and services, and to focus the strong residential growth. Partnership has also been used as a new way of developing urban land by the Autonomous Community of Madrid. The consortium formula is a way of involving landowners in the development of new urban land by giving them permission to build in some areas at market price in exchange for urbanised land for social housing. This partnership allows a considerable increase in building infrastructures with a positive short-term effect on employment in this sector. Construction accounted for 8 per cent of the total number of workers employed in 1997.

But there has been a fundamental change in the way new urban projects are developed. The regional government ruled by the Socialist Party in the 1980s and the beginning of the 1990s often formed consortiums and expropriated land in order to build new social housing projects (Mangada, 1991). However, this changed in the 1990s after the Popular Party came to power in the region and in the Madrid council. Today, the development of new urban projects is almost always in private hands, improving the activity of strong real estate entrepreneurs linked with big building enterprises and sometimes also with banks. It is noticable that Spanish land law has benefited the concentration of private entrepreneours in developing new housing projects and that public intervention is scarce (less than 8 per cent of all new dwellings built in Madrid). This is linked with concentrating the owning of land for new developments. The result is an urban landscape characterised by large, homogeneous urban areas where the same form is repeated, as a result of saving money in design and construction. Nowadays Madrid is one of the few great European Urban Regions with big real estate projects, some of them involving building more than 6,000 housing units at the same time.

This change is a result of giving a greater autonomy to private enterprises in developing the new urban areas, as a way of applying a liberal ideology for producing urban space. The result of this regional and local urban policy could be more efficient and easier to manage, in terms of improving the urbanisation process, but public authorities have lost the control of land prices and it has led to a considerable increase in housing prices. In spite of the growing prices of housing, the drop in mortgage rates has contributed to increase the housing demand. Madrid reached at the end of the 1990s the highest volume of new building with 50,000 units built in one year, representing 2.5 per cent of the existing stock.

Housing policy, with most of its resources coming from the Central State, resulted in a regional imbalance. Most of the benefits went to the poorest regions with little or no growth, whereas urban regions with the greatest housing problems were neglected by these policies. The general growth of prices of these new housing units is partially a consequence of the privatisation of the managing of new urban developments, and the proportion of households which cannot afford to own a home increases. The consequence is the overcrowding of low-income households (e.g. those of immigrants) and the delaying of young people in getting an independent life (average age of leaving parents' home reached in 2001 29 years old). The principal way to get a home is to become a home owner, but it takes time to save enough money for the deposit. Getting a new home is becoming one of the strongest social problems in the Madrid region.

Improving environmental conditions

The fourth challenge for the strategic development of the urban region was to improve environmental conditions. Environmental policies have gone through two phases in recent years. In the 1980s, the principal objective was to improve the quality of water and reduce air pollution, with the construction of purifiers and the preservation of existing natural areas in the region from which most of the water is sourced, and the change from carbon heaters to gas heaters. In the 1990s the improvement and preservation of some natural areas became a focus of these policies, with limitations on or prohibition of construction within them, especially in the areas surrounding the city already strongly affected by the growth of real estate activity. Some have been closed to public use and others have limited the numbers of visitors. The means applied to preserve the natural parks are the laws and the plans of the autonomous community but these means are not enough to prevent the degrading of the environment without a budget in accordance with the needs. Air pollution in the city centre – although it has decreased thanks to the switch from coal to gas for central heating – it continues to be a problem, primarily due to urban traffic. Suburban growth is degrading the best natural areas in the north west of the Urban Region and water resources begin to be scarce.

Conclusion

Madrid Urban Region has a public administration structure with a high capacity to coordinate the management of the strong urban growth and the strategic opportunities coming from its geographic position in the centre of the Iberian Peninsula, and for being the financial and political capital of Spain. Nevertheless, the rapid urban growth is not easily managed. In the recent past the change in the sharing of responsibilities by the three administrations (local, regional and central) has improved their efficiency in managing the Urban Region but has increased their distance from the citizens.

Madrid's governability is strongly affected by the small capacity of local councils and their limited budgetary resources. The growth of the autonomous community and its economic capacity has been brought about by the independence of local power. At the same time, citizen participation and the lengthiness of the decision-making process are growing problems. On the other hand, the continuous tensions between central government power and autonomous (regional) control has focused the political debate on the division between the two economic resources and the negotiations for them, leaving the local powers aside. Only recently the central government resolved to overcome the demands for more autonomy for autonomous communities by restarting the debate over increasing the economic power of local councils, searching for a national agreement between political parties to achieve it. This could bring about major changes in the government of the Madrid Urban Region, especially to the local councils in the second ring, and could contribute to the decentralisation of local services.

In the meantime, Madrid is characterised by a considerable urban growth, the highest in absolute terms of its history – in terms of housing, employment, infrastructures and services – most of them controlled by public administration but led by the largest enterprises, as a consequence of the liberalisation process. Most of the innovative plans in urban development are being led by private capital, especially by larger enterprises which propose new urban developments to the public authorities.

The greatest projects, like highways, new housing estates, new productive spaces, theme parks (such as the newly constructed Warner Bros. Park), etc., are managed by these big private enterprises, approved by the autonomous community and imposed upon local councils. These projects are often joint ventures between different enterprises, such as banks, builders, commercial firms and entertainment enterprises, and it is difficult to solve the conflicts between the private interests of these big enterprises and local public interests. The improvement of local councils and the increasing participation of civil society could be a way to overcome these problems.

Acknowledgement

This chapter was made possible thanks to research grant PB 980908 from the Spanish DGESIC.

Notes

1 Data from the 1991 census.
2 By the term second home I refer to houses purchased by households in addition to their principally owned home.
3 PAI: Plan de Actuación Immediata.

Bibliography

Buesa, M. and Molero, J. (1999) 'El sector industrial', in J.L. Delgado (ed.) *Estructura Económica de Madrid*, Madrid: Civitas.

Campos, J. and Camarero, C. (1991) *Recuperar Madrid*, Madrid: Ayuntamiento de Madrid.

Campos Venuti, G. (1981) *Urbanismo y austeridad*, Madrid: Siglo Veintiuno de España.

Castells, M. (1990) 'Estrategias de desarrollo metropolitano en las grandes ciudades españolas: la articulación entre le crecimiento económico y calidad de vida', in J. Borja, M. Castells, R. Dorado and I. Quintana (eds) *Las grandes ciudades en la década de los noventa*, Madrid: Sistema.

Estébanez, J. (1990) 'Génesis del modelo territorial metropolitano madrileño', in J. Estébanez (ed.) *Madrid presente y futuro*, Madrid: Akal.

Ezquiaga, J.M. (ed.) (1995) *Plan General de estrategia territorial*, Madrid: Comunidad de Madrid.

Fernández Cordón, J.A. and Blane, A. (1999) 'La población de la Comunidad de Madrid, tendencias recientes y perspectivas de futuro', *Situación*, 1999, Serie Estudios Regionales.

Iranzo, J. and Llanes, I. (1999) 'Los transportes y las comunicaciones', in J.L. Delgado (ed.) *Estructura Económica de Madrid*, Madrid: Civitas.

Izquierdo, M. and Jimeno, J.F. (1999) 'Rasgos generales del mercado de trabajo en la Comunidad de Madrid', *Situación*, 1999, Serie Estudios Regionales.

Leal, J. (1994) 'Cambio social y desigualdad espacial en el Área Metropolitana de Madrid', *Economía y Sociedad,* 10, June.

Leal, J. (1999a) 'Crecimiento económico, empleo y desigualdad social en Madrid', *Papeles de Economía*, 18, 116–28.

Leal, J. (1999b) 'Vivienda y comportamiento residencial en la Región Metropolitana de Madrid', *Situación*, 1999, Serie Estudios Regionales.

Mangada, E. (1991) 'Suelo e infraestructura metropolitana: el diseño urbanístico de las grandes ciudades', in J. Rodríguez, M. Castells, C. Narbona and J.L. Curbelo (eds) *Las grandes ciudades, debates y propuestas*, Madrid: Economistas.

Martínez Vidal, E. (1999) 'El Nuevo Plan General de Madrid, como elemento clave en la proyección de la ciudad hacia el siglo XXI', *Situación*, 1999, Serie Estudios Regionales.

Muñiz Cidad, C. (1999) 'Sector servicios, una visión general', in J.L. Delgado (ed.) *Estructura Económica de Madrid*, Madrid: Civitas.

Ruiz Huerta, R., Martínez, R. and Ayala, L. (1993) 'La distribución de la renta en España, una perspectiva comparada', in *I Simposio sobre la igualdad y distribución de la renta y la riqueza*, Madrid: Fundación Argentaria.

PART VI

Concluding part: the problem of coordination in fragmented metropolises

22 Practices of metropolitan governance in Europe

Experiences and lessons

Willem Salet, Andy Thornley and Anton Kreukels

Metropolitan coordination as the challenge of 'organising connectivity'

Metropolitan coordination is not created from a product-approach of separate territorial governments but should be perceived as a process of learning in private and public coalitions of governance. The introductory chapter characterised the challenge of metropolitan coordination as a fascinating multi-actor and multilevel game with manifold conflicting and cooperating powers. It is a complicated game with many impediments and differing values, interests and resources of power and authority. If the idea of metropolitan governance is to teach us anything, it is undoubtedly that solutions to the problems of coordination and spatial planning are not to be found in the mere establishment of new encompassing territorial government but in new methods of 'organising connectivity'. The institutional problem is not so much the fragmentation of policy actors as the disconnectedness of learning practices and policies. Metropolitan policies are made in private sector domains (in the cultural and economic diversity of international and local networks), in European programmes, in national policies and in manifold initiatives within the metropolitan setting. There is of course a lot of power asymmetry in these relationships, but they are not structured according to a one-dimensional top-down format. The main challenge to metropolitan policies is to find the keys to unlock the connections between different spheres of action.

Focusing on strategies of connectivity is not to say that formal reorganisation of local and meso-level (regional) government is necessarily irrelevant. On the contrary, many metropolitan regions are experiencing governmental innovation and many are preparing further new experiments. The formal structures of local and meso-level government encompass the governmental competences and contain many conditions that facilitate or hamper strategies of interaction and coordination. In this book, we have examined the ways governmental structures in metropolitan regions ease or complicate such strategies. In this respect the empirical case studies found a variety of significant outcomes, as will be demonstrated later.

A frequently noted problem of governmental structures in metropolitan regions is their relatively low durability. Urban and regional contexts usually contain a lot of contradictions and are extremely dynamic. For this reason metropolitan systems of government frequently deviate from the 'standard' nation-wide systems. There are many experimental forms of metropolitan government. However, continuous experimentation with governmental structures will eventually erode their social and institutional position. It may prove more prudent to rely on stable structures of government and to organise, or to participate in, flexible practices of coordination emanating from these familiar institutions. Reform of government structures should not attempt to keep pace with the social and spatial dynamics of metropolitan development, but durable institutions of government should adopt flexible policies of coordination. This strategy, however, might only be possible if the formal structures are avoiding antagonism. Here we come into an important finding of the empirical studies. Formal structures of intergovernmental relationships are never perfect, and certainly not in dynamic metropolitan regions, but some provoke conflict between governmental agencies while others seem to facilitate better coordination or association. This is a crucial key into the investigation of options for coordination. When formal conditions of intergovernmental relationships produce conflict, an urgent need will be felt to substitute the formal procedures with informal practices, but their chances of success will be relatively low under these circumstances. The subtle fabric of formal and informal strategies of coordination should not be perceived as a matter of substitution but as supplementary and mutually reinforcing.

The above discussion provides the basis for creating assessment indicators of metropolitan practices of coordination from 'good' to 'less successful'. Our empirical analyses of metropolitan experiences in 19 city-regions of Europe indicate a strong differentiation in practices, from promising to failed. As the particular challenges, historical path dependencies and institutional conditions differ from country to country and even from region to region, there are no general recipes to solve the problems of metropolitan coordination. We will identify differentiated practices and try to assess these according to the above mentioned theme of 'organising connectivity'.

Linking into global economic and cultural networks

Governments cannot simply decide upon the growth of metropoles. Metropolitan developments, and the resulting needs of policy coordination, are stimulated by global trends operating through economic, social and cultural networks. There is a good deal of unevenness and hierarchy in economic functional networks, in social patterns of international migration and in international networks of cultural activity. Models of even and harmonious spatial order, for example the objective of 'balanced patterns of poly-centered regions' in the ESDP, are abstract from what is happening in the real world. The regions of Europe are very different and extremely uneven. There are many different sorts of region. In some cases the spatial extension of urban activities in the last two decades has created new metropolitan configurations instead of the familiar central nodes of urban activity. Following the example of the American census, Europe has also felt the need to make a distinction between metropolitan and non-metropolitan regions (see the 'blue banana' and 'bunch of grapes' debate in chapter 2). Further it is also necessary to distinguish between the different metropolitan regions. In the international social, economic and cultural networks some city-regions are more centrally involved than others. Megacities such as London and Paris, are global metropolitan nodes in a wide array of different functional networks that mutually interact producing high grades of urbanity. Other regions not only differ in size, but usually also in their intensity of multi-functional interaction. Berlin for instance is becoming an international capital in cultural and political respects, but remains rather a provincial capital in its economic role. Madrid cannot match London or Paris in its global economic connections but plays a very dominant role in the Latin American world network. Prague is a centre for international tourism while remaining under-developed in other respects.

The increasing significance of these economic and global networks is that choices of spatial behaviour are not usually made within local territorial settings but through interaction with international functional (in a spatial sense: virtual) spaces. For instance, choices of economic transfusion, or splitting up international corporations, are not a matter of territorial regional policy but of functional consideration. The same goes for cultural relationships. The cosmopolitan cultural elite of downtown Venice or Amsterdam is closely linked to cultural elites in international networks but completely indifferent to what is happening in the periphery of its own metropolis. The challenge for metropolitan planning is then to link the different worlds of activity. This may be in order to fortify the city-region's strategic position in functional international networks; it may also be in order to integrate the interests and values in the functional world with local activities or goals of the region. A good example of the first strategy is to form a network of functional and governmental representatives in order to lobby national or international policy-makers. In London in the early 1990s the City Corporation, central government and business interests initiated a joint lobby network to promote London as a centre of world business (see the development of London First and the London Pride Prospectus). In a comparable way local interests in Paris mobilised the central state to provide 'world class' infrastructure to help Paris in the world-class city competition with London, Tokyo and New York (Soleil project: construction of nuclear particle accelerator; and the 'pole d'excellence' of Orsay-Saclay). The second strategy attempts to involve international corporations within the region in integrated territorial development projects; see for instance the integrated development projects in backward areas of Milan and also the mixed set-up of the South Axis in Amsterdam. At Amsterdam's South Axis, new property development of international corporations (finance, service sector) is combined with multiple uses of space: housing, even social housing, public spaces, etc. The second strategy doesn't just aim to enlarge the local significance of existing functional interests but attempts to be innovative by integrating different values and interests.

One way or another the impact of economic globalisation is having a clear impact on the governance of city-regions. In most cases this is leading to a greater emphasis on the regional level and the rise of new regional organisations. The competitive ethos now pervades many city administrations and partnerships with the private sector, in both formulating strategic priorities and implementing projects have become more commonplace (see for example the involvement of the business lobby in the new London Plan and the 'growth contracts' in Stockholm).

Supra-regional involvement in metropolitan policy coalitions

European and national governments have their own stakes in metropolitan development. Nation-states took a proactive – and in most European countries even dominant – role in directing metropolitan policies during the building up of the national welfare states. Since the early 1980s intergovernmental relationships have become differentiated. But national government is still involved in many metropolitan programmes. In London a satisfactory formula for strategic government has proved difficult to find, and in practice central government has remained the dominant governmental actor in the attempt to coordinate regional strategy. Also in France, until recently, the central state was still very manifest, although now the regions are taking a more active role in coordination (see the chapters on Paris and Marseilles-Aix). In most countries the state shares power with local and regional government. The same goes for the European Union that is used to matching its urban and regional programmes with national government and requiring direct involvement of end users or clients in all processes of decision-making. This principle of European policy is strongly in favour of multilevel methods of governance. There are however some rival policy coalitions at national and European levels. Most European programmes involving urban and regional policies promote the social and economic development of backward regions. However most national governments have downgraded their own development policies into these backward regions since the early 1980s. For the sake of international competition most national governments endorse strategic development of the best regional economic potentials (airport infrastructures, ICT infrastructures, etc.). So divergent coalitions operate at the supra-regional level.

Conversely, seen from the viewpoint of the regions in Europe, the manifest roles of national and international government create favourable conditions for regional profiling of metropolitan areas. Local governments are usually too small and too dispersed to make an impact in European, and sometimes even national, politics. The new meso-governments (for instance the regions in France) often take an intermediary position in order to link the broad national programmes and strategic projects with local policies. They often also take the responsibility for policy coordination in the context of fragmentated local government. The meaning of Europe is used in different ways by these intermediary regions. First, some regions use the discourse of the 'Europe of the regions' successfully as a visionary tool in order to mobilise more cooperation and unity of local government. The case of Wales is one good example. Others can be found in France, Italy or Spain. The notion of competition between regions in Europe functions as a cement for intra-regional cooperation and strongly endorses the, sometimes very fragile, position of regional governments. Second, the regions bid on behalf of local governments for national and European programmes and many meso-level governments raise sufficient funds to enable them to take a catalytic role in the coordination of local projects. The above-mentioned regions are good examples of this. However, in the Brussels case the 'Europe of the Regions' discourse, with its message of decentralised competences, has been drawn upon to transfer considerable power from the nation state of Belgium to the three regions of Flanders, Wallonia and Brussels. The extreme antipathy of these new regions towards central control has created more difficult conditions for coordination of metropolitan strategy.

Local and meso-level government

The local and meso-level governmental relationships still are the most controversial and complicated relationships in metropolitan governance. Here we cannot neglect the significant conditions of formal systems. Besides the above-mentioned continuation of national dominance in England (see the chapters on London and Birmingham) we distinguish the following different types of formal relationships between local and meso-level governments:

*   unity of meso-level states and local government at meso-level;
*   duality of local and meso-level government with a regional hierarchy;
*   duality of local and meso-level government with a 'mediating' meso-governments;
*   functional relationships and symbolic projects.

All models have typical advantages and disadvantages.

Unity of meso-level states and local government

Although the complaint of fragmentated government is heard frequently and loudly, there are no new experiments with forms of unitary territorial government at the scale of the whole metropolitan region. There are recently established meso-governments in diverse countries, but nowhere as unitary structures. Always simultaneously some form of local government exists with a certain degree of independence and autonomy. However, there are some good historical examples of unitary government (state and local government) and it is fascinating to analyse the implication of these governmental arrangements for the current dynamic circumstances. The cases that conform to this model in the book are 'Communidad Madrid', 'Greater Berlin' and 'Greater Prague'. Also Vienna at a smaller scale belongs to this category. Strictly considered, Madrid and Berlin do have some sort of local government as well but the unitary governments there are very dominant. In these cases, for different historical reasons, the territory of the core city was extended over suburban municipalities and combined with state government, resulting in huge unitary governments. The crucial question is how these massive territorial governments cope with the above-mentioned challenges of current economic and spatial dynamics. The first conclusion is a positive one. The metropolitan regions with unitary government appear to be the only type of regions without problems of internal coordination of material facilities. As local government is not fragmented within these regions, there are no serious problems of coordination facilities. In all cases a metropolitan-wide web of public transportation is organised systematically. Also other urban and metropolitan facilities are provided relatively efficiently. There are some complaints, however, about the low democratic quality and the technocratic nature of a unitary government that operates at great distance from its citizens. Sometimes it is felt (in Madrid as well as in Prague and Berlin) that allocative policies request more direct consideration by the involved actors. However in general, the technocratic characteristics and the unity of territorial government create sound conditions for efficient government.

On the other hand, eventually there is a limit to what can be controlled efficiently from one central position. This model draws a heavy mortgage on its 'span of control'. Next, there are political constraints on further extension. This is why in these three cases new suburbanism is not brought under the unitary governmental umbrella anymore. Furthermore there is strong opposition to new extensions not only at the municipal level, but also at the level of the surrounding municipalities and states. The further expansion of the monstrous unitary government (a metropolitan region in itself) is feared for social and political/electoral reasons. This is why the Communidad of Madrid was established separately from the surrounding Communidad of Castilla la Mancha and also the reason why the population of Brandenburg (the state that surrounds Greater Berlin) voted against the fusion of Berlin and Brandenburg. The surrounding state is often explicitly drawing spatial plans to counter the storm and stress of the metropolitan cities. So the unitary model is facing problems of further urban growth. These are serious problems, as in the cases of Madrid, Vienna and Prague where the urban expansion is exploding outside the city-region's political boundary. This was also the case in Berlin during the 1990s but the economic and housing crises recently took the pressure out of the market. We may conclude that the unitary model has the advantage of technocratic efficiency but faces serious problems because of its weak endogenous and exogenous flexibility. These problems may increase under dynamic economic and spatial circumstances.

Duality of local and meso-level government with a hierarchy at meso-level

The next model postulates a dual structure of local and meso-level government with hierarchical power residing in the meso-level government. This model may be successful in some circumstances but it may also create structural conditions for conflict. The risks are manifest. Major cities don't like to be bullied by meso-level government – there are often strong social, economical and spatial differences between core cities and their, usually more prosperous, surroundings. Often there are also political and electoral differences between 'red' cities and 'black' regions. Major cities usually have their own strategies of urban expansion that might be hampered by the meso-government. Central cities also might attempt to build countervailing power coalitions, for example by cooperation with the national government or the private sector, in order to prevent one-sided policies by meso-government. So, even if the constitution shapes formal hierarchical relationships, in practice there are many chances to develop counter-strategies that might result in lasting stalemates. These are no imaginary speculations. Problems of metro-politan-wide coordination may easily occur, certainly when strongly equipped meso-governments are positioned in a one-to-one situation with powerful urban agglomerations. We found these problematic conditions in some of the case studies.

Curiously, national states that devolved national powers to meso-level govern-ments sometimes shaped new conditions of hierarchy within the regions. The new devolved constitution of Spain established very conflictive conditions for the relationship between Catalonia and Barcelona. The same happened in the Italian cases where relatively strong regional governments in Lombardy and Veneto conflicted frequently with the cities of Milan and Venice. Unfortunately these meso-level governments regions are not capable of successfully achieving their own strategic planning perspectives but are powerful enough to prevent the success of bottom-up strategies. The formal conditions in these intergovernmental relationships generate a lot of negative energy. Under these circumstances it is quite difficult as well to find solutions to the problems of spatial coordination by using additional methods of governance. These methods of informal coordination may be successful in a few particular cases, as the Milan case demonstrates, but usually cannot overcome – at least not in a structural way – situations where conflicts are integral to the constitution itself. In the federal republic of Germany a lot of experience exists with these kinds of problems. States are the foundation of the federal republic. The constitution also recognises some municipal autonomy, but the states are in a relatively strong position to establish the intra-state relationships in their own way. The results are differentiated. Some states are notorious because of the hierarchical and very conflictive relationships with their major city-region (see for instance the relationship between Bayern and München); other regions, however, manage to achieve networks of positive cooperation (see the case of Greater Hanover in Lower Saxony).

Duality of local and meso-level government with a 'mediating' meso-government

The next model is also founded on a dual structure of local and meso-level government but with the meso-level government playing a 'mediating' role, acting as an 'intermediary' institution or sort of 'in-between' government: guiding and shaping central policies into local versions and – the other way round – representing the needs of local communities to higher tiers of government. A mediating meso-government is not equipped with large bureaucracies and budgets but attempts to link the different spheres of government and the private sector into common strategic commitments. In this model the policy competences regarding the implementation of policies and concrete projects are decentralised to local government. The political significance of this type of meso-government is in the construction of strategic spatial planning perspectives, in coordination with and stimulation of decision-making on major projects (with supra-local impacts), and in organising communication between all involved actors. Budgets and implementation programmes largely stay with central government or are decentralised to local government. In urban areas inter-municipal or city-regional forms of government usually exist in order to implement the policies in an efficient way. We found many examples of this type in our case studies: in France, the Netherlands, in some German states that decided not to go for the formal hierarchy approach, in Sweden and – albeit in a slightly different form – in Britain. So this model is applied quite frequently.

The advantage of the model is that clashes between meso-government and bottom-up metropolitan forms of government may be prevented, at least partly, as a consequence of the differentiated roles of these governments. They are not usually struggling for the same competences, although of course there still may be some frictions. A disadvantage of this model is that the lightly equipped mediating regions might be ignored by the relatively strong city or agglomeration governments. If the mediating meso-government is not backed by national government or the national government is involved in direct partnerships with city government, then the meso-level government will lose the game. This actually happened to be the case in the early 1990s in most of the urbanised regions of France (e.g. around Paris and Marseilles-Aix), the Netherlands (see the cases of Amsterdam and Rotterdam) and in the more functionally organised system in England (e.g. Birmingham), and even in Germany in the region of Hessen (see the case of Frankfurt). Within the metropolitan areas, the core cities often feel and act as prima donnas. Nevertheless, things changed during the 1990s, as national governments continued to devolve national policies to meso-level and local governments, city-regions began to feel the need for cooperation with meso-governments because of the increasing urbanisation outside their boundaries, and the pressures of increasing international competition between regions. In the course of the 1990s many mediating meso-governments became more successful in their tasks of strategic planning, policy coordination and communication. In particular, in France the regions became more and more successful, even the urbanised regions such as Île-de-France and Marseilles-Aix. In France, as always, national government is still strongly involved in transportation and other spatial policies, but central government recognises its shortcomings in allocative considerations and increasingly involves the regions in organising commitment between local communities. National–regional 'five year contracts' are made for the preparation of major projects. Also in Germany the state of Baden-Württemberg took an active role in the promotion of cooperation in the city-region of Stuttgart. In other metropolitan regions, however, major cities and agglomerations have not yet been prepared to think beyond their city-centred interests, in which case there is no evidence of strong local–meso-government coalitions (see for instance the local dominancy of Birmingham in its region, or the urban prima donnas of Amsterdam, Rotterdam and Frankfurt).

Functional relationships and symbolic projects

Finally, we note the *ad hoc* solutions to the problems of coordinating metropolitan policies in new multi-actor and multilevel contexts. A common approach is to organise cooperatively at the functional level – that is through the provision of a particular service. The advantage of functional solutions is that these strategies are not overburdened by the ambitions and 'red tape' of inter-sectoral coordination. In some governmental systems, where public policy is considered mainly as 'providing particular services to the public' (in particular the British and American systems), functional organisation even sits at the heart of the system. However, even in the most territorially integrated systems, such as the German one, functional solutions are sometimes sought as practical methods in very complex policy arenas. In many German conurbations, which as 'in-between' levels of formal governmental organisation are dependent on some kind of cooperation between municipalities or on delegated control by the states, a tradition has evolved of functional organisation of metropolitan-wide public transportation. Almost every city-region in Germany has an extended metropolitan-wide web of public transportation, and it is almost always based on functional organisation (constituted by cooperating municipalities or states or even jointly). Also in Austria and Switzerland these constructions are familiar. In practice these functional organisations serve as backbones of city-regions, and sometimes other functions – very smoothly – are added to these single purposed agencies (see Hanover for a very explicit case). Also in Britain, where functional organisations are often simply inserted by central government, the trend has been to bundle different forms of functional organisation at regional level (see for example the establishment of the Government Offices for the Regions). Sometimes, these forms of sectoral organisation even grow into new territorial governments with elected representatives (this was actually the case in the early 1980s with the birth of the new regions in France out of the previous functional economic regions). Functional organisation is a practical method of coordination in a situation of fragmented interests.

Its disadvantage is of course that it doesn't offer integration with other policy sectors. Furthermore it is often felt as distanced technocratic government without direct political control – a form of government that is not controlled by the vote of the citizen or by the discipline of the market (the well known 'quango' problem). However, these forms of organisation know about technical efficiencies (such as organising light railways) and they often serve as the anchors of cooperation in contexts of fragmentation.

Another approach to coordination is through a particular project. Single projects of strategic significance are easier to organise than fully integrated plans or frames of policy. Cooperative projects may serve as pioneers and symbolic landmarks in processes that are building new metropolitan identities. There are many successful examples of these individual projects. In the Ruhrgebiet a framework of more than 100 symbolic cultural and ecological projects has been developed through the cooperation of private and public agencies (by the Internationale Bau Ausstellung, IBA) in order to symbolise the transition of the coal and iron region into a modernised economic and cultural region. The Olympic Games in Barcelona was used as a vehicle to bring together previously disjointed governmental levels and actors. Earlier conflicts were set aside and a new consensus constructed to ensure that the development deadlines were met. One of the requirements of this approach is to ensure that all key organisations have a stake in the outcome. One of the limitations in relying on projects or key events to create coordination is that these only last for a specific time. In Barcelona one strategy for dealing with this issue has been to create a new event. The city invented the idea of a cultural festival and approached UNESCO for backing. The result is the Universal Forum of 2004 and the exhibition site is being used to coordinate action around development that will regenerate another area of the city.

Finally there are numerous different kinds of *ad hoc* informal connections that can take place in a city-region, which can contribute to coordination in some way. This networking activity can be between policy professionals across governmental levels or between different municipalities. Interest groups, trade associations or business lobbies can also get together and generate a more comprehensive approach. Such informal activity becomes more important if the formal mechanisms are lacking or leading to dysfunctional results. However, the networking processes are very uncertain and rather random in their effects. The Brussels case, however, shows how professional networking can be important where other avenues are blocked. The reorganisation of the Brussels territory into three parts, each with strong feelings of autonomy, has made coordination very difficult. However bilateral agreements, pragmatism and personal networks have been used to establish a degree of cooperation albeit restricted to more low profile issues.

Strategies of cooperation at the municipality level

Finally, we will discuss several multi-actor strategies at the local level of governance. How can cooperation between municipalities and between municipalities and private actors be improved in the fragmented metropolitan context and how can innovative policies be focused on the emerging metropolitan spatial configuration? In the introduction chapter we outlined how strategies of cooperation and innovation in metropolitan city-regions are constrained by fragmentation of interests and policies. We focused in particular on the sociological asymmetries within metropolitan areas and on the tensions between strategies of cooperation and competition. On the one hand local actors feel the incentives for more mutual cooperation within the metropolitan region in order to meet the challenges of rival international regions. On the other hand, as a result of growing local accountabilities, local actors feel the competition within their metropolitan region with its increasing inequalities. More local accountability is needed in order to improve the interrelationships between public and private sectors, but as a consequence all local actors will attempt to attract income generators to their own territory. How are these contradicting challenges of more cooperation and yet more competition to be met in practice? How can we explain the different results of the more successful metropolitan strategies in Stuttgart, Kopenhagen/Malmö and Marseilles-Aix and the relative failures of Frankfurt, Amsterdam and Rotterdam?

We may learn from the experiences of failure that bottom-up strategies of metropolitan governance should be more wary about the quintessence of the operation. What happened in the above-mentioned failing experiments is that the expanding core cities provoked the negative energy of the surrounding municipalities. The core cities followed a double strategy: on the one hand the strategies were aiming at city-regional forms of government in order to mitigate the sociological and fiscal asymmetries: they chose the strategy of regional equalisation. On the other hand these strategies were aiming at inter-municipal cooperation in order to promote joint economic developmental policies in the face of the increasing competition between regions. The two motives are contradictory. The motive of equalising the social and financial conditions within the metropolitan region presupposes hierarchical conditions as the prosperous suburban municipalities are not usually keen on sharing the distribution of welfare. The second motive presupposes cooperation between municipalities that are aiming at win–win situations. The cases of the failing experiments suggest that it may be better not to try and fuse the two motives.

On the other hand the more successful experiments of Stuttgart, Marseilles-Aix and (unfortunately not included in this book) Kopenhagen/Malmö may teach us that it is promising to focus on the strategy of cooperative development policies. Hierarchical approaches needed to create re-distribution could be brought forward by higher tiers of government leaving the bottom-up processes of cooperation free from the responsibility for such re-distributive policies. Furthermore the above-mentioned successful experiments found a solution for the uneven relationships of power between major core cities and the large number of smaller municipalities in the surrounding areas. In these cases the city-centred strategy of further expanding the central cities was dropped and creative attempts were made to establish new centres of power outside the urban boundaries. These strategies are actively preparing the transformation of urban led regions into multi-centred metropolitan constellations. So strategies of cooperation may be better embedded. In Marseilles-Aix several cooperating circles of suburban municipalities have been formed, which in their turn cooperate with the city of Marseilles. This strategy of 'double coopera-tion' is strongly supported by higher tiers of governments and is resulting in successful multilevel governance. The Stuttgart and Kopenhagen initiatives are also building on the cooperation of multi-centred coalitions.

The Stockholm case also draws out some very interesting points about the costs and benefits of municipalities joining together into some kind of cooperative effort. There has been a debate in Stockholm over whether to adopt a new form of regional government and two alternatives have been suggested – an elected regional parliament or an association of municipalities. It is interesting to see that although some experiments of the elected parliament have been set up in other parts of the country, national government seems to be reluctant to devolve its power in the Capital region. Meanwhile the city of Stockholm is reluctant to join an association of municipalities as it does not see why it should water down its considerable strength in the region by joining up with smaller authorities. This suggests that such cooperation is easier if the municipalities in the regions are more equal in size.

Conclusions

We have discussed the challenge of coordinating metropolitan spatial policies in a complicated multi-actor and multilevel game. Next the subtle interdependencies of government and governance were analysed. There are manifold contradictions, constraints and conflicting interests and power games in metropolitan arenas. It is difficult to draw general conclusions, but the first is a very important one – and curiously enough one that is rarely drawn in metropolitan studies – good practices are very differentiated, there are different ways to success. The metropolitan arena is filled with public and private actors at manifold levels of spatial scale and they are active in all sectors of urban policy. In this multi-dimensional game many different coalitions and many conflicts may occur, and actually do occur. We summarise the main points from the discussion according to the analytical categories we have established. We started at the supra-national level with the impact of international economic and cultural networks on metropolitan development, and the roles of the supra-regional government authorities, and we finished by discussing different approaches to local and meso-level governance. However, it will be clear that these analytically separated relationships actually strongly interact with each other. The main challenge for metropolitan governance is to find the keys to organising the *connectivity* between the different spheres of action.

Focusing on the different types of relationship, we can summarise the discussion by making the following observations:

- At the meta-levels of decision-making metropolitan governments cannot simply decide on the growth of metropolises. Economic decisions and cultural policies are made through international economic and cultural networks. On the other hand governmental agencies are not completely dependent on the rescaling of spatial structures by private actors. Involvement and interventions by governments do make a difference. We discussed some strategies that may successfully organise this connectivity.
- Supra-regional governments are still very strong stakeholders in the guidance of metropolitan development. However, we found striking incongruities in the supra-national policies: national governments increasingly relate to the competitive forces in regions (by stimulating airports, infrastructures, ICT conditions, etc.). At the European level the EU, having once established the overall framework of economic liberalisation, mainly focuses its specific programmes on the upgrading of backward regions and economic sectors. As the European programmes presuppose matching funds from national states, national strategies are often required to play a sort of double game.
- Within the metropolitan regions we identified four characteristic models with different impacts upon multilevel governance relationships:

a Unitary models of states and local government are relatively efficient and don't have strong problems of coordination within their (wide) boundaries. There are serious problems, however, with the endogenous and exogenous flexibility. The large bureaucratic forms of organisation may experience more problems in dynamic periods.

b Dual models of local and meso-level government within hierarchy at meso-level sometimes conflict with expanding metropolitan initiatives. Curiously, this problem may emerge in federal systems that are constituted by strong states. Some hierarchical meso-governments, however, still manage to rely on bottom-up initiatives. This situation is more likely when meso-level governments and urban governments are not mutually related in a one-to-one relationship. In the latter situation there is a risk of competing competences.

c Dual models of local and meso-level government with mediating meso-government and strongly equipped local government provide good opportunities for cooperation between the complementary roles of local and regional government. However, if frictions arise it may be difficult for meso-level government to overcome local and metropolitan coalitions of power.

d Functional and *ad hoc* models of metropolitan coordination belong to the pragmatic solutions; if successful these may grow into more integrated and durable forms of coordination.

• Finally we discussed strategies of multilevel local governance. Experimental failures in metropolitan governance may suggest that it is not advisable to mix strategies of distributive equality and strategies of cooperative development in inter-municipal exchanges. Where the first strategy presupposes hierarchical methods, the second strategy is based upon cooperation. More successful strategies chose developmental cooperation and left distributive policies to higher tiers of government. Furthermore, the successful strategies opted for 'ex-centric' strategies by stimulating a multi-centred organisation of metropolitan powers and building new cooperation on these constellations.

Index

Index

Index

Index

Index

Index